The Persian Gulf

WESTVIEW SPECIAL STUDIES ON THE MIDDLE EAST

J. C. Hurewitz
Oil, the Arab-Israel Dispute, and the Industrial World: Horizons of Crisis
David E. Long
The Persian Gulf: An Introduction to Its Peoples, Politics and Economics

This book is an introductory survey of an area of increasing economic, commercial, and strategic importance to the United States and the Western world. The first chapter describes the geographical and climatic features of the region, its peoples, and their cultures, with emphasis on the striking degree of diversity found among the peoples who inhabit the Gulf littoral. There follow three chapters analyzing the politics of the Gulf: the first focuses on the political dynamics of each of the littoral states; the second discusses regional Gulf politics; and the third analyzes the role of the Gulf in international politics from the early Portuguese, French, and British imperial interests to present day oil interests. Persian Gulf oil and the economics of the region are then discussed in successive chapters. The final chapter traces U.S. interests in the area, recent U.S. strategic and economic interests, and the development of a U.S. Gulf policy over the last eight years.

David E. Long is currently the Executive Director of the Center for Contemporary Arab Studies, Georgetown University. During 1974-75, he was an International Affairs Fellow of the Council on Foreign Relations, and was in residence at the Georgetown University Center for Strategic and International Studies, where he conducted much of the research for this book. From 1962 to 1974, Dr. Long was a member of the United States Foreign Service, serving in the Sudan, Morocco, and Saudi Arabia. From 1970 to 1974 he was in charge of research for the Arabian Peninsula, the Persian Gulf and Israel in the Office of Research for Near East and South Asia of the Department of State, Washington, D.C.

Dr. Long holds degrees from Davidson College, the University of North Carolina, the Fletcher School of Law and Diplomacy, and the George Washington University. He is a recipient of the W. Averell Harriman Award given by the American Foreign Service Association for "extraordinary accomplishment involving initiative, integrity, intellectual courage and creative dissent." He has lectured widely throughout the United States and the Washington area universities on subjects dealing with the Middle East. Among his publications are several articles and reviews dealing with the Middle East and a forthcoming book on the contemporary Mecca Pilgrimage.

David E. Long

The Persian Gulf

An Introduction to Its Peoples, Politics, and Economics

Westview Press
Boulder, Colorado

DS
326
L654

71256

Copyright 1976 by Westview Press, Inc.

Published 1976 in the United States of America by

Westview Press, Inc.
1898 Flatiron Court
Boulder, Colorado   80301
Frederick A. Praeger, Publisher and Editorial Director

Library of Congress Cataloging in Publication Data

Long, David E.
  The Persian Gulf.

  (Westview special studies on the Middle East)
  1. Persian Gulf Region. 2. Persian Gulf Region—Politics and
government. I. Title.
DS326.L654   320.9'182'4   76-6531
ISBN 0-89158-103-0

Printed and bound in the United States of America.

To Barbara, Gordon, Geoffrey, and Andrew

Contents

Acknowledgments

Anyone who attempts a broad survey study is beholden to more people than he can mention. This survey is no exception. That it was done at all was due to the Council on Foreign Relations which provided me an International Affairs Fellowship for 1974-1975. I should especially like to thank Alton Frye and John Campbell of the council for their support and encouragement. Thanks are also extended to David Abshire and the Georgetown University Center for Strategic and International Studies for so graciously providing me with a place to write and conduct research and for the excellent administrative support during my fellowship year, and to Jon Vondracek of the center for his unflagging support and encouragement. I am indebted to Richard Erb, another International Affairs Fellow and a traveling companion during our research trip to the gulf, for his excellent company and enlightenment on some of the mysteries of "petroeconomics." He also provided the economic data in the Appendix. The support and kindness of my Foreign Service colleagues all along the way—the Jack Pattersons in Tehran, who put us up for a night when we had nowhere else to go; the American Embassy staffs in Kuwait, Bahrain, Qatar, UAE, Oman (where Bob Headly also put me up and David Zweifel got me to Dhufar and Nizwa), Saudi Arabia, Lebanon, and London —all were invaluable. The embassy staffs and government officials of each of the gulf states we visited were more than generous with their time and assistance; I cannot thank them enough. I also wish to thank those of the Arabian Mission of the Reformed Church in America for their kindness and help, particularly Dr. Donald Bosch in Muscat. To Debbie Dawson, Mona Jallad, John Wetter, and particularly Blythe Jones—who suffered through deciphering most of the first draft—I gratefully acknowledge my appreciation for the willingness and cheerfulness with which they prepared the manuscript, and to Michael Burrell and Thomas Ricks, who read it in its entirety and offered valuable suggestions, I also say thank you. Finally, I should like to give my humble thanks to my family for bearing with me during the months of research, travel, and writing that went into the book.

Georgetown University
February 1976

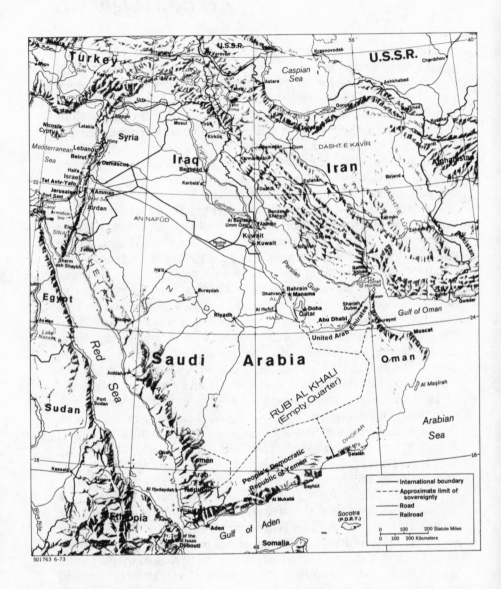

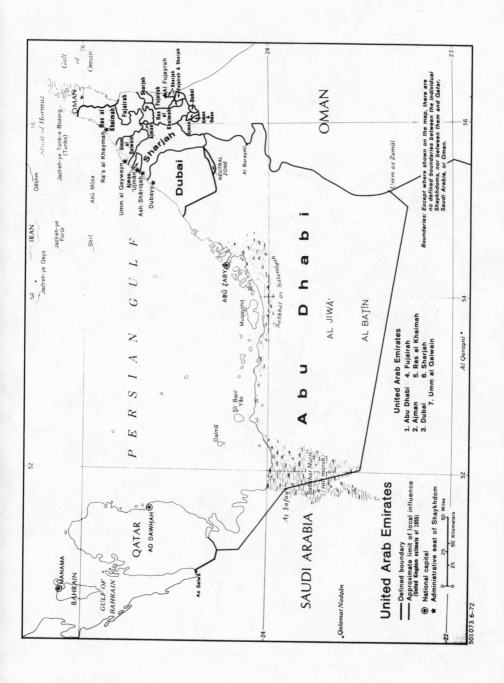

United Arab Emirates

— Defined boundary
--- Approximate limit of local influence
    (United Kingdom estimate of 1955)
⊛ National capital
★ Administrative seat of Shaykhdom

United Arab Emirates

1. Abu Dhabi   4. Fujairah
2. Ajman   5. Ras al Khaimah
3. Dubai   6. Sharjah
                7. Umm al Qaiwain

Boundaries: Except where shown on the map, there are no defined boundaries between the individual Shaykhdoms, nor between them and Qatar, Saudi Arabia, or Oman.

501073 6-72

1 The Land and People

Geography, in the words of Carlton Coon, "is the prince of disciplines, combining the fruits of geology, meteorology, anthropology, sociology, economics, and dozens of other specialties."[1] Nowhere else in the world is there a better example of the impact of geography on society, economics, and politics than the Persian Gulf. Start with geology. The gulf is situated in a sedentary basin which holds roughly two-thirds of the world's proven reserves of oil. Without that fact, the gulf would elicit little interest for any but the peoples who inhabit its shores. But because of its oil, in an energy-deficient world, it has become an area of universal importance. Understanding the peoples of the gulf has taken on an urgency never known before. And to understand them, because their societies have been molded by the lands they live in, it is necessary to start with their geography.

Stretching from Turkey to Oman, the Persian Gulf juts like a broken finger northwestward from the Gulf of Oman to the marshes of the Shatt al-Arab River. Roughly 90,000 square miles in area, it is 600 miles long and 230 miles across at its widest point. With no discernable channel or thalweg, it is shaped like a flat, shallow basin never exceeding 300 feet in depth.

The shores of the gulf are generally inhospitable, swampy in the north and desert elsewhere, occasionally broken by salt flats called *sabkhas*. The coastal population is primarily located in scattered oasis towns. Except where oil revenues have financed large-scale desalination, the lack of sweet water is the primary curb on the population growth.

Inland to the east, the Zagros Mountains separate the gulf from the high, arid plateau of central Iran. In the north, the Zagros meet the Elburz range of northern Iran, with its Mount Demavend, towering to 18,934 feet. The northern slopes of the Elburz drop off sharply to the Caspian Sea, some 85 feet below sea level, forming a lush, semitropical area rich in agriculture. To the northwest of the Gulf, beyond the marshes, lies the Mesopotamian valley of Iraq, through which flow the Tigris and Euphrates rivers until they join to form the Shatt al-Arab. Bounded on the east by the Zagros Mountains, on the west by the Syrian desert, and stretching toward the Taurus Mountains of Turkey, this valley was one of the breadbaskets of the ancient Middle East. With massive inputs of oil revenue in Iraq and a world shortage of food to spur investment, it may become so again.

The western shore of the gulf, which forms the eastern side of the Arabian Peninsula, is shaped like a giant fishhook. The Musandam Peninsula forms the tip, and the Qatar Peninsula extends northward to form the barb. Between the northern tip of Qatar and the Saudi Arabian mainland lies the Bahrain archipelago. The northern end of Bahrain is an oasis fed by underground water from the mainland, an extension of the Qatif Oasis on the Saudi side. With the extensive use of water for oil and other industries on both sides, the water table is dropping; if nothing is done, in a few years Bahrain could face a severe water shortage curtailing its agriculture.

Inland from the Saudi coast adjacent to Qatar is the great al-Hasa (or Ahsa) oasis and its principal town, Hufuf, with its crinolated mud-brick walls and forts. To the west is Najd, the Arabian heartland, dotted with oasis towns and Riyadh, the Saudi capital. Najd, bisected by an escarpment, Jabal Tuwayq, which extends 600 miles in a shallow arc from north to south, is bounded by two great pink-sand deserts, the Great Nafud in the north and the Rub' al-Khali or Empty Quarter in the south. The deserts are connected by a narrow strip, the Dahna, which extends north to south between Najd and al-Hasa. West of Najd lie the Hijaz Mountains, the Islamic holy places of Mecca and al-Medinah, and the Red Sea. The mountains form an escarpment inland from the Red Sea coastal plain. They reach an elevation of over 10,000 feet in Asir, and in the Yemen, south of Saudi Arabia, exceed 12,000 feet.

The area south of the gulf and east of the Rub' al-Khali is historical Oman, now divided into the United Arab Emirates (UAE) in the north and the Sultanate of Oman in the south. As if to complement the heights of Yemen, Oman also boasts a mountain range, the Hajar, divided into eastern and western ranges and crowned by Jabal Akhdar (Green Mountain), which exceeds 10,000 feet. These mountains curve, as Coon describes them, "like a stray member of the Zagros pack trying to rejoin its fellows."[2] East of the mountains on the Gulf of Oman is the Batinah Coast. Westward lies "Inner Oman," long isolated from the rest of the country. To the south along the Arabian Sea coast are the Qara Mountains of Dhufar, and to the west of Dhufar lie the Hadhramaut, Aden, and again the Yemeni highlands.

The climate of the gulf is harsh and, except in the mountains, generally arid. Summer temperatures (May to October) average over 115 degrees Fahrenheit in many areas and can reach 130. During a week-long sandstorm in Riyadh one summer, I saw a thermometer read 145 degrees. Some relief is found at night, when the temperature may drop as much as 50 degrees.

Contrary to the ideas of many Westerners, however, the climate is not always hot and dry. Along the coast, although the average annual rainfall is only three to six inches, the summer months are very muggy; the humidity sometimes stays at 100 percent for days. During such periods, temperatures seldom climb above 110 degrees, but as the moisture holds the heat, neither do they fall much below 100 degrees at night.

In the winter months, the climate is quite balmy. Daytime temperatures reach into the 90s, but with low humidity it is very pleasant. Many residents of the area find it too cold in the winter to swim because, even with the temperature at 95 degrees, the water on the body evaporates so fast in the dry air as to make one shiver. At night, winter temperatures drop very rapidly, and it is not uncommon for them to dip below freezing.

The climate in the mountains is, of course, much colder, and in most cases there is more rainfall. Rainfall, or the lack of it, has been the greatest single factor in molding the societies of the gulf. Precipitation is brought by two prevailing wind systems: the winter westerlies from the Atlantic and the summer monsoons from the Indian Ocean. The westerlies, having lost most of their moisture in Europe and the mountains of North Africa and the Levant, are very fickle by the time they reach the Zagros and Hajar mountains. Areas where twenty or more inches of rain have fallen annually for decades may go without any for one, two or five years. At other times, torrential downpours may cause flash floods, wiping out farms and villages. The lesson of undependable rains was well known in ancient times, when great storehouses were filled with food for the inevitable "years of want." In modern times, their lesson is reflected in the culverts and bridges which desert road builders construct over dry wadis (valleys and streambeds). Several years ago, a road engineer in Saudi Arabia who did not allow properly for the rains looked on helplessly as miles and miles of road were either washed out or blocked by the flow of waters from desert downpours. He suffered the ultimate indignity when even his own construction camp was flooded out.

The monsoons have all the dependability that the westerlies do not. Half the year they blow in a northerly direction, bringing moisture from the Indian Ocean. The other half of the year their direction is reversed. Unfortunately, the monsoons are of little benefit to the gulf region. While dumping vast amounts of rain on the Indian subcontinent to the east and the Ethiopian highlands to the west, in between they provide rain only on the Qara Mountains of Dhufar and the Yemeni and Asiri highlands. In another way, however, they have probably had as decisive an influence on the patterns of life in the gulf as any other factor. As we have seen, the area is one of mountains, desert, and an inhospitable climate. Since history began, this terrain has impeded travel and, particularly in the mountains, harbored brigands and rebel groups. The waters of the gulf, on the other hand, provided an avenue of communication and trade as Arab dhows sailed southward with the monsoons, out into the Indian Ocean to the Indian subcontinent and East African coast. When the winds changed six months later, the dhows sailed home again. Until just recently, therefore, the major external focus of the gulf was south and east, not north or west.

The peoples who inhabit this fabulously wealthy but inhospitable land share elements of a common heritage. Perhaps the single most important such element is Islam. The hold of Islam on the peoples of the Middle East cannot be overestimated, even on those who no longer are practicing believers. More than a religion, it is an entire way of life. In Islam, there is no distinction between sacred and secular. All things are the will of God. This has imbued Islamic society with a highly developed sense of fatalism. Not to be confused with defeatism, fanaticism, or passivism, this fatalism rather instills in the Muslim a sense of the inevitability of things.

The peoples of the gulf, as elsewhere in the Middle East, are oriented more closely to their extended families and tribal groupings than to any other sociopolitical structure such as province, state, region, or in the case of the Arabs, the Arab world. Above all, obligations to one's kin, regardless of political allegiances, come first.

When Americans hear the word *tribe* used in conjunction with the Middle East, it generally evokes the image of a country of desert nomads plodding along with their camels and their wives from oasis to oasis. To be sure, each of the gulf littoral states has nomadic tribesmen within its borders. But the nomadic tribe is not the decisive social force in the area. It is in the sedentary population centers that the culture of the area has its roots. It is true, however, that even the sedentary people claim a tribal lineage back to some dim, if not entirely mythological, ancestor. And for almost all, marriage and family relations reflect the dominant influence of family ties. Among the many Arabs, for instance, marriage within the extended family is more highly regarded than marriage without, and marriage to a first cousin is most highly regarded of all. Moreover, even in cities it is not uncommon for extended families to live in compounds—as many as a dozen nuclear families of uncles, cousins, and brothers all clustered together.

Another common element among the peoples of the gulf is the increasing disruption of traditional social patterns through the process of modernization. Nearly every country in the area is making a major effort to stamp out illiteracy and upgrade the standard of living. A new class of cosmopolitan and sophisticated elites has emerged in the government, the military, and the private sector, and a new class of proletarian workers can be seen in the oil fields and major cities.

Accompanying modernization is the trend toward urbanization. Urban centers are not new to the gulf area. Most of the gulf shaykhdoms were city-states from the start, and Baghdad has always been the population center of Iraq. Iran, Saudi Arabia, and Oman each possess several old and proud cities. But the last quarter-century has seen a large-scale expansion. From 1945, Tehran has grown from a mud-brick city of 100,000 to a metropolis of 3.3 million—one of every ten Iranians—and is growing by about 200,000 people a year. Riyadh has also grown from a mud-brick desert town to a city of nearly a half-million, surpassing Mecca and Jidda in size. In Oman, emerging from a cocoon of medievalism with the accession of Sultan Qabus in 1970, the capital, Muscat, has expanded as far as the mountains surrounding it on the land side will allow, and its sister city Mutrah is now becoming the country's major urban center.

Modernization is proceeding within and among different countries at different paces. Even in Iran, where the shah's development plan, the White Revolution, has produced spectacular results in some areas, most of the population is still nonurban and illiterate, and several million are still nomadic tribesmen. At the opposite pole are the nonoil shaykhdoms of the UAE and parts of Oman where the modernization process has barely begun.

Education, travel, urbanization, and other aspects of modernization, largely made possible by oil money, may eventually break down the traditional social system. But the process will take longer than even the most ardent disciples of development may be willing to admit. As the old saying goes, it is far easier to get the boy out of the country than the country out of the boy.

Also common to the gulf peoples, and to Middle Easterners as a whole, is the tendency to be more person related than problem related, in contrast to the emphasis on problem solving so prevalent in the West. This is the result of a highly developed sense of family consciousness, the Islamic belief in the inevitability of life, and perhaps a host of other factors as well. In his business and personal interactions, for example, someone from the gulf, when answering a question, would probably give more attention to what he thinks the questioner wishes to hear than to the substance of the question. He will also be careful to prevent even his adversaries from losing face. Major policy decisions are often made on the basis of personal relationships and animosities. Therefore, to attribute to gulf economic and oil policies the same type of cost-benefit analysis that Western economists might apply, or to take at face value policy statements designed to put the best face on an unpalatable policy, can be very risky. Unlike many of their advisors, no gulf rulers have graduate degrees in business or economics from American or other universities. (The only gulf ruler with any university degree is Shaykh Sultan of Sharjah.) And it is the rulers, not their advisors, who make policy.

To the outsider, the similarities of the peoples of the gulf could overshadow differences which in fact may be highly significant. For example, though nearly all of the gulf peoples are Muslim, they are divided by the great Sunni-Shi'a schism. Nine of ten Iranians and a majority of Iraqis and Bahrainis are Shi'a, or heterodox, Muslims. Shi'a Islam is the official state religion of Iran. The Saudis, Kuwaitis, and the native populations of the lower gulf are mostly Sunni, or orthodox, Muslims. Most Omanis follow the Ibadi sect, which is neither Sunni nor Shi'a, but the only surviving descendent of an even earlier schism, the Kharijite movement. Religious differences in the gulf do not have the direct political implications that, for example, they do in Northern Ireland. But in the gulf, allegiance to a particular religious group is a major determinant of one's sense of identity. And a sense of identity is the basic building block upon which loyalty to the state is constructed.

The most visible difference among peoples of the gulf is in ethnic and national heritage. The eastern side of the gulf is Persian, and the western side is Arab. At the same time, upon closer scrutiny this distinction becomes blurred. One hears Farsi (Persian) as much as Arabic in the *suqs* ("markets") of Doha, the capital of Qatar; and Arabic is the native language of many Iranian citizens on Iran's gulf coast and northward into Khuzistan and Fars. Baluchi, Urdu, Turkic dialects, and many nongulf dialects of Arabic are also heard frequently, as are the languages of western oil men, businessmen, advisors, and government officials serving in the gulf. With the dhow trade well entrenched since ancient times, the gulf has always been a cosmopolitan place. Since the coming of the oil industry, it has become one of the most heterogeneous places on earth. Indeed, in oil shaykhdoms such as Kuwait and Abu Dhabi, the resident alien population actually outnumbers the native population.

In addition to these general characteristics and differences, the societies of each of the gulf states have their own separate identities and therefore their own political dynamics. The following are merely brief sketches of an extremely complex subject.

Iran

About half of the 33 million inhabitants of Iran speak Persian as their native language, and Persian is Iran's official language. The vast expansion of public education, in which Persian language, history, and culture are emphasized, has greatly accelerated the growing Persian cultural predominance in the country.

There are, however, a number of different tribal and ethnic areas which ring the Persian heartland. In the northwest are the Turkic-speaking Azeris, kinsmen of those living in neighboring Soviet Azerbaijan. (In 1946 the Soviets tried unsuccessfully to annex the Iranian Azeris by attempting to establish a so-called Azerbaijan Republic with Tabriz as the capital.) In northeast Iran are Turkoman tribesmen, also with blood ties over the Soviet border. In the central Zagros southwest of Isfahan are the Bakhtiari tribes, and west of them to the Iraqi border are the Lurs; both speak a dialect of Persian. In the southern Zagros are the Turkic-speaking Qashqa'is.

Three ethnic groups in Iran are of particular interest to the study of the gulf. Most of the peoples along the Iranian coast of the gulf and in Khuzistan east of the Shatt al-Arab speak Arabic although many are also bilingual in Persian. Called Hawalah Arabs, many are Sunni Muslims and have close ethnic and historical ties with the Arab side of the gulf. A whole segment of the Bahrainis, for example, are originally from this area and are called locally "Lingawis," after Lingeh, a town on the Iranian coast.

North of Khuzistan and the Lurs' tribal area are the Kurds. Also Sunni Muslims, their historical tribal area includes parts of Iraq and Turkey as well as Iran. (After World War II, the Soviets also tried unsuccessfully to promote a Kurdish "republic" in Iran.) It is the role of the Kurds in Iraqi-Iranian relations that has had an impact on recent Gulf politics. The shah's support for Iraqi Kurds in their demand for local autonomy has been a principal cause of the hostile state of relations between Iraq and Iran. Although this support has been withdrawn, causing the latest Kurdish uprising to subside, the potential for Iranian involvement in Iraqi-Kurdish affairs still remains.

The Baluchi tribes of southeastern Iran also figure prominently in gulf society and politics. Mostly Sunni Muslims, they are located on both sides of the Iranian-Pakistani border and north into Afghanistan and inhabit some of the most barren, desolate pieces of real estate in the world. For centuries, Baluchis have crossed the Gulf of Oman to settle on Oman's Batinah Coast. More recently they have been drawn to the gulf oil shaykhdoms by the relatively high wages for manual labor. It has also been the practice for Baluchis to be recruited in Pakistan by the British to serve in Oman's armed forces.

Three other ethnic groups should be mentioned. Though small in number, the Jewish community is comparatively well off in Iran. The tolerance with which they are treated is a reflection of Iranian acceptance, if not support, of world Jewish aspirations and the right of Israel to exist. There are also small communities of Armenian Christians and Zoroastrians. The latter still follow the pre-Islamic religion of Persia.

Iraq

Three-fourths of the population of Iraq is Arab, but that does not give the degree of homogeneity to the population that it might suggest. The largest minority ethnic group is the Kurds, roughly 15 percent of the population. For years the Kurds have agitated for autonomy under their leader, Mullah Mustafah Barzani. In March 1971 an agreement giving the Kurds various rights was reached between the Kurds and the Iraqi government, but by 1974 the accord had broken down, and Kurdish insurgency, aided by Iran, had risen again. In March 1975, after Iranian support was stopped, the Kurdish insurgency again collapsed, and Barzani sought exile outside Iraq.

Even among the Iraqi Arabs, there is little unity. Those living in the west are mostly nomadic, belonging to the great tribal confederations which extend from the deserts of Iraq, Syria, and Jordan, south into Saudi Arabia. In the marshes of southern Iraq, the "Marsh Arabs" live in small groups of huts kept above water by rushes which must constantly be replaced. They are seminomadic people who drive their water buffalo into the marshes in the winter and retreat with the high waters to the river banks in the summer.

Most of the Arabs, indeed most of the people of Iraq, live in the Tigris-Euphrates valley. They dwell mainly in villages and towns along the river banks, but as elsewhere in the Middle East there is a growing trend toward urbanization. Baghdad, the capital, has a population of about 1.8 million out of a total population in Iraq of just over 11 million. The next largest cities, Basrah and Mosul, number about 420,000 and 340,000.

Religion is a major divisive element. From 52 to 55 percent of the population is Shi'a Muslim, compared to about 35 to 38 percent Sunni Muslim. About 10 percent are non-Muslim: mostly Christians, some Yazidis and pre-Christian Mandeans, and now only a handful of Jews. The Shi'as, which include about three-fourths of the Arab population plus some Persian elements, live mainly in southern Iraq. They are generally on the lower rungs of the scale in Iraqi society, being more rural and less educated than the Sunnis. The latter are predominant among the Arab population north of Baghdad, and among the Kurds and the Bedouins in the west. The Sunni Arabs have always monopolized political power in Iraq and continue to do so under the Ba'thi regime.

Because of the ethnic and religious cleavages, any regime faces the problem of how to get a nationwide consensus of legitimacy. The Kurds are not Arabs and strive to maintain a separate identity. Though Sunnis, they are more militant in their opposition to the Sunni Arab government in Baghdad than their eastern kinsmen are to the Shi'a Persian government in Tehran. And among the Iraqi Arabs, where the Sunnis, though politically strong, are in the minority, many Arab Shi'as have close ties with Shi'a Iran.

Saudi Arabia

Saudi Arabia is one of the more homogeneous gulf states, but even it has noticeable regional differences. The entire population is Arab.[3] Most are Sunnis, and most of the Sunnis are followers of the religious teachings of Muhammad Abd al-Wahhab, the great eighteenth century Najdi revivalist whose name has been given to his followers, the Wahhabis.[4] The Wahhabis subscribe to the most conservative of the four Sunni schools of Islamic jurisprudence, the Hanbali school.

The impact of Islam on Saudi society is all embracing, even with the growing secularization brought about by economic and social development. Islamic law is the law of the land and is practiced in the courts. Time is still often computed by the sun to facilitate the Muslim cycle of five prayers daily (the day begins at sunset, the time of which varies each day). The Muslim lunar calendar is used because it marks Muslim holy days, particularly the annual *hajj* ("pilgrimage") to Mecca which absorbs the energies of nearly everyone in the kingdom for about two months a year. Compliance with religious requirements is enforced by a religious police force, the Mutawwa'in; women are still veiled; and practices and institutions which are considered immoral (e.g., alcohol and public cinemas) are forbidden. There is public radio and television in Saudi Arabia. However, to dispel religious opposition to such innovations, large portions of the programming are devoted to prayers, religious instruction, and readings from the Quran.

Wahhabism has also come to serve as a political ideology for the Saudi state. Since the time when Abd al-Wahhab gained as his patron Muhammad bin Saud, founder of the present Saudi royal family, the Al Saud Wahhabism has given a sense of purpose to generations of Sauds as they united the warring, disparate tribes and principalities of Arabia into present day Saudi Arabia.

Saudi Arabia's 4 million or so inhabitants[5] are fairly evenly divided among city and large-town dwellers and villagers of the oases and the mountains of Hijaz and Asir. Desert nomads, once a powerful political force, are on the decline. Despite the trend towards urbanization, Saudi Arabia has no great metropolis like Baghdad or Tehran. The three largest cities in the kingdom, Riyadh, Jidda, and Mecca, have populations of less than 500,000.

Najd is the political and cultural as well as geographical heartland of Saudi Arabia. Its inhabitants, long insulated from the outside world by the deserts which surround its oasis villages, consider themselves the only racially "pure" Arabs. Unlike the Persian aristocracy, which is distinguished by a regal manner, these desert aristocrats wear their lineage simply, so secure in the superiority of their blood lines that they scarcely question it. Though aristocratic, the Najdis possess a built-in internal egalitarianism. Until his death King Faysal held a weekly open court in which any citizen could petition him, and tribesmen, not recognizing any superiority of the Al Saud blood line, have been known to address him, "ya, Faysal"—"hey Faysal." The great Najdi families are found at all levels of Saudi government and are increasingly involved in business. They are second in importance only to the royal family and to the descendants of Abd al-Wahhab, the Al al-Shaykh who dominates Saudi religious leadership.

Equally important for Najdi attitudes is that, except for a brief period (1818-1822), they have never suffered the psychological scars of foreign invasion or domination.

The Hijaz has traditionally been one of the most polyglot societies in the world, due to the annual influx over the centuries of pilgrims to Mecca and al-Medinah, the two most holy cities in Islam. It was six years after he had conquered the Kingdom of Hijaz in 1926 before King Abd al-Aziz, known to the West as Ibn Saud, risked the degenerative influence of the Hijaz on his Najdi puritans by creating the united Kingdom of Saudi Arabia. Because of its more cosmopolitan outlook, the Hijaz has supplied the kingdom with many of its leading businessmen, soldiers, and technocrats. Its less insular atmosphere has also made many Hijazis somewhat impatient of the political structure dominated by Najdi aristocrats.

The Asir Mountains south of the Hijaz comprise one of the least developed, most densely populated and scenic areas in the country. The isolation of the region, however, is beginning to disappear, as new roads and airports open up the countryside. Asiri men are highly industrious, not refusing manual labor as many Najdis do; and the Qahhabi revival still has not induced many Asiri women to don the veil.

The eastern province of Saudi Arabia is sociologically amorphous. Before the discovery of oil, its population of oasis farmers, fishermen, and mariners was a mixture of Shi'a Arabs, similar to southern Iraqis, and Sunni Arabs, who migrated or claimed to have migrated from the aristocratic tribes of Najd. Since the development of the oil industry, however, the region has seen the influx of people from all over Saudi Arabia and, indeed, all over the Middle East and the West as well. The Saudi oil company employees living in suburbs in Dammam and al-Khubar are as thoroughly middle class as any work force in the world, and centuries in time from the oasis farmers of nearby Qatif Oasis.

Kuwait

The population of Kuwait is estimated to be nearing 1 million, the vast majority living in Kuwait City and its suburbs; over half of the population are aliens.[6] The original town of Kuwait (the word is the diminutive of *kut*, or "fort") was founded by clans from the great Najdi tribal confederation, the Anayzah. These clans, who migrated from Najd in the late seventeenth and early eighteenth centuries to escape the continuing famine and tribal warfare of that period, were called the Bani Utub, "the people who migrated."

They discovered the site of present-day Kuwait in 1716, and because there was fresh water, they settled there. Kuwait also offered a safe anchorage, and by the middle of the century, most Kuwaitis had turned to the sea for their livelihood—the beginning of the great Kuwaiti dhow fleets. Though the local accounts imply that Kuwait was uninhabited in 1716, fresh water and a safe anchorage are rare commodities in the gulf, and it is more likely that the Bani Utub displaced or perhaps conquered an older indigenous population. Indeed, nearby archeological sites date back to the third millenium B.C., and a thriving city-state existed earlier on Failaka Island, near Kuwait City. (During his eastern conquest, Alexander the Great renamed Failaka Ikaros.) The town of Kazimah, near the present town of Jahra, was also important during early Muslim times.

The first-ranking clan, the Al-Sabah, became recognized as the leading family by the 1750s and has been the ruling family to this day. The Kuwaitis maintained ties with the tribal interior, and it was in Kuwait that the father and grandfather of Saudi Arabia's King Khalid sought refuge in exile in the latter part of the nineteenth century.

The non-Kuwaiti population is almost entirely a result of the oil industry. Roughly two-thirds of the labor force are foreigners. Mostly from other Arab states, they also include Iranians, Pakistanis, Indians, and other nationalities who came to provide the manpower and technical services which the new oil-based economy required and which the local population was unable to provide. The largest minority group are the Palestinians, variously estimated at around 200,000.

Whereas the aliens have no political rights, they reap many of the benefits of Kuwait's cradle-to-grave welfare system and receive relatively high wages. Thus far they have shown little inclination to agitate for more political representation. This, however, may change in the long run. Originally, the foreign workers were almost always males who left their families behind while seeking to make the family fortune. As the years go by, however, a greater proportion of aliens are residing with their families in Kuwait; and their children, while not Kuwaiti, know no other homeland. Unless the right of citizenship becomes more attainable, this in time may cause future generations of Kuwaiti-born aliens to be more insistent in demanding participation in the political process.

Bahrain

The ruling al-Khalifah family of Bahrain also claims descent from the Bani Utub. In the 1760s several Bani Utub clans left Kuwait and, after traveling south, settled on the tip of the Qatar Peninsula. There they founded a pearl-diving city-state at Zubarah. In 1783-1785 they moved to the Bahrain archipelago, where they imposed a Sunni merchant aristocracy over the predominantly Shi'a oasis farmers and pearl divers there.

Thus, like Iraq, Bahrain has a confessional split between Shi'as and Sunnis. The Shi'a community, which has a slight majority, includes several groups. There are the indigenous inhabitants, called Baharnah, who according to legend were Arabs taken captive by King Nebuchadnezzar and who later escaped and settled in Bahrain. In addition, there are many Shi'as of Iranian origin and some of Saudi and Iraqi origin. Among the Sunnis are the royal family, the Bani Utub aristocracy, and some merchant families from southern Iran, the so-called Lingawis. Some of the latter could possibly have been Shi'as, but for political and economic reasons claim to be Sunnis. There are also Sunnis who, claiming to be *muhawalah*, or "returners," say their families emigrated to the eastern shore of the gulf centuries ago and have now returned.

Indeed, Bahrain has close historical ties with Iran, which has held sovereignty over the archipelago at various times in the past and did not finally relinquish its claims to the islands until 1970. There are generally four types of Iranians in Bahrain and throughout the lower gulf: Shi'a Arabic speakers from Khuzistan; Sunni Arabic speakers from the Lingah area; Baluchis from Kirman and Baluchistan who are employed in manual labor; and Persian speakers from Fars, sometimes called "Red Iranians." Some have been on the Arab side of the gulf for generations, like the Kanoo and Fakhroo families. Most of the Farsi Iranians are merchants and relative newcomers. At any rate, Farsi can be heard in the *suqs* of Manama, the capital, along with Arabic.[7]

Unlike the situation in Kuwait and the lower gulf, a majority of the workforce are native Bahrainis. Because the oil industry was established in Bahrain relatively early, in the early thirties, the country has the largest and most sophisticated native labor force of all the gulf amirates except Kuwait.[8] Bahrain, however, may soon experience a large influx of foreign labor. New projects such as the dry dock now under construction will probably create more jobs than local Bahrainis can fill.

Qatar

Until its oil production first went on stream in 1949, Qatar was a sparsely populated backwater. Its capital, Doha, was little more than a large fishing and pearling village. The native population is mainly Sunni Arab with an admixture of Sunnis from southern Iran. Like their neighbors in Saudi Arabia, native Qataris subscribe to the teaching of the Wahhabi revival and to the Hanbali school of Sunni Islam.

The ascendancy of the ruling Al Thani family dates from the middle of the nineteenth century. Estimated to number in the thousands, it is probably the largest royal family in the gulf. Not only does it constitute the elite of the country, it also comprises a significant proportion of the native Qatari population. That the Al Thanis are not considered to have the aristocratic Arab blood lines of the Bahraini, Kuwaiti, or Saudi royal houses is occasionally a source of irritation, particularly in relations with Bahrain. However, the Al Thanis are the only Muslim ruling house outside of Saudi Arabia who are Wahhabis, and while the Qataris do not adhere to the revivalist teachings as closely as do the Saudis, a common religious bond has enhanced good relations between the two countries.

Next in line to the Al Thani family are the leading Doha merchants. Most are native Qataris, but one of the most powerful families, the Abdallah Darwish, is of southern Iranian origin. The lesser Doha merchants are to a large degree more recent arrivals from Iran, and Farsi can be heard as much as Arabic in the *suqs*. The very few inhabitants of Qatar who live outside the capital are mainly found in scattered fishing villages. Inland, most of the Qatar Peninsula is so barren that the number of pastoral nomads has never been great.

The native population of Qatar is increasingly outnumbered by foreign workers who were drawn by the oil boom. There is a relatively large Palestinian population—mostly clerks and office workers—and there are some Omanis and Yemenis, particularly in the security services, but most of the foreigners are non-Arab. They come mainly from Iran, Pakistan, and India. The Iranians, as in Bahrain, are Arabic speakers from Khuzistan and southern Iran, some of whom have been in Doha for several generations; Farsi merchants; and Baluchis, most of whom are single males engaged in manual labor. Urdu speaking Pakistanis are numerous as lower government employees and clerks and in other petit bourgeois positions, as are the Indians.

All told, the foreign labor force in Qatar is not so permanent as it is in Kuwait. For one thing, the amenities are fewer in Qatar. At the lower end of the labor force, workers typically come for several years, live very frugally, sometimes in rude dormitory conditions, and return home again when they have saved up some capital.

The United Arab Emirates (UAE)

The UAE, historically associated with Oman to the south, is a loose confederation of seven individual shaykhdoms which, before independence in 1971, comprised the Trucial States: Abu Dhabi, Dubai, Sharjah, Ajman, Umm al-Qaywayn, Ras al-Khaymah, and Fujayrah. The origins of these shaykhdoms are all tribal. Six principal tribal groups inhabit the area: the Bani Yas, a confederation of tribes of differing histories and origins; the Manasir (singular: Mansuri), a nomadic tribe which ranges into Saudi Arabia and Qatar; the Qawasim (singular: Qasimi), which has historically been paramount in the northeast; the Ali, or Al Bu Ali; the Sharqiyin (singular: Sharqi); and the Nu'aym, or Na'im (singular: Nu'aymi, or Na'imi).

Most of the Bani Yas are nomads, but by the late 1760s some of them had founded the town of Abu Dhabi as a pearling and fishing center. The head of the paramount branch of the tribe, the Al Bu Falah, settled in Abu Dhabi in the 1790s, and the current ruling family, the Al Nuhayyan, comes from this branch. Another branch, the Al Bu Falasah, settled Dubai, which by 1833 had become an independent and rival city-state, if the term *city* can be applied to a mud-brick village.

The Qawasim, further up the coast, have a proud history of controlling at one time areas on both sides of the gulf. On the Iranian side they were suzerain to the Persian shahs in a manner somewhat analagous to the Norman kings of England who were also dukes of Normandy. This duality is one factor in the territorial dispute over three gulf islands claimed by Iran and two UAE shaykhdoms, Sharjah and Ras al-Khaymah, both of which have Qasimi rulers.[9] These proud Qasimi rulers find it difficult to accept handouts from oil-rich Abu Dhabi or Dubai, or to take a subordinate role in UAE affairs. Sharjah's lot may change now that it has become an oil producer.

There is a Qasimi majority in Sharjah, but in Ras al-Khaymah the Qawasim are outnumbered by the fierce, non-Arabic-speaking Shihuh, the Za'b, the Ali, and other tribes. The Ali is also the principal tribe of Umm al-Qaywayn, which is ruled by one of their number. Ajman is ruled by a member of the Al Bu Kharayban branch of the Nu'aym tribe. And in Fujayrah, a Sharqi is shaykh.

Until very recent times, tribal warfare and violence characterized relations among the UAE shaykhdoms, and few rulers died in bed. Even today a map of the country looks like a patchwork quilt, reflecting allegiances of noncontiguous tribal areas to various shaykhs. Several shaykhdoms were at various times subject to other shaykhdoms. One, Kalba, now a part of Sharjah, was at one time independent.

The Wahhabi revival, riding the crest of Saudi political expansion, reached the frontiers of Oman proper in the nineteenth century and has retained adherents to this day. Followers of the Wahhabi school are to be found in the Buraymi Oasis, which is coadministered by Abu Dhabi and Oman and was also claimed by Saudi Arabia until 1974; the Ali tribe of Umm al Qaywayn is also Wahhabi. For these tribesmen, as well as for the Al Thani in Qatar, there is an affinity with their coreligionists in Saudi Arabia. All other Sunnis in the UAE follow the Maliki school (as did most Sunni gulf Arabs before the Wahhabi revival), except the al-Sharqiyin of Fujayrah, who follow the Shafi'i school.

Of all the UAE shaykhdoms only Dubai and Sharjah have developed an extensive *entrepôt* trade and merchant class, although Abu Dhabi merchants are beginning to catch up. Sharjah was the commercial center of the lower gulf until the late 1940s when its "creek" (most lower gulf coastal towns have a creek or estuary which forms a natural harbor) began to silt up.

At the same time the British, partially for political reasons, dredged Dubai's creek, and in time Dubai became the predominant trading center and remains so today. In fact, Dubai, more nearly than anywhere else in the world, is principally a merchant state, and its ruler, a merchant prince, is far more interested in commerce than in politics.

A high proportion of the merchant families of Dubai and Sharjah, as well as of the other UAE shaykhdoms, are foreigners, mainly from Iran, Pakistan, and India. Many have been resident there for generations. Concentrated in the oil-rich shaykhdoms, foreigners also dominate the labor force. These workers, too, are predominantly Iranians, Pakistanis, and Indians. A great proportion of them are Baluchis and Pathans, who perform much of the heavy manual labor. Most of the foreign workers have left family behind and expect to return to their homelands.

Although all the Gulf shaykhdoms have illegal aliens, the UAE probably has the greatest proportion of them. In one way, the illegal aliens aid the government in maintaining security, for they are not apt to make demands and are easy to deport. In the last decade, the number of foreign workers in the UAE has climbed steadily so that foreigners could soon reach as high as two-thirds of the population.

Oman

Oman is the only Arab state whose population is predominantly Ibadi Muslim. Until the accession of the present sultan in 1970, it was for the most part cut off from the outside world. The Omani society is basically tribal and Arab (about seven-eighths), but there is a sizable non-Arab population in the twin-city capital area of Muscat-Mutrah, comprised mostly of Iranians, Pakistanis, and Indians. All of the leading merchants of the country are located in the capital area. Most of the Omani merchants are Ibadi; there are also many foreign merchants including Liwatis (Shi'a Muslims from India) and three important Hindu families.

As mentioned above, Oman has a large Baluchi community. Omani ties with Baluchistan date back to the eighteenth century, when Oman was a regional maritime power. The last of its far-flung empire, which once included Zanzibar in East Africa, was an enclave on the coast of Pakistani Baluchistan, Gwadur, which Oman ceded to Pakistan in 1958 for $8.4 million.

There are two tribal non-Arab groups in Oman, the wild Shihuh who inhabit the Musandam Peninsula (some say they are descended from the Shuhites mentioned in Job), and the Qaras of the Qara Mountains in Dhufar. Both are nominally Sunni Muslim.

There is also a large African population, descendants of former slaves. Slavery has only recently been abolished in Oman. Offensive as the practice might seem in Western eyes, the Arab institution of slavery was not so inhumane as slavery in the West. Slaves had status, acquired from their owners, and were far superior to free men with no status. Perhaps the most inhumane part of the practice was the conditions under which slaves were shipped to Oman from Africa. During the voyage, most of them died. At present, to make amends to the former slaves, the government has adopted policies that make them one of the most pampered groups in the country.

The foreign Muslims are either Shi'as (Iranians and Liwati Indians) or Sunnis (Baluchis, Pakistanis, and Indians). The two Arab tribal groups in Dhufar, the Kathiris and Mahras, are also nominally Sunnis. These two groups have strong tribal ties with neighboring South Yemen. Most of the remaining Arab population, which comprises the bulk of the population, is Ibadi. One of the basic tenets of Ibadi Islam was the selection of an imam rather than hereditary succession. In the middle of the eighteenth century the present ruling family, the Al Bu Said, succeeded in maintaining hereditary succession. The family moved its capital from Nizwa in the interior to Muscat on the coast, and thereafter, there was periodic war between the Al Bu Said and tribes in the interior who continued to support an elected imam. The last such flare-up occurred in 1955, when a British-led force in the name of the sultan ousted the imam from his inland stronghold at Nizwa. The imam has been in exile in Saudi Arabia and Egypt ever since, but is reportedly willing to return home as a nonpolitical figure if the right import dealership can be given to him.

Only in Oman is the ancient division of the northern and southern Arab tribes still a political factor. The southern Arabs, or Qahtanis, according to legend are descended from Himyar, the son of Qahtan, and are called "true Arabs." The northerners, or Adnanis, are said to be descendants of Ibrahim (Abraham) and Ismail (Ishmael) through Adnan, and are called "assimilated Arabs." Elsewhere, the universalism of Islam had long overshadowed the split which had been a principal element in the tribal wars of the

Arabian Peninsula. In Oman, the split is still reflected in the major tribal factions, the Hinawis and the Ghafiris. The labels date from an eighteenth century civil war that pitted the chief of the Bani Hina against the chief of the Bani Ghafir. The Ghafiris attracted the northern Arab tribes while the Hinawis generally attracted the southern Arabs. The Hinawis were the staunchest supporters of the imam. The Ghafiris, among them the Al Bu Said, also are generally Ibadi, but are less strict and more receptive to outside influences. Some of the Ghafiri tribes are Sunni, and a few have adopted the Wahhabi revival.

One other group of Omanis is worth mentioning, the "overseas Omanis." During the years of imamate-sultanate civil strife and the long years of isolation imposed by the present sultan's father, an estimated quarter-million Omanis left the country to find work elsewhere. In addition, the Arab ruling class of Zanzibar, which was historically Omani, was displaced in a revolution in the 1960s. Many of these overseas Omanis have valuable skills desperately needed in Oman. Some, particularly Zanzabaris (many of whom know no Arabic), have returned. Others are more hesitant to do so. Their return would add a tremendous modernizing force to Oman. It has already been noted that returning Omanis with superior skills can create animosities among the less well educated natives. At this juncture, however, Oman can use all the help it can get.

In sum, the gulf is a polyglot of many kinds of people, cultures, and life styles. Much attention has been given in this chapter to tribal, religious, and national affiliations and loyalties. In concluding, however, it should be emphasized that these loyalties are not necessarily, or even frequently, consciously considered by gulf leaders in deciding on policies. No one will say, because I am a Shi'a, or a Wahhabi, or an Arab, or a member of the Bani Utub, I will do thus and so. The gulf leaders head sovereign states, and it is the interests of their states on which they focus in making decisions. But those interests are seen through the eyes of individuals whose own identities are, whether consciously or not, bound up in more traditional loyalties.

NOTES

[1]Carlton S. Coon, *Caravan: The Story of the Middle East,* Rev. Ed. (New York: Henry Holt and Company, 1958), p. 10.

[2]*Ibid.,* p. 11.

[3]There is a small community of central Asian Muslims locally called "Taskhandis" who were allowed to settle after fleeing from the Soviet Union several decades ago.

[4]Wahhabis prefer to be called *Muwahhidin* or "unitarians," denoting their strict monotheism, rather than Wahhabis, which to them implies deification of their spiritual founder. In their strict belief that religious reverence be reserved only for God, Wahhabis are buried in unmarked graves so that no one may come to revere the dead. This applies to kings and commoners alike.

[5]Although there was a census in the early 1960s, no figures were ever released, and estimates vary from 4 to over 8 million. The 1973 United Nations estimate was 8,443,006. Preliminary indications from the 1974 census put the figure close to 4 million.

[6]Population figures in 1970 gave the total population at 738,662, of which 347,396 were aliens and 391,266 were Kuwaiti citizens.

[7]For a more detailed discussion of ethnic groups in the gulf amirates, see John Duke Anthony, *The Arab Gulf Shaykhdoms: People, Politics, Petroleum* (Washington, D.C.: Middle East Institute, 1975).

[8]The terms *shaykh* and *shaykhdom, amir* and *amirate* are used interchangeably in describing the gulf principalities.

[9]See below, Chap. 2, p. 39.

2   The Political Dynamics
of the Gulf States

The politics of the gulf operate on several different levels. At one level are the political dynamics of each individual state. At a broader level are the regional gulf politics. And finally, there is the political impact of the gulf on states outside the region, i.e., the gulf in world politics. An understanding of all three levels is essential to a meaningful discussion of U.S. interests in the gulf. This chapter concentrates on the first level, the political dynamics of the separate states.

All gulf political regimes, whether radical or conservative, must operate with roughly the same raw materials: traditional societies and a small but growing number of educated elites. Thus, tribal, family, and technocratic relationships are as important in the operation of government in Ba'thist Iraq as in Wahhabi Saudi Arabia. Another common factor among all the gulf states is a shortage of qualified participants in the governmental decision-making process. Since the gulf area became a principal capital market, this problem has been exacerbated by the large number of foreign visitors who make demands on the time of the small number of key decision makers. Often pressing decisions are delayed simply because no one has time to focus on the problem.

Modern political ideologies play a relatively minor role in domestic Middle Eastern politics. Political actions are based more on personalities than on abstract political ideas. For example, Nasserism, once thought to be the most potent political ideology in the Arab world, did not long survive the leader after whom it was named. Even Ba'thism, which has survived the overthrow of a number of regimes professing to be Ba'thist, is essentially what the various leaders in power say it is. At the moment, there is more enmity between Syrian and Iraqi Ba'thist regimes than between them and several non-Ba'thist regimes.

The political ideology espoused by a regime may, however, give an indication of the country's foreign policy alignment. Radical regimes such as Iraq generally, though not always, side politically with communist countries, and conservative regimes such as Saudi Arabia and Iran side with the West. But this tells one very little about domestic politics. For that, one must look at the relationship between leaders and followers.

Iran

In theory, Iran is a constitutional monarchy with the shah as head of state, a cabinet government headed by a prime minister appointed by the shah, and a two-house legislature. The lower house, the Majlis, consisting of 220 members, is elected by popular universal suffrage. Though Shi'a Islam is the offical state religion, by special provision two Majlis deputies are elected by the Armenian Christian community, and one each by the Zoroastrian (the pre-Islamic faith of Persia) and the Jewish communities. Since 1963, women may also be deputies, and in 1967 four were seated.[1] There is also an upper house, the Senate, generally assigned a lesser role than the Majlis. Half of its sixty members are elected and the other half are appointed by the shah; they all must be Muslim and at least forty years of age. Iran also has an independent judiciary with a legal code based on the French system.

In practice, the present shah dominates the Iranian government, both by his control over the levers of political power and coercion and by the sheer force of his personality. The latter should not be underestimated. The shah was nearly ousted in August 1973 as the result of an abortive attempt by Premier Muhammad Mussadiq to gain control of the country. Since that time, he has steadily increased his personal authority as well as the power and prestige of Iran throughout the region. The energy crisis beginning in 1973 has to some extent given the shah the chance to play a global role. It afforded him a forum, the Organization of Petroleum Exporting Countries (OPEC), and an issue, the world price of oil. With his extraordinary diplomatic talents, he has used the oil issue to project a forceful image of power. As one long-time observer of Iranian affairs stated it, the shah is about the closest thing to an absolute monarch existing in the world today.

The shah governs through a complex network of informal, interlocking, and sometimes competing personal relationships. For example, often two cabinet ministers are asked to provide the same information or undertake the same task: in this way, the shah can safeguard against unreliable information from an official who is "putting a good face" on unpleasant news, or can create incentive through competition to get a task done as quickly and efficiently as possible. Knowing how to function within the governmental system (or for an outsider, knowing how to insure that it functions for him) therefore entails much more than merely knowing who fills what position. In many cases, one's position of influence within the informal system can be more important than the formal position or job title one holds. This, of course, also holds true for most of the gulf states.

The political security of the regime rests on the internal security and national defense forces, on the one hand, and an ambitious economic development program, the White Revolution, on the other. The White Revolution is actually a continuation of the shah's basic development program, first announced in the Land Reform Bill of 1962. Even the most cursory look at Iranian government expenditures will show how much importance the shah places on both security and development.

The shah's technocratic absolutism supercedes the older traditional system of political dynamics in which tribal, religious, commercial, and other groups participated in the distribution power. While these groups are still economically and socially very important in many respects, the consolidation of physical and economic power by the shah through the bureaucracy and armed and security forces has eliminated most of their participation in the political system.

The process has also resulted in modernization and social reform being imposed from above, which is perhaps the only way it can be effective. This has been a positive factor in that the government can override parochial interests resisting change. But it also in some cases limits the real depth of change, creating instead a façade under which traditional ideas are still very strong and bitterness and frustration remain barely beneath the surface.

Iraq

Iraq has a single-party regime under the Socialist Arab Ba'th ("Renaissance") party. The government is a branch of the same party that rules Syria, but the two regimes are not on good terms, each claiming orthodoxy with the zeal characteristic of revolutionaries. Like many revolutionary ideologies in the Middle East, Ba'-thism is an imprecise amalgamation of antiimperialistic xenophobia, nostaliga for the golden age of the Arab caliphates, and a strong commitment to redistribution of wealth and power for the benefit of the poorer classes. Its major appeal in Iraq has been among the city dwellers at the lowest and least secure end of the middle class.

As in many one-party states where party membership is a *sine qua non* for career advancement, many younger Iraqis of all socially and politically aware classes are joining the Ba'th party. However, if one considers only the party's politically committed members, it represents a small minority of the population. Despite this, no anti-Ba'thi group has the capability to overthrow the regime, and the government is careful to maintain the loyalty of the army, which does have the resources to effect a coup. By Middle East standards, the Ba'th regime in Iraq is relatively stable.

The Ba'th party of Iraq has two wings, a military wing which at the time of this writing is led by Iraqi President Ahmad Hasan al-Bakr, and a civilian wing headed by Saddam Husayn al-Tikriti, vice chairman of the party and of the Revolutionary Command Council.2 President Bakr is considered the elder statesman of the regime, but in recent years he has taken an increasingly less active role in politics. The civilian wing of the party, under Saddam Husayn, has become ascendant and currently dominates Iraqi politics.

Saddam Husayn has a reputation for ruthless pragmatism. To Western eyes, the combination may seem a bit perplexing. He has never allowed Ba'th ideology, however defined, to interfere with meeting the needs and interests of Iraq as he perceives them. At the same time, however, recent signs that Iraq may be moderating its hostility to the West should not be interpreted as a relinquishing of the radical, revolutionary spirit inherent in Ba'thism.

In recent years, despite strong foreign policy concerns over the Arab-Israeli problem, Arab world politics, Iran, and the Persian Gulf, Iraq has tended to focus primarily on domestic issues. Until the Iranian-Iraqi rapprochement announced on March 6, 1975, the most pressing problem was the Kurdish insurgency aided by Iran. As a result of the rapprochement, the situation now appears to be manageable, but the Kurdish national movement in both Iraq and Iran will continue to be a major potential security problem.

From the Iraqi regime's point of view, much needs to be done in economic development and in extending its base of support throughout the country. With vastly increased revenues accruing from higher oil prices, domestic development is going on at an accelerated pace. The effects of this development on the political dynamics of Iraq remain to be seen, but over time they are almost certain to be far-reaching.

Saudi Arabia

The kingdom of Saudi Arabia was created in 1932 from the formerly separate principalities of Najd and the Hijaz. Members of the House of Saud have ruled over Najd, however, since the mid-eighteenth century, except for periods when rivals temporarily eclipsed them. In 1818, for example, an Ottoman army invaded and burned the Saudi capital, Dir'iyya. The Sauds rebuilt their capital nearby at Riyadh, where it has remained to this day.

Saudi Arabia is one of the very few countries for which sacred Islamic, or Shari'a, law forms the fundamental law of the land. The judicial system is based on Islamic courts presided over by *qadis,* Islamic judges. Because according to the Shari'a only God can make laws, there has been no legislature in Saudi Arabia in the Western sense. The equivalent of Western legislation has taken the form of administrative regulations called *nizams*. There is, however, a practically defunct Consultative Assembly (Majlis al-Shurra) for the Hijaz, and in April 1975 Crown Prince Fahd announced plans to create a national Consulative Assembly.[3]

The king of Saudi Arabia is the chief of state and head of government. Saudi public administration did not evolve according to a master plan. Instead, institutions were created as the need for them arose. The first national ministry was Foreign Affairs, established in 1930, when the country was still the Kingdom of the Hijaz and Najd. Except for one brief period, King Faysal was foreign minister from the creation of the ministry until his death in 1975. In the last years of King Faysal's reign, however, much of the day to day conduct of foreign affairs was delegated to the late Omar al-Saqqaf (d. 1974), who was given the title minister of state for foreign affairs. Under King Khalid, Faysal's son Prince Saud has been appointed minister of foreign affairs.

The Ministry of Finance was founded in 1932 and many of the subsequent ministries began as departments under it. The most recent ministry, Justice, was formed in 1970. Under the new administration of King Khalid and Crown Prince Fahd, other changes, particularly in local government, can be expected.

The development of the Saudi bureaucracy has channeled political power into a more organized and regulated administrative system than was the case under the traditional system of personal consultation practiced by the king's father, Abd al-Aziz. Nevertheless, the functioning of the bureaucracy still has many holdovers from the traditional system. Ministries often operate independently of each other; delegation of authority is at best limited; and decision making is still highly personalized.

The king is at the apex of the Saudi political system. But since the accession of King Khalid after the assassination of King Faysal on March 25, 1975, a new element has been added. Khalid as king and prime minister must ultimately be responsible for all decisions. But his half-brother Crown Prince Fahd has been given the role of chief administrator of the government. (There is a precedent for this kind of situation in the late 1950s, when Faysal, then crown prince, was prime minister under his brother King Saud.) At the time of this writing it is still too early to tell what effect the dual Khalid-Fahd administration will have on Saudi decision making.

Because the Saudi king is supreme in national politics, it has been widely assumed in the West that he is an absolute monarch. This is not so. Shari'a law places definite constraints on the king's powers. More important, the king is answerable to the royal family, without whose support he cannot rule. Saudi royal-family politics operate completely outside the framework of Saudi national politics, although many prominent royal princes are also active in national politics.

Numbering from 3,000 to 7,000, the House of Saud is very circumspect about its affairs and little is known about its dynamics. The most powerful group are the sons of Abd al-Aziz, from whose number the past three kings and present crown prince were chosen. The sons tend to gravitate toward sibling groups of full brothers (King Abd al-Aziz had many wives). The senior brother, Prince Muhammad, is also a full brother of King Khalid. Because of health and personal reasons, Muhammad chose to give up his claims to the throne in favor of a younger brother. One of the most powerful sibling groups is the seven-member Al Fahd ("Family of Fahd," named for the eldest brother; the group is also known in the West as the Sudayri Seven, after the maiden name of their mother). Of the seven, Fahd is crown prince, first deputy prime minister, and minister of interior; Sultan is minister of defense and aviation; Naif is minister of state for interior; and three others have noncabinet positions in the government.

Other important groups within the royal family are the surviving brothers of Abd al-Aziz. Prince Abdullah bin Abd al-Rahman, the eldest surviving uncle of King Khalid, is the senior member of the family. Prince Musa'd, the former minister of finance and national economy, is another. In addition to the immediate family, there are three important collateral branches: the Bin Jaluwis, the Thunayans, and the Al Saud al-Kabirs. King Khalid's mother was a Bin Jaluwi, as is the amir ("governor") of Eastern Province. Because it is descended from an older brother of King Abd al-Aziz's father, the Saud al-Kabir branch actually claims precedence over all but the king in royal family protocol. All members of the royal family, plus leading religious figures (including the Al al-Shaykhs, descendants of founder of Wahhabism) and cabinet-ranking political figures, comprise the *ahl al-aqd wal-hall*, "the people who bind and loose." In 1964 this group deposed King Saud in favor of King Faysal.

Other important groups in Saudi Arabia include the nonroyal Najdi aristocratic families, the leading one of which is the Sudayris. Of somewhat lesser importance politicially are tribal and business leaders. The armed forces have never played the key role in Saudi politics that they have in other developing countries. As a safeguard against a military coup, however, Saudi Arabia has a tribally organized National Guard under Prince Abdallah, another half-brother of the king and second deputy prime minister.

One unique aspect of Saudi public administration is the annual *hajj* ("pilgrimage") to Mecca, attended by a million and a half Muslims. At a cost of millions of dollars a year, the *hajj* requires the entire administrative resources of the government.

It occurs annually according to the Muslim calendar, which is eleven days shorter than the solar calendar. This is one reason (the main reasons are religious) why the Saudis have not adopted a solar fiscal year. They would be too hard pressed to administer the *hajj* and produce the annual budget if both were required in the same period, as would eventually happen. Producing the budget also takes nearly all the administrative resources of the government.

Kuwait

To a large degree, Kuwait and the other gulf amirates are governed as oligarchical partnerships among the ruling families, tribal affiliations, and an old, established merchant class. The terms of these partnerships differ in each case, and the massive inflow of oil revenues is affecting far-reaching changes, but generally speaking, the business of government in these states is primarily business.

Kuwait is a constitutional monarchy with the amir as chief of state, a cabinet government, a National Assembly, and an independent judiciary. The judicial system, while theoretically based on Shari'a law, is in practiced based on a legal code adopted from the Egyptian code, which itself was largely based on European law.

The Al Sabahs, as the royal family, are at the head of the Kuwaiti political system. From their number are chosen the amir, the prime minister, and many of the more important ministers.

Two groups of cousins within the family are important politically, the Al Jabir and the Al Salim. Traditionally the two branches alternated in providing the ruler, but in 1965 Amir Sabah, an Al Salim, succeeded Abdallah, another Al Salim. Since then, attempts have been made to placate the Al Jabirs and their supporters with government appointments at the expense of the Al Salim supporters. Moreover, the crown prince is Shaykh Jabir al-Ahmad, of the Al Jabir branch.

The Al Sabahs have never dominated political decision making in Kuwait the way the Al Sauds have in Saudi Arabia. Traditionally, they shared power with aristocratic merchant families such as the Ghanims, Saqrs, Salihs, Khalids, and Jana'ts. To a great extent, power sharing has been informal. Since the 1962 Constitution, however, a new institution, the National Assembly, has been added to the system. Although the National Assembly is somewhat restricted in its legislative role, it is not a rubber stamp for the ruler and the prime minister. Very often it questions the government on policy, and places legislative impediments in the path of unpopular policies. In a showdown the government can override the National Assembly, but since the assembly is controlled by the oligarchy which shares powers and interests with the royal family, this distinction is not so meaningful as it might appear. And on issues that the government temporarily wishes to table, it has been known to claim the heated and prolonged debate in the National Assembly as a pretext for a delayed decision on the issue.

Since its inception, the National Assembly has included an opposition group noted for its progressive, leftist views. The "elder statesman" of this group is Dr. Ahmad al-Khatib, head of the Kuwaiti organization of the Marxist-leaning Arab Nationalist movement (ANM). A younger member is Sami Munayyis, editor of *al-Tali'a*. Over the years, the opposition appears to have matured. Although socialisit rhetoric is still constantly heard in the National Assembly, the opposition in recent years has also begun to focus on domestic as well as foreign issues, questioning the way in which Kuwaiti government policies affect the Kuwaiti national interest.

One of the chief restrictions of the National Assembly is its very narrow electoral base. Of a total population of nearly 1 million in Kuwait, less than half are Kuwaiti citizens; and of the latter, only about 50,000 are qualified to vote. The narrow electoral base ensures control of the government by the oligarchical power elite. But it denies participation in the political decision-making process to a growing number of educated and capable young Kuwaitis, who are largely the product of Kuwait's cradle-to-grave welfare program, which includes free education, and there is increasing concern both within and outside the government over how to deal with the problem.

The large number of aliens in Kuwait, including some 200,000 Palestinians, has been viewed by many as a potential source of political instability. But except for the growing number of long-time alien residents who, as nonenfranchised Kuwaitis, wish more participation in the political process, the alien population has not to date been a security threat. This is in part due to the government's policy of co-opting potential dissidents through its generous welfare system, many of the benefits of which are shared with non-Kuwaitis. In addition, wages and the standard of living in Kuwait are far better than most aliens could expect to find at home or elsewhere, and the threat of expulsion for any subversive activity is a considerable deterrent.

The armed forces, though only about 10,000 in number, provide the physical power behind the regime. Their loyalty is therefore quite important. The Kuwaiti armed forces are equipped with the latest equipment, and are relatively well trained and educated. Thus far, the possibility of a dissident officers' movement, though never to be ruled out, has been considered fairly remote.

In sum, the combination of the royal family-merchant family oligarchy, the all-embracing welfare system, and the armed forces has kept Kuwait relatively stable. An additional safety valve should be mentioned: the Kuwait press is among the freest, if not the most free, of any in the entire Middle East.

Bahrain

Fully independent only since 1971, Bahrain elected to follow Kuwait's lead in creating an Islamic constitutional monarchy and an elected National Assembly (Majlis al-Watini). Bahrain's assembly had even fewer powers than Kuwait's, but a far greater proportion of its population (of some 250,000) could vote. In August 1975, however, the assembly was dissolved.

The royal family of Bahrain, the al-Khalifahs, has not had to share power with the merchant aristocracy to the same extent that their royal cousins in Kuwait have. Moreover, the merchant class was not particularly interested in the new National Assembly. Thus, the Bahraini assembly did not mirror the merchant oligarchy in

Bahrain. Additionally, despite a fairly large electoral base, the assembly attracted few of the younger educated Bahrainis. This group still gravitates primarily to the government bureaucracy. Government workers had to resign their positions to take a seat in the Majlis, and generally they preferred the security of bureaucracy over the uncertainties of politics.

As a result, the Majlis consisted for the most part of traditionalists, few of whom had a Western education. Such representation emphasized—perhaps overemphasized—the religious cleavages between the Shi'a and Sunni communities.

Two other groups were represented in the Majlis, labor and the leftist intellectuals; the latter also espouse the cause of the laboring class. In the absence of labor unions, these representatives did provide some means for communication between labor and government. The grand old man of the radicals, Abd al-Aziz Sa'd Shamlan, returned to Bahrain after years of exile and was elected to the 1972 assembly, which was tasked to draft a constitution. In the 1974 elections, however, he failed to obtain a seat. A younger group of radicals were elected, including Dr. Abd al-Hadi Khalaf of the radical National Liberation Front-Bahrain (NLF-B)—it and all other parties are banned—and Yusif Hasan al-Ajaji. However, they and three others were barred by the government from taking their seats. Many in the ruling elite considered the Majlis a haven of radicalism and welcomed its dissolution.

Despite the brief experiment in constitutional monarchy, the al-Khalifahs always monopolized the power structure. Shaykh Isa bin Salman is the ruler, his brother Shaykh Khalifa bin Salman is prime minister, and Shaykh Muhammad bin Mubarak is foreign minister. Several other members of the family also hold important ministerial portfolios. The impetus for governmental reform comes in great part from the ruler, Shaykh Isa. To the extent that reform enhances the feeling of participation among the Bahraini population, it can be viewed as a long-range investment by the royal family in maintaining the regime. Given declining oil revenues, a large labor force, and a sophistication that in the past has spawned a tradition of labor unrest, reform appears very worthwhile and the dissolution of the assembly a setback. In the meantime, Bahrain has to rely on its security forces, which are aided by outside advisors, in order to maintain its internal security.

Qatar

Of all the gulf amirates, the division of labor between the merchant class and the royal family is greatest in Qatar. The ruling Al Thani family has had a virtual monopoly on government, and the business community has stuck pretty largely to business. To be sure, there was and is close cooperation between the two groups for mutual benefit, but each has remained for the most part in its own sphere. That trend is beginning to change, if only slightly. Abundant oil revenues have brought the royal family a more lively interest in business, and the merchant community a more active interest in the repository of those revenues, the government. Moreover, educated young members of both groups are beginning to seek broader horizons than those of their fathers.

For the foreseeable future, nevertheless, the government appears to be firmly in the hands of the royal family. A constitution was adopted in 1970 (before the British departure), creating a Council of Ministers and an independent judiciary based in theory on Islamic law as in Kuwait and Bahrain. Although some mention was made of a Consultative Council, there is no independent legislative branch and laws are made by decree. The ruler, Shaykh Khalifah bin Hamad Al Thani, is also prime minister, and ten of the fifteen ministerial portfolios are held by members of the royal family, including the key ministries of Interior, Defense, Finance and National Economy and Foreign affairs.

Despite the constitution, therefore, the only major constraints on the ruler's power are Islam and the royal family. Shaykh Khalifah, who is known as a forceful and dedicated ruler, ousted his cousin Shaykh Ahmad in 1972 in what is known locally as the Change. There is still some ill feeling between the two branches of the family, but not enough to threaten the security of the regime. The Al Thanis, who subscribe to the Wahhabi revival, are militantly anticommunists and keep a tight rein on potential subversion. Their security forces are among the best in the gulf amirates.

The regime is spending a great deal of its resources on education, social welfare, and economic development projects, and as yet, expectations of the people seem not to have exceeded the government's ability to meet them. The conservatism of the population, the benefits of oil revenues, and strong security measures have thus combined to make Qatar, at least for now, one of the more stable of the gulf amirates. In the longer run, however, much will depend on the regime's capability to adapt to the changing social, economic, and political conditions that its development programs are certain to create.

The United Arab Emirates (UAE)

On December 1, 1971, Britain formally relinquished its protective status over the seven lower gulf shaykhdoms known collectively as the Trucial States. The following day, six of the seven joined a loose federation, the United Arab Emirates (UAE). The seventh, Ras al-Khaymah, did not join until February 10, 1972.

There is almost as much disparity as similarity among the UAE members. None has a large population, but the range among them is fairly wide. Abu Dhabi has the most inhabitants, about 80,000, and Dubai has slightly less; Sharjah's population is around 35,000; Ras al-Khaymah has around 30,000; and Ajman, Umm al-Qaywayn, and Fujayrah all number less than 10,000. They are economically disparate also. Abu Dhabi has a huge oil income; Dubai has both an oil and a mercantile economy; and Sharjah has just come on stream with a modest amount of oil. As yet, Ras al-Khaymah has found no oil, but does have a relatively productive agricultural sector. The other three emirates are desperately poor, subsisting on fishing, nomadic herding, some pearling, and largess from their wealthier neighbors, chiefly Abu Dhabi.

The closest political analogy to the UAE in the West is the United States as it existed under the Articles of the Confederation, when each state retained a large degree of autonomy. The UAE provisional constitution, promulgated in 1971, provides for a president, vice president, Council of Ministers, and a legislative body called the Federal National Council. Of the forty seats in the legislative council, eight each are allotted to Abu Dhabi and Dubai; six each to Sharjah and Ras al-Khaymah; and four each to Ajman, Dubai, and Umm al-Qaywayn. Council members are appointed by their various rulers and meet for six-month sessions beginning in November each year. At the first meeting, in February 1972, a speaker and two deputy speakers were elected. Among the council's responsibilities is approving the budget, and it can also initiate legislation. In fact, however, with power firmly in the hands of the seven rulers, the legislative body is little more than a debating society. The president of the UAE, with the approval of the Federal Supreme Council, can dissolve the Federal National Council by decree.

Institutionally, the real power in the federal structure is vested in the Federal Supreme Council, composed of the shaykhs of the seven member amirates. In some respects this body is the continuation of collegial consultation within the old Trucial States Council, established by the British in 1952. Federal Supreme Council decisions must have the approval of five of the seven members; Abu Dhabi and Dubai have a veto power.

In theory, the UAE federal structure was originally to have control over defense,finance, and foreign affairs, with all internal powers remaining under the local jurisdiction of the various amirates. In practice, the lines of demarcation are much more blurred. Each amirate jealously guards its prerogatives and cooperates within the federal structure only to the extent that its own interests are served or protected.

The success of guiding the UAE through its birth pangs to its current state of development is largely attributed to its president, Shaykh Zayd bin Sultan Al Nuhayyan of Abu Dhabi. Not only does Abu Dhabi contribute the largest proportion of the UAE budget, but the other major contributor, Dubai, has to date never paid its share. Thus the wheels of the UAE turn almost entirely on Abu Dhabi money.

From the outset, the Ministry of Foreign Affairs has acted as the spokesman for the entire UAE in regional and international affairs. Some of the UAE ambassadors abroad, however, retain more loyalty to their amirates than to the union they represent. The Finance Ministry has never had any power, since financial policy is set by the individual shaykhdoms. On the other hand, the central bank, called the UAE Currency Board, does regulate money and banking for the entire federation.

The union's Ministry of National Defense has also not functioned very well. The minister, Shaykh Muhammad bin Rashid al-Maktum, is the son of the ruler of Dubai. The UAE inherited the British-created Trucial Oman Scouts, renamed the Union Defense Force (UDF). Its principal mission is to keep order among the tribes, and, under the British, it remained strictly uninvolved in tribal politics. Although there are still expatriates and representatives from all the shaykhdoms among its officers and men, the UDF's association with Dubai has weakened its nontribal identification. Moreover, the UDF has been eclipsed in size and capability by the Abu Dhabi Defense Force (ADDF). The latter numbers around 6,000 men, including mostly expatriate officers, and is equipped with Mirage aircraft. Shaykh Zayd, in his capacity as president of the UAE, has increasingly called out the ADDF to quell tribal disputes in the other shaykhdoms, often without waiting to consult the local rulers. In addition to the UDF and the ADDF, other shaykhdoms have small internal security forces.

One of the most successful UAE ministries is Education. It administers schools throughout the amirates, and is expanding the school system as rapidly as possible. In the long run, the federal school system could be a major contributor to political attitudes strengthening the concept of union.

Another unifying factor is the extensive program to link the UAE by an all-weather road system. Already one can drive from Abu Dhabi to Ras al-Khaymah and beyond in under three hours and to the Buraymi Oasis town of al-Ayn in little over an hour. New roads are being planned and constructed into the hinterland, including a road to link the Gulf of Oman coast with the rest of the UAE.

In late 1973 Shaykh Zayd announced measures he was taking to strengthen the federal structure. Basically they consisted of abolishing the Abu Dhabi Council of Ministers and incorporating all but his key ministries (e.g., Finance and Defense) into the UAE cabinet. The latter was increased in size to twenty-six ministries plus the prime minister and a deputy prime minister. In many ways, the larger cabinet is still window dressing in that federal-level decisions are made by the president and the Federal Supreme Council. The expansion did enable Zayd to bring into the cabinet more representatives from the poorer amirates. At the same time, jobs had to be found for the Abu Dhabi ministers whose ministries had been abolished, and some of the new ministries, while federal in name, are in practice still only

responsible for Abu Dhabi affairs. A case in point is the elevation of the Abu Dhabi Ministry of Petroleum to the federal level. The other two oil producers, Dubai and Sharjah, not only dictate their own oil policies, but neither of them have ever participated in the

Organization of Petroleum Exporting Countries (OPEC), although The UAE is a member. Thus the UAE minister of petroleum administers only Abu Dhabi oil.

Despite these beginnings of a federal structure, the locus of power in the UAE still rests at the individual shaykhdom level.

Abu Dhabi is the largest, wealthiest, and most powerful of all the amirates. Shaykh Zayd rules as a traditional Islamic monarch, the major constraints being Islam and the royal family. The Al Nuhayyan are the paramount family of the Al Bu Falah branch of the Bani Yas tribe. Not only Al Nuhayyan family politics, but also broader tribal politics, enter into government decision making. Unlike most of the other gulf states, Abu Dhabi never has developed an extensive merchant class.

Before the post-1973 oil boom, Zayd was very accessible to his subjects. The huge demands on his time since then, as both shaykh of Abu Dhabi and president of the UAE, and the shortage of bureaucratic expertise to share some of the burden, have made him far less accessible as time goes on. Though probably not serious, there are grumblings among tribal and other leaders that they can no longer get an audience as they once could.

Abu Dhabi still has some key ministries, as mentioned above. As elsewhere in the gulf, foreign advisors also play a big role. Beyond these groups, public administration is almost nonexistent except for the ADDF and security forces. In 1971 Zayd created a Consultative Council. Numbering fifty, it is entirely appointed by the ruler and has few powers other than helping to create a consensus through which the ruler makes decisions.

Dubai's ruler, Shaykh Rashid al-Maktum, was expected to be a major political personality in the UAE when it was established in 1971. He is vice president of the federation and three of his sons are the UAE prime minister, minister of finance and industry, and minister of national defense. To date, however, Rashid has not concerned himself very actively in federation affairs. His attitude toward the union appears to be ambivalent. While not actively opposed to it, neither does he support it beyond making sure that Dubai's interests do not suffer from his nonparticipation.

Shaykh Rashid is head of the paramount al-Maktum family of the Al Bu Falasa branch of the Bani Yas. He rules Dubai more as the chairman of the board and majority stockholder than as a monarch, and is much more interested in business than in government. While Rashid's authority is clearly supreme, he rules through informal relationships with the merchant-class oligarchy, expatriate advisors, and tribal and other groups. He is extremely accessible and appears to have knowledge, if not a share, of every business enterprise in the amirate.

Public administration in Dubai is haphazard. The ruler depends on a trusted group of people, including a number of expatriates, most of whom have been in Dubai for a very long time. For example, one of his closest advisors is Mahdi Tajir, of Bahraini origin, currently UAE ambassador to London. Such basic areas as public finance, customs, public works, and police functions are also administered in great part through foreign advisors or through foreign banks and companies. One of Dubai's major problems is keeping middle-ranking personnel. One expatriate advisor complained that, because of such low salaries in the public sector, it is too great a temptation for this group, once trained, to leave the government bureaucracy and seek to become millionaires.

Sharjah is just ten miles up the road from Dubai (you can see one town from the other on a clear day). Sharjah has never had good relations with neighboring Dubai, and Sharjawis still remember the days when Sharjah, not Dubai, was the leading commercial center in the lower gulf. The ruler, Shaykh Sultan bin Muhammad al-Qasimi, is the only gulf ruler to have earned a university degree. He came to power in 1972 after an unsuccessful coup resulted in the death of the former ruler, Shaykh Khalid.

In the last year, Sharjah has become an oil producer, giving its economy and its merchant community a new lease on life. While Shaykh Sultan is in close consultation with the merchant community, particularly on economic development policies, tribal politics are also a major consideration in Sharjah's politics, particularly those of the predominant Qawasim tribe, to which the royal family belongs. The shaykh administers several noncontiguous tribal enclaves, including three towns on the Gulf of Oman—Dibba, the jursidiction of which is actually split among Sharjah, Fajayrah, and Oman; Khawr Fakkan; and Kalba, once a separate amirate.

Ras al-Khaymah's royal family is also from the Qawasim. The ruler, Shaykh Saqr bin Muhammad al-Qasimi, is thus related to the ruler of Sharjah, and the two amirates have had a long history of close political association.

Shaykh Saqr is a very dynamic and independent-minded ruler. He chafes under the disability of not possessing an oil income, and his dissatisfaction with the preponderant role of Abu Dhabi and Dubai in the new federation was a major reason he refused to join the UAE for almost three months after its creation.

With only a very small merchant community and a lack of economic development, Saqr's political administration is far more traditionalist, rudimentary, and tribally oriented than the administrations of oil-producing shaykhdoms. In this regard, Ras al-Khaymah is ruled in much the same personal and informal manner as the three poorest and smallest shaykhdoms, *Ajman, Umm al-Qaywayn*, and *Fujayrah.*

Oman

Political dynamics underwent a tremendous change in Oman in 1970 when the present sultan, Qabus bin Said Al Bu Said, replaced his father, Said bin Taymur, in a bloodless coup. Prior to 1970, Said bin Taymur had ruled as an oriental despot, playing off tribes, merchants, and religious groups with the aid of his British-led army. In later years a recluse, he lived in Salalah, capital of Dhufar, 600 miles from the national capital at Muscat. Qabus, who was educated in England, also lived in Salalah under house arrest for the years preceding the coup. Under Said bin Taymur, the country languished, and even after oil production began in 1967, almost no efforts were made to modernize.

One of Sultan Qabus's first acts was to rename the country the Sultanate of Oman. The old name, Muscat and Oman, accentuated the historical political cleavage between inner Oman and the coastal area around the capital. This division had last erupted into open hostilities in the 1950s when a British-led force defeated the Ibadi imam, who fled from his "capital" at Nizwa into exile in Saudi Arabia.

In 1970 Dhufar was also incorporated into Oman. Formerly, it had the status of a separate sultanate joined to Muscat only in the person of the ruler. Qabus had thus unified the country in name. It now remained for him to unify it in fact.

Since 1970, Qabus has instituted a Council of Ministers with seventeen cabinet positions.[4] Local government is administered by forty *walis* ("governors"), and each *wilayah* ("governate" or "province") has attached to it a *qadi*, or Shari'a judge. In the major towns, there are also municipal councils whose members are chosen by the traditional means of tribal affiliation and consensus. Despite these innovations, decision making still emanates from the top. The burgeoning range of decisions to be made as a result of ambitious development programs, the tendency of the sultan to delegate authority only to a few trusted advisors, and the dearth of technocrats able to make decisions all combine to make the governing process more cumbersome in many ways than it was in the past.

The politically important groups in Oman are the royal family, the tribes, the merchant community, and key expatriate advisors. Under Said bin Taymur, an elaborate web of personal relationships was used to deal with these groups, at times playing one group off against the other. Under Sultan Qabus, much of the old system has been dropped, but because the new governmental institutions that the sultan is creating have not been functioning long enough to comprise a new system, political dynamics are for the present in somewhat of a transitional stage. In other words, decision making is still centered at the top and the same groups still have influence, but new lines of communication through the bureaucracy are competing with the old personality network, thus changing the configuration of power.

In the new configuration, the royal family still has a major influence. The sultan relies on his uncles and cousins in key positions in the government, including a number of the ministerial posts. The political power of the tribes appears to be waning. On the other hand, the merchant class is holding its own, but is having to compete with the bureaucracy to participate in economic development projects. The predominance of non-Ibadi, and in many cases non-Omani, merchants may further dilute the influence of this group as Omani nationalism grows. Moreover, oil revenues may also induce Omanis who formerly shunned commerce to compete with the old established families.

The regime continues to rely heavily on expatriates. The British, who maintain their base rights on Masirah Island, still largely run the armed forces. There are British advisors in other key positions as well. Iranian and Jordanian troops have been sent to the sultan to counter the insurgency in Dhufar, and Pakistani officers are seconded to the sultan's navy. The oil company Petroleum Development Oman (PDO), with its foreign management, plays a major role in finance. Many third-country Arabs also have influential advisory positions.

Oman, with its lack of trained manpower and development programs and its still embryonic educational system, will have to rely on expatriates for some time to come. The relationship of foreign advisors to Omanis, however, is changing. For years, the British had what amounted to a *de facto* protective role in Oman. Under Qabus, that has all changed. There is now a distinct feeling that as quickly as possible the Omanis aim to control their own affairs.

NOTES

[1]American University, *Area Handbook for Iran* (Washington, D.C.: The American University, 1971), p. 225.

[2]His official titles are assistant secretary of the Regional Command of the Socialist Arab Ba'th party and deputy chairman of the Revolutionary Command Council of the Iraqi Republic.

[3]"Policy Statement of the Kingdom of Saudi Arabia" (a paid advertisement by the Ministry of Information of Saudi Arabia), *Washington Post*, April 15, 1975, p. A-15.

[4]The sultan at the time of this writing is his own defense and finance ministers.

3 Regional Politics of the Gulf

The Gulf as a Regional Political Arena

Outside interest in the regional politics of the gulf stems mainly from interest in gulf oil. But oil is not the driving force of gulf politics, even though it does play a very important role; the politics of the region are primarily the product of internal relationships. Inherent in these relationships are a number of striking contrasts that on occasion erupt into open confrontations and even hostilities. The greatest contrasts lie among conflicting political ideologies and between the two nationalisms which collide head on in the gulf.

In the previous chapter, it was concluded that all of the political systems in the area work with roughly the same human resources and govern in much the same way. It was also noted that the peoples of the area tend to follow political leaders rather than abstract political ideas or ideologies. Nevertheless, there are distinct ideological differences among the gulf political systems. Iraq in the north and the People's Democratic Republic of Yemen (PDRY of South Yemen) to the southwest of the gulf region have radical regimes. Iran, Saudi Arabia, Kuwait, the gulf amirates, and Oman, despite differences in their political outlook and development, all have basically conservative regimes.

Parts of this chapter were developed and expanded from an earlier essay by the author, "Confrontation and Cooperation in the Gulf," *Middle East Problem Paper* no. 10 (Washington, D.C.: The Middle East Institute, December 1974).

The arena for ideological differences is primarily in the field of foreign affairs, both regionally and in gulf relations with the rest of the world. To a great degree, the political stability of the gulf depends not only on the ability of each regime to cope with internal change, but also on the amount of political tension being generated in the region as a whole. One of the key factors in determining the level of tension is the confrontation of radicalism and conservatism.

The two principal states opposing the spread of radicalism in the gulf are Iran and Saudi Arabia. They are the largest, the most influential and powerful of all the conservative states. Thus, the other conservative states, particularly in the area of security, must depend largely on the political, economic, and military support of these two countries. The peripheral states that also play a role in gulf security are Jordan, which has sent combat troops to Oman and military and public security advisors elsewhere in the gulf; and Pakistan, which has military missions in Saudi Arabia, Oman, and the UAE.

Despite the desire of Iran and Saudi Arabia and the other conservative gulf states to cooperate, particularly in the area of regional security, their capacity to do so is inhibited by the collision of Arab and Persian nationalisms in the gulf. Divided by language, culture, and historical traditions, there has rarely been a great affinity between the Persians and the Arabs. They do share a common religion, but even that is tempered by religious schism. The Iranians are predominantly Shi'a Muslims, while most of the Arabian Peninsula Arabs are Sunnis. The conservative Wahhabi Saudis particularly find some of the Shi'a practices repugnant to their strict interpretation of Islam.

The sense of national consciousness in the lower gulf states has not been as fully developed as it is farther north, but even in the lower gulf it is becoming a major political factor. Shaykhdoms which before 1973 scarcely heeded the rhetoric of Arab nationalism in its cause against Israel solidly backed the Arab oil embargo. As it continues to develop, Arab nationalism is increasingly running counter to Iranian national aspirations in the gulf. One of the best illustrations of the conflict is the dispute over the name of the gulf: the Iranians insist that it is the Persian Gulf and even take umbrage over the neutral term, "the gulf"; The Arabs have been just as insistent that it is the Arabian Gulf.

There are other factors influencing gulf politics. One, discussed in chapter 1, is the demographic differences of size, population, and attendant political-military power. Iran, Iraq, and Saudi Arabia are the "big powers" of the gulf. Of the three, Iran has the largest and best-equipped military establishment and is attempting to strengthen it even further through arms acquisitions, chiefly from the United States. To the extent that military force is effective in halting the spread of radicalism in the gulf, Iranian military power can play a stabilizing role. However, were Iran to use its military force on the Arab side of the gulf unilaterally and without adequate consultation among its conservative Arab neighbors, even against some radical threat, it could result in opposition rather than cooperation from the Arab states. Clearly, Iranian military power could be destabilizing as well as stabilizing, depending on how it is used.

In contrast to the Iranian armed forces—which, except for two rotating battalions which have seen duty in Oman, have had no combat experience—the Iraqi armed forces have had recent and relatively large-scale combat experience in the October 1973 Arab-Israeli war and at home in the Kurdish insurgency. At the same time, political purges and ethnic divisions have been an inhibiting factor in their effectiveness; many considered that the Iraqi army's actually getting to the front in the 1973 war was a major logistical accomplishment. Thus, in trying to evaluate the relative strengths of the Iraqi and Iranian armed forces, it is an open question as to whether either could successfully mount an offensive against the other, though both probably have the capability to defend their own territories. In terms of naval strength Iran appears to be more clearly preponderant.

Saudi Arabia, large and sparsely populated, has the smallest military capability of the "big three." It is, however, building up its military voice in the regional security of the gulf.

The smaller states of the gulf—Kuwait, Bahrain, Qatar, the seven UAE shaykhdoms, and Oman—have little political or military power and could scarcely resist political ultimatums from any of the three big gulf states. Nevertheless, the ideological and nationalistic confrontations in the gulf tend to balance each other in restraining any of the larger gulf powers from seeking to impose its will on the smaller states. For example, Iraqi aspirations in the gulf are checked by conservative Saudi Arabia and Iran, whereas Iranian national aspirations are restrained by Arab nationalist sentiments which are shared by the conservative Saudis and the radical Iraqis alike. The resulting political equilibrium allows the smaller gulf states some scope for independent political decision making, probably much more than they otherwise would have.

Among the smaller shaykhdoms, there is also a political dynamic. Prior to the discovery of oil, the shaykhdoms were all poor. Kuwait and Bahrain discovered oil first, and Kuwait's oil revenues caused it to develop more rapidly than the others, both economically and politically. For example, Kuwait attained full independence in 1961, a decade before the others. The other shaykhdoms, remembering the not too distant past when all were poor, began to feel resentfully that Kuwait treated them as poor relations. Discovery of oil in the lower gulf has helped to change that attitude. Moreover, as soon as the British announced their intention to withdraw from the lower gulf, Kuwait embarked on a very successful policy of helpful cooperation which largely dispelled its earlier negative image.

There still remains a dynamic of rivalry and cooperation, based on dynastic, territorial, historical, and other factors. At risk of oversimplification, one might say there is a tendency for shaykhdoms to be at odds with their immediate neighbors and to have good relations with the next shaykhdom over. For example, Qatar has a tradition of poor relations with Abu Dhabi on one side and Bahrain on the other, the latter conflict having its origins in Bahrain's historical claim to northern Qatar, site of the first al-Khalifah capital. Similarly, Dubai is an intense rival of Abu Dhabi and Sharjah; Sharjah of Dubai and Umm al-Qaywayn; and so on. At the same time, Abu Dhabi gets along well with Bahrain and Sharjah, and Sharjah with Ras al-Khaymah, with which it has close dynastic ties. This complex political pattern can be very important at times. For example, although the British tried very hard between 1968 and 1971 to effect a federation of all nine shaykhdoms, in the end Bahrain and Qatar chose to go it alone, unable to reconcile their differences.

The economics of the gulf will be discussed in more detail in a later chapter. Some general statements can be made at this point, however, on the impact of economics on regional politics. First of all, the concentration of wealth in the gulf, almost entirely from oil income, is enormous. It is therefore within the capability of nearly every ruler to co-opt potential dissidents through lavish social welfare and economic development programs. The existence of great wealth also increases the propensity of a regime to focus inwardly in its development programs. To the extent that this is the case, external disputes can take on relatively less urgency, a stabilizing factor.

On the other hand, increased oil revenues, particularly since the quadrupling of oil prices in 1973, have tended to broaden the political horizons, particularly of the bigger gulf states, not only in the context of the gulf, but in the broader Middle East region and even beyond. To the extent that such new aspirations conflict, particularly in light of the quantum increase in military arms transfers to the area in recent years, the concentration of economic wealth in the gulf could be potentially destabilizing as well.

Oil resources are not evenly divided among the gulf states. Four of the UAE shaykhdoms—Ajman, Umm al-Qaywayn, Ras al-Khaymah, and Fujayrah—have none at all. Saudi Arabia, Kuwait, and Abu Dhabi are fabulously wealthy in terms of per capita income; they are expected to accumulate foreign exchange balances in the coming years far exceeding their capability to invest them in their domestic economies, at least at efficiencies considered even minimally productive in the West. Iran and Iraq also have large oil incomes—some believe that Iraq's reserves are far greater than are presently estimated. Both countries have a greater capacity for internal investment than do Saudi Arabia, Kuwait, and Abu Dhabi, particularly in economic development. Qatar, Dubai, Bahrain, and Oman are moderately endowed with oil, and in 1974 Sharjah came on stream as the third oil producer in the UAE. Prior to the precipitous oil price rises in 1973, Bahrain, with a large, articulate labor force and declining oil production, and Oman, struggling against the Dhufar rebels, were financially hard pressed in their efforts to maintain stability. With greatly increased revenues, the economic burdens of internal and regional security have been considerably reduced.

The distribution of wealth as a factor in gulf politics is more apparent than real. This is in large part because all of the gulf states have either direct oil revenues or access to them. The only countries with no oil revenues are the four UAE shaykhdoms, and Shaykh Zayd of Abu Dhabi, president of the UAE, has been very generous in distributing funds to these poorer areas for economic and social development.

Territorial disputes have long been a basic political fact of life in the gulf. Not only are there few permanent features in the desert terrain characteristic enough to permit a definitely described boundary line, but also the need for boundary lines did not exist in the region until the development of oil resources. Traditionally, tribal affiliation rather than geography was the main determinant of political allegiance. Unfortunately, tribes often gave their allegiance to more than one political power and changed sides as they saw fit. Moreover, tribes tend to be mobile, covering large areas in their nomadic wanderings and often locating in the vicinity of other tribes with different allegiances.

The degree to which tribal allegiances transcended line boundaries until the recent past is illustrated in St. John Philby's account of the December 1922 Uqayr Conference when an attempt was made by the British representative, Sir Percy Cox, to delimit the borders of Najd with Iraq and Kuwait. According to Philby, Ibn Saud of Najd

> was by no means enamored of the seemingly meaningless proposition of a fixed frontier in a featureless desert which never had accurately been surveyed, and whose tribes had for centuries roamed over it without let or hindrance in search of water or pasture.[1]

At the time of this writing, most of the territorial disputes in the gulf region have been settled or at least allowed to lie dormant. The British, prior to their departure in 1971, had worked hard to resolve as many of them as possible. The most heated dispute at the time consisted of Iran's claim over Bahrain. The Iranians, who had controlled Bahrain off and on over the centuries, claimed that they had never ceded sovereignty nor recognized the ruler of Bahrain as an independent chief of state.[2] In the interests of gulf stability, the shah announced early in 1969 that he would not use force to promote his claim and would defer to the wishes of the Bahraini people on the issue of sovereignty. The Iranian call for a plebiscite or referendum was seen largely as a face-saving device. This, however, was not acceptable to the ruler of Bahrain, who took the position that the sovereignty of the regime was a fact and therefore not something to be bestowed by means of a plebiscite. After lengthy deliberations among the Bahrainis, Iranians, and British, it was finally agreed to allow a United Nations commission to enter Bahrain in order to ascertain the consensus of the people. On May 2, 1970, it reported that an overwhelming majority of Bahrainis supported an independent Bahrain, thus paving the way for Iran to relinquish its claim.

A second territorial dispute which the British endeavored to settle involved three small islands in the lower gulf, the Greater and Lesser Tunb Islands and Abu Musa. The Tunbs were administered by Ras al-Khaymah, and Abu Musa by Sharjah. All three islands were claimed by Iran, which having relinquished its claim to Bahrain, was all the more adamant to gain control over them. The Abu Musa claim was further complicated by an offshore oil concession dispute between Sharjah and neighboring Umm al-Qaywayn, involving an extension of Sharjah's territorial waters from three to twelve miles.[3] This extension effectively deprived Umm al-Qaywayn of any part of the oil which was discovered within twelve miles of Abu Musa. Iran warned that no Abu Musa oil should be produced until its claims were settled.

After months of negotiation, a complicated formula was worked out whereby Iran was to place garrisons under its flag on the Tunbs and Abu Musa; and Sharjah would continue to exercise administrative control over the some 200 (Arab) inhabitants of Abu Musa. Provisions were also made for Iranian financial aid to Sharjah. The aid was to be phased out if oil were produced off Abu Musa, and the revenues of the oil were to be divided between Iran and Sharjah. By the terms of the formula the Arabs did not formally relinquish sovereignty of the islands, but Iran fully expects to retain them.

The arrangement came into effect on November 30, 1971, the day before the British relinquished their protective status in the gulf. Ras al-Khaymah, however, never agreed to it, and when Iranian troops landed on the Tunbs they were met by small-arms fire from a Ras al-Khaymah police detachment. As a further consequence, Shaykh Sagr of Ras al-Khaymah at first refused to join the UAE, but after realizing he could get little Arab support for his cause, he finally joined in February 1972.

There was some bitterness in Sharjah when its ruler, Shaykh Khalid, signed the agreement with Iran. His kinsman Shaykh Sagr bin Sultan, who had been deposed as ruler of Sharjah in 1965, tried to exploit this feeling in an attempt in January 1972 to regain the throne. The coup failed, largely due to the dispatching of Abu Dhabi troops by Shaykh Zayd, but Khalid was killed. In retrospect, although the islands dispute has been resolved for the moment, Arab claims of the "Arab character" of the islands could always reopen the dispute.

On July 29, 1974, Prince Fahd of Saudi Arabia and Shaykh Rashid of Dubai, acting in his capacity as vice-president of the United Arab Emirates, initiated a preliminary agreement ending the long-standing Saudi-Abu Dhabi border dispute. Shaykh Zayd, as president of the UAE, did not initial the agreement for protocol reasons, but it was he who invited Fahd to Abu Dhabi.

At the center of the dispute historically was the al-Buraymi Oasis. Though claimed by the Saudis from the nineteenth century, the oasis had not been directly administered by them since 1871 when the then Saudi governor departed during a period of Saudi internal political strife. For the next sixty years, al-Buraymi, which consists of nine villages, lived in quasi-independence on the fringes of the political power of Abu Dhabi, Oman, and Saudi Arabia.

Another area in the dispute was al-Liwa (al-Jiwa), the collective name for a string of date palm oases in a line about sixty miles long from northwest to southeast, considerably west of al-Buraymi. Several tribes inhabit al-Liwa. Of these, the Manasir tribesmen in this area traditionally gave their allegiance to the Saudis, but the Bani Yas were loyal to Abu Dhabi, only about one hundred miles away and originally settled by Bani Yas from al-Liwa. In many cases, however, even the Bani Yas paid both traditional date crop and religious taxes (zakat) to the Saudis as well as to Abu Dhabi.

Between 1935 and 1937 the Saudis negotiated for a boundary settlement with Britain, which was the protecting power for Abu Dhabi and also Oman. The Saudis based their claim on their nineteenth century control and on continual tribal allegiance, including payment of taxes. The British countered that such allegiance and tax payments among nomadic tribes were too irregular to prove sovereignty and that sections of the tribes in question also paid allegiance and taxes to Abu Dhabi and Muscat. Moreover, no other form of Saudi authority had been exercised since 1871. At one point, the Saudis offered to give up their claim to Buraymi and al-Liwa for concessions further west, but negotiations failed. (Interestingly enough, the terms of the present agreement appear to approximate those offered in the mid-thirties by the Saudis.)

In 1951-52 Saudi-British talks were resumed but again reached a deadlock. By this time, oil discoveries in the area had considerably raised the stakes of a settlement for all concerned. In August 1952 the Saudis dispatched Turki bin 'Utayshan and some forty Saudis to al-Buraymi, where Turki assumed the title of amir or governor. In 1954-1955 Britain and Saudi Arabia submitted their cases to arbitration by a noted international jurist, Charles

De Visscher.[4] But by September 1955 the arbitration collapsed, and in October a British-led force drove out the Saudis and some 1,000 to 1,500 inhabitants of al-Buraymi, who went into exile in Saudi Arabia. The British then proceeded to defeat the imam of Oman who also fled to Saudi Arabia. From that point on, Oman and Abu Dhabi have shared the administration of the oasis.[5]

Subsequent efforts to settle the dispute failed, and counterclaims over an oil field in the disputed area (called Zararah by Abu Dhabi and Shaybah by the Saudis) further complicated matters. In recent years, pride was probably as great an obstacle as any other factor to reaching a settlement: Shaykh Zayd, before becoming the ruler of Abu Dhabi in 1965, was governor of al-Ayn, the principal Abu Dhabi town in al-Buraymi (and now the site of a Hilton hotel); King Faysal, on his part, wanted deference shown to the Saudis' historical position along with a tangible quid pro quo in return for giving up al-Buraymi. (Al-Liwa by this time was no longer disputed by Saudi Arabia.)

In the end both sides seem to have become reconciled. The Saudis have given up their claim to al-Buraymi. In return they have apparently received most of the Zararah/Shaybah oil field and a corridor between Abu Dhabi and Qatar to the Persian Gulf to pipe its Shaybah oil. The settlement of this long intractable dispute greatly enhances regional stability in that it removes a major source of friction between two conservative gulf states, enabling them to cooperate on a wide range of issues. There is every indication, however, that Zayd will continue to follow an independent course on oil and other policies when he deems it to be in Abu Dhabi's and the UAE's interests to do so.

Settling of the al-Buraymi dispute should also make it easier for Saudi Arabia and Oman to cooperate more closely. A separate Saudi-Omani border agreement is being negotiated at the time of this writing. Relations between Oman and Saudi Arabia, which had been very strained since 1955, thawed in December 1971 when King Faysal invited the new sultan, Qabus, to visit Riyadh. In May 1975 the Saudis, as a sign of good will, offered to assist and ease Oman's financial crisis. The amount of Saudi aid had been reported to be at least $100 million.

Nine months after the Saudi-Abu Dhabi border dispute was settled, a potentially even more explosive dispute was also resolved. At the March 1975 meeting of Opec in Algiers, President

Boumedienne announced that Iraq had agreed to the Shatt al-Arab River boundary with Iran in return for Iran's ending its support of the Kurdish insurgency in Iraq led by Mullah Mustafa Barzani. A formal agreement on land and sea borders and prohibition of border violations was signed by the foreign ministries of the two countries on June 12, 1975.

The Shatt al-Arab, which is formed by the confluence of the Tigris and Euphrates rivers in Iraq, forms the Iraqi-Iranian border in its lower reaches. According to an Ottoman-Persian treaty in 1847, reaffirmed by a protocol in 1913, the Ottomans owned the river to the highwater mark on the Persian side.[6] Modern Iraq fell heir to the Ottoman claim, but beginning in the 1930s Iran contested it. The present shah's father, Reza Shah, who had seized power in the 1920s, protested to the League of Nations, arguing that the center of the river (thalweg) should be the border.

A new treaty was drawn up in 1913 and extended in 1937. Iraq still retained possession of the river to the Iranian shore, but Iran was granted sovereignty out to the thalweg of those portions of the Shatt al-Arab adjacent to Abadan and Khorramshahr. It was the 1937 treaty which Iran unilaterally repudiated in February 1969, saying that Iraq had violated the treaty and, additionally, it was "contrary to all international practices and principles of International Law relating to frontiers."[7] Iraq retaliated by deporting a sizable number of Iranian Shi'a Muslims from Iraq. The dispute thereupon entered a period of more or less stalemate.

By 1974, Iranian-Iraqi relations had reached an all-time low, in large measure over Iran's support of the Kurdish insurgency. On several occasions Iraqi and Iranian troops actually exchanged fire in border areas. Evidently, however, neither side wished to pursue their confrontation to open hostilities, being more concerned with domestic and other foreign policy issues. Finally, in reaching a rapprochement in 1975, the long-standing Shatt al-Arab dispute was finally resolved.

There are still two territorial issues which have not been totally resolved. The Iraqi-Kuwaiti border dispute is one of them. Iraq has never formally relinquished its claim to Kuwait, a claim based on the territorial limits of the Ottoman Sanjak of Basrah. There was a period of tension when Kuwait obtained complete independence from the British in 1961 and Iraq briefly reasserted its claim. Over time the tension died down, but in March 1973 border tension reappeared as Iraq sought Kuwaiti territory in order to obtain greater territorial depth for the defense of the naval base it was developing at Umm Qasr. An armed clash occured on March 20, as Iraqis occupied a Kuwaiti police post on the border. The Iraqis subsequently withdrew, and although there was a brief border flurry in late 1974, they have not pressed their claims since in a hostile manner.

Iraq nevertheless appears determined ultimately to gain control over at least parts of the Kuwaiti islands of Bubayan and Warbah, which command the entrance to the estuary on which Umm Qasr is situated. Iraqis have hinted that they may attempt some sort of leasing arrangement. In terms of transfer of sovereignty, however, Kuwait could not give up the islands. It is not simply a question of national pride. Were Iraq to gain sovereignty over the islands, Kuwait would lose hundreds of square miles of offshore oil rights.

A second territorial question involves those parts of the gulf median line between Iran and the Arab side of the gulf which have not yet been agreed upon. The Saudi-Iranian median line had been hotly contested by both sides until an agreement was reached in 1968. Elsewhere in the gulf, there are large portions of the line still undrawn. Since billions of dollars of offshore oil could be at stake, a new discovery in the middle of the gulf could set off another median line dispute, threatening the stability of the area.

Another factor in gulf politics is the potential for political subversion. At one end of the spectrum of those who subscribe to political change are a host of covert political groups, some of which form and dissolve with great rapidity as internal disputes among their members wax and wane. At the other end are active insurgents such as those involved in the rebellion being waged until recently by the Kurds in Iraq, and those in Oman's southwestern Dhufar province.

Among the better-known subversive groups in the gulf is the Arab Nationalists movement (ANM). Founded at the American University of Beirut in 1948 by a group of young intellectuals, the ANM began as a small group of militant Marxist-socialists, including Palestinian fedayin leaders George Habbish, Naif Hawatama, and Ahmad Jabril. In 1968 the group began to split up, and by 1971 it had agreed to independent country-based organizations. Although their activities are theoretically co-ordinated by a higher executive committee, in fact each group is answerable only to itself. Thus, the ANM has evolved into more of a loose ideological brotherhood than a political organization.

The ANM has profoundly influenced radical groups in the gulf. In Kuwait it is overt and, under the leadership of Dr. Ahmad al-Khatib, has more or less eschewed violence in achieving its aims. There are, however, some more militant ANM members in Kuwait who take a different view. The radical National Front regime in South Yemen also had ANM antecedents, and the leadership of the Dhufar insurgency is associated with the ANM. Although all these organizations are independent, they do support each other's activities. Thus it was largely with PDRY support that the ANM rebels in Dhufar were so successful in the early 1970s.

The Ba'th party is also active in the gulf. Its members are divided into two wings, reflecting the Iraqi-Syrian Ba'th split. Each wing is supported by its Syrian or Iraqi patron and is in competition with the other. All, however, espouse the general Ba'thi goals of Arab unity, socialism, and antiimperialism.

The National Liberation Front of Bahrain is another fairly old subversive group, but unlike the ANM and Ba'th groups with outside ties, it is wholly indigenous to Bahrain. It is a Marxist organization with appeal among Bahraini intellectuals, one of the largest groups of intellectuals in the Arab shaykhdoms. Many of its leaders were exiled in the 1960s, but younger members appear to be maintaining the organization. They include Dr. Abd Al-Hadi Khalif, who was elected but not allowed to take his seat after the 1974 parliamentary elections.

The Palestinian fedayin groups are also represented in the gulf. Since their principal aim is to obtain money and political support from the gulf states and the relatively large resident Palestinian populations (e.g., over 200,000 in Kuwait alone), they are not, strictly speaking, subversive organizations in the same sense as the others. Nevertheless, there are ties between local subversive groups and the Palestinians, particularly among those with a common ANM background. George Habbash's Popular Front for the Liberation of Palestine, for example, has cooperated with the ANM in Kuwait, South Yemen's National Front regime, and the Dhufar rebels.

With the Iraqi-Iranian rapprochement in March 1975, the Kurdish rebellion has once again collapsed and its leader, Mullah Mustafa Barzani, lives in Tehran under house arrest. All the ingredients for a resumption of the insurgency are still there, however. The Kurds have always felt discriminated against by the Arab-dominated governments in Baghdad. They have periodically staged uprisings to demand a greater measure of local autonomy. The Baghdad government had agreed in March 1970 to extend more rights to the Kurds, but the agreement soon broke down and by 1974 a full-scale insurgency was in progress, supported by Iran.

Whether or not the Kurds remain subdued depends on several factors. One is the strength of the Iraqi regime; the more it can solidify its position, the less able will the Kurds be to revolt. Another is the amount of outside aid the Kurds can obtain. Iran had been the principal donor in recent years, but the availability of Iranian aid in the future will depend very much on the state of Iraqi-Iranian relations. Finally, there is the matter of Kurdish leadership. Barzani is aging and no other leader has his prestige. Though he has been given every political label from communist to conservative, Barzani is essentially a Kurdish nationalist. Depending on the political climate, if a new Kurdish leader emerges who espouses a radical litany, it could have political repercussions not only in Iraq, but in the gulf region as well.

The other insurgency in the gulf, the Dhufar rebellion, also seems to have stabilized in favor of the government.[8] It originally began as an irredentist movement appealing to the wild Qara and al-Kathiri tribesmen of Dhufar's Qara mountains who sought to oust the sultan, Said bin Taymur. The leaders of the movement were mainly Dhufaris who had found work in the post-World War II oil boom in the gulf and had come in contact with Marxist and radical Arab nationalist ideas. In 1964 the Dhufar branch of the ANM, the Dhufar Charitable Association (which had broken off from the ANM in 1962), and the Dhufar Soldiers' Organization, made up of Dhufari veterans of the army and police forces of the gulf shaykhdoms, all combined to form the Dhufar Liberation Front (DFL).

With the help of South Yemen, which became independent in November 1967, the ANM members of the DLF solidified their control of the organization. At the second party congress, held at Harmin in central Dhufar in September 1968, the DLF adopted a program to increase the scope of their operations and changed its name to the Popular Front for the Liberation of the Occupied Arab Gulf (PFLOAG). In 1970 a similar group of radical anti-Sultan subversives from all over Oman banded together to form the

National Democratic Front for the Liberation of Oman and the Arabian Gulf (NDFLOAG). This group merged with the Dhufar group in 1971, calling itself the Popular Front for the Liberation of Oman and the Arabian Gulf (also known as PFLOAG).

Operations in the north, undertaken by NDFLOAG, went poorly almost from the start, causing the movement to lose some of its sympathizers. In July 1970 Said bin Taymur was ousted and replaced by his son Qabus, enabling the government to concentrate on countermeasures. In Dhufar, however, PFLOAG was continuing to gain ground, successfully occupying most of the mountains surrounding the Dhufar plain. The rebel initiative reached its peak in July 1972 when over seventy insurgents were killed in a pitched battle with Omani troops at Marbat. By early 1974 PFLOAG was increasingly on the defensive. The quadrupling of oil prices in 1973 eased the financial burden, and the addition of Iranian combat troops in 1973 and 1974 and of Jordanian troops in early 1975 helped the government gain the initiative.

With government troops apparently establishing control in Dhufar, the insurgency seems to be entering a new phase. In January 1974 PFLOAG's name was shortened to the Popular Front for the Liberation of Oman (PFLO), reflecting a reduction in scope. Renewed emphasis was placed by the insurgents on political action in contrast to military action.

The Omani regime could be quite vulnerable to this change in strategy. It is devoting all the resources it can spare from the counterinsurgency program to developing its long-neglected economy. In any such attempt, corruption and inefficiencies are bound to crop up and development programs can easily get bogged down. In early 1975 Oman had so overextended its economy that it faced a severe cash liquidity crisis. The crisis could have had disastrous political effects had it not been for the May 1975 Saudi loan. On balance, however, Oman seems to have weathered the Dhufar crisis and its economic problems fairly well and appears again on the way to economic and social development.

The Foreign Policies of the Gulf States

One of the complicating factors in studying gulf politics is that the political relations among the states are influenced to a great degree by their interests beyond the immediate gulf area. Indeed, it has been only in the past few years that the big three—Iran, Iraq, and Saudi Arabia—began to look at the gulf as a separate area of policy interest and not merely a subcategory of Middle Eastern, Indian Ocean, or Arab and Muslim world politics. The change came with the 1968 British announcement of its decision to end its security status in the gulf and was intensified by the world focus on the gulf in the aftermath of the 1973-1974 energy crisis.

Iran's foreign policy horizons have expanded enormously over the past twenty years. In 1953 the ouster of Premier Mussadiq reestablished the authority of the shah. Initially, while the shah concentrated on consolidating his authority at home, his foreign policy horizons were largely bounded by attention to immediate external security threats to his regime. These threats were perceived to emanate primarily from the Soviet Union. To meet the Soviet threat, Iran in 1955 joined the Baghdad Pact, later known as the Central Treaty Organization or CENTO. In 1959 it concluded a bilateral defense treaty with the United States. (The United States also signed similar treaties with Pakistan and Turkey in lieu of joining CENTO.) The U.S.-Iranian treaty became the legal basis for subsequent U.S. military sales and training programs.

In the meantime, Iran set about to improve its relations with the Soviet Union. Between 1954 and 1958, the Soviet-Iranian border was demarcated. In 1962, after the shah stated that he would allow no foreign offensive missiles to be deployed on Iranian soil, Soviet-Iranian relations improved measurably. By the mid-1960s, Iran was the recipient of rather extensive Soviet aid, including the construction of Iran's first iron and steel mill at Isfahan. Additionally, Iran purchased military equipment from the Soviet Union, including trucks, armored personnel carriers, and antiaircraft guns. However, despite the shah's policy of improving relations with the Soviet Union, he remains staunchly anticommunist. He looks on his relations with the Soviets mainly as a means of avoiding tensions with a potentially overwhelming adversary and also as a means of asserting a more independent foreign policy between the communist and Western worlds.

By the mid-1960s, cold war tensions had begun to abate. In Iranian eyes, however, a new external threat to Iranian security was emerging in the form of militant Arab nationalism. Iran's cordial attitude toward Israel was a major thorn in the side of Iranian-Arab relations, particularly among the Arab militants, and in 1960 Egypt's President Nasser unilaterally broke diplomatic relations with Iran over its ties with Israel. Iraq, on January 23, 1970, expelled the Iranian ambassador over the Shatt al-Arab dispute, and in December 1971, in reaction to Iranian occupation of the Tunb Islands and Abu Musa, also completely broke relations with Iran.

Since then, Iran has initiated a cautious policy of rapproachement with the Arab radicals. Diplomatic relations with Egypt were restored on August 29, 1970, shortly before Nasser's death. In May 1974 the shah offered economic aid to Egypt and in January of the following year he paid a visit to Cairo. In Iran's eyes, the improved relations with Egypt were considerably enhanced by what it perceived to be a more moderate Egyptian stance than in the 1960s when Egypt was espousing the spread of militant Arab socialism.

In the aftermath of the October 1973 Arab-Israeli war, Iranian relations with the Arab states improved still more. Diplomatic relations were restored with Iraq, although tensions between the two countries remained high for another two years. The shah also publicly sided with the Arabs in calling for an Israeli withdrawal from lands occupied in the June 1967 Arab-Israeli war. With regard to the militant Arab states, Iran remains openly hostile only to PDRY. The hostility is most easily seen in the Dhufar insurgency in which PDRY is supporting the insurgents and Iran has provided combat troops in support of the sultan.

The British decision to withdraw from the gulf was seen by the shah as both a threat and an opportunity.[9] The threat of the British departure, as he saw it, was that the gulf would be deprived of a British security umbrella. Iran did not wish to see radicalism, whether militant Arab nationalism or Soviet- or Chinese-supported communism, spread into the area; nor did he wish to see another Western power such as the United States take over the British role.

The opportunity was that, probably for the first time, the shah felt politically secure and militarily powerful enough for Iran to achieve hegemony in the gulf, at least in a security sense. Since 1953 the shah had been building up his armed forces until they were the largest in the gulf. After 1968 he embarked on an even more ambitious military-development program commensurate with his concept of Iran's expanded security role. In the process, he had by 1975 negotiated for the purchase of over $9 billion worth of arms, mostly from the United States.

In sum, Iran's world view envisions a basic dichotomy between the powerful industrialized states of East and West and the weak states of the third world. While firmly tied to the free world economically and politically, Iran is determined to change its position from a weak third world state to a more powerful industrialized state, somewhat in the way that Japan has made the transition within the free world, and perhaps that China is in the process of doing in the communist world. For Iran, the key to that transition is oil. Therefore, more than any of the other OPEC members, Iran is politically committed to maximizing its oil revenues to the greatest possible extent. This goes far to explain why Iran has taken the leadership within OPEC for maintaining high prices but opposing the prorating of production cuts.

For all its militant ideology, *Iraq* has not really pursued an active foreign policy in recent years. Estranged from nearly all the Arab states, conservative and radical, and also from Iran, the Baghdad regime remained relatively isolated politically throughout the 1960s and early 1970s. Moreover, much of the attention of the regime was focused on the domestic problems.

The areas of policy interest receiving top priority were the Arab-Israeli war and financial and training support for subversive groups, particularly in the gulf. The Iraqi regime displayed a highly developed encirclement syndrome in which they saw themselves surrounded on every side by adversaries: Arab conservatives, Israel, Syrian Ba'thists, and Iran.

In seeking support against all their perceived enemies, the Iraqis turned primarily to the Soviet Union. Their good relations with the Soviets were further cemented by a Treaty of Cooperation and Friendship signed in 1973. The Soviets are also the major supplier of Iraqi military arms and equipment, and have supervised the construction and improvement of Iraq's naval base at Umm Qasr. Despite close Iraqi ties with the Soviet Union, however, it would be a mistake to conclude that Iraq is a Soviet client state or satellite. The Iraqis after a colonial past are highly sensitive to any perceived encroachment on their sovereignty, even by the Soviets.

Of all Iraqi foreign policy concerns, the Arab-Israeli problem probably looms largest. Iraqi troops fought in both the 1967 and 1973 Arab-Israeli wars; the government supports a Palestinian fedayin group, the Arab Liberation Front; and Iraqi policy has been consistently uncompromising against giving any concessions to Israel for the sake of a peace settlement.

Iraq has supported subversive groups since the 1958 revolution overthrew the monarchy, and the current Ba'thi regime, which came to power in 1968, is no exception. Many of the followers of the old imam of Oman, calling themselves the Oman Revolutionary movement (ORM), were trained in guerrilla tactics in Iraq. Dhufar rebels and other subversives received training and support from Iraq also. Some observers have speculated that with the collapse of the Kurdish insurgency Iraq would devote more resources to subversive activities in the gulf. Although its support of these groups is no doubt continuing, Iraq, at least for the moment, appears to be preoccupied with the Arab-Israeli dispute and internal development.

Since the October 1973 war Iraq has moved, albeit cautiously, away from its former political isolation. In part this has been motivated by the psychological victory the Arabs achieved in the October war, which restored the pride they had lost in the humiliating defeat of 1967 and enabled them to bury their differences for the sake of the common Arab cause. In addition, Iraq would like to invest its post-1973 oil revenues in more extensive domestic economic development. It has, therefore, moved to lessen tensions with its neighbors in order to concentrate more of its energies on internal development.

Saudi Arabia's foreign policy is, of all the gulf states, the most influenced by Islam, and the Saudi world view focuses foremost on the Islamic world. The Saudis follow the strict teachings of the Wahhabi revival. As keepers of Islam's two most holy places, Mecca and al-Madinah, they see themselves as protectors of the faith and the Islamic way of life.

The late King Faysal evolved a highly developed Islamic foreign policy. For him, the greatest threats to the Islamic way of life were atheism, which he saw alike in all radical doctrines from Marxism to Arab socialism, and Zionism, which he distinguished from religious Judaism as a political movement seeking to acquire sacred Arab soil. Faysal was particularly incensed at Israeli occupation in 1967 of old Jerusalem and the Aqsa Mosque, the third most holy site in Sunni (orthodox) Islam.10 He stated publicly on several occasions that he wished to enter an Arab Jerusalem to pray at the Aqsa Mosque before he died. His wish was never granted.

The dual threat, which Faysal called the Zionist-Communist conspiracy, became the underlying theme in Saudi foreign policy. To oppose Arab socialist doctrines, the King tried to submerge Arab nationalism in a broader concept of Islamic world solidarity. The Saudi-funded Muslim World League and, after 1969, the Islamic Foreign Minister's Conferences and the Saudi-based Secretariat were used for this purpose. After the Israeli occupation of Arab territories in 1967, Faysal attempted to enlist the Islamic world not only against Arab socialism, but in support of the Arab cause against Israel as well.

Since World War II the Saudis have looked on the Western world and particularly the United States as the principal bulwark against communism. They therefore do not wish to see the West weakened economically or even politically. Unfortunately for Saudi Arabia, they also see the United States as the vital supporter of Israel, the other part of the Zionist-Communist threat. This in part explains the anomaly of the Saudis being the leaders of the 1973 Arab oil embargo and the single country in OPEC to desire lowered oil prices for the sake of the free world economy.

King Faysal was so preoccupied with Islamic world affairs and the Arab-Israeli problem that he tended to overlook politics in his own back yard, the gulf and the rest of the Arabian Peninsula. The only exception was his antipathy for the Marxist regime in PDRY. The Saudis have financed dissident South Yemen groups since PDRY's independence in 1967.

Under King Khalid and Crown Prince Fahd, more Saudi attention may be focused on the gulf. It was Fahd, at King Faysal's behest, who initialed an agreement ending the Saudi-Abu Dhabi border dispute. The new administration also shows signs of deemphasizing the Islamic coloration of King Faysal's foreign policy, though at the same time leaving the substance of that policy largely untouched.

Like Iran, the Saudis have also placed a high priority on developing their armed forces. After consolidating the Kingdom of Saudi Arabia in 1932, King Abd al-Aziz had virtually disbanded his tribally based army by World War II. In 1947 the United States established a military airfield at Dhahran with a training component for the fledgling Saudi air force. A small British training mission was established the same year to create a modern Saudi army. It was replaced by the U.S. Military Training Mission in 1952. Still, the Saudis, who knew all too well how armies overthrow monarchies, saw no need to build up a powerful military force. As a precaution, they organized, parallel to the army, a tribally based National Guard as an internal security force loyal to the regime.

When Faysal became king in 1964, the Yemeni civil war pitted Egyptian-backed republicans against Saudi-backed royalists. An Egyptian military force of some 60,000 in Yemen constituted a definite threat to Saudi Arabia. By 1965 Faysal felt that the creation of a credible military force was imperative for Saudi Arabia and asked U.S. aid in upgrading the Saudi military establishment. The perceived need for a modern army and air force was reinforced during the 1967 Arab-Israeli war. Faysal kept his troops at home, realizing that they were insufficiently trained to participate; but he also concluded that in another round of fighting he would not have that option. The need for a modern army and air force was even further reinforced in 1968 by the British decision to withdraw from the gulf. In the same year, an Iranian naval vessel seized a Saudi oil rig in the gulf. The incident was resolved, but Faysal saw the need for a naval force as well, not as a weapon to be used against Iran, but rather to ensure that Saudi Arabia have an independent voice in gulf security.

The early 1970s witnessed a growing Saudi perception of its security needs. The radical threat of South Yemen and Iraq to Saudi Arabia's greater role in the Arab-Israeli dispute have all influenced that perception.

For *Kuwait*, lacking the physical power of the big gulf states, the use of oil revenues has long been the principal tool of its foreign policy. As in its domestic programs, Kuwait sees as one of the major objectives of foreign policy neutralization of potential opposition through a systematic foreign assistance program. At risk of being simplistic, one might say that Kuwaiti foreign policy operates to a great extent on the assumption that no one will wish to or allow any one else to kill the golden goose.

The policy has worked remarkably well. For example, in the

aftermath of the June 1967 war, Kuwait, along with Saudi Arabia and Libya, became a major contributor to Jordan and Egypt, based on commitments made at the Khartoum Conference.[11] Significantly, when Jordan became somewhat of a pariah in the Arab world after crushing the Palestinian commando groups in Jordan in September 1970, Kuwait stopped its payments to Jordan. Payments, however, were resumed after the October 1973 war. Kuwait has also been very generous in its support of the Palestinians, both directly and by eliciting contributions for the Palestinian cause from the large Palestinian community in Kuwait.

Kuwait has also utilized such institutions as the Kuwait Development Fund for implementing its foreign aid programs. Prior to 1973 Kuwaiti foreign aid was concentrated mainly on the Arab states. Since the quantum jump in oil prices, however, Kuwait has expanded the scope of its foreign aid program to include non-Arab members of the third world as well.

The gulf amirates—*Bahrain, Qatar,* and the *UAE*—have been engaged in foreign policy making since their independence in 1971. All pursue conservative political policies and free market economic policies. For the most part, their external interests are limited to gulf politics; international trade, particularly in oil; and the Arab cause.

Bahrain and Dubai had built up a fairly extensive *entrepôt* trade long before independence. Bahrain's international airport, for example, is a crossroads of European-Far Eastern traffic. Dubai was noted as a free port and a center for illicit gold trade to Iran and the Indian subcontinent long before the discovery of oil, and is still a principal purchaser on the London gold market. Its "free trading" dhows (the traditional Arab sailing vessels, now largely equipped with powerful engines to outrun coast guard vessels) have dealt in many other forms of contraband as well.

All of these countries are oil producers, and as with the other gulf states, international oil policies are important to them. Bahrain, however, is not a member of OPEC, and although the UAE is, neither Dubai nor Sharjah, oil-producing members of the UAE, participate in OPEC. This means that for practical purposes Abu Dhabi is the only UAE shaykhdom actively engaged in OPEC affairs. Abu Dhabi is also the only amirate with such a sizable oil income that its foreign aid program has had a major impact. Unlike the aid programs of Kuwait and other gulf donors, however,

Abu Dhabi aid, which has been extended throughout the third world, has to date not been very well coordinated nor tied to specific projects; partially as a result of large aid expenditures, Abu Dhabi experienced in early 1975 a cash liquidity problem. This problem developed despite a 1974 income of over $5 billion.

Whether or not the emirates had given much thought to the Arab-Israeli problem before independence, they were not required to do anything about it so long as Britain managed their foreign affairs. One of the first acts each country took at independence was to join the Arab League. Consequently, when the October 1973 Arab-Israeli war broke out, each of them was swept up in the Arab cause. When King Faysal called for an Arab oil embargo on October 17, 1973, they all followed suit. In the future, therefore, the emirates will no longer be shielded from Arab world politics and the Arab-Israeli problem. This will become a major determinant in foreign policy on any issue which Arabism touches.

Since its emergence from British-protected isolationism in 1970, *Oman* has had two major foreign policy aims: to gather support against the Dhufar rebels while at the same time neutralizing their supporters, and to gain acceptance of the Omani regime, particularly in the Arab world.

The counterinsurgency program, as described earlier, has been going fairly well for the government. The deployment of Jordanian combat troops has helped to reduce Arab criticism of Iranians fighting on Arab soil. Both have helped greatly in the war effort, and have also helped to lower the British profile in Oman's armed forces.

Ending Oman's political isolation is a much more complex problem, and in the opinion of at least one senior Omani official, it is one of greater long-term priority. The Arab states, led by Saudi Arabia, nearly all supported Imam Ghalib, expelled from inner Oman in 1955 by a British-led force. Oman's political isolation was reinforced by Sultan Said bin Taymur, who had become virtually a recluse in Salalah in the latter part of his reign, and by the fact that he depended on the British to administer many of the key functions of government, particularly defense and national security.

From the time he came to power in 1970, Sultan Qabus has attempted to end Oman's long period of isolation. In December of

1971 he visited the Saudi capital of Riyadh in what was to be the first step of reconciliation with Saudi Arabia. A reflection of his success in gaining Arab acceptance was Oman's joining the Arab League on September 29, 1971. Less than two weeks later, Oman became the one hundred thirty-first member of the United Nations.

NOTES

[1]H. St. John B. Philby, *Arabia* (London: Ernest Benn, 1930), pp. 290-91.

[2]Majid Khadduri, ed., *Major Middle Eastern Problems in International Law* (Washington, D.C.: American Enterprise Institute, 1972), p. 104.

[3]*Ibid.*, p. 104.

[4]Both sides presented a memorial stating their case. See *Memorial of the Government of Saudi Arabia: Arbitration for the Settlement of the Territorial Dispute between Muscat and Abu Dhabi on the one side and Saudi Arabia on the other, A.H. 1374/A.D. 1955;* and *Arbitration Concerning Buraimi and the Common Frontier between Abu Dhabi and Saudi Arabia: Memorial submitted by the Government of the United Kingdom of Great Britain and Northern Ireland, 1955.*

[5]For a pro-British account of the dispute, see J.B. Kelly, *Eastern Arabian Frontiers* (New York and London: Praeger, 1964).

[6]See E. Lauterpacht, "River Boundaries: Legal Aspects of the Shattal Arab Frontier," *International and Comparative Law Quarterly* 9 (1960): 208-236.

[7]Khadduri, *Major Middle Eastern Problems*, p. 91.

[8]For an excellent account of the Dhufar insurgency, see D.L. Price, *Oman: Insurgency and Development, Conflict Studies* 53 (London: The Institute for the Study of Conflict, January 1975). A book taking the radical point of view is Fred Halliday, *Arabia without Sultans* (London: Penguin, 1974).

[9]The following discussion is based in part on an earlier paper by the writer, "US Strategic Interests in the Persian Gulf: Problems and Policy Analysis," delivered at the National Security Affairs Conference of the National War College, Washington, D.C., July 14-15, 1975.

[10]Many Westerners incorrectly believe the principal Islamic holy site in Jerusalem is the gilded Dome of the Rock. The Aqsa Mosque actually sits to the side of the Dome of the Rock and has a much less imposing silver dome.

4 The Gulf and International Politics

Although the gulf would probably receive relatively little attention today from the Western world were it not for oil and the revenues oil generates, external interest in the gulf actually predates the discovery of oil by over 400 years. In 1498, the Portuguese sea captain Vasco de Gama, having rounded the Cape of Good Hope, landed near "Calicut," India. Another Portuguese captain, Alfonso D'Albuquerque, was subsequently appointed viceroy ofPortuguese India at Goa and set out to establish a great Portuguese empire in the East.[1] He won two major engagements in the Straits of Hormuz in 1505, and two years later subjugated Oman's Batinah Coast. In 1515 the Portuguese finally captured the key trading city of Hormuz after several attempts and concurrently extended their hold northward to Bahrain.

For nearly a century thereafter, the Portuguese maintained a virtual monopoly in European seaborne commerce with the gulf. By the beginning of the seventeenth century, however, their power had begun to decline. In 1622 Hormuz fell to a joint British-Persian force. Portugal's last two outposts on the Arabian shore, Muscat and Khasab in Oman, were lost in 1650.

Following the decline of Portuguese ascendancy, there ensued a period of rivalry between the British and the Dutch, both expanding their empires in the East. The Dutch were predominant in the gulf in the mid-seventeenth century. However, an English-Dutch treaty against France in 1688 had the effect of subordinating Dutch interests to those of the British.[2] The Dutch position in the gulf was eclipsed entirely by 1766 when the British consolidated their position in India.

The initial British interest in the gulf was commercial and was exercised through the British East India Company. Chartered in 1600, this company was amalgamated with two smaller rival companies in 1708 and became the principal instrument of British power in the gulf for the next 150 years.[3]

The eighteenth century witnessed the rise of French imperial aspirations in the Indian Ocean, rivaling those of the British there and in the gulf as well. The recall in 1754 of the governor of the French East India Company, Dupliex, ended France's ambitions for an Indian empire but did not drive them entirely out of the area. In October 1759 they attacked Bander Abbas and forced the East India Company to transfer its Persian Gulf "residency" to Bushire (Persia) in 1763. However, company factories were still maintained at Basrah and Bandar Abbas.

The French threat to British interests in the East reappeared with Napoleon's invasion of Egypt in 1798. In that year the East India Company, acting for the British crown, signed an agreement with the ruler of Oman. The agreement, the first British treaty with a gulf state, was designed to keep the French out of the gulf.[4] A treaty of alliance against the French was also concluded between the British and the shah of Persia in 1801. British interest in the gulf by that time, however, had shifted. Political turmoil in the area throughout much of the eighteenth century had resulted in a drastic decline in trade, causing the East India Company seriously to consider withdrawing altogether. At the same time, the gulf was gaining in strategic importance as a line of communication with the increasingly important Indian empire.

The French threat receded with their expulsion from Mauritius in 1810, but a new threat had already begun to appear in the form of Arab privateers. Encouraged by the teachings of the Wahhabi religious revival, Arab mariners, particularly from the Qawasim tribes of Ras al-Khaymah and Sharjah, attacked the merchant ships of unbelievers in the gulf and the Indian Ocean. Their activities earned for the lower gulf coast the epithet, "Pirate Coast." From the mariners' perspective, however, it was a religious duty to scourge the shipping lanes of unbelievers such as the British and non-Wahhabi Muslim "heretics."

Between 1805 and 1819, the British dispatched several expeditions to the gulf to quell the "pirates," but to no avail. Then, taking advantage of the defeat of the Saudis by Ibrahim Pasha in 1818 and the collapse of Wahhabi power in eastern Arabia, the British decided to crush the Qawasim privateers once and for all. They mustered a force of two men-of-war, nine cruisers, and 3,500 troops off Ras al-Khaymah in December 1819. On December 22 the Qasimi shaykh Hassin bin Ramah, whose descendants still rule in Ras al-Khaymah and Sharjah, surrendered.[5]

The result of the British victory was a treaty which became the cornerstone of the British political, strategic, and economic presence in the gulf for 150 years. Called the General Treaty for Suppressing Piracy and Slave Traffic, it was signed by the Qasimi shaykhs and their allies.[6] In addition, the shaykhs of Abu Dhabi and Bahrain, though not considered piratical by the British, were allowed to sign at their request.[7]

Although the 1820 treaty stopped Arab attacks on British shipping, it did not bring peace, for there was no provision banning the Arab shaykhdoms from making war on each other. In 1835 the official British resident obtained a truce according to which the shaykhdoms refrained from war on the seas during the six-month pearling season and the British refrained from interfering with wars on land. This truce, which was renewed each year, was so successful that in 1853 it was replaced by the Treaty of Maritime Peace in Perpetuity. This gave rise to the name, "Trucial Coast," in place of the earlier Pirate Coast.

Throughout the nineteenth century, British policies in the gulf and the Indian Ocean generally reflected their growing imperial interests. At the beginning of the century, the East India Company still administered British affairs in the gulf. In 1822, however, when Lt. John Macleod was appointed resident in the Persian gulf, his responsibility was protection of British imperial interests rather than of commercial interests. In 1858 the activities of the British East India Company were taken over entirely by the British government of India. Thenceforth, until Indian independence in 1947, British gulf affairs were the responsibility of the Indian government.

By the end of World War I, a series of interlocking treaty relationships were established with Qatar (1869, 1913, 1916) and Kuwait (1899). With Britain's position of major influence in Persia and the creation of the British-controlled Mandate in Iraq in 1920, these relationships made the gulf virtually a British preserve.

After World War II, the British position in the gulf waned rapidly. In the early 1950s Iran began to exert her independence from outside influences; the 1958 coup in Iraq ended Britain's security and political role there; and in 1961 Kuwait regained her complete independence from British protection. But in the nine Gulf shaykhdoms and Oman, the British military and political presence was still considered to be the major stabilizing force. On January 16, 1968, British Prime Minister Harold Wilson announced to the House of Commons:

> We have decided to accelerate the withdrawal of our forces from their stations in the Far East . . .by the end of 1971. We have also decided to withdraw our forces from the Persian Gulf by the same date. . . . On the Gulf, we have indicated to the Governments concerned that our basic interest in the prosperity of the area remains: and as I have said, the capability we shall be maintaining here will be available.[8]

The announcement came as a surprise to many, both in the gulf and beyond it. After 150 years, the British were relinquishing their security role. An era had ended. When the Conservative party came to power in Britain in June 1970, it considered reversing the decision, or at least postponing the 1971 deadline. It soon realized, however, that, with Iranian and Arab opinion firmly opposed to postponement, the psychological moment for a reversal had passed.

The period from 1968 to 1971, when the British actually relinquished their security role in the gulf, was one of transition. The British attempted to leave the shaykhdoms as politically strong as possible. In an effort to resolve the territorial disputes over the Tunbs and Abu Musa, discussed in the previous chapter, they used their good offices to negotiate with all parties. On the matter of al-Buraymi and the Abu Dhabi-Saudi border dispute, they were less successful.

The main concern of the British was that some of the non-oil-producing Trucial States were too poor and too small to be viable political entities. Because Britain had never colonized the shaykhdoms but had merely provided them a security umbrella, the shaykhdoms had neither been introduced to modern political institutions nor unified into a larger, more viable entity. To remedy this, the British persuaded the shaykhdoms to agree on March 30, 1968, to federate. However, subsequent efforts to turn intention into fact, led by Sir William Luce, a distinguished British colonial official, met with only partial success. Bahrain was not entirely accepted by the others because of Iran's claim to it. When the Iranian claim was settled, Bahrain demanded a legislature in which representation was based on population, since its population (then 200,000) was nearly as large as the others' combined. When this demand was refused, Bahrain decided to withdraw from the federation and so became independent in August 1971. Qatar, a rival of Bahrain, then followed suit and became independent in September. The federation, now reduced to the seven Trucial States—Abu Dhabi, Dubai, Sharjah, Ajman, Umm al-Qaywayn, Ras al-Khaymah, and Fujayrah—became fully independent on December 1, 1971. As it turned out, however, Ras al-Khaymah, piqued over having a secondary role in UAE affairs and at the Iranian occupation of the Tunb Islands, which it claimed, refused to join the federation until February 1972.

In retrospect, the British decision appears to have been wise but precipitous. Although probably taking it for granted that the British would leave some day, none of the shaykhdoms at the time had seriously focused on the desirability of independence. In fact, many of them privately expressed dismay over the suddenly imminent prospect of losing the protective shield that Britain had provided since 1820. Nevertheless, the die had been cast, and it probably did not matter greatly what timetable the British set for their withdrawal; the period of exclusive British influence in the shaykhdoms ended on January 16, 1968. Thereafter, each shaykh, and other gulf rulers also, set out to obtain the most advantageous arrangements for the coming independence.

The British announcement of its intention to end its treaty obligations and withdraw its troops from the gulf caused foreign offices throughout the world to reevaluate their interests and policies toward the gulf. The quadruple oil price rise and the Arab oil embargo of 1973 and 1974 further focused world attention on the gulf. As a reflection of this new focus, nearly anyone, it seemed, who could name if not spell the Trucial States before 1968 was considered an "old gulf hand," and his expertise was in high demand.

The following is a brief synopsis of the leading world powers' interests in and policies toward the gulf, excluding the United States, which will be treated separately in a subsequent chapter. Economic and commercial relations, though mentioned briefly below, will be discussed more fully in the chapter on the economics of the gulf.

Britain

With the independence of India and Pakistan in 1947, Britain no longer needed to play a security role in the gulf to protect the imperial lines of communication to the East. At the same time, however, a new imperative for gulf security had arisen: oil. Not only was Britain dependent to a great degree on the gulf's oil for its own energy needs, but British Petroleum (BP), a corporate descendant of the Anglo-Persian Oil Company, was a primary producer in the gulf and one of the so-called "Seven Sisters," the seven major oil companies in the world.

By 1968 the Labour Party, then in power, had concluded that Britain's oil and commercial interests would not be appreciably threatened by the British withdrawal. Recalling the difficulties surrounding the British withdrawal from Aden in 1967, and the creation of a radical regime there, the Labour party concluded that it was better to leave before being asked than to wait for a radical nationalist movement to develop in the shaykhdoms.[9]

Current British interests in the gulf, then, can be said to focus primarily on oil and commerce. Exploiting the growing oil revenue market, including both the ambitious development plans of the area states and the long-standing commercial alliances developed during the period of British protection, British economic ties with the gulf are extensive. Much of the public- and private-sector British activity in the area, therefore, is engaged in protection and extension of those interests.

In the field of security, the withdrawal of the British protective status did not automatically mean the end of a British presence. Troops were withdrawn from the former British base at Sharjah, but the British still maintain base rights on the Omani island of Masirah.

In the gulf shaykhdoms, British military and security officers have stayed on after independence, either seconded from their British services or on direct contract to their host governments. Since the major threat to the stability of the area at present appears to be from internal subversion, the role of these British officers is very important to the security of the lower gulf.

In the long run, however, the British security role in the lower gulf cannot help but diminish. A number of the British advisors and other personnel resident in the gulf have been there for many years, and while their influence is great, it is also highly personalized. As these men retire or are replaced, their successors will not have the same degree of personal rapport with the gulf leaders, which can only be developed over a long period of time. Additionally, a number of the gulf leaders are finding it increasingly expeditious for political reasons to lower the British profile in governmental advisory positions.

In Oman, the British continue to play a large and direct role in security affairs. In addition to their Royal Air Force installation on Masirah, the Sultan's Armed Forces are still largely under British operational command. The counterinsurgency effort in Dhufar, for example, is directed by British officers under a British brigadier. Even in Oman, however, a major effort is under way to Omanize the armed forces, both the officer corps and the enlisted men, and the British are cooperating with the movement to lessen their military and security role there. Not only does a high British profile in the Omani armed forces present a political liability to Oman, but to Britain as well. One of the handicaps of the British operating in Dhufar is the fear that a high British casualty rate would be very unpopular at home and could result in Whitehall drastically reducing its military support to Oman at a time when that support is still sorely needed.

In sum, the British interests in the gulf are primarily commercial and economic. The British do retain a major security role as well, but this role will probably diminish over time.

France

Despite continuing interest in the Middle East and the Indian Ocean, France after the Napoleonic period never again challenged British imperial supremacy in the gulf. In the post-World War II period, the French came to rely increasingly on gulf oil. But the long, bitter Algerian revolution and France's cordial relations with Israel precluded any real French position of influence in the region, at least on the Arab side of the gulf. To offset its negative relations with the Arabs, France concentrated on Iran as the principal object of its economic and political policies in the gulf. Iran became the recipient of considerable French economic and technical assistance.

The resolution of the Algerian war in 1962 enabled France to seek stronger relations with the Arab world in general, and under President de Gaulle, the French began to exercise around the world a foreign policy increasingly independent from its Western allies. In the gulf area, France concluded a number of economic, commercial, and cultural agreements to strengthen its new relationship.

Despite the political overtones of French policy under de Gaulle and his successors, French interest in the gulf has been primarily economic and commercial. Even the military sales programs, notably to Iran and Abu Dhabi, which purchased a squadron of Mirage fighters using Pakistan as an intermediary, have a decided commercial cast. The main French military presence in the Indian Ocean is located at Djibouti, the capital of former French Somaliland and now the French-controlled Territory of the Afars and Issas.

The economic importance of the gulf to France, as to the rest of the industrialized world, stems from oil. More than other industrialized countries, however, the French have attempted to secure oil supplies through a policy which emphasizes their good relations with the area states, their increasing disassociation with pro-Zionist politics, and their independent policy as an alternative to alliance with either the United States or the Soviet Union.

Commercially, France seeks to increase exports to the area, in particular to offset the foreign exchange drain caused by the high price of oil. The French have had some successes, such as in the sale of communications equipment to Saudi Arabia, but in the main, military sales have been among their leading exports.

West Germany

In the latter part of the nineteenth century, Germany attempted to challenge British supremacy in the gulf. Kaiser Wilhelm II's policy of *Drang nach Osten* included a "Berlin to Baghdad" railroad project, for which Germany received a concession from the Ottomans in 1902. By extending the railroad to Basrah, the Germans envisioned that they could challenge British supremacy in the gulf. But after British protests to the Ottoman government, an Ottoman-German-British agreement was worked out in 1914 protecting Britain's position in the gulf.

World War I ended all German imperial aspirations in the gulf. There was a brief pro-Nazi movement against Britain in Iraq under Rashid Ali al-Qilani during World War II, but the movement was as much Arab nationalist and anti-British as it was pro-German. It was the pro-German sentiments of the shah's father, Reza Shah, which led the British and Russians to force his ouster in 1941.

Current West German relations in the gulf are largely economic and center around oil. Germany's strong economy has put it in an excellent competitive position in the area. But politically, German relations have been slow in obtaining a foothold. After World War II, relations were restored with Iran. However, Germany's policy of giving reparations to Israel made relations somewhat strained with the Arab states, and when Germany extended full diplomatic relations to Israel in 1965, the Arab states retaliated by breaking diplomatic relations with Germany. Additionally, until it was discontinued in 1969, the Hallstein Doctrine—which in effect forced states to choose between recognizing either East or West Germany—was another deterrent to good relations. In the last few years, however, German relations with the Arabs have improved, and West Germany has diplomatic representation throughout the gulf.

Japan

Of all the industrialized countries, Japan is the most dependent on gulf oil, which accounts for over 80 percent of its total imports. Thus, the politics of oil dictate Japan's policy toward the gulf to an even greater extent than is the case for most other countries. By the same token, the gulf is a primary target for Japanese exports, from automobiles to textiles. The importance of Japan's dependence on gulf oil was underscored by its decision in November 1973 to back off politically from Israel in order to be subject no longer to the Arab oil boycott. This decision was taken despite heavy pressure from its principal ally and trading partner, the United States.

The Soviet Union

Like the British and other West European powers, the Russians have also been interested in the gulf area for centuries. Unlike those countries, however, its interest has centered to a great degree on the direct political and military threats to the Russian heartland posed by various Muslim states on Russia's southern periphery, threats that were supported from time to time by various European powers.

By the nineteenth century, tsarist Russia had defeated the Tatars of the lower Volga and was expanding southward at the expense of Ottoman Turkey and Persia. Farther East, Russian expansion began to arouse fears in British India, setting the stage for a classical confrontation of imperial interests. Russian policies regarding its "southern tier" were essentially defensive in nature, seeking to establish a buffer area of weak Muslim states within the aegis of Russian political influence. There was also an element within the Russian leadership that sought to expand even farther southward, ultimately trying to establish a "warm water port" in the gulf as an outlet for growing Russian imperial and commercial interests. For a variety of external and internal reasons, the Russian Middle East imperialists were never wholly successful in achieving their aims.

For a time, Soviet Russia paid little attention to the gulf, or the Middle East in general, being preoccupied with foreign and domestic problems elsewhere. During World War II, however, the Soviets renewed their historical interest in the area. In 1941 the Allies decided to supply the Russian front through Iran. With the British occupying southern Iran, Russian troops moved into northern Iran where they remained throughout the war. Thus, in 1946 they were able to attempt the creation of puppet states in Iranian Azerbaijan and Kurdistan, albeit attempts that failed.

Post-World War II strategy in the gulf area reflected a mixture of the traditional defensive desire to create a buffer zone between the Russian heartland and hostile powers beyond, and a newer ideological desire to export communist revolution. The perceived threat in the former context came chiefly from the United States, which was seeking to create an alliance system through the Baghdad Pact and later CENTO to control Soviet policy aims. The target in the ideological context was the "masses" of Middle Eastern peoples "under the yoke of Western imperialist-dominated dictatorships."

Throughout the 1950s and early 1960s, Soviet strategy in the gulf was largely conceived in military terms. The attempt to carve out Azerbaijan and Kurdistan reflect that point of view. By the late 1960s, however, the Soviets appeared to be developing a more sophisticated and predominantly political strategy.

necessarily mean that the Soviets were changing their ideological stripes, nor that they would eschew the use of military force if force were deemed useful to them. It was rather that West and East had reached a nuclear stalemate which not only lessened the external conventional military threat to the Soviets but also called for different strategies to further the Soviet aims of expanding its influence.

The current Soviet strategy in the gulf is aimed at seeking to increase its political and economic influence in the area at the expense of the West and particularly the United States. In the case of Iraq and PDRY, the Soviets have expended a great deal of effort in buttressing relations. The armed forces of both countries are equipped largely with Soviet arms, and extensive technical aid and assistance has also been made available. The cornerstone of Soviet-Iraqi relations is a Treaty of Friendship which was signed in 1972.

The Soviets have also supported subversive movements in the gulf, both directly and through Iraq and PDRY. For example, the Soviet Union is the principal arms supplier for the Dhufar rebels (PFLO).

These activities would suggest a continuing militant and active Soviet posture in the gulf. Such is not necessarily the case, however, for the Soviets frequently find that their interests and objectives in the area are in conflict. The chief constraint to militant Soviet policy in the gulf is Soviet relations with Iran. The Soviets attempted to use the carrot rather than the stick in their efforts to wean Iran away from its close military and political relationship with the United States. Any overt Soviet military activity elsewhere in the gulf, either directly or indirectly through Iraq or PDRY, would almost certainly drive Iran even closer to a U.S. security orbit, which the Soviets do not see in their interests.

With this conflict of interest in mind, the Soviets have attempted to establish and maintain good relations with the conservative gulf regimes,[10] while supporting radical allies and covertly supporting national liberation movements in the area. In the main, the strategy has been passive rather than active in that it seeks to exploit targets of opportunity rather than attempting to create them by fomenting political unrest or military confrontations.

There is, however, a military aspect of Soviet policy toward the gulf. For the most part, its naval force in the Indian Ocean, exceeding in capability that of the United States, is used in the context of its overall political strategy—e.g., showing the Soviet flag, with all the psychological ramifications that it implies. At the same time, from the Soviet point of view, the northern reaches of the Indian Ocean, including the gulf, comprise one of the few areas where a deterrent naval force could be deployed with the capability to strike at the heart of the Soviet Union. Thus, the Soviets are very sensitive to the *potential* U.S. strategic threat from this area. In a more operational context, the Soviets seek access to shore facilities in order to extend, if ever necessary, the deployment duration of their own ships. It was in part with this in mind that they assisted in constructing Iraq's naval base at Umm Qasr.

Oil is also a major factor in Soviet interests in the gulf. The great dilemma facing Kremlin strategists, however, is what to do about it. On the one hand, it is quite obvious to the Soviets how dependent its free world adversaries are on gulf oil, militarily as well as economically. It would be tempting for the Soviet Union to think in terms of encouraging a more militant and punitive oil policy by the gulf producers toward the Western consumers. In this context, the Western oil companies have long been a major target of Soviet propagandists.

On the other hand, the Soviets may foresee the day when they themselves will be net importers of oil, and all present indications are that production to meet future Soviet demand will have to come largely from the gulf. In the interim period, oil is still one of the major foreign exchange earners for the Soviet Union. Thus, its own energy policies could quite possibly make it a competitor with gulf producers for free world markets. Such a situation could well conflict with Soviet political aims in the gulf.

There is another, though perhaps less crucial, constraint on the Soviets in attempting to interfere with oil shipments to the West. Any effort to interdict oil tankers moving through the Strait of Hormuz, which the shah fears may occur, would violate laws of the sea regarding international straits. Since the Soviets themselves are dependent on both the Bosporus and the Dardanelles in the south and the Baltic Straits in the north, they have traditionally taken a position supporting the right of passage through international straits.

In sum, the Soviet Union is confronted with a number of conflicting interests and policy aims in the gulf. In recent years these have tended to rule out the type of aggressive destabilizing policies witnessed at the height of the cold war.

Other Communist States

Compared to the Soviet Union other communist states have had a relatively small interest in the Persian Gulf. Even China, which would appear to have every reason to pursue an active gulf policy has in fact not done so. In the early 1960s China established commercial ties with Kuwait, and in 1966 it set up an office of the New China News Agency there. On March 21, 1971, Kuwait announced its decision to establish full diplomatic relations with China. Iran, after first expressing reservations about the growing communist presence in the gulf, followed suit on August 17.

Chinese diplomacy, essentially designed to oppose both Soviet and Western influence where Chinese interests are at stake, has not been very active. After 1967, the Chinese took over the leading role in training the Dhufar rebels, but by the summer of 1973 they had withdrawn. During a visit to Tehran in June 1973, the Chinese foreign minister, Chi Peng-Pei, implied that China would no longer participate in national liberation movements in the gulf.

In addition to China, Cuba and East Germany have had military and security training missions in PDRY. Beyond that, there has been little other communist activity in the gulf or its periphery.

Other States

There are a number of Arab and South Asian countries that have special political, economic, and security interests in the gulf. Jordan plays an important security role in several countries. In addition to the combat batallion it sent to Oman in early 1975, Jordan provides engineering and training support for Oman's army. It also provided a number of military officers attached to the Saudi National Guard, and has security officers in several of the gulf shaykhdoms. Isolated in the Arab world after he crushed the Palestinian fedayin organizations in Jordan in 1970, King Husayn sought political as well as economic support from the gulf states in return for military training and security assistance. At first these states were slow to accept Jordanian overtures. But with the new wave of Arab solidarity and rising oil revenues after the October 1973 war and oil price rises, Jordanian relations in the gulf region, particularly with the Arab states, have warmed considerably.

Pakistan and India also have interests in the gulf. The Indian subcontinent was traditionally a major trading center for gulf maritime trade, and continues to be so for the dhows that sail from Dubai, Oman, and elsewhere. It is also a major source of manpower for the rapidly developing oil shaykhdoms.

In the field of security, Pakistan has had a rather large military mission in Saudi Arabia, to which it is linked through common faith in Islam. Saudi midshipmen have also trained at the Pakistani naval academy. In Abu Dhabi, the Mirage jet fighters are flown by Pakistani pilots. There is also a Pakistani military mission in Oman. The Omani navy, under British command, has traditionally had Indian naval officers. More recently, however, these have been replaced by Pakistanis, in part due to the urging of the shah, who feared Soviet influence in India. In addition, many of the Omani troops are Baluchis recruited by the British in Pakistan.

India, which has national aspirations in the Indian Ocean area as a whole and has wished to counter Pakistani influence in the gulf, has also attempted to establish closer relations with the area states. The Indians have sent a small mission to supply training and advisors to the Iraqi air force, but Pakistan has sent military advisors to Iraq as well. A potentially destabilizing factor could arise if Iran's expanding political ambitions were to conflict with India's in the greater Indian Ocean area. Such a confrontation could have a great impact on gulf politics.

In sum, many states in the industrialized world, the communist world, and the third world have strong, often conflicting interests in the gulf. Some interests have developed over the centuries, others arose because of the gulf's commanding position as an oil producer. In looking at U. S. interests in the gulf, the rapidly changing configuration of these other interests must be taken into account.

NOTES

[1]R.B. Serjeant, *The Portuguese Off the South Arabian Coast* (Oxford: The Clarendon Press, 1963), p. 15. For a historical account of this period, see also Arnold T. Wilson, *The Persian Gulf: An Historical Sketch from the Earliest Times to the Beginning of the Twentieth Century* (London: George Allen and Unwin, 1954).

[2]See A.T. Mahan, *The Influence of Sea Power upon History, 1660-1785* (London: Methuen, 1965), p. 68.

[3]Wilson, *The Persian Gulf*, p. 70.

[4]"East India Company's Agreement with Imam of Musqat for Excluding the French from his Territories—12 October 1798," in J.C. Hurewitz, *Diplomacy in the Near and Middle East, A Documentary Record: 1535-1914*, 2 vols (Princeton: D. Van Nostrand Company, 1956), vol. 1, pp. 64-65.

[5]J.G. Lorimer, *Gazetteer of the Persian Gulf, Oman, and Central Arabia*, 4 vols (Calcutta: Superintendent of Government Printing, 1915), vol. 1, pp. 658-70. The operation also had the support of Oman.

[6]The text of this and other relevant treaties are found in C.U. Aitchison, *A Collection of Treaties, Engagements and Sanads Relating to India and Neighboring Countries.*

[7]A comparison of the signatories to the treaty and the present UAE shaykhdoms presents an interesting reflection of the politics of the area. Sharjah and Ras al-Khaymah were then under joint rule. Two of the signatories, Khatt-Fulaiyah and Jazirat al-Hamra, are now incorporated into Ras al-Khaymah, whereas present-day Fujayrah has been independent only since 1952. Kalba, a dependency of Shayjah on the Gulf of Oman, was also independent from 1936 to 1951. Dubai, though signatory, was a dependency of Abu Dhabi until 1833.

[8]Great Britain, Parliament, *Parliamentary Debates* London: Her Majesty's Stationery Office, January 16, 1968), vol. 756, cols. 1580-81.

[9]The public rationale for the withdrawal decision, emanating from defense studies begun in 1966, was economic. A defense estimate published simultaneously with the message to Parliament concluded that reductions in expenditure were necessary for balance of payments reasons, and that a reduction in commitments abroad must be made concomitantly with the reduction of military capability resulting from reduced expenditures. See Great Britain, Secretary of State for Defense, *Statement on the Defense Estimates 1968* (London: Her Majesty's Stationary Office, 1967). In fact, the conditions surrounding the decision appeared to have as much to do with domestic British politics as with either economics or foreign policy.

[10]Thus far, the Soviets have not been successful in establishing diplomatic relations with Saudi Arabia, Bahrain, Qatar, the UAE, or Oman.

5 Gulf Oil and Its Implications

If the beginning of any great historical period can be dated precisely, the modern oil era in the gulf began on May 28, 1901. On that day, Alfred M. Marriot signed an agreement on behalf of an Australian financier, William Knox D'Arcy, whereby Shah Mazafaar ed-Din of Persia granted D'Arcy the first Middle Eastern oil concession.[1] The concession included all of Persia except the five northern provinces adjacent to Russia. In January 1908, oil was discovered. Three months later, D'Arcy's interests were reorganized into the Anglo-Persian Oil Company (APOC).

The strategic importance of oil came to be recognized six years later. When Winston Churchill became first lord of the admiralty in 1911, the Royal Navy was already converting from coal to oil to power its ships, yet nowhere in the British Empire was there any supply of oil. On June 14, 1914, just two months before World War I, Churchill successfully passed through Parliament a bill to purchase a controlling 51 percent interest in APOC. The company's name was changed to the Anglo-Iranian Oil Company (AIOC) after Reza Shah adopted Iran as the new name of his country in 1935.

In May 1951 the nationalist prime minister of Iran, Muhammad Mussadiq, nationalized AIOC's concessions. Soon thereafter, lacking skilled manpower and marketing facilities, which were in the hands of the oil companies, Iran's oil production ceased and its customers went elsewhere. Without government revenues, Mussadiq's popularity began to wane. His attempt in 1953 to take complete control from the shah failed when a popular uprising swept him from office, reportedly with a boost from the CIA. The shah regained power and has maintained it ever since.

On October 24, 1954, a new agreement was signed with the oil companies. Iran was to keep the ownership of its oil through the National Iranian Oil Company (NIOC). But a consortium of international oil companies was created to handle production and refining operations. Members included AIOC, which has changed its name to British Petroleum (BP), 40 percent; Royal Dutch-Shell, 14 percent; Gulf, Exxon, Texaco, Mobil and Socal, each with 7 percent; Compagnie Francaise des Petroles (CFP), 6 percent; and a number of independent American oil companies collectively called the Iricon Group, 5 percent.

In Iraq, the development of oil concessions was vastly more complex, involving intricate diplomatic and commercial maneuvers, the details of which may never be known entirely. The initial entrepreneur was an Armenian from Constantinople, Calouste Sarkis Gulbenkian. Prior to World War I, Gulbenkian interested the Anglo-Saxon Petroleum Company (the precursor of the Royal Dutch-Shell group) in exploring for oil in Iraq, then called Mesopotamia and under the control of the Ottoman Empire. The prospects appeared good. Since ancient times, "everlasting sacred fires" fueled by escaping natural gas had burned near Kirkuk; and oil seeping through rocks in that area had been used in lamps for miles around. In 1911 Gulbenkian organized African and Eastern Concessions. Deutsche Bank, which had owned oil rights in conjunction with the Anatolia Railway Company (a part of the Berlin-to-Baghdad scheme), obtained an equity in the company, and in 1912 African and Eastern Concessions became the Turkish Petroleum Company (TPC).

In 1914 Gulbenkian drew up an agreement among British, German and Dutch interests which gave APOC a 50 percent share of TPC and both Deutsche Bank and Royal Dutch-Shell a 25 percent interest. Called the Red Line Agreement, it also eliminated competition among the TPC owners in developing Middle Eastern oil resources. For his part, Gulbenkian received a 5 percent beneficiary, nonvoting interest in TPC.[2]

After World War I, France received the 25 percent equity formerly owned by the Germans. The Compagnie Française des Pétroles
(CFP) was formed to acquire these shares, and subsequently the
French government acquired a 35 percent interest in CFP. In return for its equity, the French agreed, among other things, to support the British demands that the Musul oil fields be included in
the new British Mandate of Iraq rather than in Turkey and that
Iraq honor the TPC concession. The arrangement was confirmed in
the San Remo Agreement of April 1920 and the Treaty of Sèvres
in August 1920. With the establishment of Iraq as a British mandate, the Turkish Petroleum Company's name was changed to the
Iraq Petroleum Company (IPC).

U.S. oil companies objected to the closed-door provisions of the
Red Line Agreement. After the war, seven of them—Standard of
New Jersey (now Exxon), Standard of New York (now Mobil),
Gulf Oil Corporation, Texas Oil Company (Texaco), Sinclair,
Atlantic Oil Company (now part of Atlantic Richfield or Arco),
and Pan American Petroleum (Standard of Indiana)—created a
joint venture known as the Near East Development Corporation.
With the aid of the U.S. Department of State, they pressed for participation in IPC. In 1928 IPC equity was redivided, giving the
American group (Sinclair and Texaco had dropped out) 23.75 percent equity in IPC. The British, French, and Dutch interests received an equal amount. As a condition for their share, the Americans accepted the terms of the Red Line Agreement, eschewing independent oil exploration in the Middle East. By World War II,
IPC had achieved a near monopoly over exploitation of Iraqi oil.

Bahrain was the next site of an important oil discovery. Major
Frank Holmes, a New Zealand entrepreneur and adventurer, went
to Bahrain in the early 1920s to study its water resources. He
seems to have been far more interested in oil, however, for he soon
crossed over to what is now Saudi Arabia. With the help of Ameen
Rihani, a Lebanese-American who was a confidant of King Abd al-
Aziz, Holmes was awarded a Saudi oil concession in 1923.
Holmes's company, Eastern and General Syndicate, only hoped to
sell this concession. At first Gulf was interested, until it learned
that it was prohibited from independent exploration by the terms
of the Red Line Agreement. Holmes then sold the concession to
Standard of California (Socal) in 1928. Socal was not a party to
the Red Line Agreement, but Bahrain was under British
protection, and oil exploration was limited to British Empire companies. To meet this requirement, Socal merely created a wholly
owned subsidiary in Canada, the Bahrain Petroleum Company
(Bapco). In 1932 Bapco discovered oil.

Socal also inherited Holmes's Arabian concession, which had lapsed. With the aid of the British explorer and writer H. St. John B. Philby and an American who had previously studied Saudi mineral resources, Karl Twitchell, Socal was able to obtain a new concession agreement from King Abd al-Aziz in 1933. The concession was assigned to a wholly owned subsidiary, the California Arabian Standard Oil Company (Casoc). It first discovered oil in 1935, but it was not until the seventh well was spudded in on March 5, 1938, that Saudi Arabia started on its way to becoming the world's greatest oil country. The first commercial quantities of Saudi crude were not produced until after World War II. On January 31, 1944, Casoc's name was changed to the Arabian American Oil Company (Aramco).

Socal had excess oil for its marketing facilities whereas the situation was just the opposite for Texaco. In 1935 the two companies combined their overseas interests in the Near East and Asia, placing control of Bapco and Aramco (then Casoc) under a jointly owned subsidiary, Caltex. In 1948 Standard of New Jersey (Exxon) and Standard of New York (Mobil) also bought into Aramco, after having first been obliged to modify their commitments to the Red Line Agreement.

Major Holmes was also interested in a Kuwaiti concession. He obtained the backing of Gulf Oil, for Kuwait was excluded from the Red Line Agreement. The British, however, also having a protective role over Kuwait, insisted that no non-British company be granted a concession. After several years of maneuvering, involving the U.S. State Department and British Colonial Office, the ruler of Kuwait granted a concession to the Kuwait Oil Company (KOC) in December 1934. It was owned jointly by Gulf and APOC (now PB). Even though oil was discovered in 1938, commercial production did not begin until after World War II. Subsequently, two smaller concessions were granted, but they have not produced any oil: Royal Dutch-Shell's Kuwait Shell Petroleum has a concession offshore, and the Kuwait-Spanish Petroleum Company, owned jointly by the Kuwait National Oil Company and Hispanoil, have an onshore oil concession.

Two other companies obtained onshore concessions in the former Neutral Zone between Kuwait and Saudi Arabia. In June 1948 the American Independent Oil Company (Aminoil) obtained a concession covering Kuwait interests in the zone, and in February 1949 the Getty Oil Company obtained a concession covering Saudi Arabian interests. A third company, the Arabian Oil

Company (Japan), obtained a concession from Saudi Arabia in 1957 and Kuwait in 1958 for oil rights offshore from the Neutral Zone. It began oil production in 1960.

Although the Neutral Zone later was dissolved, with Kuwait and Saudi Arabia each absorbing half, each of the two countries still retains what amounts to half-interests in oil operations in the area.

The offshore concessions in Kuwait and elsewhere in the gulf were all developed in the post-World War II period. Prior to that time, international laws stipulated that a state could claim ownership to the continental shelf only to the extent of its territorial limits (usually three, six, or twelve miles). Since the whole gulf is a continental shelf, the question of offshore oil rights was most complicated there. In 1945 the United States extended jurisdiction over its continental shelf and soon other maritime states followed suit. The British, as the protecting power for the gulf amirates, then persuaded the rulers to claim offshore rights to a median line with Iran. The claims were never contested, but the problem of establishing a median line throughout the gulf has still not been entirely settled.

Qatar was the last gulf state to strike oil before World War II. Qatar Petroleum Company, an IPC subsidiary, obtained a concession in 1935; oil was discovered in 1939. As in Kuwait and Saudi Arabia, no oil was exported during the war. And it was not until 1949 that Qatar first began commercial production.

Subsequently, oil was discovered offshore by Shell Company (Qatar), a Royal Dutch-Shell subsidiary. In 1969, Qatar Oil Company (Japan) obtained another offshore concession, and several other companies have also been involved in Qatar. In addition, Qatar shares an oil field, Bunduq, with Abu Dhabi.

The development of oil in the UAE involved a game of musical chairs by oil company concessionaires. In 1935 Iraq Petroleum Company formed a subsidiary, Petroleum Concessions. The following year this company in turn formed Petroleum Development Trucial Coast (PDTC). By 1939 PDTC had obtained concessions from most of the Trucial States, but from then through the war, little or no exploration was undertaken. In October 1960 PDTC struck oil in commercial quantities eighty miles from Abu Dhabi town. It thereupon chose to concentrate solely on Abu Dhabi, relinquishing its concessions in the other Trucial States. The name of the company was changed to Abu Dhabi Petroleum Company (ADPC). The first exports were lifted in 1962.

Offshore rights were granted to another concessionaire, International Marine Oil Company, but it withdrew and in 1954 Abu Dhabi Marine Areas (ADMA) was granted offshore rights. Originally owned by BP (two-thirds) and CFP, Japanese interests subsequently bought a 30.83 percent equity out of BP's share. ADMA went into production in 1963.

Since then several other concessions have been granted from areas released by ADPC and ADMA. They include Abu Dhabi Oil Company (Japan), with an offshore concession that came on stream in 1973; Phillips Petroleum; Abu al-Bakush Oil Company, a French-controlled consortium with U.S. and Canadian interests; and Bunduq Oil Company. The latter, formed by BP, CFP, and Japanese interests to exploit a joint Qatar-Abu Dhabi field, is operated by ADMA.

In Dubai, Dubai Marine Areas (DUMA), a sister company to Abu Dhabi Marine Areas, obtained offshore rights in 1954. Since then, however, numerous changes have been made in ownership. DUMA came under the ownership of CFP and Hispanoil of Spain. In addition, half-interest in its concession was sold to Dubai Petroleum Company (DPC). DPC was originally owned entirely by Continental Oil Company (Conoco), but Conoco later sold 40 percent of DPC to three other firms. Conoco became the operating company. Oil was discovered in the offshore concession in 1966 and production began in 1969. DPC also had an onshore concession in 1966 and production began in 1969. DPC also had an onshore concession, but it was relinquished in 1971.

The only other oil-producing member of the UAE is Sharjah, which began production in 1974. The field, developed by a group headed by Buttes Gas and Oil Company of Oakland, California, was discovered by Occidental Petroleum Corporation, another U.S. firm with concessions in neighboring Umm al-Qaywayn and Ajman. The field was originally in Umm al-Qaywayn until Sharjah increased its territorial waters from three to twelve miles to include it. Occidental sought redress, but so far to no avail.

The other producer in the gulf is Oman. The concession for onshore oil rights was granted in 1937 to an IPC subsidiary, Petroleum Concessions, which in 1951 changed its name to Petroleum Development (Oman) (PDO). By 1960 all the IPC partners withdrew except Royal Dutch-Shell, with 85 percent, and Partex (Gulbenkian), with 15 percent. In 1967 CFP again bought in, taking 10 of Partex's 15 percent. Oil was first discovered in 1963 and commercial exports began in 1967.

OPEC

Until the 1970s, world oil prices were set by the major international oil companies. Prior to World War II, oil company efforts to regulate production and market shares in the gulf—e.g., the Red Line Agreement and the "As Is Agreement" of 1928[3] —were not designed to drive the price of oil up, as one might conclude in the post-energy crisis world. There existed a glut in the international supply of oil in the 1920s and 1930s, and the Great Depression of the 1930s compounded the oil companies' plight by drastically reducing demand. The producing countries have long charged that the oil companies conspired to keep oil prices, and hence producer-country revenues, down. But actions which have since earned the oil companies the sinister epithet of "oil cartel" were originally designed to prevent the price of oil from collapsing through cut-throat price wars. Moreover, the oil-glut mentality persisted right up to the energy crisis on 1973.[4]

The oil-producing countries chafed over what was in effect the power of the oil companies to regulate their national revenues. In 1959 a Middle East oil price cut seriously affected Venezuela, which had higher-priced crude oil. Venezuela, stung by its inability to prevent the move, consulted with Middle Eastern producer countries about the efficacy of creating a producer organization to negotiate collectively with the oil companies over price. The idea stuck a responsive chord, and in August 1960 the Organization of Petroleum Exporting Countries (OPEC) was born. Its original members were Iraq, Iran, Kuwait, Saudi Arabia, and Venezuela. In 1961, Qatar joined, and a year later, membership was extended to Indonesia and Libya. Ultimately, Algeria, Ecuador, Gabon, Nigeria, and Abu Dhabi (UAE) were also to join.[5]

At first, OPEC made little impact on oil pricing. Throughout the 1960s, a glut in supply, i.e., an excess in production capacity, maintained a buyer's market. Producing countries remembered how easy it was for the companies to increase production elsewhere in 1951 when Iran nationalized its oil. The often-heard phrase of the day in the oil-consuming countries was that the producers "cannot eat their oil."

By the late 1960s, however, increases in world demand were growing faster than increases in production capacity of both known and newly discovered oil. Another factor also became crucial. For years, the United States was the world's largest oil producer. By the 1950s, however, it was thought that U.S. production would peak by about 1970, and U.S. oil imports, mainly from the Middle East, were expected to increase rapidly. This projection proved to be correct. In other words, there were signs that the long years of a buyer's market were about to end.

Following the June 1967 war and the closing of the Suez Canal, Libya found itself in a very advantageous position because of its proximity to Europe and the low sulphur content of its oil. The Qadhafi regime, which came to power in 1969, announced production cutbacks for conservation reasons. Because Middle East oil pipelines were coincidentally closed in 1970, there was a very tight oil supply in Europe, which Libya chose to exploit. In May 1970, Occidental Petroleum Corporation, one of the smaller, independent oil companies, agreed to the Libyan government's demands for a larger government income per barrel of oil and an increase in the posted price.[6] This was the first time an oil company had given in to a producing country on price. And although Occidental was a relatively small company, its action was like a hole in the dike. By September 1970, the major oil companies operating in Libya had followed suit.[7]

The Libyan settlement sparked a succession of actions and demands by other producing countries, raising both the tax rates and posted prices, in some cases retroactively. During the OPEC conference in Caracas in December 1970, a resolution was passed specifying that, henceforth, the oil companies would negotiate oil prices with OPEC members collectively.

In the face of growing OPEC power, twenty-two oil companies, majors and independents alike, had banded together in the London Advisory Group. In January 1971, the companies, fearing that any price or other agreement not including all the producers would merely precipitate an endless spiral of increasing demands, announced that they would only negotiate with all of OPEC's members simultaneously. OPEC had come of age.

The years 1972 and 1973 witnessed OPEC's exercise of power steadily increase. Then, on October 16, 1973, OPEC unilaterally doubled the price of oil. The following December the price was doubled again. For all intents and purposes, the oil companies no longer had any role at all in establishing oil prices. In the West, OPEC was viewed as the new oil cartel, though in the classical sense of the term, neither the companies in the past nor OPEC in the present can be strictly called cartels.

OPEC is very often viewed in the West as a monolithic political-economic bloc. In fact, there are relatively few mutual political or economic interests among the members. Some are capital surplus countries and some are not; the non-Arab members do not share Arab desiderata; members are located in three continents with vastly different problems confronting them. In short, OPEC is neither a political nor an economic monolith, but a rather narrowly conceived oil-price-setting organization. The collective interest that its members have in common is to maintain the price of oil at a level well above what the oil companies had set before the 1970s. Since no member is bound by OPEC resolutions, OPEC itself does not make price decisions; the locus of power lies with the members rather than with the organization as a whole. Because nearly two-thirds of the free world's proved oil reserves are located in the gulf, the gulf members of OPEC, particularly Iran and Saudi Arabia, play a major role in OPEC decision making.

OAPEC

The Arab oil producers in the gulf also participate in another oil organization, the Organization of Arab Oil Exporting Countries (OAPEC). This organization represents a mutuality of political interests not found in OPEC. Founded in January 1968 by Saudi Arabia, Kuwait, and Libya, it was originally conceived as a conservative forum to counter more activist OPEC members, such as Algeria, Iraq, and Venezuela, as well as militant Arab states that were trying to pressure the Arab oil producers to use oil as a weapon in the cause against Israel. The Saudis in particular, while no less inimical to Israel than were other Arab states, did not want others to dictate their oil policies. Petroleum Minister Yamani, discussing the ineffective Arab oil embargo invoked as a result of the June 1967 Arab-Israeli war, said, "injudiciously used, the oil weapon loses much if not all of its importance and effectiveness."[8] Implicit in his words was the conviction that the Saudis would decide when and where it was not judicious for them to use oil as a political weapon.

Following the Libyan revolution of 1969, the conservative nature of OAPEC changed. The Libyans pressed for membership to be extended to Algeria, Iraq, Egypt, and Syria. In return, Qadhafi agreed to accept Bahrain, Qatar, Abu Dhabi, and Dubai.

OAPEC currently serves two functions. One, it is a means of distributing Arab oil money to non-Arab states, and it also attempts to coordinate economic development activity. In the latter, it is not always successful: when OAPEC decided on Bahrain instead of Dubai as the site of a regional gulf dry dock facility in 1973, Shaykh Rashid withdrew from OAPEC and went ahead with plans to build his own dry dock. In past years, OAPEC members have pledged around $80 million annually to Arab economic development, still a very small amount by Arab oil standards.

The other function of OAPEC is political. From the start it was recognized that one of OAPEC's functions was to coordinate the use of oil as a means to obtain Arab political goals. Even the Saudis accepted that premise. By 1973, King Faysal, frustrated at the lack of progress toward an Arab-Israeli settlement, was beginning to speak more emphatically of the possibility of using oil as a political tool.

The most spectacular use of oil to obtain a political objective was the Arab oil embargo of October 17, 1973, to March 18, 1974. The embargo, called in the name of OAPEC, was in fact instigated by King Faysal, who was angered at the massive $2.2 billion U.S. resupply of Israel during the October 1973 Arab-Israeli war. Faysal was able single-handedly to make the embargo effective, due to Saudi Arabia's commanding share of the world market at a time of near peak production. Iraq, on the other hand, never enforced the embargo, arguing that the embargo was only a half-way measure. Iraq nevertheless was not loath to benefit financially from not cutting its production to make the embargo work.

As it developed, therefore, OAPEC is much more politicized than OPEC, and its objectives are more broadly defined. Whereas OPEC is primarily an oil-price-setting organization, OAPEC is devoted to cooperation among Arab producers toward political as well as economic goals.

The Move Toward Nationalization

The oil-producing countries did not stop at price setting. With the exception of Iran, which technically owned its oil resources, the other producers had given up title to the oil through the concession agreements. As early as 1967, Saudi Arabia's minister of petroleum, Ahmad Zaki Yamani, had announced a scheme called "participation," whereby the producing countries would gradually buy out the producing company subsidiaries of the oil companies.

After long and difficult negotiations, the Saudis and several other producers reached an agreement with the companies for immediate purchase of 25 percent equity and ultimately full ownership of the producing companies in their respective countries. The pace of transfer of equity far exceeded the original agreement, however. By the summer of 1974, Saudi Arabia and Kuwait had increased their participation share to 60 percent, and the following year, negotiations were launched for 100 percent. As the Saudis went, so went the other gulf producers.

Production facilities were still operated by the companies, but the participating countries could dispose of their share of the oil (called "participation crude") as they saw fit. Generally they sold the oil back to the companies to market. However, the "buyback price," as it was called, was slightly higher than the equity price—the price set on the companies' share of the oil produced. Moreover, the U.S. companies could claim no tax deductions on buy-back oil. In July 1974 the Kuwaitis further raised the price of their buy-back oil to 94.8 percent of the posted price, thus raising the actual price of oil even higher.

Iraq did not follow the participation route. In June 1972 it nationalized the Iraq Petroleum Company after years of negotiating over exploration, production rates, and other issues. The dispute with the owners of IPC over compensation was settled in January 1973, as a result of mediation efforts by the secretary-general of OPEC and an official of the Compagnie Française des Pétroles (CFP). The settlement included compensation to the owners and transfer of ownership of a sister company, the Mosul Petroleum Company, to Iraq.

Another sister company, the Basrah Petroleum Company (BPC), was not nationalized then, but as a result of the October 1973 Arab-Israeli war, the equity of the U.S. partners (Exxon and Mobil) and the Dutch partner (Royal Dutch-Shell) was nationalized as well. (The United States and the Netherlands were objects of the Arab oil embargo.) Nationalized production was transferred to the state-owned Iraq National Oil Company (NOC), which was formed in 1964. Finally, on December 8, 1975, Iraq nationalized all remaining equity in BPC.[9]

Another country to nationalize, ironically, was Dubai, which took title to all its oil operations on July 10, 1975. Dubai had spurned OPEC, dropped out of OAPEC on the dry dock issue, and had never shown any interest in participation. The nationalization of its oil, however, appears to have been a very shrewd move. Shaykh Rashid not only reaped political benefits for taking over the producing companies, but compensated the companies so well, through oil purchase credits and a management contract, that everyone appears to be happy.

When the Persian Gulf producers obtained participation agreements, the shah sought an arrangement with the consortium of oil companies in Iran to ensure that Iran would have a financial return no less advantageous than the participation countries. An agreement was signed in July 1973 whereby the consortium formed a company to produce, process, and transport Iranian oil under a five-year service contract. The Iranians will sell oil to the consortium over a twenty-year period on a cost-plus-fee basis, guaranteeing Iran the financial equivalent of participation agreements obtained on the Arab side of the gulf. Any change on the Arab side will automatically increase the "balancing margin" on the Iranian side to equalize the return.

In brief, the years 1968 through 1975 have seen the gulf producers not only gain control of their own oil resources, but also gain the power to set prices.

Future Trends and Gulf Oil Policies

Prior to the 1970s, oil supply-demand relationships were maintained in relative balance at an approximately stable price. All the parties involved were thoroughly familiar with the rules governing the producer country-oil company negotiations over production levels, taxes, and royalties. Long-run demand projections, however, nearly always erred on the conservative side. Spurred by low prices, demand for oil in the 1950s and 1960s grew at a much faster rate than expected, exhausting excess production capacity worldwide and creating the seller's market of the 1970s.

When the oil-producing countries seized the initiative in setting prices and production rates, the old stable order of supply-demand relationships was swept aside; and no new equilibrium has replaced the old. We are in effect living in an interim period between the old order and a new order yet to evolve. Much of the difficulty in the capitals of the major consuming countries in their attempts to form comprehensive energy policies arises from the uncertainty of future energy supply-demand relationships and the place in these relationships of oil.

The oil producers themselves concede that, in the long run, high oil prices will cause a decrease in demand for oil due to its costliness and, more important, due to a subsequent shift to other sources of energy. But they also point out that oil is a wasting asset, and for many of them their only major source of revenues. They argue too that they are actually doing the world a service by forcing it to develop alternative sources of energy now while oil is relatively abundant, rather than later when it is almost gone. After all, they point out, it will take years, perhaps decades to develop energy alternatives.

It is therefore the medium term, the next five to ten years, wherein lies the most uncertainty. This is reflected in the wide range of opinions among professional oil and financial men about production levels and cumulative revenues that will be accrued by the oil-producing countries by 1980. For example, the World Bank projected in 1974 that OPEC countries would accumulate $650 billion (current dollars) by 1980.[10] A year later, projections ranged considerably lower. Walter J. Levy, for example, projected $449 billion by 1980, while First National City Bank projected $189 billion and Morgan Guaranty projected $179 billion. Moreover, the gap between high and low projections was greater than the low projections.[11]

In part, the problem of projecting such figures stems from the uncertainty of future supply-demand relationships. Projections made with different price assumptions will naturally vary widely. In addition, there is little concensus on the price elasticity of the demand for oil. In other words, there is substantial disagreement on the relationship between the price of oil and the demand for oil in the medium term. Some economists are convinced that continued high oil prices are certain to lower demand, but at the cost of a world recession. The 1974-1975 recession is seen as evidence of this trend. Others, while conceding that high oil prices can be deflationary to the extent that they inhibit demand for higher-priced goods and services, do not think that high oil prices per se must necessarily bring on a depression. They point to the general expectation that the industrial economies will recover in the next few years, and project that, as a result, oil demand will rise despite high prices, The real unanswered questions in the medium term are to what degree will high oil prices affect the recovery and to what degree will the recovery affect oil demand and hence oil prices.

Another problem is estimating the supply of energy from non-OPEC sources over the medium term. Not only have high oil prices placed coal in a strong competitive position, but new supplies of oil from non-OPEC sources are expected to come into production, in the North Sea, on Alaska's North Slope, in Mexico, and elsewhere. Additionally, the higher price of oil has spurred the production of known but previously uncompetitive sources, particularly in the United States, and has stimulated oil exploration throughout the world as well.

Still another difficulty in medium-term projections lies in the overwhelming influence that policy decisions of the major producing and consuming countries will have on supply-demand relationships. Taxes, trade barriers, import and export subsidies, foreign investment policies and regulations will all bear on medium-term energy patterns. Yet, because these decisions will be made on political as well as economic grounds, there is almost no way to predict with certitude what such policies might be, much less what their effect will be.

These issues, if analyzed in depth, would take us far beyond the scope of this book. It is necessary to bear them in mind, however, as we turn now to the factors underlying oil policies in the gulf. These factors will be major determinants of oil policy making no matter what direction the actual policies may take. There are at least four such factors: 1) the desire for revenues to finance development; 2) the desire to conserve oil resources, which are a wasting asset; 3) the desire to avoid measures that would seriously undermine world economic stability; and 4) the desire to maintain control over price setting through OPEC.

Maximizing oil revenues involves a very complicated calculus. In purely theoretical terms, it entails establishing a rate of production over a given period of time that will balance the advantages and disadvantages of obtaining revenues while exhausting reserves. The calculus is different for each country, depending on capital needs and oil reserve positions. Iran, for example, has a relatively high absorptive capacity for capital expenditures, but at present production rates its reserves will be exhausted by the end of the century. It would seem to be in Iran's long- and short-term interests, therefore, to maintian high prices and limited production.

Saudi Arabia, on the other hand, has a relatively low absorptive capacity for capital expenditures and the largest proved oil reserves in the world (around 150 billion barrels). To the extent that high oil prices would encourage shifts to other forms of energy, leaving Saudi Arabia with unexploited reserves, it would seem to be in its interests to increase present production at somewhat lower prices.

In actual oil policy decision making, no country follows the dictates of such practical analysis to the degree that some professors of petroleum economics would perhaps like it to do. For one thing, a country's perception of its need for revenues and the estimation of its absorptive capacity for capital are based in large part on that country's subjective view of the urgency of the need for change in its own society. For example, in the West, building a hospital with an operating overhead of several thousand dollars per bed per day might be considered wasteful. But in a country with very few hospitals and billions of dollars of reserves, such expenditure might be considered reasonable. Most of the gulf states strongly desire rapid material and social benefits for their people, and are willing to pay double or even ten times what a similar project might cost in the West. Thus their capital "needs" tend to exceed most Western projections.

Conservation can also become a political and emotional issue as well as an economic one. Kuwait had begun conservation measures even before the energy crisis of 1973. However, the natural gas that it expects to use for its domestic industrial and private consumption is associated with its oil production. Thus, too great a cut in production, whether for conservation or to keep prices up, would also deprive Kuwait of natural gas for domestic economic development. Of the other producers, only Bahrain has a relatively high absorptive capacity for capital, at least in ministate, per capita terms. Having discovered oil early in 1932, it has a more advanced social and economic infrastructure than is the case further down the gulf. But its oil reserves are nearly exhausted. Roughly half the oil used in Bapco's refinery comes via pipelines from Saudi Arabia. Bahrain's oil policy, therefore, could not really influence international supply-demand relationships. Moreover, Bahrain is not a member of OPEC.

Of the lower gulf producers, only Abu Dhabi has significant production with projected earnings for 1976 in excess of $6 billion. Abu Dhabi's Shaykh Zayd, who is also president of the UAE, has been generous with the other UAE shaykhdoms in addition to developing his own country. Still, Abu Dhabi ranks with Saudi Arabia and Kuwait as having the lowest capacity of all the OPEC members for absorbing capital. It has a native population of less than 250,000. Most of the citizens of the UAE shaykhdoms are still at a rudimentary stage of social and economic development. Thus, development opportunities are simply too limited to absorb with even minimum efficiency, based on Western standards, the kinds of revenues Abu Dhabi is accruing. On the other hand, Abu Dhabi's generosity and largely uncoordinated foreign aid policies actually created a short-term liquidity problem in 1974-1975.

The other lower gulf producers—Dubai, Sharjah, and Oman—have smaller production levels and are quite able to absorb their revenues, even though in an economic sense they would probably be considered low-absorptive countries were their revenues as great as those of the major gulf producers.

The remaining gulf producer, Iraq, presents somewhat of an anomaly. Despite its radical regime, Iraqi oil policy has always been pragmatic and moderate. With the long and bitter dispute with IPC now finally settled, and with Iraq seeking to stabilize its political position domestically and regionally, many expect Iraq to pursue a very ambitious internal development policy and to adopt petroleum policies aimed at maximizing revenues. Some experts believe that Iraq may have revenues rivaling, if not equaling, Saudia Arabia's, and that it could develop into a major oil power, a role heretofore played within OPEC by Iran, Venezuela, and Saudi Arabia.

None of the gulf producers, nor any other OPEC member for that matter, wish to see the collapse of the free world economy. As a Kuwaiti stated the case, "We are all in the same boat. If it sinks, we go down too." This sentiment was made explicit in the Solemn Declaration made during the March 1975 OPEC Conference:

> The Kings and the Presidents. . . fully realize the close links between national development in their own respective countries and the economic prosperity of the world as a whole.[12]

There has been considerable debate about the sincerity of this producer point of view, given the deleterious state of the world economy after the four-fold price hike of 1973. It has been charged in the West that high oil prices had such an inflationary effect that they ultimately led to a recession, particularly in the United States, in 1975.

The producers, however, dispute the inflationary effect of high oil prices. According to an Iranian oil man, during the twelve-month period ending October 1973—i.e., prior to the energy crisis—consumer prices went up 6.6 percent in Germany, 8.1 percent in France, 9.9 percent in Britain, and 11 percent in Italy. In the same period, wages rose by 12 percent, 13.8 percent, 13.9 percent, and 26 percent in the same countries. Thus, OPEC calculated that only 2 to 3 percent of the estimated 14 percent average inflation rate in 1974 could be attributable to the rise in oil prices.[13] What the producers fail to mention, however, is that while factors other than oil may contribute more to inflation, the extra margin of inflation created by higher oil prices may turn out to be, if the reader will excuse the metaphor, the straw that breaks the camel's back.

It is evident that, although the producers tend to absolve themselves of the major responsibility for the state of the world economy, they do not wish to see it weakened. It was due to concern over the destabilizing effect of the sudden price rises on the world economy that caused Saudi Arabia to express the desire in the summer of 1974 for lower oil prices. That in the end the Saudis did not lower prices unilaterally, despite their ability to do so, was more the result of not wishing to disrupt OPEC and Arab solidarity than of a lack of concern over the effect of the high prices.

The gulf producers, as indeed all OPEC members, are absolutely insistent that they retain the power to set prices and production levels through OPEC solidarity. Some experts believe that, with new, non-OPEC oil coming on stream, that solidarity cannot survive. During the softening of demand in 1974-1975, they point out, Saudi Arabia almost unilaterally had to cut production to keep prices up, since countries like Iran had to maintain both high production and high prices to fund their ambitious development plans. At the point where the Saudis balk at bearing the burden for cutting production to maintain prices and call on the others to cut back on a prorated basis, these experts feel that OPEC solidarity will end. In the words of one State Department official, it will "bust up the OPEC cartel."

There are others who feel that this is all wishful thinking. In addition to the obvious economic incentive to work together through OPEC, there is an added psychological dimension. It is difficult to measure the psychological impact of the events of 1973 and 1974 on the OPEC members, but it does appear to be great.

After years of feeling impotent in oil dealings not only with the major oil companies but the major consuming countries as well, some of whom had been their colonial masters, the oil producers could not help but reap a great sense of satisfaction if not downright glee at being able to turn the tables and make the consuming countries squirm. Political solidarity cannot be based on such emotion, but it does appear to have strengthened the oil producers' determination to maintain a common front no matter what market forces portend.[14]

In addition, it costs only thirty cents a barrel to produce oil in the gulf, whereas much of the new oil, in Alaska and the North Sea, will cost many times that to produce. The OPEC-gulf countries will therefore still have a strong competitive advantage.

Thus, if market conditions do force a moderation of oil prices in the middle term, and there is considerable uncertainty that they will, OPEC can probably sustain a considerable diminution of its current economic power before it ceases to function as a collective force in price setting. Moreover, in order to maintain solidarity OPEC members would probably agree to moderate prices before they ever reached the point where Saudi Arabia would demand prorating production cutbacks. Algeria's President Boumedienne reflected OPEC's determination to control prices when he said, "If prices have to be frozen, we will freeze them. If they must be decreased, we will decrease them."[15]

Whatever OPEC's future, the gulf producers will play a leading role in international oil relations for the forseeable future. Having two-thirds of the free world's proved reserves, it cannot be otherwise.

NOTES

[1]The text of the concession appears as an appendix to Annex 1419c. in the League of Nations *Official Journal* 13 (1932): 2305-2307. The D'Arcy concession was actually preceded by a broader concession including rights of exploration for all minerals except gold and silver, awarded to a naturalized British citizen, Baron Julius de Reuter, in 1872. Its provisions were restricted in 1889, and the entire concession was declared void by the Persian government in 1901. See George Stocking, *Middle East Oil: A Study in Political and Economic Controversy* (Nashville, Tenn.: Vanderbilt University Press, 1970), pp. 3-8.

[2]He is often referred to as "Mr. Five Percent." See Ralph Hewins, *Mr. Five Percent: The Story of Calouste Gulbenkian* (New York: Rinehart and Company, 1958).

[3]This so-called agreement was made by representatives of Jersey Standard (Exxon), Royal Dutch-Shell, and Anglo-Persian (BP) during a weekend grouse hunt at Achnacarry Castle, England. It was intended to fix market shares among the companies just as the Red Line Agreement attempted to regulate supply. See the Federal Trade Commission The International Oil Cartel, published by the Select Committee on Small Business, U.S. Senate, 82nd Congress, 2nd Session (Washington, D.C.: Government Printing Office, 1952). Also mentioned in Stocking, *Middle East Oil,* pp. 84-85.

[4]For example, see M.A. Adelman, "Is the Oil Shortage Real? Oil Companies as OPEC Tax Collectors," *Foreign Policy* 9 (Winter 1972-1973): 69-107. Professor Adelman took a conspiratorial view that the oil companies sought in league with the producers to create a shortage in order to raise prices, despite abundant proved reserves.

[5]Although the UAE membership technically includes all three oil-producing shaykhdoms, only Abu Dhabi is an active participant. Dubai and Sharjah have never shown any interest in OPEC.

[6]The "posted price" was an artificial accounting price per barrel for computing taxes on the producer companies and royalties on the oil they produced. It was generally higher than the actual price the companies paid. Moreover, since the U.S. companies were allowed to deduct the foreign taxes from their U.S. tax liabilities, the cost of the oil to the companies was in effect even less, by the amount of their U.S. tax write-offs, than the price they paid.

[7]The so-called major oil companies, or Seven Sisters, are Exxon, Mobil, Socal, Texaco, Gulf, Royal Dutch-Shell, and BP. In addition, CFP of France is sometimes considered a major. The other companies are called "independents."

[8]*Middle East Economic Survey,* July 21, 1967.

[9]*New York Times,* December 8, 1975.

[10]See Robert McNamara's Annual Address to the World Bank reprinted in the *Summary Proceedings of the 1974 Annual Meeting of the Board of Governors,* p. 31.

[11]See Richard D. Erb, "The Financial Management Problem From the Perspective of OPEC Members," unpublished paper delivered to the Council on Foreign Relations, July 11, 1975.

[12]The text of the Solemn Declaration was published by OPEC in the *Washington Post,* March 18, 1975, p. B-16.

[13]See D. Reza Fallah, "The Energy Crisis: Its Origins and Suggested Remedies," address delivered before the Centre International d'Etudes Monetaires et Bancaires, Geneva, Switzerland, Nov. 28-30, 1974.

[14]This theme was developed from my paper, "The Politics of OPEC," presented to the Council on Foreign Relations in New York on April 24, 1975.

[15]*Washington Post,* March 3, 1975.

6 Economic Prospects in the Gulf

The economic structure of the gulf is the result of the impact of oil revenues upon the widely diverse traditional economies of the gulf countries. Preoil economic activity centered around five principal activities: agriculture, animal husbandry, commerce and trade, fishing, and pearling.

Agriculture was limited largely to well-watered areas such as the Caspian Sea coast in Iran, to irrigable river valleys such as the Tigris and Euphrates, to those mountainous areas that had both sufficient rainfall and soil for terrace farming, and to scattered oases. Animal husbandry was the principal occupation of nomadic tribes inhabiting the mountains of Iran and Iraq and the great deserts of Arabia. In the field of commerce, the gulf area lay astride the major trade routes from Europe to the Orient. One branch extended overland through Iran to India. The other moved by sea from the Persian Gulf to India and Africa. The gulf also provided a livelihood for fishermen and pearl divers. Pearling was a major industry in many of the gulf shaykhdoms before the cultured pearls from Japan captured most of the trade.

Another important economic activity was religious tourism. Before the discovery of oil, the cash economies of Saudia Arabia, and its predecessor the Kingdom of Hijaz, consisted almost entirely of receipts from the annual *hajj* to Mecca and al-Medinah.

Pilgrimages to Shi'a Muslim shrines such as the tombs of Hassan and Husayn in Karbalah, Iraq, were also important economically, albeit in lesser scale than the *hajj*.

All of these pursuits are still present to a lesser or greater degree throughout the gulf area. The coming of oil, revolutionary as it has been to the local economies, did not initiate a totally new way of life. Rather, it began the transformation of the old, a process for which there is still no end in sight.

The economic prospects of the gulf states depend on their own individual sets of circumstances, and no two states are exactly the same. But for all states, the primary determinant of economic growth potential is oil. Because there is so much uncertainty over projected oil revenues in the middle term, however, there is an equal amount of uncertainty in trying to project growth potential.

The Structure of the National Economies

As we have noted in the previous chapter, there are great differences in both the reserve positions of the various gulf states and in their absorptive capacities for development capital expenditure. To analyze fully the economies of any single gulf state would be a major undertaking all its own. The following are but brief descriptions of these economies.

Iran

With a large population and land mass, Iran has the base to develop a modern, productive economy. Its population, projected to be 36 million by 1978, is growing at roughly 3 percent a year. Although a large part of its 636,000 square miles (1,648,000 square kilometers) is arid, there is still much potential for increasing the productivity of arable land.

Iran has a free market economy dominated by the public sector. The oil industry, of course, provides the major source of revenue to promote economic growth. Beginning in 1948, the government initiated a number of development plans aimed at modernizing the economy. The first two (1948-1955 and 1955-1962) experienced difficulties, due first to the period of instability and loss of oil revenues during the Mussa diq period, and also to the lack of managerial expertise within the public sector. Nevertheless, agricultural productivity was increased, the social and economic infrastructure was greatly upgraded, and the stage was set for the impressive growth rate begun in the 1960s and sustained to the present.

The Third Development Plan (1962-1968) became the cornerstone for the rapid economic development of the 1960s and 1970s. Moreover, the impetus created by government investment spurred private investment so that it actually exceeded investment in the public sector throughout the period of the plan.[1] In agriculture, extension of irrigated lands, construction of wells and dams, and improvement of farming techniques were instituted, but the main accomplishment was in land reform.

The Fourth Development Plan (1968-1973) was designed to concentrate on the industrial sector, but continued to give attention to balanced growth in all sectors. The current Fifth Development Plan was inaugurated in March 1973 and is expected to continue to 1978. Originally, it was to involve a total expenditure of $35.5 billion, greater than that of all the previous years combined. But with the oil price rises of 1973-1974 vastly increasing revenues, the plan was revised to produce an expenditure of $68.6 billion.[2] This should greatly increase the expected growth rate under the plan beyond the originally projected 14 percent; but because of fluctuations in the world economy since the 1973-74 energy crisis, it is difficult to project what the real growth figure will be.

The political expression of economic development is the White Revolution, which the shah evolved during the 1960s.[3] In late 1961 he declared by royal decree a program which became the first six of Twelve Points for Progress of the Revolution of the Shah and the People. The heart of the program was land reform. In January 1962, after the shah himself had ceded all personal property and business interests to the nation through the Pahlevi Foundation, he instituted the Land Reform Act which was to give land tenure to the largely landless Iranian peasants. By 1967 nearly 1 million farmers held title to their lands.[4]

On January 26, 1963, the six points—land reform, nationalizing forest lands, sale of equity of state-owned factories to the private sector to raise revenues for land reform, a provision for sharing with the workers 20 percent of the net profits of industrial establishments, and universal suffrage—were passed by public referendum. Between 1963 and 1967, six more points were added.

These included creation of a Literary Corps, a Health Corps, a Development and Agricultural Extension Corps, and a legal aid Equity Corps. Other points called for nationalization and development of water resources, urban and rural reconstruction, and reform of the civil service.

Agriculture still dominates the Iranian economy in terms of the labor force. In 1971 some 3.4 million out of a total labor force of 8 million were engaged in farming, forestry, hunting, or fishing.[5] Some 60 percent of the population still live in rural areas.

Despite the great strides in modernization and land reform, the agricultural sector is still largely underdeveloped. Nearly 90 percent of all Iranian farmers are estimated to live at a subsistence level.[6] While crop levels have steadily increased over the past years, much of the increase can be attributed to increases in the land under cultivation, particularly irrigated land.

The Fifth Development Plan places particular emphasis on agriculture, partly because a rapidly increasing population has made shortages in domestically produced foodstuffs a growing problem. The first stages of land reform (1962-1967) concentrated on redistribution of land tenure. Since then, concentration has been on increasing farm mechanization and on consolidating fragmented holdings. In the Fifth Plan, farmers are being induced to join cooperatives for better efficiency, and agricultural credit is being extended. In addition, public sector agro-industrial projects are being planned, including joint ventures with foreign partners.

Forestry in Iran had not been economically productive before nationalization in 1963, and many former forests were denuded and prevented from growing back by overgrazing livestock. The Forestry Commission now supervises conservation and reforestation efforts that should make wood products a more important resource. Some 11.5 percent of Iran is currently classified as woodlands.[7]

With the exception of the caviar industry in the Caspian Sea, fishing is also very underdeveloped in terms of its potential. However, Iran is now focusing more attention on building up its fishing fleet. One survey estimated that a potential income of $200 million annually could be earned from a more developed fishing industry.[8]

It is through industrialization that the shah hopes to build Iran into an economic (and political) power. Assuming that oil resources will be available only for domestic use by the turn of the century, Iran is undertaking a major industrialization program which it hopes will match West Germany's productive capacity by that time. Special emphasis is being placed on the petrochemical industry as a means of maximizing revenues from oil and gas resources. This industry began with the opening of a fertilizer plant in Shiraz in 1961. The Fifth Plan projects a growth rate of 22 percent per year in the petrochemical industry. By 1983 Iran hopes to meet 5 to 10 percent of world demand for petrochemicals, including fertilizers, plastics, and other products.[9]

To insure markets and gain technology, the government is encouraging joint ventures with such U.S. firms as DuPont, Allied Chemical, and Dow Chemical as well as with European and Japanese firms. Iran's National Petroleum Company (NPC), a subsidiary of NIOC, is the principal public sector investor in petrochemicals. NPC hopes to concentrate on basic production, leaving intermediate and final processing to the private sector.

Iran is also expanding its iron and steel industry. The first steel mill, Arya Mahr, was established at Isfahan with Soviet credits first extended in 1965. The plant began production in 1973. Operated by the National Iranian Steel Corporation (NISCO), it is Iran's second-largest employer, following the oil industry.

Iran hopes to expand its steel-producing capacity from 2 million tons in 1972 to 15 million tons by 1982. NISCO plans to invest about $6 billion in expansion and hopes to generate another $2 billion from the private sector and foreign sources. One scheme is to set up a 3-million-ton per year plant at Bandar Abbas in an Iranian-financed venture with Italy's Finsider Corporation. Unlike the Isfahan mill, this would obtain iron ore from abroad, possibly from India. This mill would turn Iran into a net exporter of iron and steel.

Symptomatic of Iran's foreign investment policy was the announcement on July 17, 1974, of its acquisition of 25 percent interest in the steel works of Germany's Krupp.[10] Krupp needed Iranian capital, and Iran in turn hopes to utilize not only Krupp's markets but, perhaps more important, its technical expertise for Iran's own steel industry.

There is also a growing automotive industry in Iran. The first assembly plant was established in 1957 and by 1973 production reached 51,000 cars, 6,300 trucks, 5,000 busses and minibusses, and 14,300 delivery vans. This accounted for all but 8 percent of Iran's internal demand.[11] With the rising standard of living and protective import restrictions, demand is expected to grow even greater. It has already outstripped supply and is creating horrendous traffic problems, as any pedestrian in the auto-clogged streets of Tehran can verify.

The largest of twelve auto producers is Iranian National, which produces a domestic version of a Hillman, called the Peykan, under license from Chrysler (U.K.). To date, most of the components of the Iranian auto industry must be imported, but Iran National has launched a $100-million project to build its own engines and ultimately hopes to produce an all-Iranian car.

In addition to these enterprises, Iran is pushing ahead with development of a social and economic infrastructure on a broad front. Rail, all-weather road, and air links are being expanded. New hydroelectric projects are being planned and constructed, and in February 1974 Iran ordered five nuclear power stations from France at a cost of around $1.2 billion.

Iraq

Despite the radical socialist coloration of the Ba'thist regime, Iraq still has a mixed economy with an active private sector. Because of political-economic constraints on the private sector and the fact that oil revenues and economic planning are in the hands of the government, however, the public sector should continue to dominate the Iraqi economy.

Like Iran, Iraq has an oil-based economy and a largely agricultural society. In ancient times, a highly sophisticated system of irrigated farming existed in Mesopotamia ("the land between the rivers"), but the Mongol invasions of the thirteenth through sixteenth centuries virtually destroyed it, and it has never fully recovered. Nevertheless, over half the labor force is engaged in farming.

Economic-development planning began with the creation of a Development Board in 1950, and the first Five Year Plan was adopted in the following year. When the monarchy was overthrown in 1958, the Development Board was abolished and planning was undertaken first by the Ministry of Development and later by a newly created Ministry of Planning.

Between 1951 and 1970, numerous "five year plans" were adopted, but their average life span was only two years.[12] This rather spotty performance was attributable to a combination of technical and political factors. Initially lacking in technical expertise, early projects were often ill devised and poorly administered.

In the monarchical period, an attempt was made to develop the economy while leaving the traditional land-owning aristocracy largely intact. While many real gains were made, particularly in controlling the flood-prone Tigris and Euphrates rivers, the planners did not sufficiently take into consideration the social revolution of rising expectations going on in Iraq. The monarchy was overthrown in a bloody revolution in 1958.

Succeeding regimes in Iraq have continued the planning efforts begun earlier. Their plans, however, reflecting their socialist political orientation, have followed Soviet designs; and, indeed, Soviet technicians have helped prepare them. During the 1960s, development was greatly inhibited by political instability, exacerbated by periodic Kurdish insurgencies. It was also impeded by stagnation of oil revenues due to disputes with the oil companies and later with Syria over the IPC pipeline from Iraq to the Syrian port of Banias on the Mediterranean.

By the 1970s, the Ba'thist regime that had gained power in 1968 had achieved a measure of internal stability. This was enhanced by the rapprochement between Iraq and Iran in early 1975, causing the latest Kurdish insurgency to collapse. Moreover, Iraq resolved its dispute with the oil companies in February 1973, and later in the year its oil revenues increased dramatically as a result of the four-fold price increase. Thus, by mid-1975 Iraq possessed the political stability and financial resources necessary to embark on a major program of development.

Prior to 1970, economic planning had concentrated primarily on the agricultural sector. The 1970-1974 plan and the current 1975-1979 plan, however, place an equal focus on industry as well. Moreover, both reflect the quantum jump in revenues. The 1975-1979 plan calls for an investment in agriculture and industry of around $5 billion.

The agricultural sector is inhibited by land tenure practices, lack of education among the farmers, and undercapitalization. Post-1958 regimes have attempted to deal with the land tenure problem through land reform, and the original land reform measures virtually stripped the landed aristocracy of their large holdings. However, being more politically inspired than based on economic feasibility, these measures actually decreased productivity.[13]

Land tenure is still complicated in Iraq, with free holds, religious-endowment (*waqf*) land, public land, and three kinds of government tenure. Gradually, however, reform is taking hold. Over 400,000 farmers have received land, and agricultural cooperatives have been established. Increasingly, the government is turning to collective farms both for political and pragmatic reasons, but collectivization is being done mainly in newly reclaimed areas rather than areas already under cultivation.

Of Iraq's 172,000 square miles (443,000 square kilometers), roughly half is arable. Of this, only about one-fourth is under cultivation. Thus, with intensive capital investment, Iraq can increase its agricultural production manyfold and probably support a population of over twice the present 11 million. The main problems are to increase the educational level of the farmers, introduce better methods and mechanization, and expand capital infrastructure such as dams, canals, and adequate drainage to prevent salination. And ultimately, an Euphrates waters agreement must be worked out with Syria and Turkey. In the spring and summer of 1975, Iraq charged that Syria had cut the flow behind its new Euphrates dam and caused severe hardship to Iraqi farmers.[14] Though it is doubtful that the issue will lead to an open confrontation between Iraq and Syria, it looms as a potential problem which could seriously affect Iraq's agricultural development.

Industry, with the exception of oil, has never been a key factor in the Iraqi economy. Nevertheless, with vastly increased revenues, the Iraqis now wish to balance their agricultural sector with a strong industrial sector. Although industrial growth has increased by 7.5 percent a year for the past twenty years, it still represents only 10 percent of the gross domestic product and employs only 8 percent of the labor force.[15] Larger enterprises were nationalized in 1964, and future large-scale investment will be made by the government.

Iraq hopes to base its industrialization around its own natural resources, moving from production of raw materials to intermediate processing, and ultimately to final processing. Thus, agro-industry and petrochemicals will receive primary attention. Economic infrastructure, such as power and communications, and import-reduction projects will also be developed.

During the lean years of the 1960s, much Iraqi development was financed by the Soviets. Now that it has sufficient oil revenues, Iraq is turning more to the free world market place to obtain high-quality goods and services. While not allowing foreign investment in Iraq, the regime is anxious to contract for completed "turnkey" projects and service contracts with a training component for Iraqis.

Saudi Arabia

The Saudi economy is one of the most laissez faire in the entire gulf. The strict and conservative Hanbali school of Islamic law followed by the Saudis is surprisingly liberal on most business ·practices. As an example of the strength of free market philosophy, Saudi merchants regularly do business with all the major communist states, while politically the government refuses to establish any diplomatic relations with these states and one cannot even place a telephone call from Saudi Arabia to the communist world. Despite its strident capitalism, the Saudi economy is totally dominated by the public sector, by virtue of the commanding position of the oil industry.

The development philosophy of Saudi Arabia was first enunciated by the late King Faysal. Basically, it was his intention to provide for his people a twentieth century material way of life while preserving an Islamic social order developed a milennium ago. Education, social welfare, and economic development were all stressed, but strictly within the context of Islamic social values. The evolution of Saudi society can thus be seen as a head-on collision of modern technocratic ideas and ancient socio-religious beliefs.

Development projects are carried out by the various ministries and other agencies. Because each is jealous of its prerogatives, cooperation among them is sometimes hard to attain. For example, at a time when no communications network existed in Saudi Arabia, no less than four independent systems were being designed—by the Communications, Defense, and Interior ministries and the National Guard.

Comprehensive government planning first began to gain acceptance in 1968. In February of that year, Shaykh Hisham Nazir was
appointed to the previously moribund Central Planning Organization (CPO). With the technical assistance of U.S. and other consultants, the CPO produced Saudi Arabia's first development plan,
for 1970-1975. Although it had been estimated that the plan
would provide for an annual GDP growth rate of 9.8 percent, this
ultimately proved too high. Originally, some 41.3 billion in Saudi
riyals (SR) in expenditures was allocated to the plan, but
after the 1973-1974 price rises, it was expanded by 35 percent.
The main aim of the plan was to diversify Saudi Arabia's single-
commodity economy. Agricultural development and industrialization, particularly in petrochemicals, was stressed, along with infrastructure projects.

In mid-1975, the Second Five Year Plan was announced. With a
massive $149 billion allocated for expenditure, it continued along
the same lines as the first plan. The magnitude of the plan reflects
the vast increase in Saudi revenues, but given the growing
economic bottlenecks in the region generally, many observers
doubt that the plan can be fully implemented in five years.

Before the discovery of oil, Saudi Arabia was primarily an agricultural country, but its agricultural development potential is
relatively restricted. Farming is limited to scattered oases, the
largest of which is the great al-Hasa (al-Ahsa) Oasis; to a narrow
strip along the Hijaz Mountains; and to (usually dry) stream beds
flowing from those mountains. Out of some 830,000 square miles
(2.15 million square kilometers), only some 1 million acres, or 0.2
percent, are under cultivation.[16] Most of this is date palm
orchards. Nearly all of the livestock consists of subsistence
nomadic herding.

Despite limited agricultural potential, some expansion is possible.
In the 1960s a major study was made of water resources, leading
to a program for digging wells and mining archeologically stored
water in the deserts. Four major agricultural projects were also
begun: a land irrigation and drainage scheme at al-Hasa; construction of a dam at Wadi Jizan on the Red Sea; another dam
near Abha, the capital of Asir; and a Bedouin settlement and land
reclamation project at Haradh.

The al-Hasa irrigation and drainage scheme was completed in
1971, after five years of work. Costing some SR260 million

($57.7 million according to the exchange rate at the time), it reclaimed 12,000 hectares of land that had grown saline through years of irrigation without proper drainage. The project is estimated to provide a livelihood for some 50,000 persons.

The King Faysal Model Settlement scheme was completed in 1972 at a cost of SR100 million. The project area has a capacity to resettle 10,000, but the government has experienced difficulty in persuading proud and independent Bedouin to locate there. The nomadic tribesmen much prefer the freedom of wandering through the desert as whim and weather lead them.

The Wadi Jizan Dam was completed in 1971 as a first step in a larger project to develop irrigation throughout the entire valley. Costing SR42 million ($9.3 million), it has the capacity for 71 million cubic meters of water storage. The Abha Dam, completed in 1974 at a cost of SR29 million, has a capacity for 2.4 million cubic meters of water. In addition to these projects, an agricultural school has been opened at Buraydah, and a nationwide well-drilling project is being conducted.

A major boon to agricultural expansion is the growing demand for foodstuffs as Saudi Arabia's standard of living grows. Over 60 percent of the country's needs must be imported. Continued capitalization of the agricultural sector and opening up the relatively fertile Asir to domestic markets through the construction of all-weather roads will greatly enhance domestic production. However, the gap between local supply and demand will probably continue to grow.[17]

Although Saudi Arabia was basically an agricultural country prior to the exploitation of its oil resources, the main foreign exchange earner was the *hajj*, the annual Muslim pilgrimage to Mecca and al-Medinah. Compared to oil income in 1974 of nearly $27 billion, the economic importance of the *hajj* is now negligible. Nevertheless, the *hajj* still comprises the most important commercial season in Saudi Arabia, and the *hajj* service industry, both public and private, employs a large proportion of the labor force, if on no more than a part-time basis.[18] It has been estimated that over a third of all consumer-related transactions are made within the six-to eight-week *hajj* season. Thus, for Saudi Arabia the *hajj* has roughly the same commercial impact as the Christmas season in the United States. Wholesale and retail inventories are stocked in anticipation of this key selling season.

Most goods sold to *hajjis* are imported, thus reducing the economic impact of sales. Nevertheless, when considering the income-generating effect of *hajj* commercial activity, coupled with that of the annual *hajj* infrastructure and administrative expenditures made by the Saudi government, one can begin to realize its economic importance.[19] Gross *hajj* receipts probably exceed $100 million per annum, an amount equalled by government spending. Thus, the total income generated each year by the *hajj* is in the neighborhood of a quarter-billion dollars. If the number of pilgrims continues to rise, as it has in recent years, the economic and commercial impact of the *hajj* will become even greater.

The Hijaz, with its long history of *hajj* commerce, has traditionally supplied Saudi Arabia with its merchant class. There was, nevertheless, a commercial center in the Najd also. The area of Qasim had long been a key stop on the trans-Arabian caravan route, and an extensive market grew up there including one of the country's largest camel markets. Some of Saudi Arabia's leading merchant families trace their ancestry back to Buraydah and 'Anayzah, the two leading (and rival) towns of Qasim. Today the larger merchant families have branches in all the major towns, so that it is becoming increasingly difficult to talk about a single region like the Hijaz as the Saudi commercial center. For example, the capital, Riyadh, is becoming equally important, particularly for international transactions.

Aside from the oil sector and the *hajj* service industry, Saudi Arabia's industrial sector is comparatively small. The country simply lacks the natural resources and manpower to develop a large-scale industrial base. Most non-oil-related industrial enterprises are small and keyed to local consumer demand. The largest is the construction industry, which is transforming the skylines of the country's major cities seemingly before one's eyes.

The chief instrument for industrial development in the public sector is Petromin, a public corporation established under the Ministry of Petroleum and Minerals in 1962. Petromin has invested in a steel-rolling mill in Jidda; established an oil refinery, also in Jidda; and, together with the Occidental Petroleum Company, established the Saudi Arabian Fertilizer Company (SAFCO) in the Eastern Province. The latter began operating in 1969, the first two in 1968.

The primary focus of Petromin, particularly since the oil price rises of 1973, is petrochemicals. In 1974 it initiated studies for a $3 billion gas-gathering and liquefaction complex. Most of the expected 5.2 billion cubic feet per day of gas that it hopes to utilize is currently being flared in the desert. In addition, Petromin, in partnership with U.S., European, and Japanese interests, is planning a multi-billion-dollar gas-based steel plant and petrochemical installation. Oil refinery capacity is also to be expanded, with new installations planned possibly in Riyadh and Jubayl. Unlike Iraq, which prefers outside interests merely to provide technology for wholly Iraqi-owned enterprises, Petromin wishes to interest foreign partners in an equity share. In that way, it hopes to maintain higher performance levels and utilize its partners' market potential.

Industrial expansion by the private sector, which up until now has invested less development capital than the public sector, is being encouraged with favorable financing and guaranteed markets. General Motors is currently constructing an assembly plant in partnership with Saudi private interests, and expects to market its production of autos and trucks in large part to the government. Saudi private capital is also moving into fishing, shipping, and other opportunities.

One other enterprise is worthy of mention. Saudi Arabian Airlines not only provides transportation within the kingdom but is a major international carrier as well. Started in 1945, it was guided by Trans World Airlines, which still has a management contract. Saudia, as it is now called, was originally founded to provide air service for pilgrims journeying to Mecca, and, as the national Saudi carrier, it has a favorable position in chartering *hajj* flights. In recent years it has built up the largest fleet in the Middle East.

Kuwait

Kuwait looked to the sea for its livelihood prior to the discovery of oil. Before the Japanese developed cultured pearls, pearling was a major Kuwaiti industry. In 1912, Kuwait had a fleet of 812 pearl boats manned by 30,000 divers.[20] Kuwaiti shipwrights gained a reputation for making some of the best dhows in the gulf, and Kuwaiti mariners aboard those dhows developed commercial ties throughout the Indian Ocean. At home, the great Kuwaiti families developed into a mercantile class. But the coming of oil has changed all that. Even Kuwaiti fishing boats are now manned mostly by foreigners.

Because of the scarcity of fresh water, there is practically no agriculture in Kuwait. The government has an experimental farm and hopes to develop hydroponic techniques. Animal husbandry is encouraged, and there are dairy and poultry farms in the private sector. There is also a plan to use treated sewage to create a green-belt of trees around Kuwait City. By and large, however, Kuwait will always be dependent on imports to feed its people.

Fishing is more promising, being the second-largest foreign exchange earner after oil. There is a good market for gulf shrimp and prawns in the United States, Europe, and Japan. In 1972, four fishing companies merged to form Kuwait United Fisheries, thus increasing their efficiency. The government, to encourage fishing, plans to construct a new fishing port.

The government also encourages industrial diversification, and a new industrial area has been developed at Shuaiba, south of Kuwait City. The Kuwaitis are concerned that the country be adequately prepared economically when the oil, its only major resource, runs out. In 1972, conservation measures were adopted restricting maximum production to 3 million barrels per day (bpd). Current reserve estimates (70 billion barrels) would permit production for another seventy years or so at the 1974 rate of 2.6 million bpd.

A major constraint on Kuwait's limiting production too greatly, even if it does not need the revenues, is that most of the natural gas with which it hopes to develop domestic industry and serve local energy needs is associated with oil production. As a result, the Kuwaitis have had to do some rethinking on priorities for oil and gas production.

An Industrial Development Committee aids in the expansion of local industry. The private sector is chiefly involved in consumer production and construction, which, as elsewhere in the gulf, is booming in Kuwait. The public sector is focusing, not suprisingly, on petrochemicals. As early as 1963, the Petrochemical Industries Company was formed to produce fertilizers. In 1964 it created a subsidiary, the Kuwait Chemical Fertilizer Company. With a new fertilizer plant at Shuaiba, owned by Kuwait National Petroleum Company (KNPC), the national oil company, Kuwait has become the Middle East's largest producer.

More recently, a government holding company, Kuwait Oil, Gas and Energy Company, was created to oversee the development of

Kuwait's petrochemical industry. A huge new liquid propane gas plant is in the planning stage, and there are studies for constructing an aluminum smelting plant using natural gas. In these ventures Kuwait welcomes foreign investment, particularly where contributions in technology are involved. Majority control, however, must remain in Kuwaiti hands.

In addition to diversification in petrochemicals, Kuwait also seeks to increase sales of refined petroleum products relative to crude oil exports. There are currently three refineries on stream, and KNPC, which owns one of then, is considering construction of a fourth.

One other industry, which has drawn Kuwait full circle to its seafaring days, is its modern merchant marine, one of the largest in the Middle East. The privately owned Kuwait Oil Tanker Company has been in operation since 1958 and has orders to expand its fleet. Kuwait is developing a substantial dry cargo fleet as well.

As of old, Kuwait continues to be a commercial center, and many of its imports are reexported. In addition, the Kuwaitis have developed an expertise in banking second to none in the gulf. Kuwait could be a major regional banking center were it not for its prohibition of foreign banking operations located in the country; even with this restriction, it is an important banking and capital center.

The Kuwaitis foresee returns from capital investments, handled through their own banks and investment firms, as a major source of national income when the oil runs out. Already, it is estimated that Kuwait earns over $1 billion a year from its investments and reserve holdings. The desire for a return on investments as a means of preserving the national wealth sometimes cuts across Kuwait's well-organized foreign aid program, since aid programs are not generally very profitable. While sincerely desirous of aiding other countries, questions of equity and profitability can sometimes become factors in its aid policies.

Bahrain

Among the oil-producing countries of the gulf, Bahrain is something of an anomaly. It has a balanced and diversified economy and the most advanced economic and social infrastructure found among the gulf shaykhdoms. Bahrain's educational system, first developed in the 1920s, is today one of the best in the gulf. Bahraini men of letters are known throughout the Arab world. Despite these advantages, Bahrain faces a somewhat uncertain future because of the rapid depletion of its oil reserves.

A thirty-three-island archipelago, Bahrain is small in area—130 square miles (370 square kilometers)—and only 9 percent of the land is arable.[21] Because of relatively plentiful water resources, however, Bahrain has a highly developed agricultural sector. Vegetables, fodder, and dates are grown, and cattle breeding is widely practiced. The government maintains an experimental farm. Bahrain's agricultural sector faces a long-term problem, however, for if industrial water use in Bahrain and adjacent Saudi Arabia continues to expand, the water table may drop too low in the next decade to support agriculture.

Commercial fishing is also a major industry in Bahrain. Operations range from individual fishermen to the Bahrain Fishing Company. The latter, established in 1966 by British and Bahraini interests with a capitalization of $840,000,[22] exports shrimp and prawns to the United States, Europe, and Japan.

Industry naturally centers around oil. Although the wholly owned Awali field is almost exhausted, Bahrain shares ownership with Saudi Arabia of the Abu Safa field, with over 6 billion barrels in reserves. Moreover, Bahrain has a large new field of non-oil-associated natural gas, which can be exploited industrially as well as exported. Thus, while Bahrain will never be a major oil producer, it is relatively assured of a moderate income to sustain its economic development.

The large Bapco oil refinery and the Aluminum Bahrain (Alba) aluminum-smelting plant comprise the two major Bahraini industries other than crude oil production.The Bapco refinery uses Bahraini oil and also Saudi crude which is brought in by pipeline. In addition, a new desulfurization unit with a capacity for 50,000 bpd was inaugurated in 1973. Most of its production is shipped to Japan.

The aluminum plant, which is 27.5 percent owned by the Bahraini government, went into production in 1970. It was the first gas-fired aluminum-smelting plant in the gulf, and now several other countries are considering similar projects.

Another major industrial project is the OAPEC-financed dry dock, now under construction. When completed, the Arabian Gulf Repair Yards will be able to repair tankers up to 375,000 tons.

Bahrain also has some potential as a regional commercial and communications center. It has an earth satellite station. Its new airport, opened in 1971, is capable of handling jumbo jets, and Bahrain has become a major stopover point between Europe and the Orient. Gulf Aviation, now the collective national carrier of the lower gulf shaykhdoms and Oman, was originally established with participation by BOAC, the Bahraini government, and Bahraini private interests; its corporate headquarters in the gulf are still in Bahrain. The Bahraini merchants have long-established connections throughout the region, enabling them to carry on an extensive reexport trade. The principal deterrent to Bahrain's becoming a regional commercial center is its relatively limited financial resources when compared to the major gulf oil producers.

Qatar

Located on a barren peninsula, before the discovery of oil Qatar had little or no agriculture. And unlike the other gulf shaykhdoms, it had never developed an *entrepôt* trade. Pearling, nomadic herding, and subsistence fishing were its principal economic activities.

Oil revenues, which reached $1 billion in 1975, are drastically changing the way of life in Qatar. The government, particularly since Shaykh Khalifa came to the throne in 1972, has endeavored to diversify the economy to the greatest extent possible. From practically no agricultural production in 1960, Qatar now grows enough vegetables to feed its population of 115,000, and actually exports some to neighboring countries.

Industrial development and diversification are also being planned. A number of key expatriates, such as the U.S.-educated Egyptian economist Mustafa Hassan, play key roles in development planning and investment policy formation.

Qatar has a fertilizer plant, in production since 1973, and a shrimping industry, the Qatar National Fishing Company. There is also the Qatar National Cement Manufacturing Company, and the privately owned but government-protected Qatar Flour

Mills Company. In early 1975, plans were announced that a steel mill, to be fired by natural gas, would be constructed by Japanese interests. In addition, Qatar is investing in infrastructure projects such as roads, electric power, desalination, and harbor expansion to enable it to catch up with the rest of the gulf.

The United Arab Emirates (UAE)

The economy of the UAE is the least integrated among all the gulf states. On the one hand, there is the dichotomy between the traditional, largely subsistence economy and the modern, oil-based cash economy. On the other, there is the lack of integration among the economies of the seven federation members.

Abu Dhabi is by far the wealthiest, earning more than $7 billion in 1974. Dubai has a lucrative *entrepôt* trade which had brought prosperity even before oil was discovered. Sharjah, the former commercial center of the lower gulf before it was eclipsed by Dubai, is the third UAE member to find oil, going into production in 1974. The other four shaykhdoms are practically devoid of natural resources and can only break out of their subsistence economies through the generous assistance of their wealthier neighbors, particularly through the efforts of the UAE president, Shaykh Zayd.

Most of the social and economic infrastructure projects in the UAE are carried out by the federation government. Owing to Dubai's lack of financial support for the union budget, these projects are funded almost entirely by Abu Dhabi. Roads and schools in particular are being built at a rapid pace. Dubai and Sharjah, having the resources, are also undertaking extensive development projects within their own borders.

Economic planning is still at a rudimentary stage both at the federal and amirate levels. Abu Dhabi launched a five-year National Plan in 1968 with estimated expenditures of $662 million. But due to a lack of administrative expertise, inflation, and other factors, expenditures were outrunning revenues and the 1969-1970 budget was reduced by 35 percent. More recently, problems in planning and coordination of its generous foreign aid program caused Abu Dhabi to experience a short-run cash liquidity problem in early 1975, despite huge revenues in that period. Presently, with the aid of foreign consultants and advisors, a start is being made to plan and coordinate government expenditures.

The agricultural sector in the UAE can be expanded to some degree, but because of a general lack of water, its potential is limited. Abu Dhabi is attempting to increase productivity in the Buraymi (al-Ayn) Oasis, where an experimental farm was established in 1968, and in the Liwa Oasis. It has also established an Arid Lands Research Center on Sidayat Island, staffed by the University of Arizona. The greatest potential for agricultural development, however, lies in Ras al-Khaymah and along the Batinah Coast on the Gulf of Oman. Ras al-Khaymah has an experimental farm at Diqdaqqa, established by a dedicated Briton, Robin Huntington, in 1955. It is now a federation school offering a three-year course for anyone from the UAE with at least six years education.[23] There is also a more recent experimental farm at Dhayd, in Sharjah. The Batinah Coast, on which are located Fujayrah and enclaves of Sharjah, has a narrow but relatively fertile strip of land which can be exploited to a much greater extent when the new paved road now under construction connects this region with the rest of the country.

Animal husbandry is primarily limited to the nomadic Bedouin. Dairy farming has been introduced in Ras al-Khaymah with a new breed of cattle, but it is only a start. In irrigated farming areas, tick-borne diseases are especially dangerous to livestock.

The fishing industry has somewhat more potential. Natives of the UAE, as of Kuwait and Bahrain, were traditional seafarers, fishermen, and pearlers. Although pearling has all but disappeared, and gulf shrimp and prawns cannot be found as far south as the UAE, fishing is still an important occupation. In Ajman, 27 percent of the working population are fishermen, and in Umm al-Qaywayn, 460 fishermen represent 30 percent of the work force.[24]

However, fishing in the UAE is still relatively primitive. Fishermen use many types of craft, from small *shashar* made of palm trees to diesel-powered fishing dhows holding up to forty men. Traditionally, most of the catch not sold locally was dried and sold in East Africa and South Asia, but these are no longer lucrative markets. Still, the fishing industry could be vastly expanded with the purchase of a modern fleet, and with canning and freezing facilities ashore. A fishmeal industry might also be feasible. A study by the Food and Agriculture Organization (FAO) showed abundant fish resources in the lower gulf and even more so in the Gulf of Oman. The FAO recommended a high priority be placed on developing a commercial fishing industry for export.

The industrial sector dates almost entirely from the discovery of oil in the early 1960s. The rate of development since then has been impressive. Abu Dhabi, which had no paved roads in 1962, is a modern city with dual highways, a waterside drive, and modern sewage, electricity, and other facilities. The modern airport and port facilities are again being expanded.

Abu Dhabi will undoubtedly follow the example of other major oil producers with heavy public sector investment in capital-intensive export industries utilizing its oil and gas. A $3 million liquid natural gas (LNG) plant is being constructed at Das Island, and plans call for a $2 billion LNG processing complex at Riways by 1980. Abu Dhabi is also considering a steel-rolling mill and an aluminum smelting plant.

Attention is also given to consumer and construction industries. Abu Dhabi already has a flour mill and is constructing a cement plant at Abu Dhabi town and at al-Anin. In the private sector, a number of small consumer-oriented industries have grown up in Abu Dhabi. A major factor inhibiting their growth, however, is the small market in the UAE. Abu Dhabi has a population not greater than 100,000, and the UAE as a whole about 350,000.

Dubai, the commercial center of the lower gulf, concentrates its development on expanding its commercial interests and service industries. Several modern luxury hotels have just opened or are planned, and Dubai has an ultramodern airport which is being expanded. Port Rashid, a modern facility with sixteen berths, was completed in 1972 for about $70 million. Shaykh Rashid now wishes to expand the facility into a huge free port. Not satisfied with OAPEC's choice of Bahrain for a dry dock facility, he is building his own, which will be capable of handling a million-ton (deadweight) supertanker and a ship half that size at the same time. Dubai's infrastructure projects include two new bridges over and a tunnel under its "creek" (the estuary which forms the heart of its traditional port), an international communications system including an earth satellite station and an automated telex exchange, and a color television system.

It is difficult to distinguish between the public and private sectors in Dubai, so intertwined are family business interests with local government interests. As a result, Dubai's free market economy is one of the least restricted in the world. "Free trading," including smuggling of gold and luxury items to Iran and South Asia, still remains an important element in the economy. During a recent visit, I was told of private merchants interested in purchasing a launch capable of exceeding sixty knots per hour, presumably for free trading activities.

Neighboring Sharjah, now receiving oil revenues, is also attempting to diversify and expand its industrial sector. One of its first projects is to construct a deep-water port, although Sharjah town is only about ten miles from Dubai. Sharjah has a cement factory, as does Ras al-Khaymah, and is also constructing modern hotels.

Were it not for the UAE's location at the farthest end of the gulf, it could have some potential as a banking center. Its currency was unified in 1973 with the creation of a UAE dinar; a central bank was created; and thirty-nine banks are licensed, including major U.S., British, and Middle Eastern firms. The banks have been authorized to construct 250 branches throughout the country, and had opened about 150 by mid-1975. According to an official of the UAE Currency Board, there is now a moratorium on foreign banks, although it is still possible to establish a joint venture with 80 percent local equity.

Oman

Prior to the discovery of oil, fishing and agriculture were the principal forms of economic activity in Oman, and they still employ over 80 percent of the labor force. Although the first oil shipments were made in 1967, almost no efforts at economic development were undertaken until 1970, when Sultan Qabus replaced his father in a bloodless coup. Since then, development has almost become a matter of trying to do everything at once. By early 1975 government expenditures had so exceeded revenues that Oman experienced a severe short-run cash liquidity problem, which was eased by a timely loan of several million dollars from Saudi Arabia. Since then, the government has had to slow the pace of development expenditures and consolidate the gains already made.

Oman has had a very large defense burden owing to the insurgency in Dhufar. The government, however, seems to have gained the upper hand. Moreover, with the oil price increases of 1973, its economic picture is a bit brighter. Nevertheless, Oman probably never will be a major oil producer.

The agricultural sector still operates largely at a subsistence level. About 36,000 hectares are under cultivation. Since rain is sparse and unpredictable, there is very little dry farming except in Dhufar. In the interior, there are terrace farms on the mountain slopes. In the oases at the foot of the mountains, water is tapped and transported to the fields by means of underground canals known as *aflaj* (singular: *falaj*). On the Batinah Coast the fields are irrigated by deep wells. Most of the crops are planted beneath date palm groves. In Dhufar, on the other hand, there is too much rainfall for dates, and coconut groves are plentiful instead.

The government has concentrated a considerable investment in upgrading the agricultural sector. In November 1970 it created a Department of Agriculture under the Ministry of Development to coordinate its efforts in northern Oman. Two experimental farms established by the British, one at Nizwa in 1959 and one at Sohar on the Batinah Coast in 1962, have been augmented by two more farms. By the end of 1972, sixteen agricultural extension centers were established in the north. Five water resource surveys are also being conducted in northern Oman by international consultants as a basis for future planning.25

In Dhufar, agricultural development is conducted through the Department of Agriculture of the Dhufar Development Department, established in 1971. It maintains an experimental farm at Salalah for growing cattle fodder, and a U.S. firm, Farm Machinery Corporation (FMC), which has a $6 million contract to establish experimental and demonstration farms, has another fodder-growing farm near Salalah.

FMC is also working on animal husbandry projects both in northern Oman and Dhufar. There are an estimated 190,000 head of livestock in northern Oman, but due to diseases and poor blood lines, the quality is poor. At Sohar, a small beef and poultry project is under way. In Dhufar, the government hopes to upgrade the livestock of the cattle herders who live in the insurgency-ridden mountains. Part of the problem is to induce the herders to sell male calves for beef rather than butchering them as is the usual practice.

The fishing industry currently engages about 10 percent of the work force. Omani fishermen traditionally dried and salted the fish they could not sell locally and sold them in East Africa and South Asia. Currency restrictions have cut into those markets; and due to the rise in the standard of living, many Omanis no longer care for dried fish.

The Omani government, therefore, has set about to increase the market potential for small fishermen through creation of refrigeration and processing facilities and also hopes to develop a large-scale modern commercial fishing industry.

In 1972 a Fisheries Department was established under the Directorate-General of Industries of the Ministry of Development. Two firms, Mardela and Del Monte, were granted contracts to develop the fishing industry. Recognizing the need to develop managerial skills, two Omanis were sent to Britain to study fisheries management.[26]

In Dhufar, fisheries are being developed by the Ministry of Development in cooperation with the Dhufar Development Department. Storage and marketing facilities are being built and local fishermen are being provided with small boats and outboard motors. By all reports, both the Batinah Coast and Dhufar have a great potential for a lucrative commercial fishing industry.

Traditional handicrafts comprised the only industries in Oman prior to 1970. In September 1972 a Department of Industries was created under the Ministry of Development. The department has requested technical assistance from the United Nations Industrial Development Organization (UNIDO) in industrial planning, encouragement of small businesses, and preservation of the handicrafts industries.[27]

Oman has centered its efforts for large industry on three areas: cement, oil refining, and petrochemicals. A cement plant with a capacity for 600,000 tons a year is scheduled for completion in 1976. The Department of Petroleum and Minerals is considering the feasibility of a refinery. And a gas pipeline to the capital is being planned as a first step toward the development of a petrochemical industry.

Problems and Prospects

There can be no doubt that oil revenues are rapidly changing the economies of the gulf states. The rate of change will be conditioned by future oil revenues and by the other resources each country can exploit for development. In assessing future economic prospects in the gulf, there are five potential problem areas with which all the states must cope: manpower resources; administrative and physical infrastructure including communications and transportation; market forces as they affect imports and exports other than oil; non-economically productive expenditures such as military purchases and foreign aid; and investment of petrodollar reserves.

The *shortage of manpower* is potentially the most critical bottleneck to development throughout the gulf. The problem has two dimensions. The first relates to a single country's manpower resources as compared to the financial resources it can devote to development. While able to finance large programs, most gulf states except Iran have a very small population base. The problem is doubled since, as a result of Islamic social mores, only about 2 percent of the female population is employed.

Not only is the availability of manpower limited, but educational levels are low and traditional attitudes antithetical to the development of a modern technological society are prevalent. Bedouin, for instance, generally refuse to do menial tasks. Illiterates are unable to perform the highly sophisticated tasks required in many development schemes. Moreover, many of what are considered menial tasks in the West require a degree of literacy difficult if not impossible to obtain among blue-collar workers in the gulf. Even Iran, with a population of 33 million, expects to create several thousand jobs in present development plans for which there will be no qualified Iranian workers. Great emphasis is being placed on education, but raising the general level of education requires decades, and few gulf states are willing to wait that long.

Yet another aspect of the domestic manpower problem is the paucity of qualified leadership. In most gulf countries, major decisions are made by only a handful of persons. Because of the ambitious nature of the development policies, the demands on their time are staggering. Often progress on a project is halted because a key official has not had the time to make the necessary decisions.

The second dimension of the manpower problem is related to foreign labor. Thus far, the gulf states have been able to overcome manpower shortages by hiring expatriates. Kuwait and the UAE both have more resident aliens than natives, and one out of every five inhabitants of Saudi Arabia is a foreigner.

Present figures for foreign labor, however, do not reflect the quantum jump in development goals since 1973. It is estimated that by 1980 there may be over a quarter-million U.S. citizens in the gulf. As the number of foreign laborers grows, many states will have to consider the political and security impact of so many alien residents, many of whom are placed in key jobs.

In addition, many surrounding states with no oil income, which have traditionally exported skilled and semiskilled labor to the gulf, will find shortages themselves. These shortages could be further exacerbated if foreign aid from the oil producers creates jobs at home for the same skilled workers whom the oil producers are trying to hire.

Despite language and cultural problems, the gulf states will have to seek further afield for manpower if they are to maintain projected rates of economic growth. Indians and Pakistanis of all classes are flocking to the lower gulf. Pakistani doctors and veterinarians have been working for a number of years in Saudi Arabia. If economic conditions deteriorate in Europe, it is possible that expatriate European workers might enter the gulf labor market.

Inadequate administrative and physical infrastructure has long been a major bottleneck in the gulf. Port congestion, primitive internal transportation and communications, and time-consuming administrative procedures have plagued nearly every project attempted in the area. Of all the problem areas, however, the most progress has been made in this one. New or expanded ports, airports, and roads are completed or under construction everywhere. Communications systems, including telex and earth satellite stations, are making the gulf accessible from anywhere in the world. There has also been a degree of administrative reform. Clearing customs, obtaining work permits, and other procedures are becoming far more efficient, largely due to the pressure of large-scale business operations involved in development projects.

At the same time, it is doubtful whether the improved administrative procedures and new facilities can cope entirely with the vastly expanded development projects now being planned. One measure of the boom atmosphere is the availability of hotel space. Despite hotel construction throughout the gulf, rooms are fully booked months in advance and many distinguished but shortsighted visitors end the day sleeping on a sofa in a hotel lobby.

Market forces are the great unknown of gulf economic development. World inflation, not unrelated to high energy costs, is driving up the price of goods and services that the gulf states must import in order to implement their development plans. Inflation is also carrying over into the domestic economies, a growing cause for concern among the gulf states. The cost of development must constantly be revised upward.

Another key issue is future world demand for nonoil production. None of the gulf states except Iran has a sufficiently large population base to create a significant domestic market, and even Iran is concentrating on export industries. The problem is that all of the gulf states have roughly the same resources—oil and gas, but few others. Each state plans to develop its own petrochemical industry, and several are planning steel and aluminum plants. There has been little regional economic coordination, and if all these plans are implemented, there could develop a huge glut in supply. Fertilizer demand is notoriously fickle, for example, and as new plants come on stream, the price is almost certain to be undermined. For those states with such industries already in operation, however, it would be very difficult, for political reasons, to halt production and lay off workers. In anticipation of such a possibility, Kuwait has quietly abandoned the idea of a steel industry. Without more regional planning or research into entirely new products for petrochemicals, industrialization in the gulf could turn out to be a burden rather than a boon to the local economies.

Non-economically productive expenditures are hard to assess in an economic context since their justification is based primarily on noneconomic considerations. Moreover, most such expenditures have some economic value. For example, upgrading military capability entails training programs and acquisition of skills, much of which eventually carries over into the private sector.

Military transfers to the gulf have received much attention in the last few years as purchases began to escalate sharply. Although most of the debate over what is a reasonable level of arms purchases has centered on strategic and political considerations, the argument is also made frequently that defense expenditures deny funds for economic development.

With the exception of Oman, which has been fighting a major insurgency, there seems to be little convincing evidence to support this contention, at least since the increase in oil prices in 1973. Most gulf states can buy both guns and butter. Moreover, even if states with large military budgets, such as Iran and Saudi Arabia, were to divert defense funds to economic development projects, the resulting increase in the rate of economic growth would not be greatly accelerated, due to the slow pace at which these funds could be productively absorbed.

Military programs do, however, retard economic growth to the extent that they compete with the civilian sector for trained manpower. And in the case of Iran, should oil revenues begin to decline, some hard decisions would have to be made on priorities. Iran is stretching its resources to the limit in order to maintain its ambitious military and economic development programs at the same time. Since 1972, Iran has ordered over $8 billion in arms from the United States alone.

Another possible non-economically productive expenditure is foreign aid. Abu Dhabi's recent liquidity problem is an example of how insufficiently coordinated aid programs can adversely affect domestic economic development. Other gulf states have generally extended foreign aid in the form of low-interest loans. And some development loans actually involve equity holdings by the lender. At any rate, were oil revenues to contract markedly in the gulf states, foreign aid would undoubtedly be the first to suffer.

There is one other major area of nonproductive expenditure in the gulf, the extra "fees" extracted by agents and even government officials in return for services in obtaining a contract. In the eyes of the West, these practices are considered unethical and a drain on the local economies. From an ethical standpoint, they may indeed be deplorable. However, as with military expenditures, they harm the economy only when the government cannot afford the loss of such resources and still sustain economic growth. In countries with large surpluses, such practices actually aid in distributing the national income by means of a "trickle down" system. Tolerance of graft in high places is easier when it can be accomplished in low places as well.

The *accumulation of petrodollar reserves* also has two dimensions. First is the impact of large reserve holdings in the gulf on the world economy. Early in the energy crisis, fears were raised that by the 1980s the OPEC producers would hold hundreds of billions of dollars of reserves, creating a world capital shortage and forcing the industrialized countries to go hopelessly in debt. Thus, the concept of "recycling" these reserves back into the world economy was born.

The initial fears have proved to be greatly exaggerated. Reserve holdings have not increased as fast as earlier projections, and some gulf producers actually expect to be net borrowers by 1980. Also, the international banking system has been able to manage the huge transfers of capital resulting from the oil price rises.

Investment of petrodollars is still a problem area, however. Economic dislocations resulting from the 1973 oil price rises have had a deleterious effect. For example, many countries have run up large balance of payments deficits as a result of higher oil bills. As a rule, the gulf producers have avoided becoming directly involved in these kinds of problems. Proposals for lower oil prices for net debtor countries, or for low-interest, long-term loans to ease payments problems, have not met with enthusiasm from the producers. Instead, they have let the international banking system and world market mechanisms make the adjustments. Several have made loans to the International Monetary Fund as an indirect means of easing payments problems.

In terms of their own investment policies, the producers, particularly the Arabs, have been very loath to make long-term investments and in some cases have actually paid negative rates of interest on short-term deposits. The banking system is not able to absorb such large amounts on a sixty- or ninety-day basis. In addition, since large-scale movements of short-term monetary assets could be very disruptive both politically and economically, there has been a general suspicion in the West of gulf investment intentions. This suspicion in itself has had a negative economic impact.

The other dimension is the impact of capital investment on the states themselves. To a great degree, the monetary assets now being accumulated will have to substitute for oil resources as the latter become depleted. Iran and Iraq hope to utilize most of their oil incomes in developing their domestic economies. Others, while also stressing economic development, have less domestic economic potential and will be required to make more foreign investments. The best investment opportunities are in the industrial world. Kuwait and Saudi Arabia have also explored a triangular arrangement that would utilize their money and Western technology for development projects in the nonoil Arab states such as Egypt, Sudan, and Yemen. Here again, trade-offs must be made in the returns on investment, since development projects do not generally bring a high return.

Each gulf state will approach these problem areas in different ways. The political and economic variables affecting their success are so numerous that it is essentially impossible to predict the outcome. To a great extent, however, their futures depend on investment choices made today.

NOTES

[1]American University, *Area Handbook for Iran* (Washington, D.C.: U.S. Government Printing Office, 1971), p. 372.

[2]*The Middle East and North Africa 1974-1975: A Survey and Reference,* 21st ed. (London: Europa Publications, 1975), p. 333.

[3]See Pahlevi, H.I.M. Mohammad Reza Shah, *Mission for My Country* (New York: McGraw-Hill, 1961), and Pahlevi, *The White Revolution* (Tehran, 1967).

[4]Charles Issawi, in Ehsan Yar-Shater, ed., *Iran Faces the Seventies,* Praeger Special Studies In International Economics and Development (New York: Praeger, 1971), p. 55.

[5]*Middle East and North Africa,* p. 334.

[6]*Ibid.,* p. 327.

[7]*Ibid.,* p. 328.

[8]*Ibid.,* p. 329.

[9]*Ibid.*

[10]*New York Times,* July 18, 1974, p. 1.

[11]*Middle East and North Africa,* p. 332.

[12]Albert Y. Badre, "Economic Development in Iraq," in Charles A. Cooper and Sydney S. Alexander, eds., *Economic Development and Population Growth in the Middle East* (New York: American Elsevier Publishing Company, 1972), p. 288.

[13]See Rasool M.H. Hashimi and Alfred L. Edwards, "Land Reform in Iraq: Economic and Social Implications," *Land Economics* 37 (Feb. 1961): 75, quoted in Badre, "Economic Development in Iraq," p. 296.

[14]*Washington Star,* May 22, 1975, p. A-20.

15 Badre, "Economic Development in Iraq," p. 223.

16 Since not all the borders are delimited, an exact figure for land area cannot be given. For figures on arable land, see *Middle East and North Africa*, p. 593.

17 Edmund Y. Asfour, "Saudi Arabia, Kuwait and the Gulf Principalities," in Cooper and Alexander, *Economic Development and Population Growth*, p. 381.

18 For a discussion of the administrative and economic aspects of the *hajj*, see David E. Long, *The Hajj Today: A Survey of the Contemporary Pilgrimage to Makkah* (doctoral dissertation, George Washington University, Washington, D.C., Feb. 1973).

19 The Saudi Budget figure for *hajj* expenditures in 1974-1975 was only SR243.8 million ($70 million); but this does not include *hajj*-related expenses accruing to nearly every other ministry. For example, the Foreign Ministry must handle a huge volume of visas and also care for VIP pilgrims; the police must provide security and traffic control; the Health Ministry must provide sanitary measures; and so on.

20 American University, *Area Handbook for the Peripheral States of the Arabian Peninsula* (Washington, D.C.: U.S. Government Printing Office, 1971), p. 116.

21 Muhammad T. Sadiq and William P. Snavely, *Bahrain, Qatar, and the United Arab Emirates: Colonial Past, Present Problems and Future Prospects. Studies in International Development and Economics* (Lexington, Mass., Toronto, and London: Lexington Books, D.C. Heath Company, 1972), p. 46.

22 *Ibid.,* p. 58.

23 K.G. Fenelon, *The United Arab Emirates: An Economic and Social Survey* (London: Longman, 1973), pp. 49-50.

24 *Ibid.,* p. 58.

25 Sultanate of Oman, Ministry of Development, National Statistical Department, *Development in Oman, 1970-1974* (Muscat, Oman, 1975) p. 17.

26 *Ibid.,* p. 29.

27 *Ibid.,* p. 35.

7 The U.S. and the Gulf

Direct U.S. interests in the gulf originated in Oman in the 1820s. At that time, the sultanate was a leading maritime power in the Indian Ocean. Muscat, the capital, was one of the great ports of the Indian Ocean; and Zanzibar, a dependency of the sultan, was the center of the slave trade, both East and West.

In the winter of 1827-1828, a New Hampshire merchant, Edmund Roberts, seeking to recoup losses in South America, arrived at Zanzibar. Incensed at discriminatory import and export taxes levied on U.S. vessels, he sought an audience with the sultan. The latter asked him why the United States did not conclude a commercial treaty with him, a suggestion Roberts took back to the United States.

In 1832 Roberts was empowered by the State Department to negotiate commercial treaties with Cochin China, Siam, and Muscat. In order not to arouse the suspicions of the British over the nature of his mission, he sailed on the U.S.S. *Peacock* as the captain's clerk.[1]

Roberts was an able negotiator. On one occasion, when he discovered the esteem in which titles were held, he reeled off after his own name the names of the counties of New Hampshire.[2] Arriving in Muscat in 1833, he negotiated a Treaty of Amity and

Friendship that remained in force until it was replaced in 1958 by a new Treaty of Amity, Economic Relations and Consular Rights. The treaty was ratified by the U.S. Senate on June 30, 1834, and Roberts returned to Muscat the following year to exchange ratifications. As it turned out, Roberts the merchant was never to reap the benefits of Roberts the negotiator. Contracting dysentery in Siam, where he had also exchanged ratifications, he died in Macao in 1836 en route to Japan.

The treaty with Muscat provided for the appointment of a U. S. consul. Richard Waters, a Salem merchant, became consul in Zanzibar in 1837. The following year a New York merchant arrived at Muscat, but left soon after, and a British subject was appointed consul. In 1843 the position went to Said bin Khalfan, the translator of the 1833 treaty.

By the mid-nineteenth century, Oman's commercial importance had waned drastically. Slavery had been a major economic activity, but in 1822 the sultan concluded with Britain the Moresby Treaty enjoining him from further trade. In 1861, Zanzibar, the major slaving port of East Africa, was lost altogether.

In 1909 the United States decided to assign a full-time consul to Muscat. Two events had intervened. First, trade had increased measurably between Muscat and the United States as the latter became one of the chief importers of Omani dates. By 1907-1908, the value of U.S. imports from Muscat, £43,000, was second only to that of India.[3] Within a few years, however, the date trade began to decline considerably due to competition from California dates and to changing American tastes. And after 1914, World War I generally disrupted communications and trade in the area. With the death of the consul in 1915, the consulate at Muscat was closed. Not until World War II would there be a full-time official U.S. representative in the gulf.

The second event that encouraged the appointment of a full-time consul was the establishment some years before of an American Protestant Mission in Muscat. The missionaries had appealed to the U.S. government to intercede with Muscat over impediments being placed in their way by the local authorities.[4]

Though small in number and outside the mainstream of politics and commerce, the American missionaries in the gulf have contributed as much as any other group to the creation of cordial relations with the United States. To many residents of the gulf, the missionaries were the first and in some cases the only regular contact with Americans. Unlike traders and the imperial representatives of the European powers, the missionaries came to give, not to take from the gulf. Their generosity and love have created an image of Americans in the gulf that even the vicissitudes of politics and the Arab-Israeli conflict have not destroyed. Their sons, as those of other missionaries in the Middle East, became the first generation of post-World War II American "Arabists," in government, business, and academia.

The Arabian Mission of the Reformed Church in America was founded in 1889 by the Reverend Samuel M. Zwemer and the Reverend James Cantine. Zwemer, who was later known as the "Apostle to Islam," became a noted scholar of Islam and Arabic. A small mission station was established in Basrah in 1892 and another in Bahrain in 1895. The mission in Muscat was opened in 1893, and in 1910, arrangements were made to open a mission in Kuwait. A mission station was also opened at Amarah, Iraq.[5]

Within a short time, the missionaries realized the great need for medical services and incorporated medical work as one of three focuses: medicine, education, and evangelism. The modern schools and hospitals established by the missionaries were the first such facilities in the gulf.

The early years of the Arabian Mission were a less sensitive age than the present. The missionaries established close relationships with the gulf leaders of the time and often performed services far beyond their normal responsibilities. The Reverend Dr. John Van Ess, for example, contributed to the World War I effort by producing the first modern text of Iraqi colloquial Arabic at the request of the British Military Government in Basrah. The book subsequently became a classic of its kind.

Dr. Van Ess was also named acting U.S. consular agent in Basrah in 1914 when the war created a need for an official U.S. representative there. Both during and after the war, his efforts and informal advice were invaluable and helped pave the way for U.S. recognition of Iraq in 1931.

During his tenure as consular agent, Dr. Van Ess even got involved in a "spy incident," which his wife relates in an amusing reminiscence.[6] When the consulate at Muscat was closed in 1915, its effects, including a small box labeled "Consular Jewels," were shipped to Basrah. Subsequently, a lady traveler bound for

Baghdad stopped at Basrah, being unable to continue due to the fighting. "Mrs. Johnson," as she called herself, was taken in by a missionary family, but soon the British became suspicious of her. A Major Gregson had her searched and questioned, but, other than secret pockets in her corsets and sun helmet and a hollow heel in a shoe, could find nothing incriminating. She was a thoroughly hardened individual of indeterminate age and origin who teased him for not himself searching her person. "I wouldn't have minded, I am not deformed!" she said, much to the Victorian gentleman's embarrassment.

It was later deduced that she was a German spy sent to obtain the Muscat "Consular Jewels," for they had turned out to be the State Department code book. Not only had Van Ess already burned the book by then, but "Mrs. Johnson" further made the mistake of staying with the wrong missionary family. For her efforts, she spent the rest of the war as an internee in India.

Through the years, the educational and medical needs of the gulf states changed. State educational and medical facilities obviated the need for the missionary facilities. In some cases, the missionaries decided to close hospitals and schools. In others, they were asked to do so by the host governments. The hospital at Amarah, Iraq, was forced to close by the government after the 1958 revolution. On the other hand, the Shaykh of Bahrain has expressed his desire for the missionary presence to stay on.

The palace coup which brought Sultan Qabus to the throne in Oman in 1970 presented a new challenge to the American missionaries. Previously, theirs were the only hospitals available to Omanis in the country. (The oil company and British Consulate had private medical facilities.) Shortly after coming to power, Qabus wrote to the American mission:

> In recognition of the humane and invaluable assistance, which by the selfless endeavor of your Mission has been available to our people in such generous measure over the years, we wish to inform you of our gratitude in the past, and open support in the future.[7]

Despite such warm support, however, the missionaries had to decide whether to continue until the newly organized Health Ministry could supply adequate medical services, at which time the mission hospitals no longer would be needed. This had been the pattern elsewhere in the gulf. The other alternative was to offer the mission hospitals to the Health Ministry as a base on which to develop, for in fact the ministry had no existing facilities at all.

There was a division of opinion among the missionaries about whether working for the government would help or hinder their primary mission of Christian evangelism. In the opinion of the writer, it is a mark of farsightedness on the part of the Reformed Church that they elected to donate their facilities and services to the government. In that way, the government obtained an instant program and utilized the missionaries' long experience, and the missionaries participated in the ground-floor discussions and planning in the Ministry of Health.[8]

Beginning on January 1, 1971, the property of the Arabian Mission hospitals was leased to the Ministry of Health for one Omani riyal a year (then about $2.50). The missionary staff of the hospitals donated their services to the ministry and remained in charge of the administration of the hospitals. The ministry, for its part, financed all medical services provided at the hospitals.[9] Three years later, the properties were donated outright to the ministry, excepting a house and a small chapel. Members of the mission's medical staff, including members of the Danish Missionary Society who had joined in the medical work in 1965, were all seconded to the Ministry of Health without pay. They are still there serving their God and the people of Oman. In recognition of their labors, Dr. Donald Bosch, who became the administrator of the new government hospital at al-Khuli, was awarded the "Order of Oman" in 1972.

The other long-term influential American presence in the gulf has been the oil companies. Chapter 5 has outlined briefly how and when they came. The economic and technological impact of the oil companies should be obvious. Until local government services were developed, the oil companies, like the missionaries, had to create their own. Aramco, for example, built its own schools, hospitals, roads, and other facilities. Creation of these facilities in many cases laid the original groundwork for services which the government has since been able to provide its people.

There is also a human dimension. Oil company personnel provided the first, daily contact of many gulf citizens with products of a Western, secular society. Many deep and lasting personal relationships were developed which transcended oil company business. It was common, for example, for gulf leaders to seek the advice of oil company officials on a wide range of issues, on a purely personal basis. Perhaps the conviction of many in the gulf that U.S. technology and methods are the best in the world stems from long experience with U.S. oil companies and their American personnel.

The Evolution of U.S. Policy in the Gulf

In the present day, the paramount U.S. interest in the gulf is oil. Interest in oil entails concern for its price and availability. It also entails concern for regional political stability and security in order that oil price and availability not be changed precipitously for political or military reasons. A derivative economic interest is in the investment policies of gulf states with large petrodollar reserve holdings. The accumulation of large reserves constitutes a major redistribution of world economic wealth; and without careful thought to investment policies, severe economic dislocations in the world economy could result. Commercial interests in the gulf, therefore, can be seen not only as opportunities to increase sales, but also in terms of the beneficial effect that the sale of U.S. goods and services to the gulf states has on the U.S. balance of payments.

Despite these obvious economic, political, and strategic concerns, the gulf did not become a specific area of policy interest until 1968, when the British announced their intentions to disengage. Prior to that time, the United States had developed close bilateral relations with a number of gulf states, notably Iran and Saudi Arabia. Sizable arms sales and military training programs had been developed with both countries. The United States has also maintained a small naval facility on Bahrain since 1949, the Middle East Force (MIDEASTFOR), which consists of a flagship and two destroyers assigned on a rotational basis. Nevertheless, oil policy was left largely to the British, who maintained an army base at Sharjah and a navy base at Bahrain.

The initial U.S. reaction to the British decision to disengage was one of dismay. It was perceived by many that the British withdrawal would threaten the security and stability of the region by creating a "power vacuum." Unless this so-called vacuum were filled by the West, there was considerable concern that the Soviet Union would attempt to fill it, either directly or through support of Iraq, seen as a Soviet client state. The dilemma, as it was perceived, was that the U.S. public, sharply divided over U.S.

involvement in Vietnam, would not support any U.S. efforts to undertake the British security role in the gulf. This sentiment was reflected in a statement by Senate Majority Leader Mike Mansfield the day after the British announcement:

> I am sorry the British felt they were forced to take this step because I am certain we will be asked to fill the vacuum east of Suez. I don't know how we are going to do it because I don't think we have the men or resources for it.[10]

U.S. policy in the gulf as it developed after 1968 attempted to reconcile U.S. concern for the security of the area with the judgment that the U.S. public would not support a direct security role there. The emphasis on security in overall U.S. gulf policy was reflected in a statement of "five principles" by the then assistant secretary of state for Near Eastern and South Asian affairs, Joseph Sisco, in September 1972:

1. Non-interference in the internal affairs of other nations.
2. Encouragement of regional cooperation for peace and progress.
3. Support for friendly countries in their efforts to provide for their own security and development.
4. Encouragement for the principles enunciated in the Moscow Summit of avoiding confrontations.
5. Encouragement for international exchange of goods, services and technology.[11]

The first three principles provided the conceptual framework for a policy of political support and indirect security assistance with a minimum U.S. presence beyond the military training missions already in place in Iran and Saudi Arabia. The policy relied heavily on cooperation between Iran and Saudi Arabia and became known informally as the "two pillar policy," or in a broader context, "regional cooperation." It also relied on close cooperation with the British, who were expected to continue to play a major, though in time diminishing, internal security role in Oman and the gulf shaykhdoms.

The October 1973 Arab-Israeli war had a profound effect on the gulf. The shaykhdoms, long isolated from the rest of the Arab world during the years of British protection, found themselves drawn inescapably into Arab world politics and the Arab-Israeli conflict. When King Faysal announced the Arab oil embargo in reaction to the $2.2 billion U.S. military resupply to Israel, all the gulf producers except Iraq supported it.

Bahrain, moreover, terminated MIDEASTFOR's lease, to be effective in one year. This decision was reversed in the summer of 1974, but Bahrain is still ambivalent in its attitude toward MIDEASTFOR. On the one hand, it welcomes the U.S. military presence as a form of visible U.S. support for the regime. On the other, the installation, though not strictly a "base," makes Bahrain vulnerable to political attack for allowing a foreign military presence on its soil.

Despite the political changes in the gulf since 1973, U.S. political and strategic policies have remained basically the same: dependence on regional cooperation and a limited U.S. military presence.[12] Ironically, by 1975, considerable congressional opposition had developed to the "two pillar" policy on the grounds that it was creating an arms race in the gulf, particularly between Iran and Saudi Arabia. These two countries had indeed greatly accelerated arms purchases since 1973, but this was in large measure attributable to increased oil revenues rather than U.S. policy. The real question was what, if anything, should U.S. policy makers do about the situation.

The fourth principle of U.S. policy in the gulf addressed the Soviet threat and appeared to be more of an expression of hope than a principle of policy. The growing superpower detente implicit in the principle was based on mutual U.S.-Soviet interests in a global context that did not necessarily include the gulf.

Only the last principle addressed oil and economic interests, reflecting U.S. preoccupation with gulf security and relative complacency with the gulf oil situation on the very eve of the energy crisis. Mr. Sisco conceded that "we are witnessing rather dramatic changes in the terms of financial and concession arrangements between international oil companies and the producer states." But he went on to assert: "States such as Iran, Saudi Arabia and Kuwait, however, have consistently indicated by their approach to petroleum questions, their recognition of a strong mutual economic interest with the major industrial nations . . . [and] the useful role which the international companies play."[13]

Mr. Sisco was not the only one who failed to distinguish between strong political interests among these three countries in maintaining close ties with the United States and equally strong economic interests dictating oil policies not to the liking of either the United States or the oil companies. Despite the warnings of experts such as Ambassador James Akins,[14] few Americans were prepared for what was to come. The following year, the United States and the industrialized world witnessed an energy crisis from which the oil producers emerged in uncontested control of pricing and production of oil. The 1973 price rises and Arab oil embargo underscored the strategic importance of Persian Gulf oil. Since then, much of the attention of U.S. policy toward the gulf has been focused on the price and availability of oil and related economic matters.

In pursuit of overall economic goals, the United States sought to strengthen bilateral ties as well. On June 8, 1974, the United States and Saudi Arabia signed an agreement to expand cooperation in the fields of economics, technology, industry, and defense.[15] Joint commissions were subsequently established in each of the four fields. It was not intended to be a bilateral oil agreement, which would have been incompatible with the U.S. policy of seeking international cooperation both among the consumers and between them and the producers. But it was motivated by the recognition in the United States of the need for more bilateral cooperation.

The United States also signed an agreement with Iran in March 1975 to increase cooperation in various fields of economic development in Iran, including nuclear energy.[16]

A Look into the Future

Political and Strategic Interests

Given the political and strategic goals of U.S. Persian Gulf policy— to foster political and internal stability so that the price and availability of oil will not be precipitously altered for political or military reasons—the policy was well conceived and implemented.[17] None of the gulf littoral states has succumbed to radicalism. The long-dreaded but unexpected removal of King Faysal from the throne of Saudi Arabia was followed by a smooth transition in the succession of his half-brother, King Khalid. Many of the destabilizing territorial disputes have been settled or at least allowed to remain dormant. Iraq and Iran have achieved a measure of rapprochement, ending the Kurdish insurgency; and in Oman, the government seems to have the upper hand in the Dhufar insurgency. Soviet influence is no greater in the gulf than it was before the British departed. And the Chinese presence is somewhat smaller since their departure from Dhufar.

This rather rosy picture, however, fails to take into account that U.S. Persian Gulf policy was designed to maintain a "low profile," and therefore its influence on regional stability has been at best passive. One could argue that the security situation would have turned out much the same no matter what the United States did, but this is not precisely true. The fact that the United States did not become directly involved in gulf security is probably one of the most stabilizing courses it could have taken. Left to themselves, the gulf states have fared rather well, and there seems no reason why the basic approach of moderate political support and indirect security assistance should be changed.

It will be no longer possible, however, to maintain a low-profile policy in the gulf. Many fears have been raised in the Congress and elsewhere that military arms sales to the gulf will involve the United States in gulf politics in a manner that could lead to another Vietnam type of situation. Even if there were no arms sales to the gulf, perhaps a quarter-million Americans are expected to be residing in the gulf in the next decade, participating in the development projects that are or will be launched there. The human, political and economic implications of this fact alone are enough to involve the United States deeply in gulf affairs. There is a pressing need, therefore, to study the impact that a large, private American community in the gulf could have on policy options. To date, I know of no such studies being made.

In reviewing the "two pillar" policy, great as the inherent problems for Iranian-Arab, and particularly Iranian-Saudi, cooperation are, U.S. encouragement of such cooperation still provides the best security for U.S. interests, provided expectations are reasonably modest. Iran and Saudi Arabia are the two most important conservative states in the area, and by working together, they could go far to maintaining regional stability.

Evaluating the U.S. arms sales policy to the gulf is a bit more complicated. The implication of the critics is that the massive expansion of arms transfers to the area is highly destabilizing.

This is diametrically counter to the rationale of the proponents, who say that arms sales to the gulf are intended to enhance regional security and stability by giving U.S. friends the means to defend themselves. In the opinion of this writer, there has never been any convincing empirical evidence to indicate that military inventories in and of themselves are either stabilizing or destabilizing. To measure stability, one must gauge the political climate as well as the intentions of the various leaders involved. If under certain circumstances a leader might harbor hostile intentions, then and only then does one look at his military capabilities and evaluate his military options, the constraints on these options, and the possible military repercussions of hostile acts he may initiate.

In the gulf area, the most likely antagonists in a conventional war are still Iraq and Iran, despite their current rapprochement. Both sides have concluded arms agreements greatly upgrading their inventories. The problem with evaluating arms sales agreements, however, is that they represent only a commitment. The actual deliveries are generally spaced out over a considerable period of time. Even accounting for this, it is hard to estimate the capacity of the purchasers to effectively absorb the equipment. Any attempt at an estimate must take into account such factors as training, manpower resources, and experience.

In the case of Iraq and Iran, while Iran may have the edge in the quality and quantity of equipment and in training programs for many weapons system categories, no Iranians except the two battalions that have seen duty in Oman have ever had any combat experience. The Iraqi armed forces, on the other hand, despite the political and other inherent weaknesses in their armed forces (e.g., good professional officers are distrusted and retired early in many cases as threats to the regime), have had combat and strategic logistical experience, most recently in the October 1973 war. In sum, despite new military acquisitions on both sides, it would be very difficult to assess the capabilities of Iraq and Iran in a war. Most observers go only so far as to say that both could probably defend their own territory but neither could probably mount a successful offensive against the other. Thus, it is not likely that the quantum increase in U.S. arms sales to Iran has had a major stabilizing or destabilizing effect in the context of a possible Iraqi-Iranian war.

Curiously enough, it is not a war between Iraq and Iran on which so much public attention has been focused in the context of U.S. arms transfers to the gulf, but a so-called arms race between Iran and Saudi Arabia, both recipients of U.S. arms. The most commonly imagined scenario of a confrontation between the two has Iran, arrogant and jingoistic with its huge armed forces, acting unilaterally on the Arab side of the gulf, perhaps to quell a radical uprising, but in a manner forcing Saudi Arabia to react with force. The danger of Iran miscalculating the Arab reaction to a unilateral Iranian military operation in the gulf is certainly serious—hence the U.S. policy to foster cooperation. But the shah sees the need to cooperate as well as anyone in the area. More importantly, in the context of arms sales, Iran had an overwhelming military superiority over all the conservative Arab states of the gulf, including Saudi Arabia, long before the current arms buildup and will continue to have one in the future. The present arms sales will do nothing materially to change that balance, even with a greater Saudi military capability. As to a possible Saudi-Iranian confrontation, both countries, despite their differences, see themselves as allies, not enemies. As mentioned above, the Saudis want a credible force in the gulf, not to fight Iran, but to have an independent voice in gulf security. In sum, the propensity of the Saudis and Iranians to cooperate is less in-fluenced by U. S. arms sales than by a host of other factors.

The main threat to the security of the smaller gulf states is from internal subversion, not conventional military attack. Supersonic aircraft are scarcely appropriate to counter the threat of covert subversive activities; and in countering a coup attempt, a P-51 would probably be as effective as an F-14. Some of the smaller UAE shaykhdoms are so small that an F-14 would have trouble just staying within their borders at cruising speeds.

There are a number of U.S. domestic considerations relating to U.S. arms sales to the gulf which are as important as the effect of the sales on the area. One is the public image of the recipients. The shah has recently lost much of the popularity he once enjoyed in the U.S. Congress and among the general public. Long regarded as a key anticommunist ally and long-time friend, his popularity was strengthened by his cordial relations with Israel. Iran's lead in raising oil prices, however, cut into this popularity, and its more recent rapprochement with the Arab world including radical Iraq also has caused the shah's image in the United States to suffer. This loss of popularity, coming as it does in a period of general frustration over the Vietnam defeat and of determination by the U.S. Congress to play a more active role in foreign policy, even at the cost of reducing the flexibility crucial to diplomacy, has caused arms sales to Iran to be scrutinized more critically than ever before in the United States.

U.S. domestic reactions to arms sales to Saudi Arabia have always been ambivalent: positive because of Saudi Arabia's strident anti-communism, and negative because of its enmity to Israel and more recently its leadership in the Arab oil embargo. Despite the ambivalence, Saudi Arabia is undoubtedly viewed, because of its commanding oil reserves, as much more important to U.S. interests than it was just a few years ago. The domestic political shift can be seen in the irony of Vice-President Rockefeller, who boycotted King Faysal's visit to New York in 1965, representing the United States in Riyadh to extend condolences over the King's death ten years later.

U.S. domestic attitudes toward sales to Kuwait are also ambivalent, but probably less negative. This is because the principal threat to Kuwait's security comes from radical Iraq, and because its military role in any Arab-Israeli conflict would be symbolic at most. Also, the magnitude of U.S. arms sales to Kuwait is very small compared to sales to Iran and Saudi Arabia. Sales to other gulf states are even smaller.

U.S. domestic economic factors also play a role in attitudes toward arms sales to the gulf. The oil price rise was felt personally by all Americans, and further association of the price rise with the Arab embargo has produced a very negative reaction among many segments of the Congress and the public. This negative feeling was reinforced by the 1974-1975 recession, which many also blame on high oil prices. At the same time, the recession could be a powerful inducement to encourage arms sales. It may be difficult for the general public to see expanded arms sales in terms of advantages to the balance of payments, but in congressional districts with large defense industries and rising unemployment, the additional jobs created by export arms production became very convincing arguments for more sales.

In the face of all of these conflicting domestic and foreign factors, it is difficult to make specific recommendations for future arms sales policy in the gulf. Except for new sales agreements with the lower gulf states now qualifying for the first time as purchasers of arms, that policy has remained virtually unchanged for years. The principal restraint on the magnitude of the arms transfers was the ability of the gulf states to pay. Since 1973 that restraint has been removed. Should the United States react by imposing a political restraint to compensate for the removal of the economic restraint? (For example, an arms request could be refused on the grounds that more arms would be destabilizing.) This idea has a degree of support in the Congress, where there has been talk of legislation to further limit the size of arms sales transactions not requiring congressional approval (the current maximum is $25 million). Such a limitation could possibly reduce arms sales, but there is no guarantee that the gulf states would not go to Western Europe, or even the Soviet Union, if turned down by the United States. Moreover, it is not unlikely that any refusal based on political reasons, either by legislation or executive policy, would have an adverse effect on general U.S. relations with the requesting state.

It would seem to this writer that such an approach is far too simplistic. For one thing, there are already signs that some of the gulf states, despite increased oil revenues, are developing liquidity problems which will reimpose economic constraints on their ability to purchase arms. Moreover, arms requests from the others, chiefly Iran and Saudi Arabia, are too varied and complex to be treated in the aggregate.

It is quite likely, for example, that requests for more conventional types of weapons will taper off, at least for the next several years, as the gulf states' armed forces take delivery and attempt to absorb what is already on order. The integration of these new weapons systems will probably be impeded by the severe skilled-manpower shortages which have caused the public and private sectors of these countries to compete for good people.

On the other hand, Iran is already seeking to purchase F-14s to upgrade its airforce, and Saudi Arabia is looking for a follow-on aircraft for its aging Lightnings, which will become obsolescent by about 1978. The juxtaposition of aircraft purchases by these two countries will almost certainly renew public debate about a gulf arms race, although no deliveries would be made for several years, even assuming letters of offer were imminent.

In addition to aircraft, there will probably be a continuing interest, particularly by Iran, in purchasing the latest sophisticated weapons systems. The psychological appeal of such weapons is probably the greatest factor in such interest. In many cases, the United States is the only supplier, and much pressure can be applied by the prospective purchaser. Such pressure presents problems for the United States, not only politically, but also in terms of its own security requirements. One way of reacting to such requests, however, rather than refusing them out of hand, is to agree to consider sales, but only after U.S. needs and those of other allies already possessing signed letters of offers are met. In many cases, this would delay sales for a number of years, thus greatly retarding the buildup of such weapons systems in the area, without incurring unfavorable political reactions. Just meeting U.S. needs has already become a major problem in the post-Vietnam period.

In sum, each request and category of requests should be viewed on its own merits, taking into consideration the political, strategic, and economic impact of the arms transfer not only on the gulf region, but on the United States as well.

Finally, there is the question of the future of MIDEASTFOR in Bahrain. Strictly considering U.S. interests in the gulf, the question is whether the political costs of staying in Bahrain outweigh the benefits. In light of Bahrain's reversal of its request to have MIDEASTFOR leave, it would seem advantageous for the United States to stay on in Bahrain as long as the terms of the arrangement are agreeable to both sides.

In broader perspective, MIDEASTFOR is not primarily for a gulf interest but for a broader Indian Ocean interest, and as such is beyond the scope of this book. Its future basically centers around three questions: 1) Does the United States in fact need a permanently stationed naval force in the Indian Ocean, or can naval ships be rotated there on a regular basis? The latter option might become more attractive with the Suez Canal reopened, but would still necessitate a judgment of the overall benefit to the United States of greater economic costs and lesser political costs in the region. 2) If a permanent Indian Ocean force is needed, does there also need to be a permanent shore installation? And 3) if the answer to the second question is yes, where is the best location for the installation? Bahrain has been optimal to date because a) MIDEASTFOR has been there since 1949 and everyone in the area is used to having it there; and b) because the only other politically practicable alternative site in the whole Indian Ocean at the moment is Diego Garcia, which is so far to the south that its economic and strategic suitability are somewhat questionable. Whatever the determination of U.S. strategic needs in the Indian Ocean, trying to maintain an installation on Bahrain without adequate regard for the political costs would clearly be a dubious undertaking.

Economic Interests

U.S. economic interests in the gulf fall into three broad categories: oil, monetary concerns, and commerce. In each case, the policies dealing with these interests far transcend the gulf.

Energy policy. There is a strong domestic concensus that the United States should be as independent from foreign sources of energy as possible. Project Independence, inaugurated in the aftermath of the 1973-1974 energy crisis and purported to be a "framework for developing a national energy policy,"[18] concentrated on how to accomplish less dependence on foreign supplies of oil. Nevertheless, at least through the medium term, the United States will be increasingly dependent on foreign, particularly Persian Gulf, oil. The reason is simple. U.S. supplies are being depleted, and the gulf has two-thirds of the free world's proved reserves. Thus, whatever energy goals the United States ultimately chooses, this fact must be accepted.

U.S. energy policy options toward the gulf producers must be analyzed in the context of OPEC so long as the OPEC members remain determined to act in concert on setting prices and production rates. As discussed in chapter 5, uncertainty about future supply-demand relationships makes the projection of the future state of energy-related matters extremely difficult. Identification of a few operating assumptions, however, might give some indication of the policy options available to deal with the foreign-supply side of the energy problem.

The first assumption is that OPEC is a rather narrowly conceived oil cartel, not a monolithic economic or political bloc. This assumption would argue for not treating OPEC as a political alliance, lest out of self-defense it begin to act like one. Algeria's President Boumedienne, who has long wished to politicize OPEC, scored a diplomatic coup when he announced at the March 1975 OPEC meeting that Iraq and Iran would agree to a rapprochement. This "political solidarity" was repeated at the April 7, 1975, preliminary OPEC conference, when the OPEC producers refused to back down from the Algerian position that a consumer-producer conference should include more on its agenda than oil prices. These developments have led some to conclude that OPEC is developing a new political dimension. But this type of solidarity costs the OPEC members nothing economically and enables them to gain politically in support from the third world. The real measure of political solidarity comes in collective measures where both political and economic costs are involved. Except on the subject of OPEC solidarity over oil prices, there are simply insufficient mutual political interests among the members to support broader political action beyond vocal support. Thus, despite the rhetoric, Algeria was not able to expand OPEC's scope to include a broader political dimension. On the other hand, U.S. and other policies could succeed where Boumedienne could not. Consumer countries that polarize all relations with the producers into a consumer-producer confrontation, and that state publicly that their aim is to crush OPEC, are merely inviting OPEC members to unite politically to withstand the consumer threat. It makes much more sense to develop a policy aimed at increasing mutual trust among the consumers and producers so that mutual recriminations do not poison the atmosphere surrounding negotiations on the real issues with which OPEC members and the consumers must deal: the future price of oil, and coping with the political, economic, and monetary problems arising out of the present price of oil. Thus, if OPEC members wish to have a broader dialogue on issues of world economy, third world development, and the like, why not? The producers know as well as the consumers that such talks will not change the price of oil, but they could certainly improve the atmosphere within which oil price negotiations will take place.

The second assumption is that OPEC members are determined to coordinate their policies. It would be foolish for the United States either to expect OPEC's imminent demise or to encourage it. A protracted consumer-producer confrontation would be an economic and political disaster for all concerned. One prominent U.S. official expressed the opinion that the United States could indeed force the price of oil down to two dollars a barrel. All that need be done is to create a world depression! In other words, the problem is not how to get the price of oil down, but at what cost—politically as well as economically. Whereas the consumers could indeed force the producers to their knees, it would most probably be at a price that any rational man should consider too high.

Since Dr. Kissinger's interview in the January 13, 1975, issue of *Business Week*, the option of military force in the Persian Gulf has been seriously studied as one means of bringing the producers to terms. The unfortunate element in Dr. Kissinger's statement was that many on both sides began to consider an essentially draconian response as possible in less than draconian circumstances. The substance of his statement was innocuous. It was essentially a tautology: that force would be used in circumstances (i.e., "strangulation") where no other alternative but force was left.

The secretary was apparently trying to communicate in tone rather than substance the urgency of coming to grips with the energy problem. Too many Western politicians have blamed the world's economic ills solely on the high price of oil; and too many OPEC member-nation politicians, recognizing that world inflation long predated high prices, have totally absolved themselves of any responsibilities for the world's economic problems. A sense of urgency and assumption of more responsibility is needed on both sides, but talk of using military force serves only to increase the sense of confrontation, not further cooperation.

Many Westerners, particularly those fearful that the Arab oil weapon will force the United States to abandon Israel, and those concerned that the high price of oil and shift of economic power to OPEC will undermine U.S. strategic power, have seen in the military option a simple way of solving the problems of the OPEC hold on oil prices and the Arab political power derived from oil. What the proponents of developing a military option have failed to take into account is the political, economic, moral, and human cost, not of taking the oil fields, but of holding them for as long as necessary, perhaps a century or more.

The producers, many of whom in recent memory have been under foreign rule, react to the threat of war very emotionally, even if they do not take the threat very seriously. Talk of war raises fears of Western, and particularly U.S., intentions. In such an atmosphere, it would be entirely possible for the Persian Gulf producers to adopt policies against their own economic and political interest merely in response to a perceived threat. In sum, no one can win a confrontation.

Yet another assumption is that actual cooperation is a long way from simply seeking to cooperate. Throughout a series of interviews with government and business officials both of major consuming countries and gulf producing countries, the writer was struck by the unanimity of views that consumer-producer cooperation was vital, but the absolute lack of consensus about what constituted cooperation. For some it seemed to embody the idea that if enough communication could be encouraged the problem would work itself out. Communication is undoubtedly vital, and it is true that to date there has been very little of it. But it is not enough. Cooperation must accommodate several basic and in some cases inconsistent demands:

The consumers want as low a price for oil as possible, and the producers as high a price. No amount of communication will obliterate that. Some accommodation must therefore be reached on the best way to meet both interests.

Secondly, the OPEC countries have certain political constraints against cooperation. They find it currently impossible to lower the money price of oil, particularly if it were to appear that they were reacting to any kind of pressure from the consumers. In addition, they are all committed to working collectively through OPEC on oil prices, and any attempt to split them on that issue would most certainly be resisted.

Recognizing these constraints, it does appear possible that accommodations can be made on all sides for the common good. The disturbing element of it all is that if the energy and world economic problems are not solved, the causes will probably be due to political factors—distrust, chauvinism, disproportionate influence of special interests, and short-sightedness—rather than to economic ones.

Monetary concerns. Since the four-fold oil price increases of 1973, there has been concern over the accumulation of monetary reserve holdings by a few oil-producing countries, particularly in the gulf. The magnitude of the problem has not reached the draconian proportions that were originally feared, but it is still serious. For example, Saudi Arabia's reserves surpassed those of the United States in February 1975 to become second only to West Germany's.[19] By the end of 1975, Saudi Arabia is expected to have over $25 billion in foreign exchange reserves.

Since World War II, when current international monetary institutions were created, the United States and Western Europe have monopolized the monetary system. When Japan became an economic power it also joined what amounted to a very exclusive club. This group has been wrestling with the problem of petrodollar reserves since the issue reached major proportions after 1973. Now the oil producers are demanding an active role, commensurate with their new economic power, in developing whatever arrangements are eventually adopted to deal with the problem. In other words, the oil producers want to join the club.

This has been a difficult demand for the industrialized world to accept, but in the end, it appears to be inevitable and the sooner accepted the better.

One option for encouraging the recycling of petrodollars is to encourage more investment by the gulf oil producers in the United States, the largest capital market in the free world. There are, however, significant psychological barriers to such investment. For the producers, there is the fear that their natural wealth, by being converted into long-term foreign investments, will shrink due to inflation and currency devaluations. "Recycling," stated Abd al-Latif al Hamad, director-general of the Kuwait Fund for Arab Economic Development, "is a good word, only if it should not be interpreted as just syphoning back petrofunds to rich oil importers in return for doubtful financial assets."[20]

In addition to fears that the industrial world will not put its economic house in order, the gulf producers fear that some Western states, including the United States, might hold their investments hostage for political reasons. In case of another Arab-Israeli war and subsequent Arab oil embargo, for example, the gulf Arab producers fear that the United States might freeze or even seize their assets in retaliation. Proof of hostile U.S. reception to Arab investments was seen by many gulf financiers in the highly publicized U.S. public opposition to private Saudi investors seeking to purchase controlling interest in banks in California and Detroit and to the Kuwaiti purchase of an island off South Carolina in 1974-1975.

Gulf fears of investing in the United States are matched by the fears of many in the United States that the gulf oil producers seek to "buy out" the country, or in the case of the Arabs at least, to use their financial power against Jewish financial interests. In 1974, N.M. Rothschild and Sons were not invited to bid on a $40 million Eurodollar bond issue because of Arab investors' objections; and early in 1975, the Kuwait International Investment Company withdrew from a group managing two Eurobond issues because of Jewish banking participation. In addition to the Rothschild banking interests, Lazard Frères and S.G. Warburg have also been boycotted.[21] The Arabs maintain that such banks are boycotted not because they are Jewish but because of support for Israel. Such activities, nevertheless, help to increase emotions against Arab and even non-Arab foreign investment in the United States. By March 1975 nearly forty bills had been introduced in the Congress ostensibly to monitor foreign investment but in many cases designed to halt investment in the United States by Arabs and other oil producers.

The U.S. banking community has recognized the folly of limiting foreign investment and has opposed it. In fact, much of the subsequent attention given to combatting the Arab boycott, according to a prominent Jewish financial expert, was to draw efforts away from attempts to limit foreign investment.

Since the summer of 1975 there have been signs of lessening mistrust, at least on the part of the gulf investors. Previously, their investment priorities were safety, liquidity, and return on investment, in that order. Recent investments have been more diversified and over a longer term than previously. Nevertheless, the seeds of mistrust are still there, and it would behoove the U.S. government to encourage and strengthen mutual trust to the extent possible. Foreign investment will not only accelerate domestic capital formation, but it will also give the investors a greater stake in the well-being of the U.S. economy.

Commerce. U.S. commercial opportunities in the gulf are large and growing larger. The combined planned expenditure for development projects in the area over the next five years, for example, is in the neighborhood of $250 billion. In five years, annual imports by gulf states could exceed $50 billion in current dollars, making the region one of the world's major trading areas, quite apart from oil sales.

A significant proportion of U.S. exports during this period will undoubtedly be on a government-to-government basis. The Foreign Military Sales program is a prime example. But tremendous opportunities will still exist for the private sector. Sales of goods and services fall into four categories: exports of consumer goods directly to gulf merchants; equity investments; management contracts; and "turnkey projects" opened to competitive public tender.

In the area of consumer exports, U.S. firms have a growing advantage with their generally higher-quality but also higher-priced goods. As the gulf consumer accumulates more income, his preferences for quality consumer goods is increasing. For example, in Saudi Arabia during the *hajj*, there are two distinct qualities of goods in many shops—cheap Chinese and other products for the *hajjis*, and more expensive U.S. and European goods for the Saudis.

Management contracts are available somewhat on a competitive basis, but often go to firms having long-standing relationships with the countries in question. The oil companies, for example, will ultimately be offered management contracts to operate the production facilities they developed. In Saudi Arabia, TWA has a management contract with Saudi Arabian Airlines, which it helped to create.

In the field of equity investment, the gulf states, in both the public and private sectors, are not so much interested in capital inputs as they are in a firm's special technology, markets, or some other asset that can be utilized. For example, Iran's investment in Krupp's steel production was made with Iran's budding steel industry in mind. Moreover, equity holdings tend to induce the foreign participant to be concerned for the long-run success of the venture.

It is in turnkey projects where the largest expenditure will probably be made. Typically, gulf leaders, anxious to provide for the economic and social development of their peoples, are attempting to create instant progress; and because of their huge financial assets, they are willing to absorb a very high cost for it. The current Saudi five-year plan alone calls for an expenditure of $142 billion for a population of less than 4 million Saudis and perhaps 1 million resident aliens.

The United States has a general policy of export promotion throughout the world. The Department of Commerce has created an Office of Export Development for this purpose. Overseas, embassies are staffed with commercial officers to aid U.S. businessmen abroad and to report commercial information to Washington, where it is made available to the public. The Commerce Department also organizes trade fairs and other trade-promotion activities. The U.S. Export-Import Bank also has a major export-promotion function in helping to finance U.S. export portions of development projects abroad.

The creation of four new embassies in the gulf in 1972—in Bahrain, Qatar, the UAE, and Oman—was justified largely in terms of U.S. commercial interests. Nevertheless, the embassies originally were woefully underfinanced, each with a nonresident ambassador in the person of the U.S. ambassador to Kuwait. As it turned out, the American Embassy in Kuwait was incapable, from both a personnel and a funding standpoint, of adequately providing administrative and other support to the new embassies. The small embassy staffs became completely inundated after the oil price rises, as thousands of U.S. businessmen trekked to the gulf to try to tap the new oil wealth. Finally, in 1974, the new posts were enlarged with the addition of resident ambassadors. Their main function remains trade promotion.

The U.S. private sector has a great comparative advantage in the universally high regard for American technology and quality. The larger U.S. firms also have the advantage of huge assets from which they can draw in bidding for contracts. There are, however, some special disadvantages in the way business is conducted in the gulf and the Middle East generally.

The most visible disadvantage is in having to pay middlemen or "agents" huge sums in order to obtain business. In the gulf a payment for a service rendered is acceptable, whereas in the United States it may be considered a bribe. If there is U.S. government participation in the project, moreover, the U.S. firm could possibly find itself liable for criminal prosecution.

The sheer magnitude of some projects is also a problem. Some of the larger turnkey projects will cost well over 1 billion dollars, and may extend over ten or twelve years. Commonly, gulf states call for a fixed-price contract and then require a bid bond of 2 or 3 percent of the project cost, a performance bond of up to 10 percent of the project, and an advance repayment guarantee equal to the funds advanced by the contracting country. It is the performance bond that has been a particular problem for American firms because of the magnitude of the projects and the size of the assets that must be pledged to obtain financing. Moreover, agent fees often can run the cost of a project up as much as an extra 35 percent.

For projects so large and stretched over such a long period of time, it is next to impossible to predict costs. Inflation, bottlenecks (particularly manpower shortages), and other unknowns make fixed-cost contracts extremely risky. In addition, the assets which a company must have to obtain financing for such projects are so great as to dissuade many U.S. firms from competing even if they are technologically competent to provide the best product at the cheapest price.

Conflict of interest and antitrust laws preclude the U.S. government from subsidizing American firms in their bids on such projects; but the same is not true for European or Japanese firms.

Their governments regularly subsidize them with low- or no-interest loans, loan guarantees, and protection against escalating costs. Although the Export-Import Bank does participate in some debt financing, there is no comparison between its activities and the activities of those governments.

To deal with these problems, there are a number of policy options the United States could take. One is to encourage a higher standard of business practices in the gulf than is now the rule. Even without eliminating agents, fees could be routinized according to regular schedules and hence become more accountable.

The United States could also try to persuade the gulf states to improve their bidding procedures. Fixed-cost contracts of such magnitude, for example, are not only risky but unnecessarily expensive since the bidder must err on the high side of projected cost escalations; a cost-plus-a-percentage-profit contract would not only be less expensive but also less risky to the bidder. Also, large projects could advantageously be broken down to component parts, to allow more flexibility. This would additionally make bids more competitive, as smaller firms would be able to bid, resulting in lower costs.

Finally, the United States could try to persuade European and Japanese governments not to subsidize the bids their companies make. Since that course is almost certain to fail, the United States might consider broadening the mandate of the Export-Import Bank to allow loans and guarantees competitive with public financing in other countries for firms not large enough to obtain sufficient financing in the private sector.

In sum, U.S. policy toward the gulf has adequately fulfilled U.S. political, strategic, and economic interests. There is no cause for complacency, however. The gulf is politically stable only when measured by Middle Eastern standards, which are tenuous indeed. Arms race or no, the large arms transfers to the area bear watching. And not only are future oil supply-demand relationships hard to project, but equally difficult will be projecting the social, economic, and political change brought about by petrodollar development expenditures. It is vital that Americans become aware of these issues, for with two-thirds of the free world's proved oil reserves, the gulf will remain of major importance to the United States for a long time to come.

NOTES

[1]Herman Frederick Eilts, "Ahamd Bin Na'aman's Mission to the United States in 1840: The Voyage of the Al-Sultana to New York City" (Muscat, Oman: Petroleum Development (Oman), n.d); reprinted from the Essex Institute *Quarterly*, October 1962, p. 72.

[2]Thomas Bailey, *A Diplomatic History of the American People*, 6th ed. (New York: Appleton-Century-Crofts, 1958), p. 301.

[3]William D. Brewer, "United States Interests in the Persian Gulf" (paper delivered at the Princeton University Conference on Middle East Focus: The Persian Gulf, October 24, 25, 1968), p.3.

[4]B.C. Busch, *Britain and the Persian Gulf, 1894-1914* (Berkeley: University of California Press, 1967), p. 25.

[5]For an account of the early history of the Arabian Mission, see Alfred DeWitt Mason and Frederick J. Barney, *History of the Arabian Mission* (New York: Board of Foreign Missions of the Reformed Church in America, 1926). For a later period, see Dorothy Van Ess, *History of the Arabian Mission, 1926-1957* (unpublished manuscript, archives of the Reformed Church in America), and Van Ess, *Pioneers in the Arab World* (Grand Rapids, Mich.: Eerdmans, 1975).

[6]Van Ess, *Pioneers in the Arab World*, pp. 104-108.

[7]Arabian Mission, Muscat, M.S., Ltr., Jalalat al Sultan Qaboos bin Said, Sultan of Oman to The Chief Administrator, American Mission, Muscat, August 15, 1970.

[8]Donald Bosch and John Buteyn, "Reflections on Two Years Cooperation With the Oman Ministry of Health" (Muscat, unpublished pamphlet, 1972).

[9]Oman, Ministry of Health, "Letter of agreement from Said S. Shakay, Director of Administration, to the General Programme Council of the Reformed Church in America, 21 December, 1970".

[10]*Washington Evening Star,* January 17, 1968.

[11]United States, Department of State, *Bulletin* (Washington, D.C.: Government Printing Office), vol. 67, no. 1732, p. 242.

[12]See, for example, "Opening Statement of Joseph J. Sisco, Undersecretary of State for Political Affairs Before the Special Subcommittee on Investigations, House International Relations Committee, June 10, 1975."

13Ibid., p. 244.

14See James E. Akins, "The Oil Crisis: This Time the Wolf is Here," Foreign Affairs 51 (April 1973): 462-90.

15For the text of the agreement, see "Joint Statement on U.S.-Saudi Cooperation," Washington, D.C., June 8, 1974, Department of State, News Release, June 10, 1974.

16See "U.S.-Iran Joint Commission, Joint Communique, March 4, 1975," Middle East Journal 29 (Summer 1975): 345.

17Parts of this section were developed and expanded from an earlier paper by the writer, "U.S. Strategic Interests in the Persian Gulf: Problems and Policy Analysis," delivered at the National Security Affairs Conference of the National War College, Washington, D.C., July 14-15, 1975.

18See United States, Federal Energy Administration, Project Independence (Washington, D.C.: Government Printing Office, Nov. 1974).

19International Monetary Fund, International Financial Statistics, vol. 28, no. 8 (August 1975), p. 321.

20Abdlatif Y. Al-Hamad, "International Finance—An Arab Point of View" (speech delivered at the Algonquin Club, Boston, Mass., September 26, 1974).

21The Economist, vol. 254, no. 6860 (Feb. 1975), p. 82.

Appendix

Note: An attempt has been made to keep statistical data presented in the text at a minimum for two reasons. Not only is the accuracy of data from this part of the world highly uneven, but with the phenomenal pace of change in the gulf, most data tend to be out of date even by the time they become available. The following tables therefore represent only a few basic figures designed to aid the reader.

TABLE 1
THE PERSIAN GULF STATES
BASIC DATA

States	Ruler (and date of accession)	Capital	Area (sq. mi.)	Approx. Population (thousands)	Armed Forces		
					Army	Air Force	Navy
Major States							
Iran	Muhammad Reza Shah Pahlevi (Sept. 1941)	Tehran	636,000	33,000	165,000	57,000	13,000
Iraq	General Ahmad Hassan al-Bakr (July 1968)	Baghdad	172,000	11,000	90,000	10,000	2,000
Saudi Arabia	King Khalid bin Abd al-Aziz Al Saud (Mar. 1975)	Riyadh	830,000[1]	4,000	33,000[2]	6,000	1,000
Smaller States							
Kuwait	Amir Sabah al-Salim Al Sabah (Nov. 1965)	Kuwait	7,800[3]	1,000	6,000	2,000	200
Bahrain	Shaykh Isa bin Salman al-Khalifah (Nov. 1961)	Manama	213	234	1,200	–	–
Qatar	Shaykh Khalifah bin Hamad Al Thani (Feb. 1972)	al-Dowha (Doha)	4,000	159	1,200	50	50
UAE	President:Shaykh Zayd bin Sultan Al Nuhayyan (Dec. 1971)	Abu Dhabi	36,000[1]	235	1,700[4]	–	–
Abu Dhabi	Shaykh Zayd bin Sultan Al Nuhayyan (1966)	Abu Dhabi	32,000[1]	75	7,500[5]	350[5]	150[5]

States	Ruler	Capital	Area	Population	Armed Forces Army	Air Force	Navy
Smaller States (cont'd.)							
Dubai	Shaykh Rashid bin Said al-Maktm (1958)	Dubai	1,500	75	800	—	—
Sharjah	Shaykh Sultan bin Muhammad al-Qasimi (Jan. 1972)	Sharjah	1,000	35	—	—	—
Ajman	Shaykh Rashid bin Humayd al-Nu'aymi (al-Na'imi) (1928)	Ajman	100	5	—	—	—
Umm al-Qaywayn	Shaykh Ahmad bin Rashid al-Mu'alla (1929)	Umm al-Qaywayn	300	5	—	—	—
Ras al-Khaymah	Shaykh Saqr bin Muhammad al-Qasimi (1948)	Ras al-Khaymah	650	30	250[1]	—	—
Fujayrah	Shaykh Hamad bin Muhammad al-Sharqi (1974)	Fujayrah	450	10	—	—	—
Oman	Sultan Qabus bin Said Al Bu Said (1970)	Muscat	82,000[1]	710	9,006[6]	400	200

[1]In the absence of totally delimited borders, this is only an approximation.

[2]There is in addition a National Guard of approximately equal strength.

[3]Including annexed areas of the Saudi-Kuwaiti Neutral Zone

[4]Union Defence Force (UDF).

[5]Abu Dhabi Defense Force (ADDF).

[6]There were at the end of 1975 1,500 Iranians and about an equal number of Jordanians stationed in Oman.

Table 2
THE PERSIAN GULF STATES
BASIC ECONOMIC DATA

States	Oil Income 1975 (billions)	Imports 1975 (billions)	Unit of Currency	$ Exchange Rate per 1 Unit
Major States				
Iran	$19.8	$16.1	Iranian Rial	$ .015
Iraq	7.6	6.5	Iraqi Dinar	3.38
Saudi Arabia	27.1	5.7	Saudi Riyal	.29
Smaller States				
Kuwait	8.0	1.7	Kuwaiti Dinar	3.48
Bahrain	.5	.4	Bahrain Dinar	2.53
Qatar	1.8	.7	Qatar Riyal	.26
U.A.E.	6.3	2.5	U.A.E. Dirham	.25
Oman	1.8	—	Omani Rial	2.90

Source: Oil income for Oman is my estimate. All other figures for oil income and imports are from U.S. Treasury Department, January 1976.
Exchange Rates: As of July, 1975; source: *The Middle East and North Africa, 1975-76.*

Table 3
THE PERSIAN GULF STATES
BASIC OIL DATA

States	Proved Oil Reserves, end of 1975 (million bbl.)	Crude Production, 1975 (million bd.)	Capacity, Nov. 1975 (million bd.)
Major States			
Iran	64,500	5.3	6.6
Iraq	34,300[1]	2.2	2.6
Saudi Arabia	151,800	7.1	10.8
Smaller States			
Kuwait	71,200	2.1	3.3
Bahrain	312	.1	—
Qatar	5,850	.4	.7
U.A.E.			
Abu Dhabi	29,500	1.4	2.0
Dubai	1,350	.3	.3
Sharjai	1,350	.04	.05
Oman	5,900	.3	—

Source: Crude production figures from *The Oil and Gas Journal,* Feb. 16, 1976, p. 29; reserve figures from *The Oil and Gas Journal,* Dec. 29, 1975, p. 86; capacity figures from *Petroleum Intelligence Weekly,* Jan. 5, 1976, p. 7.

[1]Some experts believe Iraqi reserves are actually much greater than this.

Bibliography

The following selections are suggested for additional reading. For more comprehensive references, see the bibliographical sections of the American University's *Area Handbook for Iran* (Washington, D.C., 1971); *Area Handbook for Saudi Arabia* (1970); and *Area Handbook for the Peripheral States of the Arabian Peninsula* (1971). See also J.D. Anthony, *The States of the Arabian Peninsula and Gulf Littoral: A Selected and Partially Annotated Bibliography* (Washington, D.C.: The Middle East Institute, 1973), and C.L. Geddes, *Analytical Guide to the Bibliography on the Arabian Peninsula* (Denver, Colo.: American Institute of Islamic Studies, 1974).

DOCUMENTS

Great Britain. *Memorial of the Government of the United Kingdom of Great Britain and Northern Ireland in Arbitration Concerning Buraimi and the Common Frontier Between Abu Dhabi and Saudi Arabia.* 2 vols. London, 1955.

Iran, Ministry of Foreign Affairs. *Iran's Foreign Policy: A Compendium of the Writings and Statements of His Imperial Majesty Shahanshah Aryamehr.* Tehran, n.d.

Oman, Ministry of Development, National Statistical Department, *Development in Oman. 1970-1974.* Muscat, Oman, 1975.

Qatar, Ministry of Information. *Qatar in the Seventies.* Doha, Qatar, 1973.

Saudi Arabia. *Memorial of the Government of Saudi Arabia in the Arbitration for the Settlement of the Territorial Dispute between Muscat and Abu Dhabi on One Side and Saudi Arabia on the Other.* Cairo, 1955.

United Arab Emirates, Ministry of Foreign Affairs. *United Arab Emirates.* Prepared by the Centre for Documentation and Research. Abu Dhabi and London: Finsbury Printing Company, 1972.

United States, Congress, House of Representatives. *Means of Measuring Naval Power with Special Reference to U.S. and Soviet Activities in the Indian Ocean.* Prepared for the Subcommittee on the Near East and South Asia of the Committee on Foreign Affairs by the Foreign Affairs Division, Congressional Research Service, Library of Congress. Washington, D.C., May 12, 1974.

——————. *New Perspectives on the Persian Gulf.* Ninety-third Congress, 1st Session, June 6, July 17, 23, 24, and Nov. 28, 1973. Washington, D.C., 1973.

——————. *U.S. Interests In and Toward the Persian Gulf.* Hearings before the Subcommittee on the Near East of the Committee on Foreign Affairs, February 2, June 7, August 8, 15, 1972. Washington, D.C., 1972.

——————. *The Persian Gulf 1974: Money, Politics, Arms and Power.* Ninety-third Congress, 2nd Session, July 30, Aug. 5, 7, 12, 1974. Washington, D.C., 1975.

United States, Federal Trade Commission. *The International Al Cartel.* Published by the Select Committee on Small Business, U.S. Senate, 82nd Congress, 2nd Session. Washington, D.C., 1952.

United States, Department of Treasury, United States-Saudi Arabian Joint Commission on Economic Cooperation. *Summary of Saudi Arabian Five Year Development Plan (1975-1980).* Washington, D.C., 1975.

BOOKS AND MONOGRAPHS

Abir, Mordechai. *Oil, Power and Politics: Conflict in Arabia, The Red Sea and the Gulf.* London: Frank Cass, 1974.

Abu Hakima, Ahmad M. *A History of Eastern Arabia.* Beirut, Lebanon: Khayats, 1965.

Aitchison, C.U. *A Collection of Treaties, Engagements and Sanads Relating to India and Neighboring Countries.* Vol. 11. Calcutta, 1892.

Amin, Abdul Amir. *British Interests in the Persian Gulf, 1747-1778.* Leiden, Netherlands: Brill, 1967.

Anthony, John Duke. *The Arab States of the Lower Gulf: People, Politics, Petroleum.* Washington, D.C.: The Middle East Institute, 1975.

Bayne, E.A. *Persian Kingship in Transition.* New York: American Universities Field Staff, 1968.

Belgrave, James H.D. *Welcome to Bahrain.* 8th ed. Bahrain: Augustan Press, 1973.

Bill, James A. *The Politics of Iran: Groups, Classes and Modernization.* Columbus, Ohio: Charles E. Merrill, 1972.

Burrell, R.M. *The Persian Gulf* The Washington Papers, no. 1. Washington, D.C.: Center for Strategic and International Studies, 1972.

——————, and Cottrell, Alvin J. *Iran, The Arabian Peninsula and The Indian Ocean.* Strategy Papers, no. 14. New York: National Strategy Information Center, 1972.

Busch, Briton C. *Britain and the Persian Gulf, 1894-1914.* Berkeley: University of California Press, 1967.

Chubin, Shahram, and Zabih, Sepehr. *The Foreign Policy of Iran: A Developing State in a Zone of Great Power Conflict.* Berkeley: University of California Press, 1974.

Coon, Carlton S. *Caravan: The Story of the Middle East.* Rev. ed. New York: Henry Holt and Company, 1958.

Cooper, Charles A., and Alexander, Sydney S., eds. *Economic Development and Population Growth in the Middle East.* New York: American Elsevier Publishing Company, 1972.

De Gaury, Gerald, *Faisal: King of Saudi Arabia.* London: Arthur Barker, 1966.

Fenelon, Kevin G. *The United Arab Emirates: An Economic and Social Survey.* London: Longman, 1973.

Freeman, S. David. *Energy: The New Era.* New York: Vintage Books, 1974.

Halliday, Fred. *Arabia without Sultans.* London: Penguin Books, 1974.

Hawley, Donald F. *The Trucial States.* New York: Humanities Press, 1971.

Hay, Sir Rupert. *The Persian Gulf States.* Washington, D.C.: The Middle East Institute, 1959.

Hewins, Ralph. *A Golden Dream: The Miracle of Kuwait.* London: W.H. Allen, 1963.

——————. *Mr. Five Percent: The Story of Calouste Gulbenkian.* New York: Rinehart and Company, 1958.

Holden, David. *Farewell to Arabia.* London: Faber and Faber, 1966.

Howarth, David. *The Desert King: Ibn Saud and His Arabia.* New York: McGraw-Hill, 1964.

Hurewitz, J.C. *Diplomacy in the Near and Middle East, A Documentary Record: 1535-1914.* 2 vols. Princeton, N.J.: D. Van Nostrand Company, 1956.

Kelly, John B. *Britain and the Persian Gulf, 1795-1880.* London: Oxford University Press, 1967.

——————. *Eastern Arabian Frontiers.* New York: Praeger, 1964.

Khadduri, Majid. *Independent Iraq.* London: Oxford University Press, 1951.

——————, ed. *Major Middle Eastern Problems in International Law.* Washington, D.C.: American Enterprise Institute of Public Policy Research, 1972.

——————. *Republican Iraq: A Study in Iraqi Politics Since the Revolution of 1958.* London: Oxford University Press, 1969.

Knauerhase, Ramon. *The Saudi Arabian Economy.* New York: Praeger, 1975.

Lambton, A.K.S. *The Persian Land Reform, 1962-1966.* Oxford: Clarendon Press, 1969.

Landen, Robert G. *Oman Since 1856: Disruptive Modernization in a Traditional Arab Society.* Princeton, N.J.: Princeton University Press, 1967.

Lenczowsky, George, ed. *Political Elites in the Middle East.* Washington, D.C.: American Enterprise Institute of Public Policy Research, 1975.

Long, David E. *Confrontation and Cooperation in the Gulf.* Middle East Problem Paper no. 10. Washington, D.C.: The Middle East Institute, 1974.

Longrigg, Stephen Hensley. *Oil In the Middle East: Its Discovery and Development.* London: Oxford University Press, 1968.

Lorimer, J.G. *Gazetteer of the Persian Gulf, Oman and Central Arabia.* 2 vols. Calcutta: Superintendent of Government Printing, 1915.

El-Mallakh, Ragaei. *Economic Development and Regional Cooperation: Kuwait.* Chicago: University of Chicago Press, 1968.

Marlowe, John. *The Persian Gulf in the Twentieth Century.* New York: Praeger, 1962.

Mason, Alfred DeWitt, and Barney, Frederick J. *History of the Arabian Mission.* New York: Board of Missions of the Reformed Church in America, 1926.

Mikdashi, Zuhayr M. *The Community of Oil Exporting Countries.* Ithaca, N.Y.: Cornell University Press, 1972.

Nakhleh, Emile A. *Arab-American Relations in the Persian Gulf.* Foreign Affairs Study no. 17. Washington, D.C.: American Enterprise Institute for Public Policy Research, 1975.

——————. *The United States and Saudi Arabia: A Policy Analysis.* Washington, D.C.: American Enterprise Institute for Public Policy Research, 1975.

Owen, Roderic. *The Golden Bubble: Arabian Gulf Documentary.* London: Collins, 1957.

Pachachi, Nadim. *The Role of OPEC in the Emergence of New Patterns in Government-Company Relations.* London: Royal Institute of International Affairs, 1972.

Pahlevi, H.I.M. Muhammad Reza Shah. *Mission For My Country.* New York: McGraw-Hill, 1961.

——————. *The White Revolution.* Tehran, 1967.

Philby, H. St. John B. *Arabia.* London: Ernest Benn, 1930.

——————. *Arabian Jubilee.* London: Robert Hale, 1952.

Price, D.L. *Oman: Insurgency and Development.* Conflict Studies, no. 53 London: The Institute for the Study of Conflict, January 1975.

Qubain, Fahim. *Education and Science in the Arab World.* Baltimore: Johns Hopkins Press, 1966.

Ramazani, Rouhallah K. *Iran's Foreign Policy 1941-1973.* Charlottesville: University of Virginia Press, 1975.

——————. *The Persian Gulf: Iran's Role.* Charlottesville: University of Virginia Press, 1972.

Sadik, Muhammad T., and Snavely, William P. *Bahrain, Qatar and the United Arab Emirates: Colonial Past, Present Problems and Future Prospects.* Lexington, Mass., Toronto, and London: Lexington Books, D.C. Heath Company, 1972.

Stephens, Robert. *The Arab's New Frontier.* London: Temple Smith, 1973.

Stocking, George W. *Middle East Oil: A Study in Political and Economic Controversy.* Nashville, Tenn.: Vanderbilt University Press, 1970.

Tahtinen, Dale R. *Arms in the Persian Gulf.* Washington, D.C.: American Enterprise Institute of Public Policy Research, 1974.

Thesiger, Wilfred. *The Marsh Arabs.* London: Longmans, 1964.

Van Ess, Dorothy, *Pioneers in the Arab World.* Grand Rapids, Mich.: Eerdmans, 1975.

Wilson, Arnold T. *The Persian Gulf: An Historical Sketch from the Earliest Times to the Beginning of the Twentieth Century.* London, Allen and Unwin, 1959.

Winder, R. Boyly. *Saudi Arabia in the Nineteenth Century.* London: Macmillan; New York: St. Martins Press, 1965.

Yar-Shater, Ehsan, ed. *Iran Faces the Seventies.* Praeger Special Studies for International Economics and Development. New York: Praeger, 1971.

Zonis, Marvin. *The Political Elite of Iran.* Princeton, N.J.: Princeton University Press, 1971.

ARTICLES, PAPERS, AND SPECIAL REPORTS

Adelman, M.A. "Is the Oil Shortage Real? Oil Companies as OPEC Tax Collectors." *Foreign Policy,* no. 9 (Winter 1972-1973), pp. 69-107.

Akins, James E. "The Oil Crisis: This Time the Wolf is Here." *Foreign Affairs* 51 (April 1973): 462-90.

Amouzegar, Jahangir. "The Oil Story: Facts, Fiction and Fair Play." *Foreign Affairs* 51 (July 1973): 676-89.

Anthony, John D. "The Union of Arab Amirates." *Middle East Journal* 26 (1972): 271-87.

Bosch, Donald, and Buteyn, John. "Reflections on Two Years Cooperation with the Oman Ministry of Health." Unpublished pamphlet of the American Mission in Muscat.

Brewer, William. "Yesterday and Tomorrow in the Persian Gulf." *Middle East Journal* 23 (1969): 149-58.

Chase Manhattan Bank. *Capital Investment of the World Petroleum Industry.* New York, December 1974.

──────────. *The Profit Situation: A Special Petroleum Report.* New York, April 1974.

Erb, Richard. "The Financial Management Problem From the Perspective of OPEC Members." Paper delivered to the Council on Foreign Relations, New York, July 11, 1975.

Fallah, Reza. "The Energy Crisis: Its Origins and Suggested Remedies." Address delivered before the Center International d'Etudes Monetaires et Bancaires, Geneva, November 28-30, 1974.

Hashimi, Rasoul M.H., and Edwards, Alfred L. "Land Reform in Iraq: Economic and Social Implications." *Land Economics*, vol. 37, 1 (Feb. 1961).

Khadduri, Majid. "Iran's Claim to the Sovereignty of Bahrain." *American Journal of International Law* 45 (1951): Supplements, pp. 631-47.

Lauterpacht, E. "River Boundaries: Legal Aspects of the Shatt al Arab Frontier." *International and Comparative Law Quarterly* 9 (1960): 208-236.

Liebesny, Herbert J. "Administrative and Legal Development in Arabia: The Persian Gulf Principalities." *Middle East Journal* 10 (1956): 33-42.

Long, David E. "The Politics of OPEC." Paper delivered to the Council on Foreign Relations, New York, April 22, 1975.

──────────. "U.S. Strategic Interests in the Persian Gulf: Problems and Policy Analysis." Paper delivered to the Second Annual National Security Affairs Conference, The National War College, Fort McNair, Washington, D.C., July 14-15, 1975.

──────────. "United States Policy Toward the Persian Gulf." *Current History*, no. 402 (Feb. 1975), pp. 69-85.

McNamara, Robert. Annual address to the World Bank reprinted in the *Summary Proceedings of the 1974 Annual Meeting of the Board of Governors.*

Middle East Institute. *The Arabian Peninsula, Iran and the Gulf States: New Wealth, New Power.* A Summary Record of the 27th Annual Conference of the Middle East Institute. Washington, D.C., Sept. 28-29, 1973.

──────────. *The United States and the Middle East: Changing Relationships.* Proceedings of the 29th Annual Conference of the Middle East Institute, Washington, D.C., Oct. 3-4, 1975.

—————————. *World Energy Demands and the Middle East.* Proceedings of the 26th Annual Conference of the Middle East Institute, Washington, D.C., Sept. 29-30, 1972.

Searby, Daniel M. "Doing Business in the Mideast: The Game is Rigged." *Harvard Business Review* 54, (Jan.-Feb. 1976): 56-64.

Breach of Promise

Breach of Promise

Roy Hart

St. Martin's Press
New York

Library of Congress Cataloging-in-Publication Data

Hart, Roy.
    Breach of promise / Roy Hart.
        p.   cm.
    ISBN 0-312-05393-2
    I. Title.
    PR6058.A694857B74   1991
    823′.914—dc20   90-48399
                                                                         CIP

First published in Great Britain by Macmillan London Limited

First U.S. Edition: January 1991
10 9 8 7 6 5 4 3 2 1

Breach of Promise

Chapter 1

The snow had stolen silently out of the north during the night. Now, at daybreak, the wind clattering over the hills was lifting the feathery upper layers that had not quite settled and turning them into a scudding spindrift that spun and cavorted in the lane ahead of her.

Already the cold had penetrated her old tweed coat, and her outward breaths had condensed into an icy crust over the red woollen scarf that muffled her mouth. But it took more than mere weather to deter the slight but stalwart Miss Kingsley. When you are seventy-three, every morning is a morning to be savoured and this one was no exception. Despite the snow she plodded briskly, and her Labrador, as old as Miss Kingsley herself, in dog-years, zig-zagged along beside her in an ecstasy of mystified excitement, sniffing and snuffling at unfamiliar white landscape.

The two of them reached the rusty iron gate set in the hedgerow, as they did each morning. Miss Kingsley lifted the latch, opened it, guided her dog through, then carefully closed the gate and latched it behind her. Then, with surprising agility, she stooped to unleash the Labrador.

'Off you go,' she urged enthusiastically, giving its rump a slap. 'Go find Ziggy.'

The Labrador sped off like a greyhound between the naked trees.

Miss Kingsley would have followed it had she not glanced back and seen the white Metro with the blue lamp on top coming up the lane behind her; so she stopped and waved a cheery hand. Conversation was a rare luxury around here, especially at this hour of a winter morning.

Her sharp weatherbeaten face creased into a smile as the thickly set and blue-uniformed driver pulled into the verge and wound down his nearside window.

'Morning, Miss Kingsley,' he called. 'Weather cold enough for you?'

She tugged down her red muffler. 'Wait till you're my age,' she called. 'You'll love it.'

'Brrr,' he grumbled. 'You've got to be joking. How's Jack?'

'Oh, not good,' she said, a little sadly. 'He had one of his bad days yesterday. I've left him in bed.'

'Perhaps I'll call in and see him on my way back.'

'Yes,' she called. 'Thank you, Mr Peasgood. He'd like that. Off to something exciting?'

'Sheep rustling again. Fred Jackson lost ten last night, so he reckons. Don't suppose you happened to see anything?'

'Oh, the buggers,' she exploded with unladylike vehemence. 'No. Didn't see a damn thing. Sorry. I wish you luck, though. Hope you find 'em.'

'They're probably in the next county by now. On your way to see Mr Komarowski, are you?'

'Yes, I am. Or rather *we* are.'

'Wish him a merry Christmas from me and the missus, in case we don't see him beforehand.'

'Yes,' she said. 'I shall.'

'And tell Jack I'll be along about ten o'clock.'

'I will.' She raised her gloved hand again as the window of the Metro was wound up and Sergeant Peasgood continued on his way to Jackson's farm.

She lifted her muffler back into place and set off after the Labrador.

It seemed a longer hike than usual this morning, the trees all about her with their black gaunt branches

8

stretched towards the leaden sky, and the snow between them giving an illusion of shortened perspective, so that a tree that looked only a dozen paces away took nearer twenty to reach it. At first she felt no sense of foreboding, merely a stitch in her side and a little breathlessness. And when the other sensation did come it was not so much foreboding as an undercurrent that all was not quite as it should be.

The dog had not barked; and Miss Kingsley was of the age when she preferred things to be much the same as they were yesterday. And yesterday, and for hundreds of mornings before yesterday, Max had barked. Not that Max was a hysterical barker; like his owner he was stolid and down to earth, but he always barked to announce his arrival and until Ziggy let him in to the caravan and gave him his digestive biscuit and saucer of tea. After that he would curl up in the warm under Ziggy's folding table while his mistress and her host put the world to rights over a mug of lemon tea. It was part of an unchanging ritual. Like a clock it regulated the beginning of each new day.

But not today. As she trudged closer to the clearing she began to hear Max's muted and persistent whine. She walked faster, wrenching down her muffler to breathe more easily, the cutting wind flapping her tweed coat about her boots. Under the snow the earth was as hard as cement.

'Max!' she called. 'Max! Come, boy! Come!'

Max did not come. He barked once, then took up his anxious whine again. And as Miss Kingsley drew closer still she heard the rasp of his claws scrabbling against the door of the trailer. That was when Miss Kingsley felt the foreboding and recognised it for what it was.

She broke stride as she at last reached the edge of the clearing. The door of the old yellow caravan, despite Max's blandishments, was still firmly shut. The windows ran with condensation. The curtains were closed. But

Ziggy's antiquated black bicycle was padlocked to the yoke of the towing-bar, so he couldn't be far.

With her arrival Max became more frantic, circling her feet and getting between them and leaping up and barking as she rapped on the door. Her anxiety heightened. A key, yes, there was a key . . . somewhere . . . She found it tucked out of sight behind the rim of the wheel near the door. As she climbed the two metal steps with it Max almost bowled her back down them again.

The door opened outwards. She could feel the heat spilling out, and smell stale cigarette smoke. Ziggy'd always had the caravan aired by now . . .

'Ziggy?' she called, still hesitant to go in too far in case the old chap was on the lavatory or something. 'Ziggy?'

The ceiling light was on, but very dim – the battery must be flat – and it took a moment for her eyes to accustom to the semi-dark. The bunk was empty; and made up. And Max was sniffing fretfully around a huge bundle of wet red rags that filled the little space between the bunk and the folding table.

And, for a second, Enid Kingsley's heart stopped and her horizon tilted, so that with one hand she had to grip the rim of the diminutive steel sink to stop herself keeling over. Her other hand flew to cover her mouth and her mounting horror.

'Oh, dear . . . '

So much blood. Blood everywhere. So cruel . . . Who could ever . . . ?

'Oh, God,' she whispered, scarcely able to breathe. 'Oh, Ziggy. Oh, you poor old boy.'

But fear and panic both have their boundaries, and Miss Kingsley steeled herself to step back over them. She reached for the Labrador's collar and drew him away.

'Come, Max,' she said softly. No tears. Not now. Not yet. There was too much to do. 'Come, boy. We have to go and tell somebody about this. And very, very pronto.'

10

Chapter 2

'Kingsley,' she said, in as firm a voice as she could summon. The giddiness had passed. All she felt inside now was the cold black void of loneliness. 'Enid Amelia Kingsley.'

The fair-haired young man in the front seat wrote that down. In all the confusion she had forgotten his name; Rice or Price or something like that. Of the two, she preferred the older, leaner man seated beside her.

'And your address, Miss Kingsley?' he asked, now passing her a blue plastic mug of tea that Sergeant Peasgood had poured from his vacuum flask and just handed in through the open window.

'Thank you,' she said, grasping it in both hands and taking a sip and trying not to let them see how much she was shaking. 'The Gatehouse. Wormsley Lane.'

'That's here in Upper Gorton, is it, Miss Kingsley?'

'Yes,' she said. It had all seemed to happen so very quickly. Up among the trees a squad of pink-cheeked young policemen, little more than boys they all looked, were stringing up boundaries of red and white tape to mark a path. It all looked very efficient and workmanlike; and so terribly final . . .

'The old gentleman up there; you call him Ziggy.'

'Yes,' she said. The man next to her spoke softly and with infinite kindness and seemed prepared to wait for her answers. 'He was properly Zygmunt Tadeusz Komarowski.' She had to spell that for them, and explain that the 'w' was pronounced like an English 'v'.

11

'Polish, was he?'

'Yes,' she said. 'Yes, Polish. But English. He took out papers.' She told them, perhaps unnecessarily, that he had come originally from Lodz.

'Relatives?'

She shook her head sadly. 'No,' she said. 'None.' Except her. She was a relative, she supposed. It had been a beast that war. Johnnie still had nightmares about it now; for her and Johnnie the war was still going on, indeed would never end. She sipped again. She much preferred her tea with lemon, but it had been kind of Sergeant Peasgood to think of her . . .

'A sort of hermit, was he?'

'Oh, by no means,' she protested roundly. 'More independent. He used to have a cottage in the village – until he had to sell it. Then he bought the caravan and rented that little piece of ground off Mr Henneker. It was private, you see. And he had his books and his typewriter . . . ' The backs of her eyes prickled sharply.

The man next to her gave her pause. She could feel the warmth coming off his overcoat. She herself suddenly felt very cold.

The young man in the front seat was less patient. He sounded faintly Welsh. He was a Chief Inspector. She had forgotten what the man beside her was, except that it had sounded terribly important.

'When did you last see him alive, Miss Kingsley?' the man in the front seat asked, over his shoulder.

'Yesterday,' she said. Fifty years ago suddenly seemed like yesterday. Yesterday felt like a lifetime ago. 'Yesterday afternoon. About half-past four. Teatime. His back light wasn't working.'

'His back light?' The man next to her again.

'On his bicycle. It wasn't working. I called after him to tell him, but I don't think he heard me. He'd been up to have a game of chess and a chinwag with Jack.'

'Jack?'

'My brother,' she explained.

12

'Ah.' He gave her another pause, this time for a sip of tea. 'He didn't happen to say where he was going? After he'd left your brother.'

She shook her head. 'I presumed he was coming back up here. To the caravan.'

'He was a regular visitor? To your place?'

'Oh, yes,' she said, wistfully. 'Every day.'

'And this morning, Miss Kingsley,' he said, and she had the distinct feeling that the question that was coming next was as uncomfortable for him as it would be for her. 'What time do you think you found him?'

'Eight o'clock,' she said. A most unforgettable eight o'clock . . .

He lifted an eyebrow.

'Oh, for Heaven's sake,' she scoffed – and made herself feel giddy again – they probably thought she was just another silly old woman with a clutch of cats and a walking frame. 'I'm not so damned old that I can't read a wristwatch. At five to eight this morning I was behind that gate there and talking to Mr Peasgood. Ask him.'

He made no response. His name was Roper, she remembered belatedly. Not that it mattered. Nothing mattered any more. Zygmunt was gone. Brutally taken. And she would have to go on, getting older and lonelier and more decrepit. Only now did old age hold terror for her. The man next to her hooked her up on his eyes again.

'You found the caravan door open?' he said.

'Oh, no. There was a key. Tucked behind a wheel. I let myself in. I felt sure something was wrong, you see.'

'The key was always there, was it?'

'Yes,' she said. 'He was very absent-minded about little things like that. He was always forgetting his keys.'

'Did you touch anything inside? D'you remember?'

'The doorkey . . . the door . . . the sink,' she said, trying hard to remember exactly.

'Nothing else?'

'No. Definitely.' She was sure she had not.

13

'Good,' he said.

A set of knuckles rapped on the window, and the door was opened from the outside. She felt the cold drift in around her knees. It was Sergeant Peasgood again. Beyond him two more policemen were wiring a black and yellow sign to the gate. 'No Admittance Without Authority' it read. 'Scene of Crime'. Then a distant movement caught her eye, further along the lane, through the windscreen. A silhouette, with a carrier-bag, just standing there watching. It looked like that terrible Allgrove man – only it couldn't be because he was still in prison. And then she blinked. And when she opened her eyes again he was gone . . . she wondered if she ought to say something . . .

Sergeant Peasgood touched his cap as he stooped to look into the car. 'Mr Wilson says you can go up now, sir,' he said.

'Right, Sergeant,' said the man beside her. 'Thank you.' Then, to her: 'We'll have somebody drive you and your dog home, Miss Kingsley; and drop in on you later on, if that's all right.'

'Yes,' she said. 'Certainly. And whoever did that,' she pleaded earnestly, plucking at his sleeve as he swung his legs out of the car, 'you will find them, won't you?'

'Oh, we'll find 'em, Miss Kingsley,' he said, and sounded as if he meant it. 'Don't you worry yourself.'

He twitched a smile as he closed the car door, and she watched him and the Inspector cross the verge and go through the gate, then start up the snow-clad slope between the ribbons of coloured tape.

'Game old lady,' observed Price.

'Certainly got her head screwed on,' agreed Roper. 'Got a feeling she was more than a bit fond of our Polish gentleman, too.'

'At her age?' said Price, with a younger man's scorn.

'Why not?' said Roper. 'Wait till you get a few more years on your back. You don't know the half of it yet.'

14

To the left of the marked track they were taking were two sets of Miss Kingsley's footprints, one set going up the slope and another coming down. The ploughed wake and patterns of paw prints had been left behind by the Labrador.

'Get in touch with the area Met station some time,' said Roper. 'Might be useful to know when it started snowing around here last night.' Because if the snow had started to fall before Komarowski had been murdered, there was a faint hope that it might be a help; if it had fallen afterwards it was going to be Hell's own hindrance. Already the snow on the taped-off path was a jumble of boot prints where the cadets had been, everywhere else it was virgin white. The wind was still lifting the sharp white dust between the trees and the weather forecast was heralding a heavier fall by lunchtime, which might have to mean a very contracted morning programme.

They came to the clearing. Miss Kingsley was clearly not only game but remarkably fit. Even Price was winded.

From the outside the battered yellow trailer looked almost derelict. A woman's ancient black bicycle was chained by its back wheel to the towing-bar. Crouched in the shadowy doorway, Wilson the pathologist was tucking a few instruments back in his case.

'How goes it?' asked Roper, at the foot of the steps.

'A bad 'un,' said Wilson grimly, snapping shut the catches of his case. 'Shotgun. Twice. Can't tell you when, I'm afraid. It's still like an oven in here.' He stood up and drew back into the little lavatory cubicle to give Roper room to step up and look inside. 'All I've done is to open the curtains and turn off the cooker.'

Cigarette smoke, stale and pungent, mixed with the smell of a butcher's shop . . .

The bearded Komarowski lay sprawled along the floor, his head against a pile of books stacked against the back bulkhead, and the rictus of horror still on his face. His stomach had been blown open and there was another wet cavernous wound higher up in his chest. It looked as if he

15

had put up a hand to protect himself. The right one was shot to ribbons.

Roper grimaced and whispered softly, 'Jesus,' and it wasn't a blasphemy and perhaps it wasn't a prayer either, but if there was anybody up there listening he hoped they would hear and take due note. He moved a little aside so that Price could look past him around the edge of the door-frame.

The squarely built old man had to be seventy if he was a day. Trimly bearded, his steel-framed spectacles askew and hanging from one ear, eyes still open, dry and lustreless.

'The bastards,' said Price.

'Bloody right,' said Roper.

Komarowski lay between a narrow bunk and a little folding table with a typewriter on it, an old grey, crackle-finished Remington with yellowed keys. There was a bloody hand-print at the edge of the table, blood on the made-up bunk, blood on the heap of books against which his head rested. Blood on the grey linoleumed floor. Muddy paw prints, too; that dog of Miss Kingsley's, most likely.

'How close?' asked Roper, over his shoulder.

'The stomach shot, about a yard away,' said Wilson, still wedged in the lavatory compartment behind him. 'The chest wound I'd say was only a few inches. There're powder-burns around that one.'

In the confined space the noise of the two shots would have been deafening. The entire little box could not have been much more than ten feet by six. Apart from the blood, it was all shipshape and clean. The grey linoleum had been recently polished, the sink shone, the tap over it gleamed, and the bed had clearly been made by someone whose watchwords were neatness and order.

'Photographs?' asked Roper.

'I've taken some Polaroids,' said Wilson. 'You'll have some copies this afternoon. And when the Coroner's Officer turns up I'll push for an instant PM.'

'Good,' said Roper. 'Thanks.'

Price backed off down the steps, Roper followed him, the bespectacled Wilson came after. It was good to breathe the icy fresh air again after the malodorous warmth in the caravan. It was a minute to nine o'clock. The sun was trying to struggle through. Roper lit a cheroot, Wilson a small cigar, while they waited for the Coroner's Officer to arrive and the body to be taken off to the mortuary.

'Going away for Christmas?' asked Wilson.

'Only Christmas Day,' said Roper, not meaning to sound curt, but he was not at the moment in a mood for small-talk. His still envied the cynical hard-nosed copper who could take outrages like this in his stride. Even after most of a lifetime at the job they still made him chillingly and bitterly angry and soured his stomach.

'Reckon you'll crack this by then?'

'I wouldn't make a book on it,' said Roper grimly. 'But I'm going to have a bloody good try.'

They fell to silence. Roper could feel the cold striking up through his shoes. Over by the caravan Price was organising a couple of cadets with shovels and a sieve to sift through the contents of Komarowski's little plastic dustbin, although the chance of them finding anything significant in that was remote.

Wilson glanced past Roper's shoulder towards the well-trodden path. 'The cavalry's on its way by the looks of it.'

Roper turned. Trudging up the rise was the Coroner's Officer, and a few paces behind a Scene of Crimes Officer with his equipment case, their outward breaths turning momentarily to vapour before the wind blew it away.

After a brief handshake, the Coroner's Officer went into the caravan with Wilson. The Scene of Crimes man stayed outside with Roper.

'What's the form?' asked the SOCO, a small neat bearded man in a grey anorak and gilt-framed spectacles.

'Shotgun,' said Roper. 'Twice.'

The SOCO wrinkled his nose distastefully. Nobody who had seen the end product of a shotgun on human flesh was exactly enamoured of shotguns.

'I'd like you to work inside the caravan first,' said Roper. 'Footprints . . . dabs . . . whatever you can come up with. And a few more photographs before they take him away.'

The SOCO took in the scene. 'Might do better to tow the van back to the vehicle-shed,' he said. 'I could give it a more detailed going over there.'

'Not that simple, old lad,' said Roper. 'That caravan must have been lifted in here on a crane. Take another look.'

The SOCO did. 'Yes,' he said. 'See what you mean.' The caravan was hemmed in by trees and shrubbery. The only way in – and certainly the only way out – was skyward.

Roper called over Sergeant Peasgood who was talking to Price by the caravan.

'Where's the nearest road, Sergeant?'

'Not exactly a road, sir,' said Peasgood. 'But there's an old cinder track about thirty feet on the other side of the caravan. You can't see it from here. The ground sort of falls away a bit sudden over there.'

'Common land, is it?'

'No, sir. It's Henneker's farm. Like this. Mr Komarowski rented this bit from Mr Henneker.'

'Know Komarowski, did you?'

'Yes, sir. Everybody did. What you might call a bit of a character around here, he was.'

'Liked?'

'Nothing to dislike, sir,' said Peasgood. 'Help anybody. Cheerful. Nice old bloke all round. Never any trouble.'

Roper looked askance at him. 'So why did somebody take a shotgun to him?'

Peasgood looked baffled. 'I don't know, sir. I haven't got the faintest bloody idea.'

18

'Enemies?'

'Doubt it. Or if he had, they weren't from around here.'

Miss Kingsley had telephoned him, from the box in the lane, soon after he had arrived at Jackson's farmhouse, about ten past eight.

'Did you touch anything?'

'No, sir,' said Peasgood. 'I only poked my head around the door. Didn't need to do much else, I could see he was dead.'

'And what are you on now?'

'Well, I ought to go back to Mr Jackson if you don't want me here.'

'Do that,' said Roper. 'And thanks for your help. I'd like a copy of your report some time.'

'Yes, sir,' said Peasgood, and after a cursory salute, turned and struck back down between the ribbons to the lane and his car.

It was already eleven o'clock by the time Roper and Price could get back into the caravan. Komarowski, shrouded in the final indignity of a plastic body-bag, had been taken off to the mortuary, his bed-covers and several bloodstained books had been despatched to the Forensic laboratory, mud and blood samples had been scraped from the grey linoleum and now the SOCO was dusting around the sink and typewriter for fingerprints and lifting off what he found on to acetate tape.

With latex gloves stretched over their hands like another skin, Roper and Price opened drawers, cupboards, lifted what was movable and looked underneath. In a drawer under the bunk where Komarowski kept his shirts and underclothes, Roper found a couple of slim medal-presentation boxes covered in scuffed leatherette; in one, lying on a velvet pad, was a Distinguished Flying Cross. In the other some kind of wartime Polish decoration. The DFC was engraved with a date on the back: 10th September, 1940. So Komarowski had obviously spent his war in the RAF; and DFCs were not a decoration that came up with the rations as a matter of course. All the shirts in the drawer were neatly folded and in plastic bags, as if they had just come back from a laundry. In the adjacent drawer, socks and a few pullovers. And an elderly Nikon 35-millimetre camera with a lens like a small cannon strapped to its front. Roper lifted it out of the drawer, aimed it through the window and looked through its viewfinder. A distant tree-trunk leapt sharply into focus, close enough to see every pore and split in the bark. The lens was almost a foot long.

'Wonder what he used this for?'

'Birdwatching, probably,' said Price, down on his hunkers by the heap of books at the back end of the caravan against which Komarowski's head had been. He was holding out a handful of small notebooks.

Roper laid the camera on the bunk and took one from him. It was a birdwatcher's notebook. Date. Time. Location. Weather. Species. Every page was crammed with small neat writing, here and there a tiny, immaculate sketch of a head or a beak or a set of claws. Several Latin tags indicated that the late Mr Komarowski had been something of a scholar.

'And take a look at these,' said Price.

He was holding up two thick and dog-eared textbooks with the spines towards Roper. *Advanced Chemical Engineering for University Students*, he read. Volume One and Volume Two. Their author was Z. T. Komarowski. This year of publication had been 1958.

'No slouch, was he?' said Roper.

Price flipped a few pages of one. 'Guess who they're dedicated to.'

'Enid Kingsley?' hazarded Roper.

'Dead right,' said Price.

'I told you. They go back a long time together those two.'

'She seemed to take it all pretty calmly to me,' said Price.

'The hell she did,' said Roper. Enid Kingsley was

of another generation, another breed. If they ever wept they went away somewhere and did it privately.

At the door end of the bunk was a narrow wardrobe, only wide enough for clothes to be hung in end-on. One navy blue suit in a polythene cleaner's-bag. One brown leather overcoat. One Harris tweed sports jacket, vintage, and a pair of green corduroy trousers with frayed bottoms. Standing on the floor was a pair of well-worn wellingtons, one with a pair of seaman's oiled-wool socks balled into the top. A pair of stout brown walking boots. A pair of black brogues, newly soled and heeled and polished like mirrors. And a pair of binoculars – except when Roper opened the case what he pulled out was a pair of well-worn German Navy night-glasses, still faintly embossed with the Nazi eagle and swastika. War-loot and probably some more of the old man's birdwatching equipment.

All the inch marks of a man's life. And they were important because, paradoxically, Zygmunt Tadeusz Komarowski, for the moment, was more important than his murderer; who he was, what he was, where he had come from, who his friends were, and what he had been doing after he had left Miss Kingsley's house at 4.30 yesterday afternoon with the back light not working on his battered old bicycle.

And what there was about him that had sent someone up here in the dark last night to blast him out of existence with two rounds of lead-shot.

Had he not been, after all, such a harmless old man?

Chapter 3

Roper focused on the distant farmhouse with Komarowski's night-glasses. An old grey Land-Rover stood outside, and drawn up behind it was Sergeant Peasgood's white Metro. The intervening fields lay under an untrammelled white blanket, glinting here and there where it was caught by the watery sunlight. It was a lonely place up here.

Where he stood was virtually the edge of an escarpment, probably left behind by an old landslip. Some twenty precipitous feet beneath him was the cinder track to Henneker's farmhouse that Peasgood had mentioned; and some thirty feet and a few conifers behind him stood Komarowski's caravan.

It was an excellent viewpoint. In the clear crystal air, through the glasses, he watched a single scavenging crow totter clumsily down like a piece of black rag and land on the farmhouse chimney stack. With the glasses down he could scarcely make out the farmhouse.

Whoever had been up here last night would never have come this way. Barely negotiable by day, the steep incline would have been almost impossible in the dark. Before the frost and the snow there had been two days of rain and sleet and the grass would have been like a ski-run.

Behind him he heard the occasional call of one of the cadets to another come through the trees as they quartered the ground around the caravan. It was a cold job, on hands and knees despite the weather, and the most thankless task that went with coppering. In fiction they would find a particularly unique cigarette stub, or a cast-off matchbook, or a perfect size-nine footprint, but real life wasn't like that. Most villains knew the form these days. It was a rare one who left anything behind that was an instant give-away, perhaps a hair here, a fibre there, and a fingerprint or two if he was really unlucky, none of them much use without a lot of legwork and midnight oil.

He watched Peasgood shake hands with someone at the distant farmhouse door then hurry back to the Metro tugging on his gloves. A cloud of blue exhaust gouted and was snatched away in the wind.

'Super,' a voice said behind him. It was Price. Fair haired and fair skinned, his cheeks and nose were flushed with the cold.

'Found something?'

'His cash-box.'

'Empty?'

'Doesn't sound like it. The SOCO's still looking for the key. And one of the cadets has just found a hide. About a hundred yards over that way.' Price gestured with a thumb over his shoulder. 'Looks like the old boy's birdwatching place.'

'Anything in it?'

Price shrugged. 'The end of a Kodak box, a few toffee papers and about two hundred cigarette stubs – and a lot of tyre marks. Looks as if they might have been caused by a wheelchair. Found anything up here?'

'No,' said Roper. 'I was just scouting out the land. Let's go and look at that hide.'

From the outside it was a ramshackle little hut of woven branches draped strategically with flaps of green hessian as extra camouflage, and with a green tarpaulin roof to keep out the rain. Roper held aside the hessian curtain that served as a door. Inside, it smelt of earth and damp. As Price had said, the earth floor was a mosaic of trodden-in cigarette stubs. Two viewing slots, one at standing eye-level and another at a height to suit someone sitting down. Both were draped over with old net curtaining that had been dyed dark green, so that whoever was looking out could not be seen from outside. The earth floor was criss-crossed with narrow tyre marks. Several were so exactly parallel with each other and consistently about two and a half feet apart that Price was probably right about the wheelchair.

Roper came out again into the daylight. The watery sun was gone and it was starting to snow again. He looked up at the sky. It was lowering and ominously grey now for as far as the eye could see.

'Better call off the cadets for a couple of hours,' he said. 'They won't find anything in all this. Tell Sergeant Hume to drive 'em off somewhere for a cup of tea and a warm-up.'

Price went off. Roper returned to the caravan.

'Any luck?'

'Nothing that feels important,' said the SOCO. He was sitting on the pan in the cramped little box of the lavatory and jotting some notes. 'There was a fragment of red wool snagged on the top door-hinge on the way in. But according to Inspector Price the old lady who found him was wearing a red woollen scarf; so it's probably hers.'

The fragment of red wool was in a transparent plastic envelope lying on the bunk mattress. There had been nothing made of red wool in Komarowski's wardrobe or drawers. Beside it was a plain white banker's envelope, and next to that another small evidence-bag with a tiny scrap of paper in it.

'What's this piece of paper?'

'I found it in the typewriter,' said the SOCO. 'I gave the platen a turn when I was looking for dabs and that popped up. I wouldn't have kept it; except there was that envelope tucked under the typewriter.'

'Perhaps he was typing a letter just before it happened.'

'Might have been,' agreed the SOCO.

'Did he run to a waste basket?'

'Under the table. It's empty.'

'How about a cover for the typewriter?'

The grey linen typewriter cover had been fitted with a loop of tape and was hanging from a hook under the table. Neat, and out of the way, like everything else, except that pile of books up against the back bulkhead. And Komarowski, from what Roper had observed of his lifestyle so far, had not been the kind of man who would leave a typewriter uncovered unless he was using it. So he had probably been in the throes of writing a letter.

'Could he have chucked the rest of the sheet down the toilet?'

'Doubt it,' said the SOCO. 'It's good quality bond paper. There's a box of it in the cupboard under the bunk. And this is a chemical toilet. I don't reckon he'd have taken the risk of blocking it.'

Nor did Roper. Mr Komarowski had been a most orderly man. And he'd had a wastepaper bin. And maybe it wasn't even important.

Under a newly laundered drying-up cloth on the tiny draining board two inverted cups sat on saucers on a tin tray, a spoon in one saucer but not in the other. An expected visitor. Miss Kingsley, most likely. And one of them didn't take sugar.

'Where's this cash-box?'

'Here.' The SOCO reached down beside him. Presently bagged in polythene, it was a heavy grey steel affair, the sort of thing one could buy in any good stationer's. Roper shook it gently. The soft rasp of papers, the noisier clink of something metallic.

'No key?'

'I'm not even sure it's here,' said the SOCO. 'I've even had all the drawers out and looked underneath in case it was taped up somewhere. I can't think of anywhere else to look short of taking the whole place to pieces.'

Robbery somehow didn't seem a likely motive. The cash-box was still here, the binoculars, the Nikon camera with its expensive piece of glass on the front. On a shelf above the window, over the typewriter table, stood a black and chrome stereo radio-cassette-player, high-tech and pristine new. That, surely, would have gone. There was not much else to take. Apart from the typewriter, the radio and the books, Zygmunt Komarowski must have lived a very Spartan existence up here.

The little sitting-room was warm and cosy.

'And this is my brother John,' said Miss Kingsley.

Only just was Roper able to stifle the frisson of shock as the black-wigged, unkempt, elderly man in the wheelchair by the fire turned his scorched and twisted face to briefly regard him.

'Superintendent,' said the old man curtly.

'Sir,' said Roper. Kingsley's right hand, in a black leather glove, lay curled on his lap like a dead bird. Coming along here in the car, Roper, from a great distance, had recalled the name of a particular John Kingsley. Now he was certain that this man was the very one. 'And this is Chief Inspector Price, sir.'

Price, too, managed manfully to disguise whatever he felt inside.

'How do you do,' said Kingsley, brusquely. 'Sit, if you want to.'

There was a soft buzz as he tilted the joystick on the arm of his chair, and it rolled back a few inches from the fireplace to make more room.

'Would you like some tea?' asked Miss Kingsley, too brightly and too brittly.

'Bless you,' said Roper. 'Thank you.' She had aged ten years since he had left her in the lane; and the paint which she had bravely applied in the meantime did little to disguise the fact that she had had her tidy weep, alone and unobserved.

'Smoke?' asked Kingsley.

'No, sir, thank you,' said Roper. Price shook his head. Both of them watched as Kingsley clamped the packet against his knees with his black-gloved right hand

26

and deftly clawed out a cigarette with the other. He made it look like a conjuring trick.

The bright flame of the lighter brought the stretched and featureless right-hand side of Kingsley's face into all its terrible prominence. Price seemed to be having trouble finding an empty page in his pocket book. On the piano, a silver-framed photograph showed two young men in sheepskin jackets and white silk mufflers leaning raffishly against the leading edge of the wing of a wartime Hawker Hurricane. The taller of the two still bore a striking resemblance to the left-hand side of Jack Kingsley. Age had wearied him, the years condemned. It was a rough justice for doing right by your King and Country.

'Please ask whatever you have to,' said Kingsley, and again that pithy, irritable voice came out of the scarred and twisted face. 'Enid said it looked like a shotgun.'

'Yes, sir,' said Roper. 'It was.'

Kingsley closed his charcoal shadowed eyes and turned his face away towards the fire.

'You saw him yesterday, sir?'

'Yes, I did.' The cigarette glowed brighter, the hollow cheeks sank deeper. He coughed briefly and hackingly. From his good left-hand side he looked the seventy he must surely be. And for fifty of those years he must have been imprisoned in an invalid chair.

'Did he drop any hint of where he might have been going afterwards, sir? Or mention anyone he might have been meeting?'

'No,' said Kingsley. 'I thought he was going back to the caravan. He told me he had a couple of letters to type.'

'How about friends, sir? Other than you and Miss Kingsley.'

'Friends? Few. Acquaintances? Many.'

'I understand from your local bobby that Mr Komarowski was a popular man, sir.'

'He was,' said Kingsley, still with the right side of his face turned away. He sent a cylinder of ash winging

27

from his cigarette unerringly into the fire; he probably sat for most of the days doing little more than that. 'But isn't that the *secret* of being popular?' He turned his face back and smiled. 'To know everyone – and yourself to remain unknown?' The smile was cynical and hideous and the right-hand side of his mouth had no part in it. Whoever had repaired him had done a good job; but plastic surgery had been in its infancy then.

'But he was generally liked, sir?'

'Yes,' agreed Kingsley. 'He was liked. He played the buffoon. And everyone likes a buffoon, don't they? The dotty old foreigner especially.'

'Anybody dislike him?'

'Who ever knows if anybody dislikes him?' said Kingsley sourly, turning his face back to the fire. Roper wondered how he could still bear to look at fire after what it had done to him. 'I catch people looking at me sometimes. I see distaste; I can recognise distaste. Dislike is more easily hidden. Do you follow?'

Roper made no reply to that. If anyone had a God-given right to be cynical, Jack Kingsley certainly had.

'Did he have some kind of daily routine, sir? We're still trying to establish when he might have died.'

'He was like me, Superintendent. A free spirit.' It was a cruel joke. That smile again, not so bitterly cynical from this side but only wry. 'We come and go as we please. Well, almost. Early to bed, early to rise, a little birdwatching in between, a game of cribbage, a trip down to the pub – before it gets busy, of course. The usual things old men do to spin out their dotage.'

'He was fully dressed when we found him, Mr Kingsley. A red and black checked shirt, jeans and a pair of carpet slippers. Was that what he was wearing when he left here yesterday afternoon? Bar the slippers, of course?'

'Yes, I think so,' said Kingsley, having scowled about it for a moment. 'And his overcoat. An old leather thing. And his walking boots. And a scarf.'

'Did he have any valuables?'

'Anything worth stealing, you mean? Hardly.'

Roper rose as Miss Kingsley came in with four brimming white breakfast cups on a wooden tray, and took it from her while she fetched a bamboo-legged coffee table from under the window and set it down beside Kingsley's wheelchair. The sugar came the old-fashioned way, cubes and a pair of silver tongs. Miss Kingsley took hers with lemon, but no sugar.

The tea was welcome, the room a little too warm for real comfort. The windows were narrow and stone mullioned and barely adequate. The grey stone cottage had looked from the outside as if it had once been the lodge of a long-defunct manor house. Several amateur watercolours hung about the walls. The only concessions to Christmas were a few greetings cards standing on the piano.

'May I ask you how long you'd both known Mr Komarowski?' asked Roper over his tea.

'What would it be . . . ?' Kingsley frowned. 'Ten years?'

'Twelve,' said his sister, much too quickly. 'Nearer twelve.'

Price glanced up sharply. Roper, barely perceptibly, shook his head at him.

'And he was retired?' said Roper.

'Yes,' said Kingsley. 'He was some sort of chemist. Don't know the ins and outs exactly.'

'Do you know if he belonged to any expatriate organisation?'

'Yes, he did. Some Polish club up in London. He went up there once a month. Usually stayed over the weekend.'

'You don't know the address?'

'Sorry.'

If Kingsley was right, the Polish war medal that Roper had found in the drawer under the bunk was a *Virtuti Militari*. It was the Polish equivalent of the Victoria Cross. Neither of the Kingsleys knew the story of how he had won it.

'He was the kind of chap who didn't talk about that sort of thing,' said Kingsley.

'No, sir, quite,' agreed Roper, well aware now that he was talking to a man with a sizeable collection of medals of his own; and he probably wouldn't have talked about it either.

They left with Miss Kingsley's red woollen muffler in an evidence-bag, and a set and a half of sample fingerprints.

'I wonder what that little bit of kidology was about?' said Price as they settled themselves back in the warmth of the car. 'According to those textbooks, she must have known Komarowski for a hell of a sight more than twelve years.'

'Aye,' said Roper, reaching over his shoulder for his seat belt. 'She did. And her brother didn't; and perhaps she didn't want him to know about it. And still doesn't.'

'Why not?' said Price. 'It's a whole new world out here these days.'

'And perhaps they don't want to join in.' The Kingsleys were another generation, almost another species. They had handled their lives differently, and observed more stringent proprieties, and now they were too old to change.

Price switched on the windscreen wipers. They hummed protestingly for the first couple of sweeps. Outside, the snow was fast becoming a blizzard.

'Where now?' asked Price.

'Henneker's farm,' said Roper. Mr Henneker was Komarowski's landlord. He might just know something.

The tyres slithered in the snow as Price made a three-point turn in the narrow lane. It was only a quarter-mile or so back to the gate in the hedgerow. Peasgood's white Metro was parked against the verge, a red mail van behind it. As they drew closer, the bulky figure of Peasgood stepped out into the lane and flagged them down.

Roper wound down his window.

'Some post for Mr Komarowski, sir,' said Peasgood.

'Looks like a batch of processed photographs. Postman's not sure what he ought to do with it.'

The postman came up beside Peasgood. 'I normally dump his mail behind the gate,' he said. 'But he always likes his photographs dropped off at the caravan. If he's not in I usually leave them underneath, near the steps.'

'Can I see the packet?'

The postman passed it in through the window. It was postmarked in Chiswick, West London, the day before yesterday. It had been self-addressed in the same neat handwriting that Roper had seen in Komarowski's notebook.

'What happens if I open this?'

'I get into a lot of trouble,' said the postman. 'Unless I drop it over the gate first.'

'Do that,' said Roper.

A brief pantomime ensued as the postman took back the packet and dropped it over the gate. Peasgood retrieved it and brought it back to Roper in the car.

Roper slit it open. Glossy prints. Seven by fives. All of birds. Two prints from each negative; perhaps one set for Komarowski, the other for Kingsley, for it could only have been Kingsley's wheelchair that had left those tyremarks up at the hide. They were excellent photographs, almost professional, perfectly exposed, perfectly printed. And totally irrelevant to the matter at hand.

31

Chapter 4

Roper, Price and Sergeant Peasgood stood huddled under Henneker's porch. The falling snow had reduced visibility to a few yards.

'What's his other name?' asked Roper.

'Austen, sir,' said Peasgood. 'Austen Henneker.' He lifted his gloved hand and slammed the door knocker again.

'All right, all right!' someone bellowed from deep within the house. 'I'm bloody coming!'

'And not a moment too bloody soon,' Price muttered into his upturned raincoat collar, stamping his feet. 'We're freezing to death out here.'

'Get in there!' the same voice shouted. A door slammed. A dog barked.

Rubbery footfalls approached the door from the other side, and it was snatched open impatiently. The man's boozy, irritable face relaxed slightly. His black hair was awry and he had still to shave. His already substantial bulk was made larger still by the several baggy old pullovers he wore over a faded khaki shirt with a frayed collar.

'Oh,' he grumbled. 'It's you again.' Thus far, he had only addressed the uniformed Peasgood. His slightly out of focus eyes swivelled to Roper, then Price. 'Who are you? The heavy mob?'

'County CID, Mr Henneker,' said Roper, flipping open the holder and showing his warrant-card. Henneker took it and looked at it blearily before handing it back again. Roper thought he could smell whisky on him.

'I've already told Peasgood,' growled Henneker. 'If Jackson can't look after his bleeding sheep that's his own bloody fault. I don't know anything about the bloody things. OK?'

'We're not here about Mr Jackson's sheep, Mr Henneker,' said Roper, tucking the card back inside his overcoat. 'We're making routine enquiries into the death of Mr Komarowski. Wondered if you might be able to help us.'

Henneker's face clouded. 'I don't know about that, either. I told Peasgood that an' all.'

'Perhaps we could step inside, sir. Just for a couple of minutes.'

For a moment it looked as if Henneker was going to be difficult; but only for a moment. Then he stood aside, grudgingly, and made room for them to pass him in the dark narrow passage. An outstretched hand pointed towards the scullery at the back of the house. Roper passed the door of a room on the left that still had its curtains closed. The house felt chill and smelt musty. There was no woman here. Too sparse, too much dust, not enough light. There might have been a woman once, but she was long gone.

Behind a door on the right a dog growled and clawed at the woodwork.

'Quiet!' shouted Henneker. The growl dropped to a whine.

Roper stepped down into the scullery. A faint warmth came from a lit gas oven with a greasy hob. Several days' crockery heaped in the china sink. Crumbs on the uneven quarry-tiled floor. Grubby net curtain over the window above the sink. Fly-specked parchment lampshade over the deal table. And a half-empty whisky bottle and a used glass on the dresser.

'Take a pew if you're staying,' said Henneker.

Roper pulled an old kitchen chair from under the table and tipped it to dislodge some breadcrumbs from the seat. Until that previous spring Roper had lived alone all his life; but never like this. Price sat opposite, Peasgood at the end of the table near the door, clearing a small space of more crumbs and débris in order to lay his cap down.

'Can I get you something?' asked Henneker slurrily. He probably meant whisky. There was only one teacup in evidence; and that was dirty.

'No, sir, thank you,' said Roper.

Henneker looked disappointed. He sprawled himself down on the chair at the opposite end of the table from Peasgood. His wellington boots were crusted with mud. He made no move to take them off, merely observed them.

'So what do you want to know?' he asked, looking up. The boots, like the pile of crockery in the china sink, were clearly something else he could put off until tomorrow. His voice was gravelly, or perhaps it was simply thick with drink.

'You were Mr Komarowski's landlord, sir,' said Roper.

It took a moment for Henneker to work out if that was a question or not.

'Yes,' he said. 'I am . . . was. But I minded my business and he minded his.'

'He paid you rent?'

'Peppercorn,' said Henneker. 'Ten pounds a year. My old man made the arrangement with him.'

He spoke as if the arrangement displeased him.

'Your old man?'

'Aye,' growled Henneker. 'My father. He ran this place then. Dead now.'

Henneker looked somewhere in his middle fifties. Florid faced, heavily built, the fine veins of his nose already breaking up. A thick gold wedding ring on the third hairy, stubby finger of his left hand.

'Since when?' asked Roper. 'This arrangement.'

Henneker's forehead corrugated. 'Six . . . seven years.'

'No trouble?'

'Like I said: he minded his business, and I minded mine. We didn't bother each other much.' He paused.

'Mind you, I did see the sun shining on those binoculars of his sometimes when he was looking this way. Can't say I cared for that all that much, mind. And he was a funny old bugger.'

'Funny?' said Roper.

'Well,' growled Henneker, 'living up there all on his own, like, in that bug-hutch. A man needs space to breathe, don't he? It's sardines that go in little tin cans, not men.'

'You thought he was spying on you, Mr Henneker?' asked Price.

'That's not what I said,' growled Henneker. 'I just didn't like the idea that he might be, that's all.'

'Did you hear anything last night, Mr Henneker?' asked Roper.

'Can't say I did; can't say I didn't. Didn't hear a shotgun, if that's what you're asking.'

'You knew about the shotgun?'

'Aye,' said Henneker. 'Sergeant Peasgood here told me when he came earlier about Jackson's sheep. First one he came to, I was.' He looked balefully along the table at Peasgood. 'Thought I was getting my own back on Jackson for stealing mine. Ain't that right?'

'Yours weren't stolen,' said Peasgood. 'They wandered because you hadn't shut a gate.'

'You've only got Jackson's word for that,' said Henneker.

But Roper, at the moment, was not concerned with what was clearly a long-term feud between a couple of farmers.

'When did you last see Mr Komarowski alive, Mr Henneker?' he broke in.

'Yesterday – afternoon. About two o'clock. Might have been after. Saw him turning into the Kingsleys' place on his bike. He usually went along there in the afternoons . . . Regular thing, it was. Thick together, they were. Him and the Kingsleys.'

Again he sounded grudging, as if he didn't like the Kingsleys much either.

'Did you see any lights burning in the caravan last night?' asked Roper.

'I wasn't looking,' said Henneker. 'No reason.'

'Some background, Mr Henneker,' said Roper, changing tack for a moment as Henneker took a thirsty furtive glance towards the whisky bottle on the dresser. There was another bottle, empty, Roper saw, sticking out of the chockful waste bin under the sink. Mr Henneker was clearly a dedicated drinker. 'This arrangement of Mr Komarowski's and your father's; in writing, was it?'

'Aye,' said Henneker. 'The old man signed a contract with him. Ten quid a year; fixed rent. He was a war-hero, see. The old man thought he owed him. Buddies, they were, him and the old man.'

'How did the caravan get up there?'

'Crane,' said Henneker. 'We had a crane in to build one of the barns. They used that. Bloody performance it was an' all. The old man paid for that too. Silly old sod.'

It was obvious that the friendship between Komarowski and Henneker's father had not rubbed off on to the son; and he was taking no pains to hide the fact.

'Your father's been dead how long?'

'Three years,' said Henneker.

And it looked as if the farmhouse had been left to go derelict ever since. Back along the passage the dog had started to whine louder and claw at the door again.

'When you saw Mr Komarowski yesterday afternoon, did you speak to him?'

'I was in the Land-Rover,' said Henneker. 'I only saw his back.'

'Do you know if he was worried about anything?'

Henneker shrugged. 'I wouldn't know,' he said.

'Did you ever see anybody up there with him?'

'Enid Kingsley, her brother. Old Stan Rydz.'

'Ritz, like the hotel?' asked Price.

No, it was spelled with a 'y' and a 'd'. Rydz was another Pole. A pig farmer, over in Lower Gorton.

36

'Nobody else?'

Henneker shrugged dispassionately again. 'They might have done,' he said. 'I wouldn't know for sure, would I?'

Roper stifled his impatience with difficulty. So far as he was concerned, ignorance was one thing, stonewalling another. He wasn't overly keen on Austen Henneker.

'Perhaps you ought to tell Mr Roper about your bit of business, Mr Henneker.' This contribution came unexpectedly from Sergeant Peasgood.

'My business is me own,' said Henneker tartly. 'Besides, it's got no bearing.'

'What is this business exactly, Mr Henneker?' asked Roper, having noticed how sharply Henneker had shot an irritated glance along the table at Peasgood.

Henneker made no response.

'Mr Henneker's selling up,' said Peasgood, speaking for him.

'Retiring, are you, sir?' asked Roper.

'Aye,' grumbled Henneker. 'Had enough. It's not all fun these days, trying to run a farm.'

'Did Mr Komarowski *know* you were selling up?' asked Roper.

'I wrote him,' said Henneker. 'My solicitor did. Offered to buy him off. But the old bugger still hadn't replied . . . And he won't now, will he?'

'So you *were* trying to get rid of him, Mr Henneker?'

Henneker's lip curled. 'Not like that, I wasn't. I wasn't trying to *run* him off. There'll be a copy of the letter over at my solicitor's. You can look if you bloody want. Can't sell a place with a bloke playing gypsies on it, can you?'

'Had he told you he wouldn't go?'

'Didn't say yes, didn't say no. Just said he'd think about it.'

'I see,' said Roper. 'Was he prevaricating in writing?'

'Told you,' said Henneker. 'He still hadn't put it in writing. That's what I was waiting for.'

'But you'd spoken with him.'

37

'Aye,' said Henneker. 'And he said he'd got the letter and he'd like a couple of weeks to think about it. I told him it could wait till after Christmas.'

Well, it was a motive of sorts. On a couple of occasions Roper had come across men who had been murdered for a sight less than sixty square feet of useless land in the middle of nowhere . . .

'Do you own a shotgun, sir?' asked Price.

'Aye,' growled Henneker. 'Two. What about 'em?'

'Can we see them, Mr Henneker?' asked Roper.

Henneker glowered at him. 'I've got a permit,' he said. 'Ask Peasgood.'

Roper waited in silence. Then, reluctantly, Henneker shoved his chair back, levered himself out of it and clomped off into the passage. 'Shut up!' he shouted again, and hammered on the door as he passed the room where the dog was.

'Bit of a charmer,' observed Roper, as Henneker went on upstairs out of earshot.

'He's had a bad time, sir,' muttered Peasgood. 'His missus and his lad walked out on him about a year ago. They're both shacked up with the wife's boyfriend along the way a bit. The lad used to help him out here. It left him short-handed.'

'I see he's on the bottle.'

'That's new,' muttered Peasgood. 'The last six months or so. He didn't used to be like that before.'

'Behave himself, does he?'

'Had a bit of trouble with him about a month ago. Banging on the wife's boyfriend's door at three o'clock in the morning. I had to go along and sort him out for 'em. He'd about kicked the door in by the time I got there.'

'Drunk?'

'*And* the rest,' said Peasgood. 'I had to put the irons on him to get him in the car.'

'Charged, was he?'

'Bound over on the promise of good behaviour.'

'Nothing since?'

Peasgood shook his head as the clomping footfalls sounded across the landing and started back down the stairs.

Henneker came in with the two shotguns. One was an elderly twin-barrelled weapon with a break action, the other almost new with a bolt-action, single barrelled. Both were twelve-bore. One of the barrels of the twin had been choked down to provide a narrower spread of shot. Both were well kept, smelt of gun oil.

'What shot do you use?' asked Roper, apparently disinterestedly, sliding back the bolt of the single-shot and slipping his thumbnail in the breech and looking down the barrel; and hoping that Henneker subscribed to the myth that a keen nose could detect whether a gun had been fired in the last twenty-four hours or not.

'Eley Alphamax,' said Henneker. 'And I haven't used either of 'em since last week. So you can sniff all you bloody want.' Roper broke open the twin and looked up both barrels, and put his nose to the breeches. Henneker took them back and laid both amongst the litter on the dresser. Then clomped back and dropped on his chair again.

'What were you doing last night, Mr Henneker?'

'I was here.'

'Alone?'

'Aye,' said Henneker.

'And you didn't see or hear anything?'

'I wouldn't have, would I?' There was almost a sneer in Henneker's voice. 'I was sparked out most likely. Doors shut, windows shut. Like I say, I mind my own bloody business.'

He saw them out as sullenly as he had seen them in.

'What did you make of him?' asked Roper, as he and Price settled themselves in the car. Behind them Peasgood was getting into his. The only piece of ground for miles that didn't have a coating of snow was the few square yards under Henneker's Land-Rover.

'Didn't like him much,' said Price. 'Easy to see why his wife did a runner on him. Didn't seem exactly inclined to help, either, did he?'

'Well, he didn't get on with Z. T. Komarowski,' said Roper. 'And that's for certain.' In the rear-view mirror he watched the white Metro back away, turn, and head off towards the cinder track throwing up two wakes of dirty snow that were blown sideways on the wind.

'Be interesting to see what the ballistics man comes up with,' said Price, as he sorted out the ignition key.

'Shotguns are common enough,' said Roper. But he knew what Price was thinking because his own mind was running on a similar track. The problem would be proving it. But malice was there. He was sure of that, and that was certainly a start.

'This snow's a bit of a bugger,' observed the Assistant Chief Constable (Crime), sourly, from under his umbrella.

'Yes, sir,' agreed Roper.

The two of them stood surveying the yellow caravan. The wind, mercifully, had dropped at last. There was only the snow now.

'Can't work from here,' said the ACC.

'I thought the MIC, sir. Up in the village.'

'Yes. Right.' The ACC was a man of few words, and expected those about him to be similarly economical. 'What's your strength?'

'Price. Ten cadets under Sergeant Hume. DS Makins'll be here tomorrow.'

The ACC sucked on his teeth. 'Not enough. Long way from A to B around here. Door to doors'll take for bloody ever. How many bodies, d'you think?'

'Six men. Four cars.'

'Good. Right.' With a military flourish the ACC shot his cuffs to see his glittering space-age wristwatch. 'It'll all be here by three o'clock. What's next on your agenda?'

'Another Pole, sir. A Mr Rydz.'

'Good. Right.'

The ACC turned away and started back down the track between the red and white ribbons. Roper fell in behind him.

They reached the gate to the lane.

The ACC peered up at the sky, as if he was about to prophesy a change in the weather. 'Hope you haven't arranged a heavy Christmas schedule, Douglas.' His pinched narrow face smiled coyly; he had always been an uneasy man when it came to a joke. 'Crack it, will you? Finish the year with a bang?'

Roper smiled back. 'That's an order, is it, sir?'

'Like to see you do it, Douglas. Really. Show the young 'uns. Eh?' For a moment, the ACC showed something that approximated, very roughly, to emotion. 'Life in us old dogs yet.'

'Yes, sir,' said Roper solemnly. The ACC was still a stripling forty-four.

'Good. Right.' The ACC took the few paces to his car, briskly collapsed his umbrella and shook the snow off it. He said something else, it might have been 'good luck', but the words were lost in the slam of the car door.

There was a roar, a puff of blue exhaust, a hand waved curtly.

'There was snow on his overcoat,' remarked Price, coming up at Roper's shoulder, as the ACC's white Jaguar receded down the lane.

'What about it?' asked Roper.

Price sniffed. 'Nothing,' he said. 'Means he must have stood still for a couple of seconds to let it settle, that's all. Doesn't often do that, does he?'

Chapter 5

Roper stretched the map flatter on his knees, traced the narrow road with a forefinger, then peered out past the sloshing windscreen wipers. As the ACC had said, from A to B around here was a damned long way. This was Lower Gorton, although there was little to distinguish it from Upper Gorton except a signpost half a mile back down the road, and that had been almost illegible under a dusting of snow.

'This one,' said Roper. 'Coming up on the left.' On the map on his knees, Peasgood had circled Rydz's bungalow with a red ballpoint. Rydz was a pig farmer, and a successful one if the smart white bungalow beyond the hedge was anything to go by.

Price stopped the car in the bell-mouthed layby in front of the wrought-iron double gates. Some thirty yards of drive led up to the porched front door. An illuminated Christmas tree stood in the right-hand front window.

A woman answered Price's ring at the doorbell. A tall, close-cropped blonde, thirty-fiveish, with broad Slavic cheekbones.

'Yes?'

'Superintendent Roper, madam, County CID.' Roper held out his card. 'We're making enquiries into the death of Mr Komarowski. We rang earlier.'

Her face fell. 'Oh, yes,' she said glumly. 'You'll want my dad. You'd better come in.'

They stamped the snow from their shoes. The passage was warm.

'He's in the office,' she said, leading the way towards the back of the bungalow. 'You'll find him a bit shattered. He's taken it badly, poor old guy.'

She stopped at a half-open door on the right, and rapped on it before going in.

'It's the police, Dad,' Roper heard her say softly. 'They've come about Ziggy. Do you want to see them in here?'

A chair creaked. 'Yes,' a tired voice said. 'Better in here. You get another chair, eh?'

'I'll get one.' Rydz's daughter opened the door wider for them. 'Please go in,' she said.

The mountainous figure of Rydz rose from behind his battered old desk as they entered. The curtains were closed, all bar an inch or so, so that the room was in semi-darkness. In the old man's hand was what looked like a balled-up white handkerchief.

'I am Rydz,' he said in a voice choked with emotion. 'Please . . . ' He gestured towards a wooden chair. 'My daughter is bringing other chair. You like some coffee?'

'No, sir, thank you,' said Roper. 'I apologise for troubling you. The name's Roper, sir. Superintendent, County CID. And this is Chief Inspector Price.' Roper proffered his card; the old man brusquely waved it away. The handkerchief was stuffed out of sight in a trouser pocket. With another gesture at the solitary chair on the other side of the desk, Rydz subsided into his own.

'Why?' he said, with a dry catch in his voice. 'Why somebody *do* this? He was old man like me. Never do any harm to *nobody*.'

'Don't know, sir,' said Roper. 'But we're doing our best to find out.' He sat down on the solitary chair as Rydz's daughter came in with a dining chair for Price.

'Shall I open the curtains, Dad?' she said.

Rydz flapped a weary hand as if he didn't care one way or the other and screwed up his eyes as the stark white daylight poured in. Like Henneker, he hadn't shaved this morning. And, like his daughter, he had

43

a big-boned Slavic face and big white Slavic teeth. He could not have been far off seventy himself, but was still vigorous and bursting with life. The hands he clasped tightly together on his desktop looked as if they had done a lifetime of work. His eyes were bloodshot, his sparse grey hair uncombed.

'He was good man,' he said bitterly. 'I tell anybody who ask. I tell *you*.'

'When did you last see him, Mr Rydz?' asked Roper.

The old man considered, the front of one thumb absently massaging the back of the other. 'Yesterday. Morning. 'Bout ten o'clock. He drop in for beer. And chess move.' He nodded disconsolately towards a chessboard set up on a rickety old circular table in the corner beside the window. 'Is a game we never finish, that one. I was winning, too. Today I was going to take his king's bishop. For two years I never win. Now . . . ' He shrugged massively and sadly. His grey shirt was unbuttoned to the waist. He had an expanse of chest like an all-in wrestler. It was difficult to imagine him weeping; but he surely had been.

'What did he talk about, Mr Rydz? D'you remember?'

'Same as old men always talk about. The old days. Politics. The war. The price of pigs. Bloddy gov'ments. Nothing special. Except we do it in Polish.' He seemed to drift away dispiritedly. 'I only got old Zygmunt to talk Polish to any more. The missus is gone too now. Just my daughter – but all she speak in Polish is yes and no and t'ank you very much. Brought up English, see. She and her husband got two kids – they don't know where Poland is, even.'

'He didn't mention any trouble he might have had with somebody?'

Rydz scowled.

'Somebody who want to shoot him? Ach, nobody. Me, I got enemies; but Zygmunt? Never on your bloddy *life*. It was somebody breaking into caravan, I bet. Some hooligan kid with a gun.'

Roper forebore to dispute the illogicality of that. He waited for Rydz's moment of anger to subside. The desk was a muddle of papers. On the wall behind it hung a brass and copper ikon. Over the curly grey hairs on Rydz's chest dangled a silver crucifix, and there was another cross, a carved wooden one, standing on the mantelshelf.

'Did he have any kind of routine, Mr Rydz?' asked Price. 'Something that would help us to fix the time?'

'He was free agent. He go to bed early and get up early. Watch his birds with Mr Kingsley. Talk a lot. Drink a bit.'

'You say he went to bed early, Mr Rydz,' broke in Roper. Kingsley had mentioned that too. 'What sort of time would that be?'

'He come along at nights sometimes. And always at ten o'clock he get on his bicycle and—' Rydz's two clenched ham-like fists pedalled at the air.

There was a sound of a car pulling up outside, the slam of doors, the excited chatter of children.

'Is Christmas,' said Rydz nostalgically, peering sadly from under eyebrows that were like two grey ferrets. 'For kids, sir, yes? Not for killing though, eh?'

'No, sir,' agreed Roper. Tragedy was like a stone tossed into the sea; nobody ever knew where the last outward ripple would reach. It had certainly lapped as far as the godly Stanislaus Rydz.

'And this is aeroplane,' said Rydz proudly. His tatty old scrapbook was out and a thick stubby forefinger stabbed at the ancient newspaper cutting that looked as if it had spent many years folded in a wallet before ever going into the scrapbook. 'Is P37 – from Second Air Regiment. Warsaw. Ziggy was only Cadet-Pilot. He never even fly a bomber before. Not ever. And we don't even got a map.'

The creased and yellowed clipping showed a gimcrack, antiquated, twin-engined bomber with the chequered insignia of the pre-war Polish Air Force on the tail fin.

45

The locale was the edge of a pine forest, the caption in Swedish. The date-line above was the 16th of September 1939. The two smiling young men standing triumphantly beside it, albeit flanked by two armed Swedish guards, were Komarowski and Rydz. By mid-October of the same year, both had arrived in England and had joined the RAF, Komarowski to fly Hawker Hurricanes and Rydz to work as an engine fitter. They had both finished up in the same squadron.

'Is a long time to know somebody,' said Rydz wistfully.

'Yes, sir,' agreed Roper sympathetically. 'It certainly is.'

They had parted company after the war, Rydz to open a garage in North Wales and Komarowski to study up in London at the Polish University.

'He was chemical engineer,' said Rydz. 'Degrees and everything. Got it—' he tapped his temple '—in here. Brains. Not like me. He writes books even. Me, I don't even write a proper letter – except in Polish.

'Then, one day – 'bout ten, twelve years ago – I am in Dorchester. I only buy this place, two, three days before, so I'm new here, see? And there in street is Ziggy. With Enid. Although I do not know at first it is her. Only Ziggy I recognise. We embrace. We cry a little. We do not see each other in t'irty-five years, but *still* we know each other. Then we go for lunch together. Get very drunk. It was like a miracle. From God. You understand?'

'This lady . . . ' said Roper.

'Was *Miss Kingsley*,' said Rydz. 'She was ferry pilot during war. She fly in new Spitfire from factory one day, meet Ziggy in officers' mess – and whoosh! It is big romance.' He shrugged dolefully and hugely. 'But when I see them in Dorchester she is still *Miss* Kingsley. It was her brother, see. He got burned up. She have to look after him. Still does. Bloddy sad.'

'How come he chose to live in that caravan, Mr Rydz?' asked Price.

'Ach, with money old Ziggy is *not* so clever. He buy

46

shares for his old age. I tell him pigs are safer – you can't eat shares, I tell him. Shares go—' Rydz lifted his right hand and swooped it down, 'and Ziggy go broke. I say come and live here with me, but *he* won't do that. Bloddy independent, see. Then Neville Henneker tell him he can have that bit of no-good land 'long there on his farm; ten pounds a year for life. So old Ziggy moves in there with his caravan. He say he don't need more than that. He got his birds, his books and some place to sleep. And from time to time he do a little bit of work for somebody – chemistry work. Bring in a few shillin', so he don't go short.'

'Get on all right with Mr Henneker's son, Austen, did he?' asked Roper.

Rydz's lip curled. 'Ach, that Austen Henneker. He no good. Don't like work. His son and missus live over there a bit.' Rydz jerked a stubby thumb towards the window. His two grandchildren, a boy and a girl, were out there now playing snowballs. 'She got fed up, his old woman. Took up with another man. The son went with her. The Jackson's place. Big spread Jackson's got. Plenty money, too.' Rydz rubbed finger and thumb together in the age-old gesture of the market place. 'Mrs Henneker, she wear smart clothes these days; and young Trevor Henneker, Jackson made him farm manager.'

'But there was no quarrel between Austen Henneker and Mr Komarowski?' Roper repeated patiently.

'I don't think so,' said Rydz. 'I know Ziggy was worried about Henneker selling up. He get a letter from solicitor couple o' weeks back saying how Henneker'd pay two t'ousand if Ziggy'd move out. I told him to take the money and come along here with me so we can talk a lot of Polish. But all he'd say was he'd think about it. He was upset, see; 'cos the contract with Neville Henneker was for life, see? And what the hell . . . Didn't have all that much longer life left, did he? Ten years? And then some *bastard* goes shoot him, so he don't even got five *minutes*.'

The old man's eyes lit angrily. Roper waited for him to calm down again.

'We think he might have been writing a letter when it happened, Mr Rydz,' said Roper. 'Any ideas?'

'Letters?' Rydz, clearly a man of mercurial emotions, flung out both arms wide. 'Ach! He was always writing bloddy letters! Buckin'ham Palace, the Prime Minister, the newspapers, the local bloddy council even. He was very environmental, was Ziggy. Mad on environmental. Anybody even chop down a tree an' old Ziggy'd be writing a letter to *somebody*.'

'A bit of a conservationist, was he?'

'A bit!' Rydz stared back at Roper as if he suspected him of unwarrantable irony. 'He was *crazy* conservationist!' Then, for a few moments, the old man's emotions seemed to overwhelm him. He sat back in his old swivel chair, a great hairy hand gripping the carved end of each arm, and his eyes shining. He looked carved himself, huge and monumental; and perhaps even immortal.

'Sir,' he said gravely to Roper. 'And you, sir,' to Price, before fixing Roper again with his moist grey eyes. 'You find who kill old Ziggy. I make reward – two, t'ree thousand pounds. You tell everyone that. An' I tell you, I *love* that man.' A clenched fist was laid with awesome solemnity over the silver crucifix on his chest. 'An' this I tell to God, too; if *I* find the bastard first, you only get what's left; maybe an arm or a leg, or a few fingers. Or maybe—' a finger and thumb snapped together like a pistol-shot '—I don't even let you have *that* much. And afterwards I see priest; then I come along and you do what you like with me. Eh?'

And the old man meant it; every passionate word.

The ACC was also a man of his word. By half-past two in the afternoon the big white mobile incident-centre was drawn up on the village green at Upper Gorton. By a quarter to three it had been taped off, by ten to its generator was quietly puttering and by five to the telephones were being connected to the nearest pole. By half-past three it was fully operational and the uniformed sergeant, whose pride and joy the vehicle was, was able to bring Roper a freshly brewed cup of tea from the galley.

The Formica-lined office, little more than a cubicle, was almost as cramped as Komarowski's caravan, but it was bright and warm and air-conditioned and there was everything on the van from a first-aid box to a micro-computer. The door-to-door enquiries were well under way, and Price had driven off to see what he could find out from the priest to whom both Komarowski and Rydz made their weekly confessions.

After the tea Roper drove back to the scene of last night's crime.

'How goes it?' he asked the SOCO, in the caravan.

'Just wrapping up.' The SOCO was perched back on the lavatory again, and making notes of the odds and ends he was taking away with him. 'Anything new at your end?'

'Not a lot,' said Roper, looking around. 'He was a decent enough bloke by the sounds of it. How about these?' He had idly picked up the packet of photographs that had arrived that morning and that was lying on the bunk.

'No use to me,' said the SOCO. 'Do what you like with 'em.'

'Any film in that camera, was there?'

'It was empty,' said the SOCO.

At four o'clock Roper was sitting on Komarowski's only movable chair between the bunk and the folding table, looking at the chalked outline on the lino and trying to get the feel of what might have happened in here last night. Outside, the darkness was gathering and what little light was left seemed to flow upwards from the snow, pale and artificial. An occasional breeze made the open door flap gently against the outside cladding. There was a small petrol-driven battery-charger outside. Nobody had been able to make it work. Another secret that had died with Komarowski.

There had been violence wreaked in here last night. You could feel it, even if you hadn't heard about it, or hadn't seen it. You could feel it in the cold oppressive air and the occasional desultory flap of the door.

Someone had called here last night, perhaps with the intent to kill; or perhaps the intent had come later. At some time after half-past four, after Komarowski had cycled back from the Kingsleys'. The bunk had been made up when Roper had seen it this morning, and Komarowski fully dressed. Ergo: the old man had been killed at some time between, say, 4.45 yesterday afternoon and perhaps some time around midnight – since both the Kingsleys and Rydz had said that Komarowski was early to bed and early to rise. And when Wilson had arrived this morning the caravan was like a sweat-box, so the gas cooker must have been alight all night, which was further evidence, surely, that the shooting must have been perpetrated last night; the other alternative, that it had all happened in the few hours before daybreak, could be dismissed. Komarowski wouldn't have been up *and dressed*, much before six o'clock. And it had certainly snowed by then – 2.30 a.m., according to the local Met station; and whoever it was would have blazed a trail of footprints, even if they had been later smudged by more snow. And there was still that cooker. No man could have slept comfortably in all that heat. So it had to have happened last night. Some time.

Komarowski would have been in here, perhaps sitting where Roper was now, perhaps at the typewriter. The door would have been shut. A knock with gloved knuckles; he – she – would have been unlikely to have known about that spare key. Komarowski might even have been expecting whoever the caller had been, and let him – or her – in without suspecting anything was amiss. Anybody with sense would have worn an overcoat last night; a shotgun was easily hidden under an overcoat. There wasn't a lot of room to wave a shotgun about in here, and Wilson had said that that stomach shot had

50

been fired from a distance of a couple of feet. So even if the killer had been standing near the door, in front of the lavatory, say, Komarowski would have to have been halfway along the caravan. Roughly beside the folding table; and there had been a bloody handprint on that table. Perhaps Komarowski had even made a grab for the gun as his assailant had squeezed the first trigger and taken a lot of the shot through his hand.

At that range it would have blown him off his feet. Hurled him back against the rear bulkhead before he had subsided to the floor.

Then had come the second shot; the one that made certain. A first shot was sometimes an accident. A second one never was.

Despite his overcoat Roper shivered in the dark. The caravan now was as chill and depressing as an empty house.

'Cup of tea, sir?' a youthful voice said. It was one of the cadets, standing at the foot of the steps, a capped black shadow sharply delineated against the snow. He was holding the steaming cup from the top of his vacuum flask.

'No, thanks, son,' said Roper. 'You'll need that yourself.' This lad and four others would be keeping an eye on the caravan overnight; one hour on and four hours off, and cat-napping as best they could in the MIC. It wasn't the best way to spend the night before Christmas Eve. 'Appreciate the offer, though.' He got up from the chair, ducked as he felt the top of his hair brush the ceiling; Komarowski had been only about five feet eight; Roper himself could have lived in here only with his neck permanently bent.

He ducked under the door-frame into the brighter dark outside. It was a crystal-clear evening, already pricked with stars, and the merest sickle of a new moon low down on the horizon. The temperature was likely to drop to minus-ten by midnight, so the forecasters had threatened. At the foot of the steps he closed the caravan door and made sure the catch had worked. At midday

51

tomorrow the vehicle was being winched out and taken away to the laboratory for more tests.

'Radio working all right, laddie?'

'Yes, sir,' said the cadet.

'Call in every fifteen minutes. Anybody comes up here, or anywhere near, I want to know.'

'Yes, sir.' He was only a boy. Nineteen. He might just have been pushing twenty.

'And keep on the move, son. I don't want a sick-note from your mother telling me your feet have dropped off. Right?'

The cadet, flask in one hand and cup in the other, and not quite sure what to do with either, forebore to smile. 'Yes, sir,' he said.

'Good,' said Roper, and turned away and trudged back in the eerie half-dark with his shoulders hunched against the cold.

Price was back. Komarowski's priest had assured him that the only sin the old Pole had occasionally committed was to vent his spleen upon the authorities. A polluted stream, a long-stagnant pool, poison laid down with too little consideration for creatures other than the vermin to which it had been directed. These had been Komarowski's hobby-horses. He was an active member of the church and occasionally stood in when the organist was sick or away on holiday; he played uncommonly well. Mr Komarowski had clearly been a man of many talents. Last week, dressed as Santa Claus, he had supervised the bran-tub at the Sunday-school Christmas party.

'Mr Clean, then,' said Roper.

'Everybody seems to think so,' said Price.

The door-to-door men started to drift back in twos and threes in the darkness round about six o'clock. Of the two hundred or so inhabitants of Upper and Lower Gorton, there had been few who had not been at least on nodding acquaintance with Z. T. Komarowski. The general consensus of opinion seemed to be that he was

52

slightly crazy, good for a laugh and the soul of charity. The emotion generally roused by his passing was a corporate dismay; quickly followed by a corporate anger. Two farmers, other than Rydz, had offered further modest sums towards a reward for the detection of his killer.

'Why?' asked Roper, who, over many years, had learned to be suspicious of even the least base of human motives.

'He did jobs for 'em, sir,' said the uniformed sergeant sitting on the other side of the desk, a mug of tea in one hand and his pocket book in the other. 'Investigations, mostly. He was a chemist, sir.'

'What sort of investigations?'

'Pollution problems, sir. A fouled-up water course. Komarowski sorted it out for 'em. With Mr Carslake.'

'Carslake?'

'He's the local vet, sir. Him and Mr Komarowski solved it together. Someone had dumped a sack of nitrate upstream.'

'Did you have words with this Carslake?'

'No, sir. But I dropped a note through his letter-box. Asked him to call in here some time.'

'Bully,' said Roper. 'Thanks.' Carslake could be useful.

By seven o'clock he had spoken with all the knockers-on-doors. Most of the information was innocuously routine. Several people had seen Komarowski about Upper Gorton on his bicycle yesterday. He had bought a lemon, a pound of Brussels sprouts and four pounds of potatoes in the greengrocer's at lunchtime. In the newsagent's he had settled his last week's newspaper bill and bought sixty Disque Bleu cigarettes and an aerosol of gas for his lighter. In the pub on the other side of the green, the Gorton Arms, at a quarter to two, he had bought two cans of Guinness, as he did every day. According to the Arms' landlord, these were to take along to the Kingsleys' to be shared with the Squadron Leader over a game of chess.

There had, however, been one sighting of Komarowski *after* he had left the Kingsleys' cottage. A Mrs Brake had

53

seen him posting a letter, up here in the village, at – she was guessing, but doubted she was more than five minutes out either way – five-fifteen yesterday evening. She had noticed the incident particularly because the mail van was already there and Komarowski had only just caught the last collection of the day.

Wilson rang at seven-thirty. He had completed the autopsy on Komarowski. From the shot he had recovered, he was able to estimate that there had been roughly 2400 pellets to the ounce, and that each pellet was 0.05 inches in diameter. He had also recovered two felt cartridge wads from Komarowski's stomach and chest. From which evidence, according to the firearms expert at the Forensic laboratory, the shotgun had been a twelve-bore, and it was logical to suppose that it had been twin-barrelled. Which did not help all that much. Twelve-bores were in common use, especially around here with so many farms and so much woodland.

'How about time of death?' asked Roper.

'Estimate only, I'm afraid, Douglas,' said Wilson. 'Between about six o'clock yesterday evening and one o'clock this morning.'

'Can't get closer?'

'Sorry,' said Wilson. 'And I found a couple of keys, if you're interested. One's a Yale, and the other one might be a key to a desk or something.'

'Like a cash-box?'

'Could be,' agreed Wilson.

'Odd, that,' said Roper, frowning. 'The SOCO went through all the old boy's pockets before they carted him off. They were empty.'

'He must have been carrying them in his *shirt* pocket,' said Wilson. 'They'd been blasted straight between his ribs by that chest shot. Pure fluke.'

Roper grimaced. It was late, and he hadn't eaten all day.

'Nothing else to tell me?'

'Sorry,' said Wilson.

Chapter 6

The office door was shut. Beside him on the desk were two cheese and pickle rolls from the Gorton Arms, one half-eaten. It was half-past eight.

'I could be late, old love,' he said, into the telephone. 'Sorry.'

'It's all right,' she said stoically. 'I'll probably wait up. There's a late film on the box. Have you eaten?'

He eyed with repugnance the half-eaten roll peeking out of the paper bag. There were times in this job when he was past eating. 'Yes,' he lied. 'I've eaten.' If he hadn't told her that, she'd probably be rushing around the kitchen at midnight. They'd known each other ten years, married only lately. It wasn't fair to expect a woman to be a copper's wife for too long. The aggravation quotient was too high.

She had heard about Komarowski earlier in the day on the local radio. 'Bad, was it? They said he was shot.'

'Bad enough,' he said. 'It was a shotgun job. He was seventy-odd. Came over from Poland in 'thirty-nine. Fought in the war. Poor old sod.'

'I'll ring Marion,' she said. Marion was her sister with whom they had arranged, with some reluctance, to spend Christmas Day. 'I'll tell her we may not be able to make it.'

'We'll make it for lunch,' he said. 'Can't promise more, though. Not yet.'

They bandied the weather about. It was already down to minus-ten in Bournemouth, where she was, and the forecasters were promising it would go even lower before daybreak.

'I'll ring Marion tonight. If you're sure.'

'We'll be there. One way or the other.' He broke off and covered the mouthpiece as someone rapped on the door.

It was Price. He stopped short when he saw that Roper was on the phone.

'Oh, sorry,' he said. 'Important?'

'Sheila,' said Roper. 'What's up?'

'The vet's here. Carslake. Says he'd like a few words.'

'Wheel him in.' Roper uncovered the mouthpiece as the door closed again behind Price. 'Sorry about that,' he said, 'but I've got to go. Something's come up. See you about midnight.'

'Drive carefully.'

'I will.' The phone went back on its rest, the two cheese rolls hidden away in the top drawer of the desk. He would have preferred a few more moments of quiet domesticity; but they didn't go with the job. Never had.

Price knocked, and this time came all the way in and stood aside to usher in the squat plump figure standing in the narrow passage behind him.

'Mr Carslake, sir,' he said.

Carslake waddled in ponderously, his several chins bouncing, a podgy hand extended. Sixtyish and bespectacled under a battered tweed pork-pie hat that looked as if it had been the object of numerous rugby scrums.

He apologised for the lateness of the hour. He had only just read the note that had been dropped through his letter-box. He had spent the day up in London buying Christmas presents for his nephews and nieces, and had only just arrived back.

'Terrible business,' he said with a shudder, as he sat down and unbuttoned his sheepskin driving coat. 'Monstrous.' The tweed hat was plucked off and laid on the desk. Under the sheepskin he was wearing a garish Lincoln-green suit, a red and navy blue striped shirt with

56

a crumpled collar and a yellow bow-tie. A few strands of hair had been carefully arranged over a pink head that was otherwise devoid of it.

'You'd known him for a long time, Mr Carslake?' asked Roper.

'Oh, yes,' said Carslake reminiscently. 'A damned long time. Twelve years. He was a fine man. Very bright.' He hunched forward on his chair, his hands clasped on his plump knees, and gazed sadly at the floor.

Price came back with another chair and a notepad.

His full name was Julian Maurice Carslake. Field Cottage. Upper Gorton. He gave Price one of his business cards.

'Had you seen Mr Komarowski recently, sir?' asked Price.

'Yesterday,' said Carslake. 'Yesterday evening.'

'Time?'

'He arrived at half-past eight. Left about half-past nine.'

Which shrank the period of time that Wilson had estimated by three and a half hours, and left only another three and a half to account for. It wasn't much, but it was certainly a help.

'I presume the two of you talked,' said Roper.

'He came along to ask me about his contract with old Neville Henneker; he rents his caravan-site from the son. He's selling up; the son.'

'Yes, sir, we know about that,' said Roper. 'He was worried about it, was he?'

'Well, yes, he was. Quite worried. On the face of it Austen Henneker had made him a fair offer – two or three thousand pounds, I think it was; but of course that kind of money doesn't go far these days, does it? And the old chap's real problem was that he had nowhere else to go. And, to be frank, Austen was pressing him *very* hard.'

'I understood this contract was in writing, Mr Carslake,' said Roper.

'Yes,' said Carslake. 'It is. But it was something cobbled together by Neville Henneker late one night on his kitchen table, I suspect. It's written in pencil on a scrap of notepaper. Lots of heretofores and therebys, and really quite meaningless if Henneker ever took it to court.'

'And Mr Komarowski called on you last night to discuss it with you, did he?'

'Well, not me exactly. My brother. He has a solicitor's practice up in Salisbury. I rang him while Ziggy was there and read him the contract over the phone.'

'And?'

'He wasn't sanguine,' said Carslake. 'He could only suggest that Ziggy got himself a solicitor and used the contract to buy himself a little more time by litigating. But he'd probably have to go in the end, and a court case might prove costly.'

'And what was Mr Komarowski's reaction?'

'Bleak,' said Carslake. 'I made a pot of coffee. Then he went back to the caravan. And that,' he added, wistfully, 'was the last I saw of the old chap.'

'Was he on foot, sir, or on his bicycle?'

'His bicycle.'

'Did he actually *say* he was going back to the caravan?'

'Yes,' said Carslake. 'He told me he had a letter to write.'

That letter again. Or another letter.

'We understand that you did some kind of scientific work with him from time to time.'

'Oh, not quite *together*,' said Carslake modestly. 'Old Ziggy was the boffin. I only supplied the facilities.'

Carslake had a small laboratory, a sophisticated microscope, a few electronic gadgets for some basic biological tests. He was quite isolated down here. The nearest other veterinary surgeon lived five miles away, the nearest specialist laboratory was closer to thirty.

' . . . Although I did do an occasional post-mortem examination for him. Birds, mostly; and a couple of rabbits. He thought they might have been poisoned. He was very deeply into conservation.'

'And had they been poisoned?'

58

'In several cases, yes. In most, no.' Carslake plucked off his spectacles and held them up towards the fluorescent lamp on the ceiling. From somewhere in the Lincoln-green suit he fished out a crumpled paper handkerchief and began to clean them.

'This poison . . . ?'

'Oh, it was nothing sinister, nothing deliberate. Pesticide over-sprays, mostly.' The spectacles were held up to the light again. 'There was, of course, the business of the nitrate. Perhaps you haven't heard about that? That was definitely planted. Deliberately.' The spectacles went back on Carslake's button of a nose, the handkerchief returned to its source in the green suit.

'This was when, this business with the nitrate?'

'Last September,' said Carslake. A farmer with a valuable dairy herd noticed that a lot of fish were dying in the stream that went through his property; and, more particularly, the stream formed one of the boundaries of his grazing land. His herd drank from it. A check of the herd by Carslake had detected a higher concentration of nitrate than would normally be expected. Three other farms had been similarly affected.

'Is nitrate a poison? I thought it was a fertiliser.'

'It's found in nature all the time,' said Carslake. 'It's only a nuisance when man flings it about to excess. Given sufficient, it can be a killer. Especially to wildlife.'

'And you and Mr Komarowski found the source, I take it?'

'Not quite,' said Carslake gravely. 'We found the bag. What we didn't find was who put it there.'

The bag of nitrate, plastic, but strategically perforated so that its contents would leach out slowly, had been found weighted down with stones under a footbridge on Jackson's farm.

'That's upstream from here, or down?' asked Roper, making a note. Jackson, allegedly, had recently become the protector of Mrs Henneker and her son.

'Upstream,' said Carslake.

'So Mr Jackson wasn't affected?'

'No,' said Carslake.

'How about Mr Henneker?'

'Badly, said Carslake.

Roper jotted another note. It sounded like another incident in that feud. Henneker's wife and son had left him, his stream had been polluted, his sheep were given to wandering. He seemed to be a man with more than his fair share of life's vicissitudes, did Mr Henneker.

'D'you happen to know why Mr Henneker's selling up, Mr Carslake?'

'A man can only put up with so much bad luck, Superintendent. Henneker's had more than his fair share.'

'Do you know who's buying the place?'

Carslake shook his head. Henneker had become a very close man of late. Almost a hermit. Not that he had ever been a particularly sociable . . . But just lately . . .

Roper tacked back to Komarowski.

'Do you know if he had any enemies?'

'To a few people he was definitely an irritant,' Carslake conceded. 'I wouldn't like to say more than that. And certainly none of those would be likely to kill him. Generally speaking he was much liked. Personally I admired him. Always on the go. Tremendous energy.'

'Did he have many visitors up at the caravan?'

'Few, I'd say,' said Carslake. 'Myself, very occasionally. Stan Rydz – he's a pig farmer in the next village. And of course the Kingsleys; Jack and Enid. And if you *really* wanted to know about Ziggy I'd say your best bet was to talk to her. I think she knew him better than anybody.'

But Roper had already worked that out for himself. There seemed to be little else that Carslake could tell him that he did not already know.

'I'm sorry,' said Carslake. 'I only wish I could help you more.'

'You've helped a great deal, Mr Carslake,' Roper said, as Price showed Carslake out. Carslake had filled in three missing hours. It was better than nothing.

It was ten o'clock. Roper had finally forced himself to eat the two cheese and pickle rolls. From time to time the slam of a car door and the sound of voices came from the direction of the Gorton Arms. It didn't feel at all like Christmas. In two hours' time it would be Christmas Eve.

His desktop in the MIC was a mosaic of photographs, copies of the Polaroids that Wilson had taken this morning showing Zygmunt Komarowski's body in all its hideous detail, and the fifty or so that the SOCO had taken during the rest of the day.

Komarowski had obviously been at his ease, in his carpet slippers, his gas oven alight to keep him warm, his curtains closed. He had smoked a lot of cigarettes. And perhaps he had written a letter – typed a letter. He might even have posted it, although that seemed unlikely since he wouldn't have arrived back at the caravan, after his visit to Carslake, much before 9.45 last night. It would have been cold. He was an elderly man.

The scrap of paper caught up in the typewriter might, of course, have been torn from a letter written some time before – even days before. But Komarowski had certainly done – or had been about to do – something at his typewriter. The blank envelope tucked partly underneath it was evidence of that. Further evidence was the tidiness of his bunk. Apart from that rickety old chair, the only other place to sit was the bunk which, during the daytime, served as an upholstered bench seat. Apart from the splashes of blood over them, Komarowski's bedclothes had been undisturbed. And since he was unlikely to have been simply standing about, the only other place he had been likely to be was sitting in that chair.

And then he had been disturbed. He had got up from the chair and gone to answer the knock at the

61

caravan door. Or he had heard something outside and opened the door to see what it might have been.

He had been confronted, or had himself confronted someone, out there in the dark. He might not, initially, have known they – he – she – had been armed.

Whoever it was had come into the caravan. The door would have been closed, or surely someone somewhere would have heard the two shots? A quarrel.

Bang.

Bang.

Then the killer had made his exit, and the next person to see Komarowski, albeit dead, was Enid Kingsley at a few minutes past eight this morning.

And the motive: not robbery; there had been too little to steal. Yesterday lunchtime Komarowski had collected his old-age pension from the local post office. The SOCO had found the four ten-pound notes, still tucked in the old man's pension book, in the drawer under the sink. A crime of passion was unlikely. Given his hobby-horse, it *was* just possible that he had upset somebody. He had obviously done a lot of nosing about, perhaps on land where he had no business, and what one man saw as working for the general good another might judge to be rank interference.

Or perhaps it went even deeper than that. Komarowski had obviously been a bit of a detective; Austen Henneker had not only wanted Komarowski off his land, he had also suspected, rightly or wrongly, that the old Pole had occasionally spied on him. Carslake the vet had used the word irritant about Komarowski. So perhaps to someone he had been more than just an irritant, more, even, than a downright nuisance. To that someone he might even have been a potential threat. A dangerous man who had had to be silenced in the only sure way.

By killing him.

In the warmth of the Gorton Arms it at least felt like Christmas. A decorated tree in the corner by the blazing

62

fire, tinsel around the dartboard, the clink of glasses and the buzz of a dozen half-heard conversations, an occasional raucous hoot of laughter.

Price fought his way out from the press around the bar with a fruit juice and a half of bitter and came across to the fire.

'Cheers,' he said.

'Pros't,' said Roper. The bitter tasted home-brewed, potent and out of the wood. It was an old-fashioned pub. No fruit machines, no piped music, a wooden counter that probably dated back a hundred years and white-china pump-handles of a similar vintage. When Roper and Price had first come in, an eerie silence had fallen. It had only been fleeting while the two of them were covertly sized up and recognised as strangers, but it had been palpable, too. They were coppers from the big white van with all the aerials parked on the green across the way, looking into that murder business; which was all very well, but they were still coppers and beer never tasted quite the same with the law breathing down your neck.

'He could be among this lot, somewhere,' said Price, over his glass.

'I was thinking the same,' said Roper, looking around as he sipped at his bitter, hoping against futile hope that someone might finish his drink quicker than was meet and sidle out with a guilty look on his face. Not that he was likely to be that lucky. Apart from himself and Price everyone seemed to know everybody. Farmers, farm workers, a couple of City-suited gentry sitting in a corner hugging whisky tumblers. Only two women. The Gorton Arms was the only pub for several miles; so if Komarowski's killer was a drinking man, and this was his local, he was just as likely to be in here tonight as not. The ornamented brass cash-till beside the spirit optics rang almost continuously.

Roper felt Price's nudge at his elbow.

Austen Henneker had just come in, cloth capped, sheepskin overcoated and mufflered to the chin. He

barged his way through to the counter with little cere-
mony and only a curt reply to the few other customers
who spoke to him. He was clearly in a hurry. He pushed
a plastic carrier-bag over the bar, and a fistful of blue
banknotes. Mr Henneker bought his Scotch a half-dozen
bottles at a time by the looks of it. The till rang, his change
was passed back the other way across the counter, and
with his head down and the carrier-bag tightly embraced
he was gone again into the night and the bar door was
flapping behind him.

Several customers had turned to watch Henneker come
and go with more than usual interest. Now they turned
back to resume their conversations and their beer.

'I don't reckon the world'll see much of him till after
Christmas,' said Price.

Roper was left with the distinct impression that the
world wouldn't care all that much if it didn't, especially
around here. A glance at his watch told him that it was
ten to eleven. It was time to make tracks for home.

He and Price crossed the lane to the green and the
MIC, and he left Price scraping the snow off his windscreen while he made a last visit to the van to see if there
had been any calls or messages while they had been over
at the Arms.

'No, sir,' said Sergeant Blackett, who had driven the
van here and tonight would bunk in it. 'But I was just
coming across to fetch you. There's a Miss Kingsley to
see you. Says she won't keep you long; got the impression
she's got something she wants to get off her chest. She's
in your office. I could tell her I missed you . . . '

'No,' said Roper. 'I'll see her.' If Miss Kingsley had
come on foot, she had had a long cold walk, and he
already had a hunch as to what had brought her out at
this late hour.

She was sitting in his cubicle. Her dog was with her.

'I'm so sorry, Mr Roper,' she said. 'It's so very late . . .
But there's something I have to say that I should have told

64

you this morning. And if I don't tell you now, I shall never sleep.'

'We're open all hours, Miss Kingsley,' said Roper as he hung his overcoat on the door. 'Can we get you a cup of tea?'

She shook her head. 'No . . . I'd rather not . . . but thank you.'

Roper settled himself behind his desk. Her eyes fixed on him levelly. They were pale blue, very bright, very dogged, and it was not so difficult, after all, to imagine her, fifty years ago, busily ferrying fighter planes around the Battle of Britain airfields. There was something indomitable about Enid Kingsley.

'I told you a lie this morning, Mr Roper,' she said. 'At the time it seemed such a little lie; but it's grown, and I could never go to sleep on it. I'm sorry.'

Roper waited.

'You asked how long my brother and I had known Zygmunt. My brother told you the truth. I could not; at least not in front of Johnnie. He has never known, you see. About Zygmunt and I.' Her gaze dropped briefly, rose again. 'I first met Zygmunt in nineteen-forty. The August. Two days later we became engaged. And the day after that, while I was writing to Johnnie to tell him about us, the telegram came to tell me that Johnnie had been shot down over Canterbury and was seriously wounded.'

'So the letter was never finished?'

'No,' she said, with a sad little shake of her head. 'It never was. Zygmunt and I weighed things; and I finally decided that my brother needed me more. But we kept in touch, Zygmunt and I. We saw each other as often as we could, and neither of us ever married. So . . . ' Her voice tailed away, she lifted her shoulders under her old tweed coat, and she looked, for a moment, on the verge of tears, but again she managed to stifle them. 'The only other person who knew was Mr Rydz,' she said, 'who rang me after you'd left him this morning, poor man, to tell me that he'd let the cat out of the bag and told you everything.'

'No,' Roper hastened to assure her. 'Not everything. Mr Rydz was very discreet. I think he honestly believed he was helping us.'

'Yes,' she said wistfully. 'I'm sure he did. Mr Rydz is a very dear man.'

Roper gave her a breathing space. 'Is there anything else you'd like to tell me, Miss Kingsley?'

'No,' she said. 'Certainly nothing that could help you . . . Except that Zygmunt only came to Gorton because of me. Because I simply couldn't manage Johnnie on my own any more. Zygmunt took an early retirement and bought a little cottage at the back of the village; and when he had to sell that he bought the caravan and made that arrangement with old Mr Henneker. It was so that he could always be on hand for me, you see. To help me. To take Johnnie off my hands sometimes. And then, about a week after Zygmunt moved into the village, so did Mr Rydz. And we were all back together again. It all seemed so very fortunate. And then, a few weeks ago, Mr Henneker went up to the caravan and told Zygmunt that he would be hearing it formally from his solicitor, but that he thought it would be better if he told Zygmunt himself that he wanted that piece of ground back. The piece of land where the caravan was, that is. Do you know about that?'

'A little,' said Roper. 'Apparently Mr Komarowski went along to see Mr Carslake last night and discussed the contract with Mr Carslake's brother – he's a solicitor.'

'Yes,' she said. 'He told me he was going to.'

'Do you think Mr Henneker was pressing him harder than we know about?'

She shook her head. 'No,' she said. 'I wouldn't like to say that. I'd hate to get Mr Henneker into trouble.'

'But do you think he might have?'

'I only know that Ziggy was very worried about it. And Mr Henneker is a *very* strange man these days. His wife left him, you see . . . So sad.' She reached out sideways and the Labrador pushed up its head sympathetically into her cupped hand.

'He was going to spend Christmas with us,' she said absently. 'Ziggy, I mean. We'd all *so* much looked forward to it.'

Roper could think of nothing to say except an inane few utterances of sympathy, and Miss Kingsley wasn't that sort. Looking after her brother for more than half a lifetime could not have been easy. It was difficult to judge which of them had made the greater sacrifice.

'There's no need for my brother to know, is there?' she asked anxiously. 'Not now, especially.'

Roper shook his head. 'None,' he said.

'You've been very kind,' she said. 'Thank you. Now I must go. I've already kept you too long.'

Roper offered to have her driven back.

'No,' she said. 'Thank you. I've left my brother asleep. He doesn't know I've come out.' She had risen, Roper too. 'There is one thing,' she said. 'My brother and Zygmunt were waiting for some photographs to come back from the printers. They would have come by post.'

'They arrived this morning,' said Roper.

'Only, one set was destined for Jack,' she said hesitantly. 'He was wondering what the legal position was.'

'I don't think the legal position comes into it, Miss Kingsley. I've got them here. You can take a set now, if you like.'

'Oh, no, thank you,' she said. 'I'll pick them up in the morning, if I may. If I took them now I'd have to tell another lie, wouldn't I?'

He smiled. 'Yes,' he said. 'I suppose you would. If I'm not here when you turn up in the morning they'll be here on top of the desk. I'll leave a message with the duty sergeant.'

'Thank you,' she said.

Roper saw her safely down the aluminium outer steps and watched her cross the road towards the Gorton Arms, where she struck off to the right with her dog. Despite the snow she walked briskly away into the darkness.

'Shush,' Miss Kingsley whispered, as she closed her front door stealthily behind her and the Labrador keened softly to be let off the leash. 'Shush.'

She bent and unclipped him, and he padded out to his basket in the kitchen. And as she hung her old tweed coat on the hallstand it came to her that tomorrow, for the first time in many, many years, she would not be seeing Zygmunt. And that, tomorrow, she and Max would do better to walk in another direction altogether when they took their morning stroll. She could not bear to pass that gate ever again.

And she wondered, as she had all day, off and on, if it really had been that terrible Mr Allgrove standing in the lane this morning, or if she had only imagined him. She had confided her suspicion to Johnnie this afternoon; his jaw had dropped and his eyes had almost started out of his head.

'You sure?'

'No. Not for certain. But it did *look* like him.'

But the more she had thought about it since, the more certain she had become. It *had* been Mr Allgrove standing there in the lane.

Chapter 7

He was back at 8.30 the next morning, Christmas Eve. No more snow had fallen during the night but the overnight frost had put a fragile icy crust on the snow that had lain since yesterday, so that it crackled underfoot like thin glass. It had taken him an hour and a half this morning to drive thirty miles.

In the MIC, at the far end, by the galley, Sergeant Peasgood was chatting to Sergeant Blackett. Both held steaming mugs of tea.

He hung up his overcoat behind his door. The photographs had gone from the top of the desk. Miss Kingsley had clearly taken her morning walk.

'What's the agenda?' said Price, at 8.45. Raring to go, he had still to take off his scarf and raincoat.

'I don't know,' said Roper, around the cheroot he was lighting. And nor, at that moment, did he. All the locals had been questioned yesterday, with little significant result. There was not, to date, any obvious motive – apart from Austen Henneker's – except that Komarowski might have put his nose into some kind of dirty business. There was little physical evidence, a couple of felt shot-wads, an ounce or two of lead-shot, a strand of red wool. The public at large, secure in the knowledge that every police officer carried a crystal ball about with him, would probably deem such infinitesimal evidence more than sufficient to nail a suspect. But it wasn't like that. According to Peasgood's records there were more than forty authorised twelve-bore shotguns on his patch. And according to the WPC who was collating the door-to-door statements, over sixty inhabitants of Upper and Lower Gorton had admitted to being out and about between six o'clock and midnight on the night in question, and of those, twelve had a permit for a shotgun or two. Although the chances of the real villain readily admitting to both on his own front doorstep had to be remote. And, besides, there was nothing to indicate that Komarowski's killer was a local man – or woman. He, or she, could have come from anywhere.

'How about a few more words with Austen Henneker?' suggested Price.

'On the strength of what?' said Roper. He had been at the business long enough to know that you could question a suspect – which Henneker was not, yet – until Hell froze up, and unless you could confront him with some iron-hard evidence you might as well talk to yourself.

Jackson, however, might be worth a visit. It had been on Jackson's land that the plastic sack of nitrate had been found by Komarowski. And it had been to Jackson that Mrs Henneker and her son had turned after they had walked out on Henneker. And the fact that Mr Jackson had yesterday added £500 to the reward money put up by Stanislaus Rydz was no criterion that he had been exactly a friend of Komarowski.

Another useful contact might be the landlord of the Gorton Arms across the way. Listening to hearsay and gossip with a ready ear was part of a landlord's stock in trade. There would be a lot of both in a little place like Upper Gorton. Around these parts a stranger couldn't go unnoticed for much longer than it took to say knife. The landlord had been interviewed yesterday, but only in the broadest terms like everyone else. A few more pointed questions might drag something out of him that he had not realised he knew. It often happened like that.

They were at Jackson's farm soon after 9.30. As Rydz had said, it was a big spread, with its own private road and Jackson's lonely house standing on a snow-clad rise in the distance, a two-storey rambling place of Purbeck stone, surrounded by a clutter of outbuildings and stock-sheds. Parked in front of the wooden weather porch was a green Range Rover with an open wooden trailer hooked behind it.

Price pulled in behind the Range Rover. Somewhere at the back of the house a couple of dogs started barking, and a net curtain to the right of the porch was briefly lifted at one side as a man peered out.

In the shelter of the porch, having looked for either a bell push or door knocker on the new front door, and finding neither, Price rattled the flap of the letter-box; although there had been no need. The door was opened almost immediately by the man Roper had seen at the window.

'Mr Jackson?' asked Roper.

'What about it?' the man grunted suspiciously. His dark scowl looked like a fixture. Roper had expected some kind of village Lothario, but Jackson was endowed only with an indifferent ordinariness. He might have been a couple of years younger than Henneker, a short, squat, square man with a pair of luxuriant, greying sideburns.

Roper introduced himself and Price, and proffered his warrant-card. The card was regarded only cursorily before it was handed back again.

'Come about my bloody sheep, have you?'

'We're making a few routine enquiries into the death of Mr Komarowski—'

But Jackson had already heard enough. 'I spoke to a couple of coppers yesterday,' he broke in. 'Can't help you any more. Sorry.'

Roper pointedly lifted a foot to the doorstep.

'I believe you have a Mrs Henneker living with you, Mr Jackson.'

'So what?' retorted Jackson. 'None of your business, that, is it?'

'She was out when the other officers called yesterday,

71

sir,' Roper explained patiently. He had read somewhere once that folk who conducted extramarital affairs were usually making the same mistake twice. Mrs Henneker obviously had. 'Perhaps we could talk more comfortably inside.'

There was a pause. Jackson lifted his shoulders. 'If that's what you want,' he replied grudgingly, 'I've got nothing to hide.' He backed a pace and took the edge of the door with him.

Roper and Price wiped the soles of their shoes on the coconut mat. The rest of the passage was carpeted in green Wilton with a strip of plastic protector over it. A pair of muddied gumboots stood by an old-fashioned mirrored coatstand with several coats and jackets hung on it. There was a faint smell of pine disinfectant.

'Better come in here,' said Jackson, standing aside with a curt flap of his hand towards the open doorway of a room beside the narrow staircase.

It was a sitting-room. Spacious. More Wilton carpet. A jungle of furniture, a lot of it past its prime but all spotlessly clean, a low, beamed ceiling, a log fire crackling in the grate, new curtains at the windows. There was a rustic cosiness here that had not been at Henneker's; so perhaps Mrs Henneker had taken it from the one place and brought it to the other.

Jackson went straight to the wooden shelf above the fire and took down a crumpled packet of cigarettes and a lighter. 'You can park your backsides if you want to,' he said. 'So long as you don't bank on staying too long.'

Roper and Price lowered themselves to the bagged-out leather settee in front of the fire. Jackson remained standing. He lit a cigarette, then put the packet and lighter back beside the clock. From somewhere upstairs came the muted whine of a vacuum cleaner.

'Well,' grunted Jackson, 'I've got a business to run. Routine enquiries, you said.'

'Mr Komarowski,' said Roper. 'Anything you can tell us about him?'

'Aye,' said Jackson. 'He was a bloody good bloke. There's some as wouldn't say so, mind; but I got on all right with him.'

'And the people who didn't?'

'Not all that many,' said Jackson. 'And none that I know would have taken a shotgun to him. If I was you I'd be looking further afield.'

'Like where?'

Jackson sketched a shrug with his cigarette. 'I wouldn't know, would I?' he said. 'You'll have to ask about.'

'Had you talked to him? During the last week or so?'

'Aye,' said Jackson. 'Day before yesterday. Late morning. Along by Lower Gorton. I stuck his bike on the trailer and gave him a lift back.'

'Did he say what he'd been doing in Lower Gorton?'

'He'd been to get a book. The travelling library. Comes every Tuesday.'

'And where did you drop him off?'

'Outside the post office down in the village. Told me he was going to get his pension.'

It sounded right. It fitted in.

'You didn't see him after that?'

'Only his light.'

'Light?'

'Up there.' Jackson tilted his head towards the windows. 'His caravan.'

'You can see it from here?'

'Only after dark. Just the light.'

Roper rose from the settee and went to the window. Jackson followed him and lifted the net curtain aside. 'Over left a bit,' he said. 'About eleven o'clock.'

Roper could just make out the distant misty hummock and grey-green of the conifers on top of it. It was a good mile from here.

'What's that place further over?'

'Henneker's place,' said Jackson sourly. He obviously wasn't much enamoured of Austen Henneker. He let the curtain fall back again.

73

'Komarowski's light was burning all evening, was it?'

'I wouldn't know,' said Jackson. 'I wasn't looking. Got the impression it might not have been, though. I saw it go on a bit before ten.'

'Did you see him close the curtain?'

'They must already have been,' said Jackson. 'The light was only faint.'

Komarowski's curtains had been only cheap chintzy things, and the light would have shone through them, and even been visible from here in spite of the conifers in the way. Out here in the country, with no streetlights, a night could be like black velvet, and you could see a man lighting a cigarette a mile off. So what Jackson had probably witnessed was Komarowski's return from Carslake's surgery.

Jackson had gone back to stand in front of the fire. Roper joined Price again on the settee. Upstairs, the vacuum cleaner note changed as it was trundled into another room.

'Do you have a shotgun here, Mr Jackson?' asked Price.

'Three,' said Jackson. 'I've got two and the boy's got one.'

'Your son?' asked Roper.

'Becky's lad,' said Jackson. 'Trevor.'

'That's Mr Henneker's son, is it?'

'Aye,' said Jackson, sourly again at the mention of Henneker.

'Twelve-bores?' asked Price. 'These shotguns?'

'Got a twelve-bore and a four-one-o.' Trevor Henneker also owned a .410, a single-barrelled bolt action. Both Jackson and Trevor Henneker were in possession of current certificates. 'I can show you 'em, if you like.'

'If you wouldn't mind, sir.'

Jackson went off willingly enough. Roper decided that his doorstep impression of him might have been wrong. He was merely a laconic man by nature. Now that he had relaxed a little he was almost forthcoming.

A lot of the furniture in the room was handcrafted,

country style, probably handed down from one generation of Jacksons to the next. Some of it looked collectable. The pair of pots that flanked the clock on the mantelshelf were Royal Worcester, early Edwardian; a Christmas tree standing in the corner near the window was waiting to be decorated.

Jackson came back with the trio of shotguns. His own twelve-bore looked as if it had not been used for some time. The two .410s had both been used last Monday, by himself and young Henneker, for a spot of rabbiting.

'How about the twelve-bore?' asked Roper.

'A couple of months,' said Jackson. 'The spring's gone on the left-hand firing-pin.'

Roper cocked it, and squeezed the triggers. The right-hand percussion pin clicked sweetly, the left-hand pin not at all. It didn't seem likely to have been the weapon that had killed Komarowski. He handed it back and Jackson stood it with the other two beside the fireplace.

'You were home all that evening, Mr Jackson?' asked Price.

'Apart from about twenty minutes,' said Jackson. 'I went across to see Austen; he wasn't in. Least he didn't answer the door.'

'What time would that have been, Mr Jackson?' asked Roper.

'Not sure,' said Jackson. 'Bit after ten, I suppose it was.'

'After you'd seen Komarowski's caravan light go on?'

'Aye,' said Jackson. 'It would have been. That's what I'd gone to the window for; to see if Austen had come back. It was lights in his place I was looking for. I'd been ringing all evenin'. And he wasn't answering. I got all worked up waiting, so I went over there to sort him out.'

'On foot?'

'The van,' said Jackson. 'I bashed on his door half a dozen times. Then went round the back. Got no answer either way, so I put a note through his letter-box saying I wanted to see him. Then I came back here.'

'You concluded Mr Henneker was out?' Jackson

'Or he knew who was knocking,' said Henneker, darkly. 'Could have just been sitting there with his lights out, couldn't he? Or he might have just been stoned out of his mind again, mightn't he? I can't say, can I?'

'The reason you needed to see him, was that something to do with Mrs Henneker?'

'If it was, it'd be none of your business, would it?'

The reason for Jackson's late-night call on Henneker was a matter of fences. A few weeks ago Henneker had backed his tractor along his and Jackson's common boundary and taken out fifty feet of wooden fencing. He had told Jackson he would repair it, and still had not.

'I still reckon he did it deliberate,' said Jackson, half-turning and tossing his cigarette-end into the fire. 'Or he'd been on the juice again; either way I'm going to make him fix it, even if I have to go to law.'

So Henneker might have been lying when he had told Roper that he had not gone out at all on the night Komarowski had been shot. He might, of course, have been so paralytically drunk that he had heard and seen nothing of Jackson's telephone calls and, later on, the visit Jackson had finally made. There was, equally of course, the possibility that Jackson himself was lying to get Austen Henneker into trouble. There was clearly little love lost between the two of them, although, for the moment, Roper was human enough to let his sympathies lie with Jackson. Short of kidnapping, a man couldn't take away another man's wife unless she wanted to go.

'Mrs Henneker was here with you the other night, sir?'

'No,' said Jackson. 'Neither of 'em were. Her nor the boy. I was here on my own.'

'Until when?'

'Midnight,' said Jackson. 'Thereabouts. Beck was over at her mother's at West Knighton; young Trevor was up in Dorchester, at some disco place. Got back about one o'clock, he did.'

Which also tended, Roper's sympathies aside, to put

76

Jackson himself squarely in the frame. He had been alone here for the few hours straddling the time when Komarowski was killed. It was an isolated place. If he'd been careful, no one would necessarily have seen him come and go. He could even have cut across the fields in the darkness and never gone near a road. He might have another twelve-bore tucked away somewhere, one with two working firing-pins.

Upstairs the vacuum cleaner had been switched off. There was a metallic clatter, and someone started heavily down the stairs.

'I'll be back,' said Jackson, and hurried out to the passage.

'Told you not to go carrying that thing, didn't I?' Roper heard him say softly. 'Give it here.'

Then a woman's anxious voice said something, it sounded like a question.

' . . . couple of p'licemen,' replied Jackson, in a hoarse stage-whisper.

' . . . what?'

'Old Ziggy Komarwoski.'

' . . . me?'

'Come on . . . ' Jackson wheedled, still in that whisper. 'Nothing to worry about. They only want to talk to you.'

Then came the sound of the vacuum cleaner changing hands on the stairs, then the squeak of its wheels as it was set down in the passage.

The waif-like Mrs Henneker nervously preceded Jackson into the sitting-room, her face shiny with perspiration. From the neck up she was clearly in her early forties; the rest of her would have passed for an undernourished thirteen. A few black hairs escaped from under the pink turban she was wearing. The gloating Jackson, who was clearly still in the first fevers of enchantment, steered her into the armchair to the right of the brick fireplace; and perched himself on the arm beside her with an arm draped protectively across the back.

77

Roper, after effecting the introductions of himself and Price, resumed his place on the settee. Mrs Henneker sat like a tightly clenched fist, and his reassuring smile met little response.

'Mr Jackson tells us you were over in West Knighton the other night, Mrs Henneker.'

She nodded, and looked as if she was struggling to swallow a large pebble.

'And how did you come home?'

She swallowed again, and looked up at Jackson for what seemed to be moral support.

'Go on,' he urged softly. 'Tell 'em. It was the bus, wasn't it? Tell 'em you came on the bus.'

She cleared her throat nervously. 'Yes,' she said. 'The bus. I came back on the bus.'

'And you got off the bus where?'

'The village,' she said.

'Along by the Arms,' Jackson explained. 'Along by the Arms, the bus stop is.'

'And what time would that have been?' asked Roper, still resolutely addressing Mrs Henneker. 'Can you remember?'

Jackson's right hand stole forward and squeezed her shoulder fondly. 'A bit before twelve, wasn't it?' he prompted. 'Eh?'

'More like half-past eleven,' she said, but addressing Jackson rather than Roper. 'That's when the bus got in. It was twelve, nearly, when I got back here.'

'I told her to ring me from the bus stop,' said Jackson, still practically drooling down at her and talking to her in the third person. 'But she didn't. Did she? Eh?'

'I didn't want to bother you,' she said.

'That's daft,' he simpered. 'That's what I'm here for. Isn't it? Eh?'

Roper felt his stomach squirm. According to Peasgood, Jackson had been a staid old bachelor all his life and with never a breath of gossip about him. And then, out of the blue, he had taken up with Mrs Henneker. That she warmed his bed with some gusto was evident from the now fixed, fatuous expression that Jackson wore on his grizzled face.

'So you walked from the Arms,' said Roper, with a commendable show of patience. 'You must have passed the gate to Mr Komarowski's caravan site.'

'It's the only way to come,' said Jackson, to Roper's mounting irritation. 'Told you to ring me, didn't I? Didn't I?'

'Did you see anyone, Mrs Henneker?' Roper persisted valiantly. 'Or a car you might not have seen before parked anywhere near? Anything like that?'

She mulled that over. And, for the first time, Jackson was unable to answer for her.

'A man,' she said, after a long hesitation.

Roper's interest quickened. 'Where did you see him exactly?'

She thought lengthily again. 'He was crossing the road,' she said.

'Near the gate to the caravan site?'

'A bit after.' The man had been walking towards the village, on the same side of the road as her, but obviously in the opposite direction. As she had glimpsed the shadowy figure so it had crossed to the other side of the lane.

'To avoid you, d'you think?'

'He might have. I don't know.' Jackson squeezed her shoulder in fond approval.

So there had been a lone man walking towards the gate to Komarowski's caravan some time between 11.30 and midnight. And as he'd seen Mrs Henneker he'd crossed over to the other side. Which might be significant or it might not. It was a grim reflection on the times that many a man went out of his way to avoid presenting a threat to a woman walking alone, especially at night.

'Could you describe him, Mrs Henneker? Anything at all about him?'

'He was carrying a bag,' she said. It had been a sort

of long bag. Like a cricket-bag. She lifted up her face to the adoringly transfixed Jackson. 'Like the one Trevor had. You know.'

'You could hide a shotgun in one of those,' said Jackson, knowingly. 'Couldn't you, eh?'

'Any idea what colour the bag might have been, Mrs Henneker?'

Sort of lightish, she thought. Grey, or something like that. It had been dark. There were no streetlamps along that stretch of road. She couldn't be sure.

'How about his clothes?'

Again, she wasn't certain. But some kind of shortish jacket. Perhaps with a hood, because his head had seemed a funny shape. And, yes, it *might* have been an anorak. The lightest thing about him had been the bag he was carrying. And he had been walking fairly briskly. Sort of businesslike. You know. As if he'd been in a hurry to get somewhere. And he'd seemed very tall. And thin. Ish.

Roper brought out Peasgood's map and unfolded it, and asked her to show him more precisely where she had passed this mysterious man. Again, she was vague, but with some loving encouragement from Jackson she finally decided that she had first glimpsed him as she was passing the telephone box, which was fifty yards or so beyond the gate; or before it if you were walking from *Lower* Gorton. You know?

'You had some trouble with a polluted stream a while back, Mr Jackson,' said Roper.

'I did,' said Jackson. 'Although it wasn't me as had the trouble; more the land downstream of here.' He added bitterly, 'A lot of fingers were pointed my way over that. There's a few about here still who reckon I dumped that bloody sack. To get my own back on Austen. 'Cause of the way he treated Beck here. Used to knock her about, didn't he?'

At that revelation two spots of colour blazoned brightly at Mrs Henneker's cheeks, and she shot a distraught glance up at Jackson. 'Don't, Fred, please,' she pleaded. 'They don't want to know about that. It's past. I don't want any more trouble.'

But Jackson was determined to pour it all out now that he had started. 'He came here,' he said. 'Few weeks back. Three o'clock in the morning, it was. I had to call Sergeant Peasgood. And next day, I had to call in a chippie and get a new front door fixed. Cost me, that did.'

'Your husband's a violent man, then, Mrs Henneker,' said Roper.

'He was out there shouting he was going to kill her,' railed Jackson.

'Is that true, Mrs Henneker?' persisted Roper, willing her to speak for herself, if only to get some kind of character reference for her husband.

She hung her head, and dropped her gaze to her thin white shiny knees. Then, in scarcely more than a whisper, she said, 'Yes. Yes, he did.'

But now that it had come to the crunch it appeared that Jackson himself hadn't actually heard what Henneker had been shouting, because he had been in his office at the back of the house trying to drum up Sergeant Peasgood on the telephone. 'But Becky here heard. *She* heard. *You* heard, didn't you, eh?'

She didn't reply. And that was when Roper caught her eye and realised that she was looking at him not with anxiety but shrewdly and calculatingly, as if she was measuring his immediate reaction to what had just passed about her husband. And an instinctive, momentary thought was that Mrs Henneker, at least on that particular score, might not be telling him the whole ungarnished truth.

In the flint-cold air the three of them, Roper, Price and Fred Jackson were crouched on their heels at the eastern end of the old snow-clad wooden cattle-bridge under which, a few months back, Komarowski had located the perforated plastic bag of nitrate.

'Just there, it was,' said Jackson, pointing under the planks. 'Wedged against the bank; and a couple of house bricks on top to stop the current taking it away.'

Roper straightened up. The stream was six feet or so wide, steeply banked at this point, and, at the moment, a couple of feet deep, although, according to Henneker, it was often a lot deeper after a few days of rain; and it would be again when the thaw came. The surface was thinly iced over. Here and there a few reeds and weeds showed above the ice.

'Did you call in the local water authority, Mr Jackson?' asked Price.

'Should have done,' agreed Jackson. 'But we like to sort our problems out ourselves around here. Especially with old Ziggy on the spot, like. Don't like government people poking about any more than we have to.' He lifted a shoulder to shrug off grey officialdom. His only concession to the cold was an old tweed jacket with leather patched elbows, and, perhaps more pertinently, around his neck and crossed over his chest under the jacket, a hand-knitted red scarf that bore a striking resemblance to the colour of Miss Kingsley's.

At 11.00 they were back in the village where, according to Jackson, young Trevor Henneker would probably be found in the snooker room of the Gorton Arms. There were a few women about catching up on the last of their Christmas shopping, a queue across at the post office, several cars already parked on the gravel apron in front of the Gorton Arms. From somewhere came the sound of carols.

In the MIC, there was a welcome fresh face with its nose buried in a mug of tea outside the galley. Detective Sergeant Makins, newly returned from a spell of Duty Elsewhere on a drugs-bust, and scarcely recognisable behind a recently cultivated blond beard.

'Morning, George,' called Roper.

Makins lifted his mug cheerily. 'Morning, guv'nor.'

Roper left Price to give Makins a quick briefing while

he turned into his cubicle to phone Craig across at the Forensic laboratory. While he waited to be connected he leafed through the half-dozen envelopes that Sergeant Peasgood had dropped off earlier with a note, and which represented this morning's mail delivery to Zygmunt Komarowski which Peasgood had thoughtfully intercepted. One by one he held them up to the fluorescent lamp in the ceiling. Four were clearly Christmas cards, one postmarked in London, three locally. The handwriting on one looked like a woman's. It had been posted here in Upper Gorton the day before yesterday. Probably from Enid Kingsley. Another was some kind of advertising brochure; that had been posted in Dorchester. The last envelope had been postmarked in Wareham yesterday lunchtime, and carried the return address, on the flap, of a solicitor's in Wareham; perhaps another hustle from Henneker's solicitor. With the telephone receiver huddled against his ear he was about to slit that one open when Craig was at last put through, his voice accompanied, as it invariably seemed to be, by the distinct tinkling of a teaspoon in a china cup.

'News?' said Craig. 'Yes, I have news. But not the sort that'll rock you on your heels, I'm afraid.'

'The SOCO found a piece of red wool,' said Roper.

A rustling of papers came down the line. ' . . . Wool and nylon, actually,' said Craig. 'Could have got snagged up any time lately, so it might not be evidence. And I don't know if it pleases you or not, but it doesn't match the scarf you sent along. Miss E. Kingsley's, so the label on the bag says. That's pure wool.'

'Ah,' said Roper.

'Is that ah, good; or ah, bad?'

'Can't say, Mr Craig,' said Roper, drawing a jotter closer and scribbling 'red scarf – Jackson', and underlining it, twice. 'But I've just left a gentleman wearing a very similar item. What else is there?'

'The cartridges,' said Craig. 'They were definitely twelve-gauge.'

83

'I know about those,' said Roper. 'Have you checked out the bloodstains . . . ?'

'All group A, as was the old chap's. Can't say for certain that it was all his without a lot more tests, of course, but I think it's safe to assume that it was for the time being. We've certainly found none from another group.'

'How about his cash-box?'

'Nothing significant. A will. His money, books and medals to an Enid Kingsley – whom I presume is she of the scarf – and his photographic equipment to a John Kingsley. And a quaintly handwritten contract between Komarowski and a Neville Henneker for a lifetime lease of land and a water supply thereto.'

There were a few other things: a wad of old bank statements, a building society paying-in book with £1300 recorded in it, a receipt for the purchase of the caravan and a few certificates and documents in Polish which Craig was still pondering about the necessity of having translated.

'I heard something metallic rattling about,' said Roper.

'You did,' said Craig. 'A ringful of small keys. Four of them. Well used. Might be ignition-keys. Two of them certainly are.'

'He didn't have a motor,' said Roper.

'Well, he obviously felt a need to lock them away, whatever they were for. I'll send them to you, shall I? You might just find the matching locks lurking about somewhere.'

'Do that,' said Roper. 'Otherwise, it's back to the drawing-board, is it?'

'Afraid so,' said Craig.

Chapter 8

Still wearing his overcoat, he slit open the letter from the Wareham solicitor and unfolded the single sheet of stiff white bond paper that had been inside it. He had been right; it was a hustler.

Dear Mr Komarowski,

Further to our letter of December 12, we feel it necessary to point out to you that Mr Henneker is seeking an exchange of contracts on January 31 next. As you are aware, the intending purchaser of Mr Henneker's property requires full vacant possession in its strictest sense. As we have already made clear to you, your contract with the late Mr Neville Henneker has no substance in law, since it does not make clear to which 'lifetime', yours or the late Mr Henneker's, this document refers.

However, Mr Henneker has instructed us to make clear to you that he understands the difficult circumstances in which you find yourself, and in the light of this is prepared to increase his compensatory offer to you, generously, in our consideration, by a further one thousand pounds, making a total of three thousand pounds in full and final settlement.

Your immediate decision is requested.

Yours sincerely,

L. Barkworth (Senior Partner)

L. Barkworth clearly had a different definition of 'generous' from most other folk. As offers went, this one was pretty meagre. Roper had little idea of current land prices but that property of Henneker's surely had to be valued in *hundreds* of thousands, in proportion to which the three thousand offered to Komarowski for turning him out of house and home seemed downright miserly. But what the letter did imply was that Henneker had needed to get Komarowski off his land with some speed in order to be able to sell it.

He and Price crossed the village street to the Gorton Arms. A pale watery sun shone, although it did nothing to warm. Back at the van, they had left George Makins to find out what he could from L. Barkworth (Senior Partner) over the telephone.

Apart from two women taking morning coffee, the little snug-bar was empty. In the adjacent saloon-bar a barman was stocking up shelves with more bottles in preparation for the Christmas Eve lunchtime rush. There was presently a lull, and the tall, rangy, shirtsleeved man who had been pouring a bag of small change into the till slammed it shut, came along the bar towards them and braced himself with both hands on the back edge of the counter.

'Yes, gents?'

Roper ordered a single Scotch and the use of the water jug for himself, a small rum for Price. The man offered a couple of tumblers up to the optics beside the till.

'Mr Painter?' asked Roper, as the two tumblers came one way across the counter and his five-pound note went the other.

'That's right.' Poised still with the note in his hand, Painter looked worriedly down at the warrant-card Roper had discreetly opened on the counter. 'Trouble?'

'No, sir,' said Roper, as discreetly tucking the card back inside his jacket. 'Saw your name over the door. We'd like a few words, if you can spare us a couple of minutes.'

'Sure,' Painter said. 'Always glad to help the law.'

86

'And pull up one for yourself on that.'

'Thanks.' Painter went back to his till, rang it, counted out Roper's change, then stopped on the way back to draw himself a half-pint of bitter. Beside Roper, one of the two women who had been drinking coffee brought their two empty cups back to the counter. There was a rush of cold air as the two of them went out.

'Merry Christmas,' said Painter.

'Pros't,' said Roper, tipping water on his whisky and then lifting it.

'If it's about old Ziggy,' said Painter, standing his glass back on the counter, 'I spoke to a couple of your lads yesterday.' He was fiftyish, gaunt-faced, and with pale moist eyes. One of his bony knees came up as he rested a foot on a shelf beneath the counter. 'I only knew him as a customer. I told 'em that.'

'But you hear a lot,' said Roper.

'Can't help it,' said Painter. 'Not in this job.'

'He was in here the day before yesterday.'

'About a quarter to two. Lunchtime. Bought a couple of cans of Guinness to take along to the Kingsleys'. Every weekday he did that.'

'How about the evening?'

Painter shook his head. 'Didn't see him.'

'How about talk?'

'Gossip, you mean?' Painter broke off to sip ruminatively at his beer. 'There's plenty just now. We don't often get a murder in these parts.'

'Any fingers pointed anywhere?'

Painter shrugged. 'Would be, wouldn't there? He'd upset a few people in his time.'

'Like who?'

Painter stretched his mouth dubiously. 'I don't pay a lot of attention to gossip. Goes in one ear and out the other. Know what I mean? If it didn't, it wouldn't be worth opening up the bar. Bit like being a priest, this job.'

'You said he'd upset a few people, Mr Painter,' said Price. 'How many's a few?'

'If I could have put a number to it, I wouldn't have said a few would I?' said Painter. Behind him, a customer was impatiently tapping a coin on the counter for service. The barman crouched at the shelves, got up and went to serve him.

'Can you put a name to any, Mr Painter?' asked Roper.

'Look,' said Painter uncomfortably, 'perhaps I shouldn't have said anything. It's all bloody hearsay anyway. Most of the people around here liked old Ziggy.'

'But a few didn't,' persisted Roper.

Painter sent a shifty glance over his shoulder towards his saloon-bar. 'There's talk,' he conceded, dropping his voice a pitch as he turned back again. 'Always is in a little place like this.' He leaned closer across the counter. 'Me,' he said, 'I just listen.'

Roper, too, had leaned encouragingly closer to Painter. 'So what do you hear?'

'It's just something I've heard, so don't start getting ideas. It was a while back. Somebody dumped a bag of fertiliser up along Fred Jackson's place. It fouled up Gort Stream all the way to the river. Done in all the fish.'

'I've heard about it,' said Roper.

Painter dropped his voice another cautious pitch. 'The land it caused most trouble to was Austen Henneker's. He's Jackson's neighbour. Gort Stream goes straight through his place. Thing is – it's just a rumour, mind – folk are saying that Henneker did it himself; to get the finger pointed at Fred – Jackson, that is, like.'

'And why would he have done that?' asked Roper.

'Henneker's missus, Becky,' said Painter. 'She moved in with Jackson. Her and Henneker's boy. Both of 'em. Had enough of Austen, see? He used to knock her about. That's what they say.'

'And Mr Komarowski fitted in there somewhere, did he?' asked Roper.

'Austen – he's been putting it about ever since – reckoned that old Ziggy was spying on him. Like he's waiting for him to make the same mistake again.'

88

'Did Komarowski ever accuse Mr Henneker of dumping this bag?'

'Not that I ever heard,' said Painter. 'I had more the idea that it was something Austen got into his head and couldn't get out again. He's like that, these days; since his old woman took up with Jackson. He's been on the old fire-water a lot lately, too. Comes in here, buys himself half a dozen bottles of Scotch, and that's the last anybody sees of him for three or four days. Funny bloke, is old Austen, lately.'

'How about his farm? How does he manage to run that?'

'He's selling up,' said Painter. 'He can't get out of it fast enough. It's starting to get a real rack and ruin of a place. They say the house is like a tip.'

Well, not quite, thought Roper. Not exactly a tip. Not yet. But it showed the power, around these parts, of rumour and gossip. And he had seen for himself Austen Henneker slipping out of this very place last night with a carrier-bag full of Scotch bottles.

'Who else might have had it in for Komarowski, Mr Painter?' asked Price.

Painter's mouth tightened in another momentary show of reluctance. 'Well,' he said. 'There *is* Charlie Allgrove. He got out about a couple of days ago.'

'Out of where?'

'The nick,' said Painter. 'Three years, less remission. He always swore to get his own back on Ziggy Komarowski when he came out. Mind you, he always did have a lot of mouth, did Charlie.'

'What was he sent down for?'

'Dog-fighting,' said Painter.

'And where did Komarowski come into it?'

'It was Komarowski who nobbled him,' said Painter. 'He came across him on the heath burying a couple of weighty-looking rubbish sacks. One of 'em was split and there was a dog's head sticking out. Komarowski reported it to the law a bit sharpish. Thing was, you see, old Ziggy had taken a couple of photographs of Allgrove doing the burying, so he didn't have a leg to stand on.'

'And Allgrove didn't know he'd had his picture taken?'

'Not till afterwards.'

'Anybody else involved? Anybody from around here?'

'Austen Henneker . . . and a bloke called Colin Snow, from Lower Gorton. Henneker got a fine for conspiring, and Snow got off with a warning. It was Snow who spilled all the beans, that's why he got off light. I shouldn't think *he*'s all that popular with Charlie, either.'

'What does this Allgrove do for a living?' asked Roper.

'He's in the removal business,' said Painter. 'Got a couple of big vans. Least, he did have. Don't know what he's up to now. I've only had the word he's out. I haven't exactly seen him myself yet.'

Price wrote down Allgrove's address. It was a mile or so off the lane between here and Lower Gorton. Mr Allgrove certainly sounded worth a visit. If anybody had a motive, then he certainly had.

'Mr Henneker's son still on the premises, Mr Painter?' asked Roper, in passing. 'It's only that we missed him on the door-to-door enquiries yesterday. We'd like a word.'

'Him and my lad are having a knock-up in the snooker room. Want me to fetch him?'

'No, sir, there's no rush. But if he's got a minute or two perhaps he could drop in and see me in the van.'

'Will do,' said Painter.

Back at the MIC, Roper dropped in on the WPC who was operating the CAD cubicle officially, but less officially was painting her fingernails for want of something more useful to do.

'Get on the blower to Hendon, Constable. I want all that's known on a Charles Allgrove—' He broke off to take Price's open pocket book and hand it over to the WPC. '—this address. He's a dog-fighting man. Tell Hendon to fax it. And preferably before lunch.'

In Price's cubicle, Makins, with a mug of tea in one hand, was dotting the i's and crossing the t's of the notes

90

he had scrawled during his telephone call to Henneker's solicitor.

'Any luck, George?' asked Roper.

'Not a lot,' said Makins. 'I think I was interrupting the office party.'

'But?' said Roper.

'But the contract between Komarowski and Neville Henneker was about as watertight as a paper bag. It reads as if the lease was for old Henneker's lifetime, not Komarowski's. Also – I quote – Mr Henneker needn't have paid any compensation at all, but had only offered to do so – and this is the best bit – out of the goodness of his heart.'

'Cobblers,' said Roper. 'What else?'

'That Mr Henneker's intending purchaser is planning to clear all the old trees on the land where the caravan was and turn it into a conifer plantation.'

'Who's buying?' asked Roper.

'He wouldn't say,' said Makins. 'And won't, unless we call in personally and wave a warrant under his nose.'

None of which was particularly useful. And it didn't seem likely that anybody who wanted Henneker's land wanted it badly enough to kill for it. That Henneker was desperate to get it off his hands – now that was a different matter entirely.

Price showed in young Trevor Henneker on the dot of midday. He was somewhere in his early twenties, short, dark and powerfully built, like his father, but there the resemblance ended. Personable and coolly articulate, he brushed Roper's apology aside. Calling in here was no problem. Apart from feeding the livestock and getting the cows into the milking-plant on time, farming wasn't exactly labour intensive over the few days of Christmas. Anything he could do to help; when he had been at school it had been old Ziggy who had coached him through the A-level chemistry examination that had helped him get a place at the local agricultural college.

'So I guess I owed the old boy.'

'You're Mr Jackson's farm-manager, Mr Henneker?' asked Roper, when Price came back after retrieving his pocket book from the WPC in the CAD room.

'I've worked for him for eighteen months. Since I came out of college.'

'And you were where, the night Mr Komarowski was murdered, Mr Henneker? Just for the record.'

'Dorchester,' said Henneker. 'At a disco. I was with Greg Painter. That's Harry Painter's son. The governor over at the Arms.'

'What time were you back here in Upper Gorton? Roughly.'

'Roughly . . . about one o'clock, I suppose. Perhaps a bit before. Greg and I talked a bit outside the Arms. Then I dropped him off and drove home. To Fred's, that is.'

'You'd have passed the iron gate up to Mr Komarowski's caravan.'

'Yes, but I didn't give it a thought. I didn't see anyone, if that's what you're asking.'

'You didn't see a man carrying a bag? Anything of that sort?'

Henneker shook his head. 'No,' he said. 'Nothing.' Certainly more forthcoming and helpful than his father, he lacked even his parents' Dorset burr. A slight cast in his left eye looked like the result of an accident.

'You obviously knew Mr Komarowski well.'

'Very well,' said Henneker. 'Since I was about twelve. Soon after he moved down here. He was a nice old guy. My grandfather was alive then; it was him who got old Ziggy to coach me through school.'

'And your father inherited him from your grandfather,' said Roper.

Henneker weighed the statement carefully before he admitted: 'My father didn't like him much; well, not him, exactly. It's the way the caravan site overlooks the house. My father's always been a bit paranoid about his

92

privacy; he used to think old Ziggy was spying on him. Said he'd seen him up in the trees sometimes with his binoculars trained on the house. But, like I say, my old man's obsessed with his privacy. Old Ziggy wasn't the sort to spy on anybody.'

Oh, but he had been, thought Roper. He'd lain in cover once and painstakingly photographed Charles Allgrove burying a couple of savaged dogs out on the heath.

'Your father's an obsessive man, is he, Mr Henneker?'

Henneker didn't seem keen to answer that; until Price, shrewdly, made a showy business of closing his pocket book and laying it on the corner of the desk beside him.

'More difficult,' said Henneker. 'He really wasn't cut out to be a farmer. When my grandfather died, and my father realised that he had to manage the place himself, he started to go to pieces; and so did the farm. He doesn't really like work. The place is becoming a shambles.'

'You were never inclined to help him?'

Henneker had the grace to blush slightly. 'It wasn't an easy decision,' he said. 'I'd done three years at agricultural college, and I knew that my father was twenty years behind the times. Fred Jackson's bang up to date with everything. And I've got ambitions.'

'How about the relationship between your father and your mother, Mr Henneker?'

Strictly speaking, at that question, Henneker could have got up and walked out; but he didn't.

'My mother's had a pretty bad time with him,' he said. 'Most of the village knows that, so it isn't exactly a secret.'

'Violent man, was he, Mr Henneker?' Roper asked sympathetically.

'There were times.'

'You never thought of reporting them; on your mother's behalf?'

'She expressly forbade it. She thought if I did – or she did – it would only make things worse.'

93

'Did you ever hear or see any of these goings-on?' asked Roper.

Well, no, he had not. He had never been an *eye-witness* exactly. But he had known for a long time that his father had been making his mother's life a misery. Nor had he seen or heard anything of the incident when his father had called at Jackson's house that night and all but kicked the door in. He had spent that night with an erstwhile girlfriend down at Swanage. Few, it seemed, even her closest next of kin, would have been much help to Mrs Henneker in a court of law.

'Your mother's filed for a divorce, I suppose, has she?' asked Roper, still pursuing his role of commiserating father-figure.

'No,' said Henneker. 'Not yet. But she's thinking about it.'

Which caused Roper no little surprise, seeing how Mrs Henneker seemed so comfortably ensconced with Fred Jackson, and had been for some little time. Surely an abused woman, in those circumstances, would have ditched one husband for another with some speed. That she had not, led Roper to doubt that Henneker was quite as bad as gossip had painted him. He still recalled that brief moment when he had caught Mrs Henneker slyly weighing him up. For all her coyness, he had got the impression just then that Mrs Henneker was a sharp little lady.

Sergeant Peasgood called in soon after Trevor Henneker had left. He had spent the last half-hour sorting out Jackson's wayward sheep from Henneker's.

'You found 'em, then,' said Roper. 'Henneker nicked 'em after all, did he?'

'Can't say for sure, sir,' said Peasgood. He was capless and gumbooted and the knees of his uniform trousers were soaking wet. 'I found them wandering about with Henneker's flock; but Henneker doesn't know how they got there.'

94

'He wouldn't, would he?' said Roper. 'How did you get on to them?'

'Chap called Colin Snow,' said Peasgood. 'He spotted them earlier when he was cycling home for breakfast. He used to work for Henneker, but now he works for Jackson.'

Snow. The name rang a bell; but Roper couldn't immediately put a finger on it. Snow had noticed several sheep with Jackson's blue dye-patches on them wandering among Henneker's yellow-patched ones. Henneker had let Peasgood cast an eye over his flock yesterday, and Peasgood was certain that none of Jackson's allegedly rustled ten had been on Henneker's property then; or if they had been they were tucked away somewhere well out of sight.

'Perhaps they just wandered,' said Roper.

But Peasgood reckoned that was unlikely. Jackson wintered his sheep in a secure enclosure with a warm and well-stocked feed shed. Jackson won prizes with his sheep. Of the ten ewes stolen the other night, eight were due for a February lambing, and ewes like that were like gold on the hoof.

'Is Jackson making a formal charge?'

'He might,' said Peasgood. 'He's going into Wareham first thing after Christmas to see his solicitor. I told him he was on a hiding to nothing so far as cast-iron proof was concerned; but one way or another he wants Henneker nailed to the nearest wall.'

All of which seemed to bode yet more ill for the unfortunate Austen Henneker.

'Did you know about this, Sergeant?' asked Roper, sliding the summary of Allgrove's past misdeeds across the desk to Peasgood.

'No, sir,' said Peasgood, having scanned a few lines of the fax. Lower Gorton wasn't on his patch, so he had not been officially notified that Allgrove had been released. And the sergeant whose patch Lower Gorton was had only been on that beat for the last six weeks or so, and hence wouldn't necessarily have known about Allgrove's promise to get his revenge on Komarowski. And since Peasgood himself had only been the beat officer around here for eighteen months he only knew of Allgrove's threat by hearsay.

Roper drew the fax back again. Allgrove's record went back to the middle seventies. All the known offences concerned organised dog-fighting and illegal betting on the results; and each time Allgrove had been caught he had moved on to another county. He had been charged and convicted on five occasions; the fifth time, on the initial evidence of Zygmunt Komarowski, he had been given a three-year custodial sentence, of which one had been remitted for good behaviour.

And now Allgrove was out, and Zygmunt Komarowski was dead.

Chapter 9

Even cloaked in white snow Allgrove's isolated cottage looked a bleak and sombre place. Several dilapidated sheds and lean-tos had been tacked on to the sides like afterthoughts, the net curtains at the dirty upstairs windows were grey and rotting, and over on the right two high wooden garages with double doors and corrugated asbestos roofs had been neglected for so long that their creosoted planks had curled and split. From one of them, as Roper climbed out of the car, came the steady crashing of a hammer on sheet metal overlaid with the sound of pop music.

Peasgood, gloved and overcoated, climbed from his own car and joined Roper and Price in front of Allgrove's rusty iron gate. The snow on the front path showed only two sets of smudged footprints, one set coming out and the other going in; more snow had fallen since they had been made, and filled them in, which probably meant that they had been made some time early yesterday. When Roper opened the gate the bottom of it ploughed an arc in the snow. The thumping beat of music grew louder.

Price took the path to the cottage, Roper and Peasgood to the garages. The hammering had stopped. Peasgood rapped on the garage door from which a brass padlock and a swinging steel hasp hung loosely.

The volume control of the radio was turned down and the flimsy door was shoved open a cautious inch from the inside.

Roper held up his warrant-card to the slit. 'Mr Allgrove?' he said.

One inimical eye, set in a half of a narrow pugnacious face, stared hard at the card, then out at Roper.

'What if I am?'

'Routine call, Mr Allgrove,' said Roper. 'We'd like a few words.'

The one eye took in Peasgood at Roper's shoulder. 'I'm busy. What's it about?'

'Zygmunt Komarowski, Mr Allgrove,' said Roper. 'Believe he was a friend of yours.'

'Yeah,' said Allgrove scornfully. 'Guessed it wouldn't be long before I got a visit about that.' He shouldered the door open wider and stood aside. He picked up a piece of rag from a plywood tea-crate littered with tools and wiped the black grease from his hands as Roper and Peasgood followed him in. The vehicle he was working on was a semi-derelict removal van. Allgrove's Removals. From Your Place to Anywhere. Free Quotations Given. A wire-caged inspection lamp dangled from a length of flex over the opened engine compartment. The front nearside tyre was almost treadless. The smell of paraffin came from an old stove with a kettle on it beside the tea-crate.

'Getting back into business, are you, Mr Allgrove?' asked Roper.

'Not getting back to anything around here,' said Allgrove surlily. 'Selling up, aren't I?' He was fractionally taller than Roper, spiky haired, lean and sinewy and fortyish, and wearing a motheaten red pullover and a pair of frayed and tattered jeans with bits of white flesh showing through here and there, and a failed fly-zip.

'You're moving on, then?' asked Roper, still looking around, weighing, tagging, and not missing the two wire dog-cages stacked one on top of the other in the dark corner at the back of the garage.

'None of your bloody business,' said Allgrove, tossing down the rag amongst the tools on the crate. He looked witheringly towards the door as Price joined them after making an exploratory tour of the outside of the cottage.

The tax disc on the pantechnicon was two years out of date. Roper opened the door of the cab. It smelled damp and cold. There was mildew growing on the split upholstery of the passenger seat.

'You're wasting your time,' said Allgrove. He was tilting the tin kettle over an unsavoury-looking enamelled mug. Close behind him, Roper fancied he could still smell the sour odour of prison on him. 'I didn't do it.'

'Didn't do what?' asked Roper.

'Kill that bloody Pole,' said Allgrove.

'But you told him you were going to, didn't you, Charlie?'

'I've been there,' sneered Allgrove. 'I've done it, haven't I?' He turned slowly, stirring his black coffee with a bent spoon. 'And it was only talk. I just wanted him to spend a couple of years wondering. And I'm *Mister* Allgrove now, by the way. Only my friends call me Charlie.'

'The night before last,' said Roper. 'Where were you?'

'Here,' said Allgrove. He sipped defiantly at his coffee.

'Anybody with you?'

'Nobody,' said Allgrove.

'Wife?'

'Buggered off, didn't she? The day after I got banged up.'

'How long have you had that pullover?' said Price.

'Bloody years,' said Allgrove.

'Wearing it the other night, were you?' asked Roper.

Allgrove's mood changed. He looked suspiciously from one to the other of them as he lowered his mug. Roper hemmed him from the front, Price to his left, and Peasgood had just appeared around the back of the pantechnicon and blocked off his other side.

'Found this,' said Peasgood, holding a closed fist over Roper's open palm and letting what he was gripping drop into it.

It was a bundled length of thin, grubby white cord,

a small, cylindrical lead weight at one end and a short strip of oily rag tied to the other. Roper held the frayed strip of rag and let the weight dangle down by his knees where it swung like a pendulum.

'Been cleaning out the barrels of your shotgun lately, Charlie?' asked Roper.

'I haven't got one,' said Allgrove. 'Never had. And that bloody thing's not mine, either.'

Roper sniffed at the rag. He could only smell damp. The smell of oil was long gone. He jerked at the cord and caught the weight up again.

'I'll get a search warrant, if you like, Charlie,' he said. 'How d'you want to play it?'

'I don't get any peace until you lot have looked around, that it?'

'Right,' said Roper.

Roper sat on an upturned orange-box in the empty scullery and watched Allgrove feed a couple of logs into the old-fashioned iron range. From what he had seen so far, there was no furniture anywhere. If it had been movable, including the light bulbs, Mrs Allgrove had taken it with her. The hollow sounds of footsteps coming from upstairs were Price's and Peasgood's; Makins was here now, too. He was having a more thorough poke around amongst the rubbish in the two wooden garages and the outbuildings.

'Where's your missus gone?' asked Roper.

'None of your business,' said Allgrove. 'I've told you, I've done nothing. You want to find out anything, you bloody find it out for yourself.'

'You're a card-carrying villain, Charlie,' said Roper. 'I've got a form-sheet on you as long as my arm.'

'And that makes me a bloody suspect, does it?' sneered Allgrove. 'I told you: I've been there and I've done it. Two bloody years. And I'm not that stupid enough to want to go back again. OK?'

Roper fetched out his cheroots. He offered the open

100

packet to Allgrove. Allgrove shook his head. Roper struck his lighter. A cupboard door was slammed shut upstairs and echoed all over the empty house like a gunshot.

'You threatened Komarowski. The judge heard you, the jury heard you. Bad news, that is, Charlie.'

'The old bastard had been spying on me, hadn't he? If it hadn't have been for him, I'd never have been sent down in the first place. I'd got a gripe. And I got it out of my system, didn't I?'

'Did you?' said Roper. 'Or did you spend the last couple of years hatching out how you were going to do it?'

'You're stupid,' sneered Allgrove. 'Don't think I'm that bloody daft, do you?'

Roper took a long draw of his cheroot. 'That pullover's a dead ringer,' he said, aiming the tip of the cheroot at it.

'For what?'

'A piece of wool we found up at Komarowski's caravan,' said Roper. 'The villain left it behind. Caught up on the door-frame.'

'Not from this one, it wasn't,' said Allgrove. He had brought his mug in with him. He turned his back on Roper and gave it a token swill under the cold tap, then stood it upside down on the wooden draining board. On the flagged floor by the door stood a plastic carrier-bag with Allgrove's Christmas groceries in it; mostly tins, mostly baked beans and tomato soup.

'When did you buy those?' asked Roper.

'Yesterday,' said Allgrove. 'Morning. Early. There's a till receipt in there somewhere. It's got the date on it. You can look if you like.'

'I'm more interested in what you were getting up to the day *before* yesterday,' said Roper. 'After dark.'

'Told you,' said Allgrove. 'I was here.'

'Watching the box? Listening to the radio?'

'Radio,' said Allgrove. '*She* took the telly.'

'And what was on the radio?'

'Music,' said Allgrove. 'It's all I ever listen to. Breaks the silence.'

'Name me a programme.'

'How the hell would I know?' said Allgrove. 'They all sound the same, don't they?' He reached up to the window ledge over the china sink, took down a battered tin tobacco box, and from it a cigarette roller, a packet of Rizla papers and a few strands of tobacco. The cigarette he made was old-lag style, thin and meagre. The protruding wisps of tobacco were nipped off with a finger and a thumbnail and dropped back into the box for later.

'Got kids, have you?' asked Roper.

'No, thanks,' said Allgrove.

'I forgot,' said Roper. 'You're a dog-lover.'

Allgrove smiled ironically around the cigarette as he lit it, and the tip flared into momentary flame. 'You've got nothing on me. Believe it.'

'Convince me,' said Roper.

'Not down to me, is it? If you reckon you've got something on me, it's your job to prove it.'

Roper let the silence hang while Allgrove puffed away truculently at his wisp of a cigarette. Roper's viscera, usually a reliable indicator, tolled a warning bell. Allgrove wasn't his man. The warmth of the iron stove was making the bare white walls weep with condensation.

'Your missus gone far?' Roper asked.

'Not far enough,' said Allgrove.

'Still local, then?'

'Took up with that bloody Colin Snow. Over at Jackson's place.'

Snow. Of course. Roper remembered now. It had been partly on Snow's evidence that Allgrove had been sent down and Austen Henneker fined for conspiring with him.

'That's the Snow who used to work for Austen Henneker, is it?'

'Labourer,' said Allgrove. 'Least, he was till he shopped

Austen and Austen sent him packing. Serves him bloody right and all. Helped to shop me an' all, he did. Two-faced bastard.'

'And now he works for Mr Jackson,' prompted Roper. 'And your wife's gone with him, eh?'

'He's Jackson's stockman,' said Allgrove contemptuously. 'She chucked all this—' A wave of his cigarette encompassed the run-down empty cottage as if it were a mansion, '—for a little tinpot two up and two down. Got two kids to look after, an' all, the silly cow. She always used to say she hated bloody kids.'

'Had these kids by this Snow, did she?' The subject of his errant wife, at least, appeared to be something of which Allgrove was prepared to talk at great and bitter length.

'Snow's two kids. His missus died. About three years back.'

'And now he's pinched yours,' said Roper.

'And he's bloody welcome,' sneered Allgrove. 'If he gets all I did out of her he's in for a few cold nights.'

'Like that, was it?' asked Roper.

'Aye,' said Allgrove. 'Bloody was, an' all.'

'Made you feel like getting your own back, I'll bet.'

But Allgrove was quicker and smarter than that. 'Told you,' he said. 'I'm getting out. Selling up. She's made her bloody bed and now she can lie on it.'

A thunderous double knock sounded at the front door. Someone came down from upstairs to answer it. It sounded like Price. The grim voice that answered him was George Makins'.

'Where did you find it?' asked Price.

'In his other van,' muttered Makins. 'Rolled up in an old blanket. Where's the guv'nor?'

'In the scullery with Allgrove.'

Allgrove, one ear cocked towards the ominous exchange in the passage, suddenly looked a lot less sure of himself. Roper rose expectantly from the orange-box as Makins' footfalls sounded hollowly along the bare boards outside, then came into the scullery. He was carrying a scuffed grey canvas cricket-holdall, and whatever was inside it was rigid enough and long enough to make a bulge at each end. And from the way Makins was carrying it, it looked just about the right weight and length for a shotgun.

The bag went down with a thud as Makins set it on the orange-box and held the handles apart so that Roper could look inside. It *was* a shotgun, twin-barrelled, a rust-freckled old twelve-bore with its split wooden stock held together with a whipping of copper wire and varnish. The canvas of the bag felt cold and damp.

'Touched it?' asked Roper.

Makins shook his head.

Roper crooked a finger in the direction of Allgrove. 'Things are looking a bit dire, Charlie. This thing yours, is it?'

Allgrove shuffled forward anxiously with his neck craned as Roper stood aside to give him a view into the holdall. Makins held the top wider open. Price had appeared at the doorway, Peasgood at his back.

Allgrove shook his head vehemently.

'So what was it doing in your van?' said Roper.

Allgrove had visibly crumpled. 'It ain't mine,' he protested. 'Honest, it ain't mine. I've never had a bloody shotgun. I had a record for Christ's sake, didn't I? I wouldn't have got a bloody permit, would I?' His eyes flicked to Roper, to Makins, to Price, to Peasgood, to the door to the garden behind him; only the door was bolted and Peasgood was already moving in to intercept him if he tried.

'And supposing it's got your dabs all over it?' said Roper.

Allgrove's head started shaking again. 'It won't have.'

'Why not?'

'Because I've never *touched* it. I've never bloody *seen* it before.'

'Or you've cleaned it,' said Roper. 'That it?'

Allgrove's head was still shaking. Scared he certainly was, but bewildered he also was; and the bell began tolling again in Roper's gut and conspired to add to his feeling of unease. It was all somehow too convenient, too pat and too ready-made. Allgrove was a villain, Allgrove had made a threat on Komarowski's life as they'd taken him down from the dock. Allgrove was out of the chokey for only a couple of days and Komarowski was dead of a shotgun. And now a shotgun – and Roper did not doubt for a moment that the one in the grey holdall was the very one – had been found wrapped up in an old blanket in one of Allgrove's sheds, and Allgrove didn't have even a shred of alibi for the hours during which the Pole was shot.

'In the pantechnicon, was it?' Roper asked Makins.

'In the other shed,' said Makins. 'He's got an old white van in there. Looks like a gutted ambulance.'

'Van have its doors locked?'

Makins shook his head. 'Bit of old clothes-line wound round the handles.'

Roper's unease lingered. Too much had come together too quickly. It was like opening up a new jigsaw puzzle and finding the pieces already put together. From what he had seen of the two clapboard garages, both of them had been neglected for so long that they had started to fall to pieces. The van doors had been tied together, not locked. And if the shotgun was Allgrove's, and it was the weapon that had been used to kill Komarowski, it wouldn't have been lying around this place so crudely hidden. Allgrove wasn't smart, but he was smarter than that.

But indisputably the shotgun was evidence of something or other, and it was here. And so was Allgrove.

'Have you got a coat, Mr Allgrove?' asked Roper.

Outside now it was too cold even for snow. The converted ambulance stood on thick oak duckboards laid over a concreted pit that took up most of the floor area.

He climbed into the back of the white van behind Makins. From the few odds and ends inside, a stack of old folded blankets, a couple of plywood tea-crates, a two-wheeled dolly of the sort used to shift pianos, it was obvious that Allgrove used the vehicle for light removal jobs, or, rather, he had before he was put away. But in the last couple of years the van had been nowhere. All four tyres were down on the wheel rims, the windows were almost impenetrable with grime and dust and the knob was missing from the top of the gear-stick.

'It was wrapped up in this,' said Makins. He was down on his heels by a motheaten pink blanket. Like the ones on the pile behind him, it had been folded so long that its rectangular pattern of dusty creases looked as if they had been ironed in. One rectangle was almost black with dust. The remainder were relatively clean. And so was the top of the topmost blanket on the pile.

'It was a plant,' said Roper.

'You reckon?' said Makins.

'I can practically smell it,' said Roper.

The strip of worn grey institutional carpet glued along the middle of the floor probably dated back to the days when the van had been an ambulance. It was covered with stains and dust, and felt damp to the touch when Roper put the backs of his knuckles to it.

He stepped out into the shed again. Daylight showed through gaps and chinks in the clapboards here and there but nowhere was there a hole large enough for anything but a fox or a cat to slip through. There was certainly no way in for a grown man, except the doors.

There was a creak of springs as Makins climbed down after him.

Roper crouched and peered down between the oak duckboards. 'Got a torch?' he said.

Makins passed down his Maglite, and Roper flashed its bright pencil beam around the inside of the pit. Black streaks around the walls were probably animal bloodstains; there was six or seven inches of water in the

106

bottom, stagnant and with a film of green slime over it. It looked as if the water had been higher still once, and had evaporated away. He stood up and handed the torch back to Makins.

'What do you think, George?'

Makins stretched one side of his mouth doubtfully. 'Dunno,' he said. 'He's a career villain. And he certainly had it in for Komarowski. And an alibi would have helped, too. If I had to stake odds on it, I'd say it was fifty-fifty. He might just be a bloody good liar.'

'And hid the shotgun himself to make it look like a plant.'

Makins shrugged. It wasn't impossible. The ways of villainy were many and devious.

Roper looked at his watch. It was one o'clock of the afternoon. Price had taken Allgrove back to the MIC for a protracted interview, and the shotgun, Allgrove's red pullover and samples of his fingerprints were on their way to Forensic. Tomorrow was Christmas Day and most of the machinery of the law would grind to a halt for twenty-four hours. Time, especially for Roper, was fast running out.

Back at the MIC he collected a welcome mug of tea from the galley and joined Price and Allgrove in the interview cubicle. Bent over a notepad at one end of the table was a WPC, and behind Price a neon glowed on the tape-recorder. Allgrove sat miserably hunched with his clasped hands pressed between his knees.

'Has he changed his story yet?'

Price shook his head.

'I'm not going to, either,' said Allgrove, still not looking up. 'I didn't go out that night. And that's *not* my bloody gun.'

'We'll see,' said Roper.

'You don't frighten me,' said Allgrove. 'You can keep me here all night if you like. You still won't get anywhere.'

Roper was inclined to agree with him, and so, with a

discreet shake of his head over Allgrove's arched back, was Price.

He left Price with it and returned to his own office, sipped at his mug of tea and lit a cheroot, feeling like a man who was trying to work with both hands tied behind his back. He had spoken to a lot of people, asked a lot of questions. He might even have spoken to Komarowski's killer and not known it. He had still to establish a motive. He had – his intuition was almost screaming its certainty aloud – the weapon. Mrs Henneker had passed a tall thin man in the dark. Allgrove was a tall thin man. He didn't have an alibi. The man had been carrying some sort of long bag. Allgrove had been in possession, in the eyes of the law at least, of a long bag. And the bag had a gun in it.

Everything pointed to Allgrove; except the finding of the gun and bag in his garage. Crudely hidden. If Allgrove had really wanted to hide that gun it would have been miles away from here by now, and even if he hadn't had the time or the wit to do that he was surely bright enough to have hidden it less obviously. And there was something else: if he *had* killed Komarowski he would have realised that he would be the law's first port of call when the body was found . . .

Roper glanced up as a brisk rap sounded at the door, and it was slid back on its runners.

'No joy?' asked Roper, as Price slid the door shut again behind him.

'I don't think there's going to be,' said Price. He dropped into the chair on the other side of the desk. 'I've given him several chances to change his story.'

'And?'

'He won't. He says he was in all that evening. He got himself a couple of cans of lager from his local grocer's earlier in the day; he drank those and listened to his radio, and climbed into his sleeping-bag round about ten o'clock. That's the last thing he remembers. He reckons the lagers must have knocked him out. He went out shopping early the next morning, got back around nine o'clock, and he hasn't been out since.'

'D'you believe him?'

'We can't prove otherwise, can we? And we certainly can't hold him if his dabs aren't on that shotgun.'

'But we keep him here until we find out,' said Roper; because gut-telegraphs were one thing, and a bagful of evidence quite another.

Chapter 10

'What's up?' Roper asked, as Makins, for perhaps the third time in the last mile or so, reached up and gave yet another tweak to the angle of the driving mirror. They were on their way to Snow's cottage.

'That white van,' said Makins. 'We seem to be seeing a lot of it.'

Roper turned against his seat-belt and looked over his shoulder. Before a sudden sharp curve in the road, when it went from view behind a hedge, he had a brief glimpse of a small white van. It might have been an old Austin.

'First time I've noticed it,' he said.

'It followed us to Allgrove's place,' said Makins. 'It was parked down the lane in a layby.'

But Roper hadn't seen it there, nor did the white van reappear during the remainder of the drive to Colin Snow's cottage.

It stood alone, and lonely, well back from the road, a little box of a place that a new coat of pebbledash and fresh white paint did nothing to distinguish. In the front garden an elderly and snowbound yellow Toyota stood with its front end jacked up on a pair of axle-stands and its front brake drums open to the elements. It looked as if it had taken root there.

Snow, when he opened the door to them, viewed Roper's warrant-card with patent trepidation. Dark, stooped and slight, he looked like a man who spent most of his waking hours braced for the next disaster to overtake him.

'What's it about?' he said, anxiously taking in Makins

110

at Roper's shoulder as he handed the card back again.

'Routine enquiries, Mr Snow,' said Roper. 'We're investigating the death of Mr Komarowski. Wondered if we could have a word with you and Mrs Snow. Just a chat, sir.'

'Yeah . . . Well . . . I suppose.' With a marked lack of enthusiasm he let them into the cramped narrow hallway. A child's tricycle blocked off the stairs and the two front wheels of the Toyota, newly tyred, were leaning against the wall. A smell of cooking turkey wafted along from the kitchen.

'You'd better go in there,' Snow said. 'I'll get the missus.' He went on along the hall. A slight drag of his right leg made his gait uneven.

Snow's two children were playing with a Lego set in front of the gas fire in the general-purpose room into which he had shown them. The little boy was about six, the girl a couple of years younger. Both viewed Roper and Makins with only passing interest. The room had been newly wallpapered, and the Christmas tree on the table at the window seemed to be well hung with presents.

A muttered exchange from the kitchen preceded the return of Snow with his wife, the erstwhile Mrs Allgrove. He was around thirty-five, she several years older, a big flamboyant woman with a grim gash of a mouth that would brook no nonsense, least of all from a couple of policemen. It was immediately obvious that Colin Snow had warmer nights with her than Charlie Allgrove because she was also regally and sumptuously pregnant. She lowered herself into an armchair, and the little girl climbed on to her lap, and stuck her thumb in her mouth contentedly as Mrs Snow draped a motherly arm about her and drew her closer.

Snow perched himself on the arm of the chair opposite her. He still looked uneasy. Roper and Makins sat on a couple of dining chairs. Makins took out his pocket book. Roper could feel Mrs Snow watching him like a circling vulture.

111

'You work for Mr Jackson, Mr Snow,' Roper said, by way of a gambit.

Snow considered that with his forehead puckered. 'About two years,' he said.

'And before that?'

'Up Henneker's place—'

'And *he* sacked him,' broke in Mrs Snow. Snow looked embarrassed. It didn't take much imagination to work out who the boss was here, and it wasn't Colin Snow.

'Because of the dog-fighting business, was that?' asked Roper.

Snow nodded. 'I only went the once, an' all. And that was only after a couple of drinks; I didn't even stay to see all the first fight. When Charlie was arrested a few weeks later, I got scared the law'd pick me up too. So I turned myself in.'

'And he gave evidence in court,' said Mrs Snow. 'And serve 'em all right. Only Austen Henneker was there too, and because of what Colin said he got fined. And that's why he sacked Colin. Not that he said so, mind, but it was. Said Colin was lazy, which he isn't.'

'And your ex-husband was sent down, so I hear.'

Mrs Snow's jaw stiffened rancorously. 'All his doing, it was. Whole house used to smell of dogs. I hated it. Sent him to prison, they did, and bloody good riddance, that's what I said. Except he left me with all his debts – *and* no money. Debts up to his ears, he had. Allgrove never could handle money. I had to do all that.'

'Did you know he'd threatened Mr Komarowski, Mrs Snow?' asked Roper.

'Colin told me he had,' she said. 'I wasn't in court.'

'I heard,' volunteered Snow. He was like a man grabbing at a conversational lifebelt. 'I heard him say it.'

'Can you remember what he said exactly, Mr Snow?'

Snow's eyebrows came together. He looked a ponderous thinker. 'I'll bloody kill you for this, you old bastard. Something of that sort, it was.'

112

Roper regarded him speculatively, wondering how reliable he was.

'A violent man, was he, Mrs Snow?'

'Not with me, he wasn't,' she retorted tartly. 'He wouldn't have dared.'

'Did he ever have a shotgun?'

'Once,' she said. 'About five years ago.' She had never liked guns, especially in the house; and when she'd nagged him for days about a permit for it, and finally forced it out of him that he hadn't got one, she had ordered him to get rid of it. Sharpish. She thought he had, in any event she had never seen it again. But she had, when she was clearing out the house to get the money to pay all his bills, found a half-empty cardboard box of cartridges tucked out of sight on the top shelf of his wardrobe. She couldn't describe the gun, except that it was a bit knocked about, had two barrels and broke in half to be loaded. He'd bought it off a man in a pub, so he'd told her. Fifteen pounds it had cost him, half a week's housekeeping money. He'd always been a fool with money, had Allgrove.

So Allgrove had lied this afternoon. Mrs Snow-ex-Allgrove was sharp-tongued and malicious – at least towards Allgrove – but forthright and honest she also was.

'Did he ever threaten you, Mr Snow?'

Snow shook his head. Roper glanced across at Mrs Snow. She did the same. 'I told you,' she said. 'Anyway, him and me had stopped talking towards the end. It wasn't worth the bother.'

'Did you know he was back in circulation?'

Their reactions were poles apart. Snow paled. His wife only looked disgusted.

'Neither of you have seen him about?'

Mrs Snow shook her head. 'If he comes near here I'll kick him where it hurts,' she said. 'He don't scare me.'

'How long's he been out?' Snow asked anxiously.

'A couple of days,' said Roper.

113

'I'd better watch out for myself, then,' mumbled Snow. 'Bloody hell.'

'You're worth two of him,' his wife rejoined contemptuously. 'Don't you worry.'

Snow seemed to draw some comfort from that. Still with her thumb in her mouth the little girl was droopily asleep on her stepmother's ample lap.

'You're Mr Jackson's stockman these days, Mr Snow?' said Roper.

'Jack of all trades, more like,' said Snow. 'Always been in farming. Bit o' this; bit o' that. You know. He pays good too, old Fred—'

'Not like that Austen Henneker,' broke in Mrs Snow. 'Had to chase *him* every Saturday for his wages, didn't you, Col?'

'They don't want to hear all that,' grumbled Snow, lifting his face and scowling at her. 'They haven't come for gossiping.'

'Bit close with his cash, is he, Mr Snow?' asked Roper, to whom all information was grist of one sort or another, even gossip.

'Aye,' said Snow. 'He is, an' all.'

'That's why *she* left him,' said Mrs Snow. 'And took up with Fred Jackson. That's what all the arguing's about now. Austen's never forgiven him for taking Becky.'

'This feud between Mr Henneker and Mr Jackson, you mean?'

'There ain't no feud,' Snow broke in. 'Takes two to make one o' those. Fred wouldn't feud with nobody. He don't have the time. It's Austen Henneker. All on his own. It's like Dot says, he's getting his own back on Fred Jackson for taking his missus.'

Some more judiciously interjected promptings made Snow almost loquacious. Jackson was the good guy, Henneker the villain. When Jackson's stock was let out into the road it was because Henneker had crept along in the night and opened the gates. When Henneker's stock was let out it was Henneker who let it out and

114

put the blame on to Jackson. When Henneker's stock was found among Jackson's it was Henneker who put it there. It was the same with that bag of fertiliser that had fouled up Henneker's stretch of Gort Stream. Henneker had put it there himself, with the sole object of pointing the finger at Jackson. Stood to reason, didn't it?

Reason, so far, had not come into it, but Roper didn't disillusion him.

'Did you ever work for Mr Henneker's father, Mr Snow?'

'I did,' said Snow. 'Years and years. Started with him as a boy. Good bloke, he was. Henneker's farm used to run like a piece o' clockwork in those days.'

'So you'd remember Mr Komarowski moving in with his caravan.'

'I helped,' said Snow. 'We all did. Old Neville got a crane in. Bloody great thing it was. Him and Mr Komarowski knew each other in the war. In the Air Force, they were, the two of 'em.'

'Then old Mr Henneker died,' said Roper.

Snow nodded glumly. 'Things were never the same after that,' he said. 'Place started to go to rack and ruin. Austen was never cut out for farming, not like Fred Jackson. He's a lazy bugger, Austen.'

'And violent?' Roper prompted hopefully.

'They say,' said Snow.

'Did you ever see him behaving violently – towards Mrs Henneker, for instance?'

'Saw her once with her arm in plaster. Another time she was limping. When I asked her she said she'd fallen down the stairs.'

'Fallen down the stairs?' said Roper. 'Both times?'

'Aye,' said Snow. 'That's what she said.'

'She told me the same,' said Mrs Snow. 'But she would, wouldn't she? Scared of him, she was. Ain't that right, Col?'

Col agreed that it was. Dead scared.

115

'How did Austen Henneker got on with Mr Komarowski?'

'Had a couple of barneys the two of 'em,' said Snow. 'Austen's making, mostly. I heard Austen went up there to see him a couple of months back – with his dog. Told old Ziggy if he caught him spying on him again he'd have him off his land altogether. Least, that's the story that's got about.'

'Who'd you hear that from?'

'Heard it up the Gorton Arms; forget who told me.'

And doubtless it had been well doctored and filtered before it had even arrived there. Truth, as ever, was determinedly elusive.

Roper fastened his seat-belt and lit a cheroot. 'We're running around in circles, George,' he said. He preferred spirals. With a spiral, eventually, you got to an end. With a circle you trod the same stretch of ground over and over.

Makins turned the ignition key and the rear wheels slewed sideways in the snow and rubbed against the kerb before he managed to pull away. Neither of them saw the waiting man return to the white van a couple of hundred yards behind them.

'Don't give me the old moody, Charlie. I'm a busy man.'

'I told you,' retorted Allgrove. 'I've never had a bloody gun.'

'Fifteen quid,' said Roper. 'A bloke in a pub.'

Realisation dawned in Allgrove's eyes. 'You've been to see her, haven't you? My bloody old woman.'

'I'm plugged straight in to the grapevine, Charlie,' said Roper. 'And you'd better believe it.'

Allgrove was still in Price's cubicle, a mug of tea in his hands. Roper sat close beside him, his eyes boring into the side of Allgrove's head, knee to knee and elbow to elbow. Makins and Price sat opposite.

'All right,' Allgrove finally conceded. 'I did have a

116

shotgun, and I didn't have a permit for it. But I only had it a couple of days. The old woman found it and made me sell it.' Allgrove's anxious eyes watched Makins write that down on a fresh sheet of paper.

'The gun we found this afternoon? Or another one?'

'Another one.'

'How do you know?'

'Because that one was broken, wasn't it? It had wire round the stock to hold it together, didn't it?'

'And yours didn't?'

Allgrove shook his head. All he knew about the gun he'd once had was that it was a twelve-bore side-by-side – and to the best of his memory had been made somewhere on the Continent; Italian, it might have been.

'That's all I remember. And that's the truth.'

'But you lied, Charlie,' said Roper equably. 'You told us you never had a shotgun in the first place. Now you're telling us you did. So which is it?'

Allgrove set his mug on the table but kept his hands around it, his fingers working nervously at its rim.

'I had a shotgun . . . I sold it . . . That's the truth. I fired it once, to try it out. Then the missus found it. That's when I sold it.' He turned his face away anxiously again to watch Makins commit him to paper.

'You bought a box of cartridges,' said Roper.

'The bloke chucked 'em in when I bought the gun. And it was only half a box. It wasn't full. I used two. When I tested it.' His head slowly swung back so that he and Roper were eye to eye again. 'Honest.'

'What did you do with 'em?' asked Price. 'These cartridges.'

Allgrove pondered. 'I dunno,' he said, eventually. 'I don't remember. Straight. I think I put 'em away somewhere.'

'You didn't hand them over when you sold the shotgun?'

Allgrove pondered again. 'No,' he said. 'Don't think so.'

Roper shifted sideways to give Allgrove more room. 'Don't spoil it, Charlie,' he cautioned. 'I'm almost believing you . . . Who bought the gun off you?'

'It was over Honiton way,' said Allgrove. 'I don't know his name.'

'Try remembering,' said Price.

'It was a dog-fight,' said Allgrove. 'Nobody hands out visiting cards at those, do they? He was just a face.'

'How about that cleaning pull-through Peasgood found?'

'It came with the gun. I'd forgotten I had it.'

'How d'you reckon the gun got in your garage? Walk in on its own, did it?'

'Of course it bloody didn't.'

'So how did it get in there?'

Allgrove licked his lips. 'I can't answer that,' he croaked. 'You know I bloody can't. It was *put* there. Somebody's setting me up.'

'No signs of a break-in, Charlie,' said Roper. 'Perhaps you left the garage unlocked.'

It was a lifeline, had Allgrove chosen to make a grab for it. But he did not. 'I always keep it locked,' he said. 'Told you: somebody's set me up for this.'

'The other night . . . The night Komarowski was shot. Tell us about it.'

'I already did.'

'Again, Charlie.'

They bounced Allgrove between them like a rubber ball, but he didn't change the story he had told Price. He had worked on his pantechnicon that night until 9.30. In the kitchen, he had heated a tin of soup for his supper. After that he had broached two cans of lager he had bought that afternoon, then he had climbed into his sleeping-bag, unrolled on the kitchen floor, around about ten o'clock, after which he remembered nothing until he had woken the next morning with the radio still going.

'Two lagers laid you out, did they?'

'That's right. I hadn't had a drink in two bloody years, had I?'

There was a momentary hiatus as someone rapped on the door and Price got up to answer it.

'Who d'you think is setting you up, Charlie? One of your old dog-fighting buddies?'

'Don't bloody know, do I?' said Allgrove miserably. 'If I did, I'd bloody tell you, wouldn't I?'

Price's hand dropped on Roper's shoulder. 'Phone,' he said, loud enough for Allgrove to hear. 'They've got some results on that shotgun.'

Allgrove didn't react at all. Roper rose. Price followed him out and slid the door shut behind them.

'I've got a sneaky feeling he's on the up and up,' said Price.

'So have I,' said Roper.

Preliminary tests on the shotgun had revealed not a single latent fingerprint, nor were there any on the two empty twelve-bore cartridge cases that had been found still in the breeches.

'They were old, by the way, the cartridges. Made with waxed-cardboard cylinders; they're mostly made of plastic these days.'

'How old?' asked Roper.

'Twenty years,' said Craig. 'Perhaps even older. They must have been kept uncommonly well.'

The weapon was older still, fifty or sixty years, made by a firm of gunsmiths that had long since gone under. So far no serial number had been found on it.

'Any idea when it was last fired?'

'Well, the two cases still have a strong smell of propellant. Say within the last week at most.'

'How about shot-pattern?'

'I'll let you know,' said Craig. 'Give me another hour or so.'

He rang in again at five o'clock. His firearms technician had failed to establish any kind of regular discharge

119

pattern from the shotgun; the request on Roper's part had only been a long-shot anyway. But the gun had definitely been fired recently. And a speck of dried blood, on one of the barrels close to the muzzle, had now been identified as recently deposited and of blood group A, as had been Komarowski's. Neither result was proof positive. The gun could have been fired at any time during the last few days and 42 per cent of the population of the United Kingdom, give or take a few, had group A blood coursing around its pipework, but the two findings together made it highly likely that the gun found in Allgrove's van was the one that had been used to kill the Pole. More definitive blood tests might render it a certainty; but those would take several more days.

'How about the bag?' asked Roper.

'No prints that we can make anything of. And the leather handles had been well wiped.' In Craig's opinion the bag was almost as old as the shotgun; no plastic had been used in its manufacture, the zip-fastener was a good old-fashioned metal one, heavily corroded in places with verdigris, and the eight studs that protected its bottom were made of brass and not chromium-plated tin the way they were these days. And the bottom, on the inside, was reinforced with a sheet of plywood lined with the same grey canvas with which the bag was made. The canvas was stuck to the plywood with fish glue, which was again evidence of the bag's antiquity. Removal of the plywood reinforcement had revealed the débris of many years. Dust, human hairs, splinters of wood, a couple of diminutive green rubber spikes – genuine unalloyed rubber, faded and perished and crumbling to the touch, so they were probably as old as the bag – probably broken off years ago from a pair of wicket-keeper's gloves, several fragments of varnished red leather.

'And an old tram ticket,' said Craig. 'A fourpenny one.'

'You're sure it's not an old bus ticket?'

'It reads "London Passenger Transport Board, Tramways Department. Route Number Sixteen".'

'Must be over thirty years old,' said Roper.

'It certainly means the bag had been up to London. Or came from there. But what I think you *are* looking for, by way of an owner, is – or was – a dedicated cricketer.'

It sounded likely.

'How about Allgrove's pullover? Any chance of it matching that piece of wool we found at the caravan?'

'No. Sorry. The pullover's made entirely of nylon.'

Allgrove was still in Price's cubicle, a fresh mug of tea in his hands and a uniformed constable for company. He looked up hopefully as Roper appeared in the doorway.

'You can go whenever you like, Mr Allgrove.'

'Told you, didn't I?' said Allgrove triumphantly. 'I've a bloody good mind to sue for wrongful arrest.'

'I didn't say I'd finished with you,' said Roper. 'I only said you could go. Only don't go too far, eh?'

Allgrove's face fell again.

'D'you want a lift back?' asked Roper.

'Not bloody likely,' said Allgrove. 'I'd rather bloody walk.'

Chapter 11

By seven o'clock the MIC was incommunicado. The telephone lines had been disconnected, the radio and computer terminals switched off, and Sergeant Blackett was stowing away all the movable furniture prior to driving the vehicle back to County for the Christmas break.

Roper, too, was calling it a day. He dropped his briefcase into the boot of his Sierra. A few yards away on the green the local schoolchildren were assembling for a torchlit carol concert, and at the fringe of the small crowd that had already gathered was the hardy figure of Miss Kingsley with her Labrador. Beside her, hunched, heavily muffled and overcoated, was her brother in his electric wheelchair.

It was like a furnace in the Gorton Arms. Apart from two men sitting at the far end of the counter and two of the village elders playing dominoes by the fire, the saloon bar was empty.

'Quiet night,' he observed, when the young barman brought back his half of bitter and his change.

'It's the kids and the carols,' said the barman. 'Give it another hour and there won't be room to breathe in here.'

Roper sipped at his half of bitter. He could feel the warmth of the fire at his back, and through the frosted glass of the windows see the haloed lights of the torches and home-made lanterns bobbing about on the green. One of the two men at the end of the bar was regarding

122

him suspiciously, but as Roper's eyes met his square on he looked away quickly. There was a click as a domino piece went down on the table by the fireplace.

The fire was reflected in the mirrors at the back of the bar, the thick, warped oak mantelshelf, the array of old prints and photographs on the panelled walls either side of it. It was the prints that drew him. Several times he had come across precious and sometimes unique prints carelessly hung on a wall to brighten a place up a bit without the owner ever realising he'd got a gem on his hands. He rose and ambled idly across to them with his beer. One print depicted a vista, viewed through its gateway, of the manor house of Upper Gorton and its surrounding parkland. The little grey stone lodge just inside the gates was instantly recognisable as the Kingsleys' place. Another showed the Gorton Hunt taking its stirrup cup outside this very pub on a fine autumn morning in 1838.

The photographs documented some more recent history of Upper Gorton. The village main street hung with bunting in honour of Queen Victoria's Golden Jubilee in 1887, the children's party in the church hall on the occasion of Edward VII's coronation in 1902. The Upper Gorton cricket eleven, a motley, bearded and moustachioed bunch of desperados, all in black trousers and waistcoats and rolled white shirtsleeves and staring hypnotised at the camera, captained by one Jos Painter, a formidable and black-bearded young Moses who sat with implacably folded arms at centre stage. The date on that was 1906.

Upper Gorton plainly took its cricket seriously and passed on its skills to the next generation with rigid nepotism. The 1938 eleven all had the same surnames as the team of thirty years before, with the exception of J. A. Kingsley – looking even more boyish than he had standing beside his Hawker Hurricane a few years later. Jos Painter was still in evidence that year, too, although his role had been reduced to Hon Captain and Treasurer and his beard was white and sparser. There was a younger

Painter standing behind him; and Roper, recalling that the present landlord of the Gorton Arms was also a Painter, presumed that the two of them were related.

Another cricket team, another generation. All boys this time. The surnames had changed, bar three, all of them probably the sons of the team of '38. Henry Painter, Austen Henneker and Frederick Jackson, all of them nearly forty years more cherubic and youthful than they were now. The team, composed of schoolboys from Upper and Lower Gorton and several other towns and villages at this end of the county, had played in the South of England Junior Boys' Schools Championships in 1951, and had reached the dizzy heights of the quarter finals . . .

Roper, who had taken a pace sideways, took a pace back again.

The photograph had been taken inside the Oval cricket ground – those gasholders stamped against the sky could only belong to Kennington gasworks – and in 1951 when electric trams had still been racketing around the streets of London.

He continued to sip at his beer; cool speculation told him that he could not be that lucky. A born, bred and now lapsed north-Londoner himself he had, in his youth, made many a trip across the river to watch cricket at the Oval. He himself had travelled down on the tube in those days, but he clearly remembered seeing trams, as well as buses, passing the ground in the early fifties. Folk in general didn't travel far in those days; a fortnight's holiday by the sea was a luxury indulged in by a privileged few, and if you owned a car you had to be dripping money. For a country lad, the hundred-and-thirty-mile trip to London, let alone to play cricket at the Oval, would have been momentous.

Had one of those lads carried a grey cricket-holdall with him, and taken a fourpenny tram ride for the last stage of that momentous journey, back in 1951? And dropped the ticket into the holdall, perhaps as a souvenir; and later forgotten all about it, or thought that he had lost it because it had worked its way under the plywood reinforcement in the bottom – where it had lain ever since? Because, if that was the way it had been, that tattered grey holdall was more traceable than it had at first appeared. A man would never forget that as a schoolboy he had once played cricket at the Oval.

He ambled back to the bar and resumed his wooden stool. Out on the green, with a little more enthusiasm than sense of pitch, the carollers had launched themselves into 'Silent Night'.

'Seem to like your cricket around here,' he observed to the barman who had just finished polishing a pint glass and was holding it up to the light.

'They used to.' The young man's tone was curt; he was plainly not a cricket fan. He picked up another glass from the pewter shelf under the counter. 'Better things to do, these days.'

'I see the Boys' Eleven made it to the Oval back in fifty-one,' Roper said casually, after another sip of his beer.

'And they still talk about it. You'd think it was the only thing that had ever happened around here.'

'You don't play?'

'No. Squash and tennis, me.'

Roper had already marked him down as a touch up-market for a country-pub barman. He was well-spoken, a little on the flash side, and had served Roper his bitter as if he were frightened of getting his hands dirty. Another glass was subjected to a scrutiny against the light.

'I noticed a Henry Painter in that team,' said Roper. 'Would that have been the lad who's the landlord of this place now?'

'My old man,' said the barman.

So unless Henry Painter had another son, the barman was young Greg Painter, the lad who had been at the disco in Dorchester with Trevor Henneker the night Komarowski was shot; and to whom young Henneker had given a lift home in his mother's paramour's Range Rover.

125

'So you're not the regular barman,' said Roper, hopefully appealing to Painter's obvious dislike of serving behind his father's bar.

'Just helping the old man out over Christmas.'

Like Trevor Henneker, young Painter was easy to draw out and quick to hint at a glittering future far away from Upper Gorton. He had taken his Law Finals back in the summer and was working for a solicitor over in Wareham. A couple of years there and he was moving up to London.

'Where the money is, eh?' prompted Roper companionably.

'Too damn right,' said Painter.

But then, just as Roper had wound him up like a gramophone, the senior Painter appeared through an arch beyond the till, and Roper quickly switched the topic to the better weather that was forecast over the holiday. For the time being, he preferred that the subject of cricket, and the grey holdall that had been to London, were put on the back burner. What he certainly didn't want, for the next twenty-four hours at least, was one suspicious member of the team talking to another.

He closed the refrigerator door and padded back to the table with a carton of milk and a tumbler. It was Boxing Day morning, 2 a.m., and sleep still eluded him after the tedious drive back from Southampton where he and Sheila had spent Christmas Day with her sister's family. The sister was a gloating grandmother four times over and seemed not to notice what spoiled little brats her four once-removed offspring were. By the early evening Roper had been gritting his teeth and developing a strong rapport with Herod.

Tomorrow – today – he was turning in to work again. Price wouldn't be there, but George Makins would. High up on the agenda would be another talk with Austen Henneker and Fred Jackson; and perhaps even Harry Painter.

126

Austen Henneker had sworn that he hadn't left his house the night Komarowski was shot; but when Jackson had called there about his broken fence Henneker hadn't answered the door to him. Henneker may have been too drunk to answer it; he might simply have seen who the caller was and chosen not to answer it. Or he might have been lying to Roper and Price and not been in the house at all. Jackson on the face of it, had no motive for killing the Pole. If Jackson was involved in a feud of any sort it was more likely to be with Henneker. Painter, the other member of the boys' cricket eleven who still lived locally, had seemed like a man who, outside his business and because of it, kept himself very much to himself. And Charlie Allgrove wasn't involved; Roper was as certain of that as he was of drawing his police pension in a few years' time. Whoever had planted that shotgun had probably known of Allgrove's threat to Komarowski, and known that he had recently been released from prison. It had been a good idea, badly timed and clumsily set up.

And still there wasn't an obvious motive anywhere in the offing. That Komarowski had put his nose too deeply into someone else's business was a possibility.

A slippered footfall shuffled into the kitchen behind him.

'Can't you sleep either?' he said.

'Headache,' she said. 'Those damned kids.'

'They weren't kids,' he grumbled. 'They were midgets from the bloody Mafia.'

She tipped a couple of tablets into a tumbler and poured some lukewarm water from the kettle on top of them, and brought the fizzy concoction back to the table. She winced as the chair struck a table leg as she pulled it towards her.

'You going in tomorrow?' she said, gingerly sitting.

'Today,' he said. 'I thought I would. A couple of hours.'

'Don't wake me,' she said. 'I'd like to die; till about two o'clock this afternoon.'

They sat in companionable silence while she drained

127

her potion and he his glass of ice-cold milk. An image of sun, sand and sea came and went. He grabbed it by the heels and brought it back again and savoured it. 'When d'you think the travel agents'll be open again?' he said.

'Apropos of what?' she said, frowning.

'Greece,' he said. 'A couple of weeks.' They had met in Greece. 'When this thing's finished with.'

'I'd kill for it,' she said fervently.

'No need to be too ambitious,' he said. 'I think they'll only want a deposit. How's your headache, by the way?'

'What headache?' she said.

Enid Kingsley woke with a start, and the sure knowledge that something was terribly, terribly wrong. She fumbled for the switch of the bedside lamp in the dark; although it wasn't dark, not quite, but she felt sure it ought to have been because it was only five o'clock, or her alarm clock had stopped.

Johnnie! He was her first thought as she thrust her arms into her dressing gown and quickly girded it. Something had happened to Johnnie. She hurried out to the landing. Stopped as she caught sight of the wavering vermilion glow shining through the little window. Saw now why she thought it might have been the dawn glimmering pinkly through the curtains. There was rising black smoke, too, in the direction of where Ziggy'd had his caravan. Then suddenly, in the second she had paused to take it in, a single ball of brilliant blue flame leapt skyward and was instantly extinguished. The explosive thud of air rattled the window . . .

She found the light switch.

'Johnnie,' she called, 'Johnnie,' as she hurried feverishly down the stairs, but of course Johnnie couldn't do anything to help, although it was a natural reflex to knock on his bedroom door and call his name again in the moment before she picked up the telephone and dialled 999 for the fire brigade. The voice that replied to her was almost drowned out by something that sounded

128

like a motor-cycle revving up as it was manoeuvred in the lane outside. She heard its door slam, so it wasn't a motor-cycle, it was a car . . . 'The Fire Brigade, please . . . I think it's at Henneker's farm . . . or it might be Jackson's . . . no, I'm sorry, I'm not sure. All I've seen are the flames in the sky. And I think there's been an explosion . . . '

Then Johnnie's muffled voice was calling: 'What the hell's going on out there?' in that fractious, whining way that so irritated her . . . he was so demanding sometimes . . . 'Yes,' she said. 'Upper Gorton. Please come quickly . . . '

With Makins tagging behind in his own car, Roper drove along the frozen cinder track to Henneker's farmhouse. It was Boxing Day morning, ten o'clock. A lot of heavy vehicles had passed this way since five o'clock this morning and the track was like a ploughed and gouged-up ice-rink.

He passed the escarpment, on his left, on top of which Komarowski's caravan had been, then dropped into the depression in which the farmhouse lay, or, rather, what was left of it. Most of the roof had disappeared, the end wall had gone and the lintels of all the windows he could see were black with soot, and festooned with icicles from the overspray of the firehoses. There was a red, County Fire Brigade tender parked on the concrete apron outside, and behind that the white van of the Fire Investigation Unit from Regional Forensic. Fred Jackson's Range Rover was standing further over by the stock sheds, near a white Metro that looked like Peasgood's.

He pulled in behind the white van. As soon as he opened his door he could smell the lingering stench of smoke and soot. Makins' car door slammed shut behind him. Over on the right, near some more stock sheds, young Trevor Henneker was talking deedily to Sergeant Peasgood.

The roof of the house had not so much fallen in as been blown out, certainly at the end of the house where the wall had collapsed, where shards of broken slates lay at all sorts of crazy angles in the snow round about. Close to the house, the snow had melted in the heat, then frozen back into puddles of black ice.

At the slam of Makins' door, a yellow-wadered and white-helmeted fire-officer had appeared in the charred doorway, a clipboard in one hand and an extended steel measuring tape in the other. His name was Beevers.

Roper showed him his warrant-card and introduced Makins.

'Anybody hurt?'

'Just a dog. And a couple of our lads. But we're still looking. The dog was locked in his office. Suffocated, poor bastard.'

The passage walls, with their scorched wallpaper, were still faintly warm to the touch, and ice was already forming in the cracks between the clay tiles of the floor just inside the front door. The stairs were just a few more charred timbers. Access to the upstairs was presently given by an aluminium ladder poked through a hole in the ceiling between the joists.

'Must have gone up like a torch,' said Roper.

'It did,' said Beevers, over his shoulder as he led the way.

Voices from the sitting-room belonged to a couple of Forensic technicians. One was taking flashlit photographs, the other, with a clipboard, was taking measurements and drawing a floor plan. In front of the fireplace, with its back to the door, stood the gutted wooden skeleton of a sofa with a few springs and bits of scorched hessian still attached to it.

'No sign of the owner?'

'Not yet?'

'Any idea where it started?' asked Roper.

'In here, we think.' The senior of the two technicians jotted a couple of figures on his clipboard. The word

'Cyril's' was splashed in red paint on the side of his yellow hard hat. 'Somebody left the sofa too close to the gas fire, amongst other things.'

'What other things?'

'Gas stove was turned on in the kitchen, according to Mr Beevers. Looks like somebody'd put a meal in to cook and forgot to light the gas.'

'What sort of meal?' The idea of Henneker cooking himself a decent meal didn't seem likely somehow.

'Don't know,' said the technician. 'We haven't found it yet. It's probably splattered all over the walls, the state it's in out there.'

'Can I take a look?'

'Be our guest.'

Beevers was still in the doorway. Roper stepped back over the débris of ceiling-plaster to join him. Above his head the smoke-blackened ceiling joists were still dripping water.

'Anybody out looking for Henneker, Mr Beevers?'

'The local bobby,' said Beevers. 'And the son. They haven't tracked him down yet.' He led the way past the charred staircase towards the kitchen. This was the end of the house where the wall had collapsed; ceiling and roof timbers had fallen in with it and this morning there was a clear view out to the sky and open fields. Three firemen were salvaging anything that was still intact and carrying it outside.

'Looks like a bomb's hit it,' said Roper.

'It did,' said Beevers. 'More or less. Mind how you go.'

Roper followed him over more débris of wood, plaster, roof slates, broken glass and crockery. The buckled gas cooker, thick with fallen dust and leaning to one side, was where Beevers stopped. The oven door hung open.

'This could have been the bomb,' said Beevers. 'The gas oven was turned full on, and the kitchen door was halfway along the passage before we cleared it away, so it was probably shut at the time.' The unlit gas had built up in the kitchen. A little of it would have leaked out under the door. It would have been like a time bomb. The unlit gas had drifted one way, the fire had licked the other. The subsequent explosion when the two had met, as well as taking the roof and wall out, had ripped the cooker from its incoming gas pipe, which had presented another hazard to Beevers' men this morning. The gas cock was under the stairs, together with the meter, and by the time the brigade had got here the stairs were already blazing and close to collapse. A Miss Enid Kingsley had reported hearing and seeing an explosion in the few seconds preceding her 999 call, so the fire must have been well under way by then.

This was the scullery where Roper and Price had interviewed Austen Henneker the other day. It was unrecognisable now. The remaining walls were flecked with black, the dresser a skeleton of warped and paint-blistered planks surrounded by shards of crockery, the china sink hanging from one bracket and a water pipe. The door out to the back-yard, according to Beevers, was lying twenty yards away in the snow where the blast had carried it like a piece of cardboard.

They picked their way carefully back to the passage, and Roper copied the sequence of events from Beevers' clipboard into his pocket book. A sudden gust of breeze blustering through brought more dust and drips of water wafting down from upstairs.

Two firemen had been injured, one by a falling roof timber, another by the firecracker explosions of a box of shotgun cartridges up in the front bedroom. The fire had been reported at 5 a.m., the brigade had arrived with two tenders at 5.15, and another tender had been requested at once. That had arrived at 5.30. The fire had finally been extinguished a few minutes after six o'clock.

It had been Beevers who had requested the attendance of the Fire Investigation Unit from Regional Forensic. Besides the suspicious circumstance of the gas oven having been turned on at full bore – and the probability of the scullery door having been shut on it – Beevers had also noticed that the sitting-room window had been left open at the top.

'How much?' asked Roper.

'Eight or nine inches,' said Beevers. It had let in sufficient fresh air not only to sustain the fire in the front room but to turn it into a blowtorch. Without fresh oxygen the fire might, just might, have been confined to the one room before its own smoke had extinguished it.

'Eight's a lot of inches,' said Roper. It had been a cold night last night. And from what he had heard, Henneker wasn't a man given to throwing his money about; what he certainly was unlikely to have done was to have had his gas fire on and a window wide open at one and the same time.

Makins was climbing down the aluminium ladder as Roper tucked his pocket book away. Two firemen were clearing up in what was left of the bedrooms.

'What's it like up there?'

'Dodgy,' said Makins, slapping his gloved hands together to shake the dust off. 'There's a couple of places where you can look straight up and see what the weather's like.'

Roper sent him off to scout around the outside and went back into the sitting-room. The younger technician had risen from the front of the sofa. Dangling precariously from the end of a ballpoint pen he was holding was a heat-crazed Johnnie Walker bottle. He carefully lowered it into a polythene evidence bag and ran a finger and thumbnail across the patent fastener to seal it.

'Anything new?' Roper asked, from the doorway.

'Could be,' said the older man. 'Can't be certain, but from the dents in the carpet it looks as if the sofa's a couple of feet nearer the fire than it used to be.' Both the sofa and the two armchairs ranged either side of it had been upholstered with highly inflammable plastic foam and covered in some kind of nylon-based velveteen. With ingredients like that the sofa would have become an incandescent ball in a matter of minutes. And he agreed with Beevers: the thick toxic smoke that would have been generated, had the sitting-room door been shut – and that window closed – might have extinguished the fire, or at least confined it to this one room.

More and more it was beginning to look like arson; and crudely executed at that. And there was still a chance of someone finding a body.

Roper went out to the only marginally colder outdoors and walked the hundred yards or so to where Peasgood and Trevor Henneker were still deep in conversation by the stock sheds.

'No sign of your father, Mr Henneker?'

Henneker, pale and drawn and shivering, shook his head. 'No,' he said. 'Not yet.' The shivering looked like shock rather than the cold. He had been here for the last hour seeing to the milking and feeding of his father's animals. His father, these days, was running the place with just one part-time labourer, and he had been given the day off.

'You've no idea where he might be?'

'None,' said Henneker, through chattering teeth. 'But his Land-Rover's not here, so he's got to be somewhere.'

Neither he nor his mother, nor Jackson, had seen or heard anything in the early hours of this morning. They all slept at the far end of Jackson's house. They had known nothing until Sergeant Peasgood had come knocking on Jackson's front door at six o'clock this morning. It was now nearer eleven. Henneker ought to have been here by now, but he wasn't. And that was ominous.

But, strictly speaking, unless Henneker turned up dead somewhere under the rubble, the fire was none of Roper's business. Henneker might have started it himself, perhaps for the insurance money, or it might, after all, have been an accident. It might even have been yet another incident in the feud between Henneker and Jackson, although that didn't seem likely, either, simply because it was too extreme. Jackson surely would never have been that stupid. Glancing sideways, he saw the distant figure of Makins beckoning to him from the cinder track, and excusing himself he ducked deeper into his upturned collar and went back across the front of the house and down the track to join him.

By the time he reached him, Makins had walked thirty or forty yards further down the track and was slowly walking back again, stopping every now and again and dropping to his heels to examine the snow between the mess of tyre tracks and the marks of the crane that had lifted out Komarowski's caravan the other day.

'Found something?'

'Might have,' said Makins. 'Footprints. Three just there.' Makins dropped to his heels and pointed to three frozen depressions in the snow. Two were smudged from back to front, the one in the middle was perfect, albeit splashed and dirty. The ones ahead and behind had been obliterated by vehicle tyres.

Makins levered himself up and walked back towards the main gate. Roper followed him. Makins stopped again. 'Four more,' he said. Again, all four had been spoiled with vehicle splashes. But again, each alternate one, the right foot in each instance, was smudged from back to front. The heel imprint at the back was knife sharp, the toe end blurred, as if the right foot had been dragged rather than lifted. Over several dozen yards similar patterns of bootprints, some walking towards the house, some walking away, meandered in and out of the tyre tracks. Whoever it was had not walked in a straight line. Over one stretch, enough prints showed between the tyre gouges to show that whoever had left them behind had wandered from one side of the track to the other and back again. They looked like impressions of wellington boots, with a barred sole and heel, fairly well worn.

Roper crouched and touched the rim of one impression with his finger. It was frozen hard. What seemed fairly certain was that they had been made before the fire brigade had arrived this morning. Which had been around 5.15.

'He was probably pissed,' called Makins. 'Looks as if he fell flat on his face. Just here.'

Stepping carefully, Roper walked further down the track to join him. Makins was down on his heels again.

'Hands, right forearm, knees,' said Makins, pointing to the scatter of depressions. It needed a little imagination to work out their geography, but once you'd done the imagining it was easy to see that someone had skidded in the snow just here and stumbled to his hands and knees. On his way out. And he had cut his right hand on the sharp snow if the rusty blotch with the pink edges was anything to go by.

'Get the camera, George.'

There were times when coppering gave Roper little pleasure; and this was one of them, because he knew where to find the man who was probably sporting a bandage on his right hand this chill Boxing Day morning. He might, of course, have had business here yesterday, but somehow Roper doubted it. And he was hardly likely to have dropped in to wish Austen Henneker a joyous Noël. All the signs were of a man unsteady on his feet; so perhaps Makins was right. The man had been drunk. And he limped as well, and his right leg was the favoured one.

And one local man who fitted that description was Colin Snow.

Colin Snow, who certainly had an axe or two to grind with Austen Henneker, who had just started to carve a fresh slice of life for himself with Fred Jackson, and a new wife with a baby on the way, and who had probably just broken himself at the bank by buying a pair of new tyres for his old banger of a Toyota.

Roper preferred his villains to be hard cases like Allgrove. Men like Snow were victims, permanently floundering around in a sea of misfortunes. It wasn't fair, it wasn't right; but life wasn't, either, and it wasn't the time to be standing about and philosophising on the human condition – whatever that was – because a vehicle was thundering up the track behind him at a great rate of knots.

It was Henneker's Land-Rover, bouncing and joggling over the rutted ice, and accelerating, and it looked as if Henneker wasn't going to stop despite Roper's upraised palm. There was a split second when he made up his mind to jump clear because Henneker hadn't seen him, but in that split second Henneker's horrified eyes lowered and fastened on Roper's through his windscreen, and there was a thud as he slammed on his brakes and braced himself against the back of his seat, and for a couple of seconds more the Land-Rover skidded inexorably on before finally stopping with a jolt that sent Henneker lurching forward in his seat.

He stayed in the cab only long enough to push the release of his seat-belt. He climbed down on buckling legs, eyes wide, mouth agape, not really crediting what he saw past Roper's shoulder.

'Christ!' he raged dazedly and thickly. 'Christ! What the bloody hell's going on?'

Roper opened his mouth to answer, but before the first word came Henneker had reached out, pushed him aside and stormed up the track towards the wreckage of his house. Roper caught up with him breathlessly, snatched hold of Henneker's sheepskin cuff.

'Hold on, Mr Henneker.'

It took several paces more to drag Henneker to a stop. His jaw was no longer slack, his eyes no longer wide but sheer bloody murderous. His hand went to close over Roper's wrist to wrench himself free, but Roper was fractionally quicker and warded it off.

'Bloody Jackson,' Henneker hissed through gritted teeth, as they wrestled in silence. 'I'll bloody kill 'im!'

'You'll do nothing of the bloody kind, Mr Henneker,' grunted Roper, finally seizing Henneker's other wrist. 'Just be bloody sensible for a minute, eh?'

137

For a few moments longer the two of them struggled, not with each other but for breath in the air that was like breathing icy needles. The engine of the Land-Rover was still running.

'How about the animals?' gasped Henneker, suddenly going slack.

'They're all right. Your son's here. He's looking after 'em.'

'When did it happen?'

'About five o'clock,' said Roper. 'This morning.' He loosed Henneker's wrist and cuff by way of an experiment. Henneker didn't move, except to cast another angry glance at his farmhouse.

'Got a cigarette?' he said.

'Cheroots.'

'That'll do.' Roper brought out the packet and his lighter. Henneker tugged off one of his leather gloves between his teeth, and plucked a cheroot from the open packet with trembling fingers. It took several attempts before he finally succeeded. Roper struck his lighter and cupped his hands around the flame, and held it to the wavering tip of the cheroot. Henneker inhaled, and slowly let the smoke seep out again.

'I'm really going to do it, you know,' he said truculently, looking up at Roper. 'You won't bloody stop me.'

'Do what?'

'Bloody Fred Jackson,' said Henneker. 'I'm going to bloody kill 'im. You bloody see if I don't.'

Chapter 12

They sat in the shelter of the Land-Rover's cab. Henneker was still smoking the cheroot.

'What's *he* doing?' asked Henneker, nodding beyond the windscreen towards the figure of Makins, who was still taking photographs of the limping man's bootprints.

Roper didn't answer. 'You took your time getting here, Mr Henneker. Where've you been?'

'Over with Charlie Allgrove,' said Henneker.

'Since when?'

'Yesterday afternoon. About four o'clock. I took over a couple of old armchairs and some bits of furniture to help him out.'

'Full house, was it?'

Henneker shot him an angry glance. 'I don't like the way you're bloody talking. Don't like what you're asking, either.' He jerked the cheroot towards the windscreen. 'Think I did it myself, all that? For the bloody insurance money or something? Think I'm bloody crazy or something? Think I'd have left my dog in the house knowing all that was going to happen?'

'It's been done before, Mr Henneker,' said Roper.

Henneker looked away again. 'I didn't have it insured,' he said bleakly. 'I let it slide the last time the premiums came due.'

'Why?' asked Roper.

Henneker shrugged. 'Didn't think it would ever happen, did I?' he said. 'I was selling up. It seemed like pouring good money after bad. Six months and I'd have been out of it.' He closed his eyes and tipped his head back against the seat-rest. 'Christ,' he sighed. 'What a *bloody* mess.'

Well, that was certainly one motive out of the window, if it was true; and from what Roper had heard about Henneker it probably was.

'Did you have any visitors yesterday, before you went to Allgrove's?'

Henneker shook his head. 'That's why I went,' he said. 'I was all on my own here. Got brassed off looking at the walls.'

'Not much more to look at at Allgrove's, was there?'

'Yeah,' said Henneker. 'He told me you'd been there. Said you'd found a twelve-bore in a bag.'

Roper ignored that. 'What did you do, the two of you? Besides looking at the walls?'

'Played cribbage. Talked. Had a few drinks.'

'Where did you sleep?'

'On the chairs I took. In the kitchen.'

'Comfortable?'

'Not very.' Henneker swivelled his bloodshot eyes to Roper's. 'But a bloke gets a few bevvies down, it don't matter a bugger where he lays his head down, does it?'

'So you'd had a few?'

'I took two bottles over,' said Henneker. 'I left a half-empty one with him. Yeah, we'd had a fair few. Haven't slept that sound in years,' he added bitterly.

'Did you go out at all? Either of you?'

'What for?' said Henneker. 'No point, was there?'

'So you just stayed in Allgrove's kitchen, played cards and got pissed together.'

'That's it,' said Henneker.

'And you left Allgrove when?'

Henneker looked at his watch in the bleary manner of a man who is not even really sure what day it is. 'A bit before ten,' he said. He hadn't shaved; and probably hadn't shaved yesterday, either. In the close confines of the cab, Roper could smell the whisky on him.

140

'Did Allgrove go out?' Roper asked again.

Henneker smiled twistedly. 'You reckon *he* did that? You're off your bloody rocker. Why'd he bother? He's got no gripe with me. We're mates. Have been for years.'

'Did you do any cooking? Yesterday, before you went to Allgrove's?'

'I knocked up some toast. Mid-morning. After I'd seen to the stock.'

'How about the gas oven?'

'Haven't used that since the old woman went,' said Henneker.

One thing was certain: that gas oven hadn't been left turned on at the time Henneker had left for Allgrove's. Because Enid Kingsley had told the emergency services that the fire was well under way before she had heard the explosion; and if the oven had been turned on since yesterday afternoon, unlit, enough gas would surely have leaked from the kitchen between then and 5.00 a.m. this morning to have blown Henneker's house to kingdom come the moment it reached the burning gas fire in the front room. In which case, Miss Kingsley would have heard the explosion before the fire had started . . .

'Did you leave your gas fire burning? The one in your sitting-room?'

Henneker wasn't sure. He thought he might have done. He hadn't exactly gone to Allgrove's sober.

Henneker's brows beetled belatedly as he ground out the cheroot in the ashtray. 'Here,' he said, as realisation suddenly came to him, 'what's all this *gas* business about?'

Roper sketched in the details for him, as much, that is, as Henneker needed to know for the moment; the unlit oven, the sofa that might have been shifted closer to the gas fire, the open window—

'What open window?' said Henneker breaking in.

'In your sitting-room,' said Roper.

'This weather?' scorned Henneker. 'Never on your bloody life. The missus, she was always opening bloody windows; but then she didn't pay the bloody gas bills, did

141

she? In my line of work I get enough bloody fresh air as it bloody is.'

Henneker was certain about the window. It hadn't been opened since the cold weather had clamped down, a week ago. Abruptly he came to life, a rigid finger aimed through the windscreen. Roper followed the direction of the finger. Henneker's son was standing by the fire brigade's tender and shaking hands with Peasgood.

'That's who you want to talk to,' he said. 'Him and his mother's new fancy-man.'

'He came here to see that your animals were all right,' said Roper.

'Oh, yeah,' sneered Henneker. 'Him? He's never done a day's work for me in his life. Put him through college I did, too, and never got a penny back for it. Cost me a bloody fortune, he did.'

'And you reckon I should talk to him?'

'And Fred Jackson,' said Henneker. 'You make sure you talk to him, an' all. They're in this up to their necks, both of 'em. And I'll tell you something else.' He turned his head again to look Roper squarely in the eye. 'You want to know who killed that Pole – you ask one or the other of 'em. They'll know.'

'You reckon?'

'Yeah,' said Henneker. 'I reckon.'

Trevor Henneker had climbed into Jackson's Range Rover and driven as far as the end of the cinder track, where Makins had stopped him and, by the looks of it, was asking him to keep well in the middle to avoid obliterating the limping man's bootprints until he was safely past them.

He drove by slowly. There was not a great deal of room. As he passed, he and his father could have been no more than a yard away from each other. Neither of them acknowledged the other by even a glance.

'While we're on the subject of Mr Komarowski, Mr Henneker, you had a visitor the night he died. He called here. And he didn't get an answer.'

'I know,' said Henneker. 'Fred Jackson. The bugger'd been ringing all evening. He's chasing me to fix a fence.'

'He said when he arrived here all your lights were out.'

'I turned 'em out,' said Henneker. 'The phone started ringing every couple of minutes in the end. I guessed he'd come over. So I locked up and turned all the lights out. Didn't want to talk to him.'

'He turned up here at nine o'clock, so he tells us,' lied Roper.

'Then he's a liar,' said Henneker. 'It was a couple of minutes after ten. He went all round the house. Trying all the doors. I heard him. Then he got back in his van and went off. He left a note in the letter-box. I watched him sit in his van with his courtesy-light on and write it.'

So Henneker *had* been at home when Jackson had called on him the other night. Henneker also knew that Jackson had come in his van and not his Range Rover.

'What are you going to do now?' asked Roper.

'I don't know,' said Henneker wearily, scratching his stubble. 'Cost me a bloody king's ransom, this lot will. And I'm in hock with the bank as well. When I've sold up I'll be lucky to clear six figures.'

'Got a buyer in view?'

'Did have,' said Henneker. 'Bloke up in Wales. But he's got five kids. He's not likely to want it now, is he? He was expecting a proper house, with bedrooms. Stands to reason, don't it? If I'd been insured, I'd have been all right.' He sighed, dropped his head back against the rest and closed his eyes to blot it all out. 'What a bugger,' he said. 'Eh?'

Roper sombrely agreed that it was. Austen Henneker was indeed a hard-pressed man. And someone, in Roper's opinion, was doing the pressing.

He and Makins took an early lunch in the front seats of the Sierra; the inevitable turkey sandwiches and a Thermos of coffee, lovingly assembled by Makins' latest

143

conquest, probably the very last in a long line because Makins declined to divulge even her name in the canteen and had been seen, on several occasions lately, furtively using the payphone in the corridor outside, and with an expression on his face that many witnesses had described as one tortured by untold passions. It was generally agreed that one thing was certain: to have caught old George, whoever she was, she had to be a lady who was very fast on her feet.

Through the windscreen Roper watched Henneker, in the distance, checking over the sheep that he had just let out from their shed to the pen in front of it.

It was a few minutes before midday. On the Sierra's back seat, bagged in polythene, was a pair of plaster-casts taken from the limping man's bootprints. A similar pair were locked away in the Forensic van.

'He might have been put up to it by Jackson,' said Makins. 'If those prints are Snow's.'

As a theory, it was all too plausible. Jackson had a profitable farm. Henneker's land was adjacent to it. If Jackson wanted to spread his wings, the first place he would look to do it would be next door. Henneker's land and stock were up for sale. Without a house on it – and Jackson already had a house – the value of Henneker's property, without any insurance on the house, had been reduced overnight by £100,000, perhaps more. According to the fire officer, Beevers, the house was in too dangerous a state to repair. It would have to be totally demolished and re-built. From the damp-course up.

If Snow *had* come here last night he might have done it for money. It needn't have cost Jackson much – a few hundred, a thousand, say. Even a little money would have been a lot to Snow. He had a wife, two children, and another one imminent, a car to run; he had just spent close to £100 for two new tyres, and there were all those presents on that Christmas tree in his front parlour. Even as Jackson's stockman he wouldn't be earning a great deal.

Roper rolled his post-prandial cheroot thoughtfully against the rim of the ashtray. 'D'you think Snow might have killed Komarowski?'

'I wouldn't have thought so,' said Makins. 'He's not the sort of bloke to wander around with a shotgun, is he? Or is he?'

'No,' said Roper. 'I don't reckon, either. And who'd want Komarowski dead most? Jackson or Henneker?'

'I suppose Henneker,' said Makins. 'If either of 'em did.'

'And if neither of them did?'

'It's back to the drawing board,' said Makins.

'Right,' said Roper. He reached for the Sierra's door catch.

'Where're you going?' asked Makins.

'Tell you when I come back,' said Roper. He swung his legs out and slammed the door shut behind him. Through the windscreen Makins watched him start off along the cinder track towards the farmhouse and then walk around the side of it, where, a few minutes ago, they had seen Henneker go. A few moments afterwards they both reappeared, Henneker wheeling a sack trolley; he had just started salvaging a few bits and pieces from his house and was stacking them in the Land-Rover. The two of them conversed for several minutes, during which time Henneker shook his head a lot.

Makins leaned across and opened the door as Roper came back. 'What was that all about?' he asked, as Roper climbed back in and settled himself.

'Wife-beating, whisky, cricket and cricket-bags,' said Roper. 'His wife really did fall down the stairs and break her arm. And the limp she had a few weeks later was because she'd sprained her ankle on the wet kitchen floor. He swears he's never laid a finger on her. And he's never bought a bottle of Johnnie Walker in his life; he always drinks Bell's. And he did have a cricket-bag like the one we found at Allgrove's. And he remembers *exactly* who he gave it to.'

'Who?' said Makins.

'His lad,' said Roper. 'Young Trevor.'

Makins backed his car down the track towards the road; Roper followed in his, the occasional puddle of ice cracking under the Sierra's tyres like pistol shots. The frozen ruts of snow were like tramlines; once in them it was difficult to wrestle the tyres out again, and when Makins thumped his horn twice, loudly and lengthily, Roper braked and stuck his head out of the window.

'Trouble?' he called.

Makins was gesturing with his thumb towards the road. 'That bloody white van again,' he shouted. 'Just seen it flash across my mirror.'

'Going which way?'

Makins aimed his thumb towards Lower Gorton.

'See if you can catch him.'

After a couple of wheelspins, Makins shot off backwards, swung into the road, slid broadside on into a hedge, extricated himself, after another wheelspin, and headed off towards Lower Gorton.

But the driver of the white van clearly knew his way about these parts a lot better than Makins.

Driving more sedately, Roper caught up with him a half mile further on. Makins' car was parked a few yards short of the Y-junction from which two high-hedged lanes went off to left and right.

'You lost him?' called Roper, pulling in beside.

'Like a hole in the ground,' said Makins. 'He just went.'

'How about his number?'

But Makins had not got close enough to make out even a part of it.

There was no sardonic smile today, barely an acknowledgement. The scorched side of John Kingsley's face glistened from either the heat of the fire he was huddled over or the whisky bottle he had within arm's reach on a side table.

Roper and Makins sat on the settee and loosened their coats. Two steel needles, some knitting on them, were plunged into a ball of pink wool on Miss Kingsley's chair, a small box of chocolates with half the top layer eaten sat on the carpet beside. There had been a few additions to the greetings cards on the piano, but, at a guess, the Kingsleys had had a very quiet Christmas without the company of Ziggy Komarowski.

Miss Kingsley came back with three mugs of tea. Her brother morosely topped up his tumbler and lit another cigarette from the stub of the last. Of the two of them it was only Miss Kingsley who was certain of the time when she had woken this morning. It had been a few minutes to five. Which tallied to within a few minutes of the time when the emergency services operator had logged in her telephone call.

'What woke you in the first place, Miss Kingsley?'

'Nothing,' she said. 'At least, I don't think so.'

'Other than the fire, did you see or hear anything suspicious?'

Miss Kingsley glanced across at her brother. 'Well . . . ' she ventured, 'there *was* that car, wasn't there, Johnnie?'

Kingsley didn't answer.

'What about this car, Miss Kingsley?' asked Roper. 'Something special about it, was there?'

Again she deferred to her brother, but he only shrugged.

'There was something wrong with it,' she said. 'Johnnie says it was probably the exhaust. It stopped a few yards along the lane,' she added.

'That right, sir?' asked Roper, when Kingsley still declined to add anything. A car on the road at five o'clock in the morning of a public holiday, and one that stopped on this quiet stretch, had to be regarded with more than usual interest.

'That's what it sounded like,' Kingsley replied gruffly. He was plainly going to be a man of few words this morning.

147

'What time was that, sir?' asked Roper.

Kingsley performed a deft sleight of hand with his cigarette and the whisky tumbler. 'I couldn't say.' He sipped from the tumbler. 'But it was well before Enid came down.'

'And it came back again,' said Miss Kingsley. 'We both heard it that time.'

'It might not have been the same bloody car,' said Kingsley.

His sister looked exasperatedly at him. 'But you said it was,' she protested. 'At breakfast. You said.'

'That right, sir?' asked Roper.

'It was the exhaust,' said Kingsley testily and unhelpfully, and lapsed back into silence. Miss Kingsley had already told Roper that her brother had good days and bad days. This was obviously one of the bad ones.

'It sounded like a machine gun,' said Miss Kingsley. 'Pop-pop-pop . . . '

'It was only after the door slammed, when it stopped,' said Kingsley, his slurred voice now raised in argument. 'The first time, it drove up quietly enough.'

'Did it stop outside when you heard it the second time?'

'Yes,' said Miss Kingsley. 'And the door slammed. And then it sounded as if it was turning round; it went back the other way.'

'Which way do you think it was travelling, Miss Kingsley?' asked Makins. 'After it had turned round?'

'I think that way,' she said, pointing. 'Towards Lower Gorton.'

Roper glanced towards Kingsley. 'Mr Kingsley?'

'Yes,' said Kingsley, disinterestedly. 'Probably.'

Roper had to prise it out of them piecemeal. It was Miss Kingsley, mostly, who answered, paraphrasing sometimes what her brother had told her, and he affirming grudgingly when Roper pushed him hard enough.

Kingsley had slept in fits and starts last night, despite the pills he had taken. Some half an hour – it might have been less – before his sister had noticed the fire, he had been woken by the sound of a car coming along the lane. It had stopped. One of its doors had been slammed shut. It had turned in the road. It then drove off, but with a different sound. As if its exhaust had just been holed.

Miss Kingsley herself had heard its return. She had been in the hall calling the fire brigade on the telephone. A car with a noisy exhaust had stopped not too far away. A door had slammed. The car then drove off again, having turned, noisily, towards Lower Gorton.

Perhaps it was nothing. A coincidence. But around five o'clock on Boxing morning most honest folk were curled up in their beds and sleeping off the excesses of the day before. And it was one of the few days of the year when there were no early-morning deliveries of newspapers, or milk, or much else for that matter.

Kingsley slept across the hall, downstairs. He had drifted in and out of sleep all night, and had just dropped off again when the approaching car had woken him. He conceded, reluctantly, that the car might have come from the direction of Lower Gorton the first time he heard it.

'And you reckon it was almost half an hour before you heard the explosion, do you, sir?' asked Roper.

'Less,' said Kingsley, irritably. 'It might have been twenty minutes.'

'And it came back again a few minutes after the bang,' reaffirmed Miss Kingsley. 'We both heard it.'

'And the slamming door?'

'Definitely,' said Miss Kingsley. 'Both of us.'

'Mr Kingsley?'

'Yes. Both times.' Wedged between two of his black-gloved fingers, Kingsley's cigarette rose and fell again as his other hand reached out for his whisky bottle. He clamped the bottle between his knees to take off the cap. His sister watched him with an expression somewhere between dismay and despair – perhaps anger, too.

Roper affected not to notice. He had been right the first time; the two Kingsleys had had a miserable Christmas.

'This car . . . ' he addressed Miss Kingsley, now that her brother had so clearly disassociated himself from the remainder of the proceedings, 'd'you think it might have been picking someone up; or letting someone down? Did you hear any voices? Footsteps? Anything like that?'

'Someone coughed,' she said, her eyes brightening as she suddenly remembered that. 'I heard someone coughing. After the door slammed.'

Again, it might be important; or it might not. It sounded very much as if someone had driven up close to the cottage at some time around 4.40 this morning, picked up a passenger, turned and driven away again towards Lower Gorton. And, from here, Henneker's farm was in the same direction as Lower Gorton. A few minutes after 5.00, the same thing had happened in reverse. And in the time between, someone had set fire to Henneker's farmhouse. It all sounded to Roper highly germane to the matter in hand. From here, too, Colin Snow also lived in the direction of Lower Gorton. And Snow had a car, and he would have had time by now to get the front wheels back on it.

Enid Kingsley saw them out, closing the sitting-room door behind her in order to make her apologies for her brother's bad manners.

'I shouldn't say it,' she said, anguished, at the front door, 'but he's been *atrocious* – all over the holiday. I think he misses Zygmunt. And his leg's been playing him up abominably; the worst for years. I really am terribly sorry.'

'Don't worry about it, Miss Kingsley,' Roper assured her, briefly clasping her proffered hand. It was something he did rarely, always wary that he might be shaking hands with the opposition; except that Enid Kingsley was more likely to be numbered among the saints of this world than the sinners. She seemed genuinely sorry to see them both go.

'Where now?' said Makins, fishing out his car keys. 'Snow's place?'

'No,' said Roper, who had taken out his own keys; then abruptly changed his mind again. 'You take a walk up this side, and I'll have a wander up the other. A couple of hundred yards each way.'

'What are we looking for?' said Makins.

'Signs of a car turning round,' said Roper. 'Twice. It shouldn't be difficult.'

Nor did it take long. Plenty of traffic had used the lane over Christmas, and crushed the settled snow into a thin glassy crust, except for a narrow band at the crown of the carriageway where it was an inch or so thicker. It was not a stretch of road where anyone driving a car would have much reason to stop and turn around. But someone had.

It was Makins, quartering westward, towards Upper Gorton village, who found the first set of transverse tyre depressions in the thicker crust of snow in the middle of the road; and Roper, twenty or thirty yards further on, who came across the second set.

And, if what he noticed on Makins' side of the lane was what he thought it was, it was the set that he had found that had been made first; and would have accounted for the sudden burst of noise that Kingsley had heard when, on the first occasion, the car that had woken him was driven away.

This side of the lane was a kerbed, flagged footpath, no more than three or four inches above the level of the carriageway. Over on Makins' side there was no path, merely a grassed bank, perhaps a foot or more higher than the road. And someone had backed a vehicle into it. Hard.

By now Makins had also spotted it, and Roper went over to join him as he dropped to a crouch in front of it.

'No wonder his exhaust made a noise,' said Makins. 'Looks like he crumpled it.'

In either direction, for as far as the eye could see, apart from tyre splashes, the bank of the verge was blanketed

151

with a thin layer of snow clinging to the grass; but not here. Here it had been disturbed. Here a rear fender had scraped the top of the verge as it had backed over it, perhaps on tyres that had slithered as they lost their purchase on the icy crust of the carriageway. And a few inches lower, on the sloping face of the bank, were the clear residues of soot and rust left by the outlet of an exhaust pipe that had been rammed into the frozen bank hard enough to scoop a semi-circular gouge out of it, upward, over several inches. Some more flakes of rust, in the gutter, would probably have dropped off the exhaust when the driver had pulled away again.

It looked as if the driver had made a three-point turn here. And travelling on this side of the lane, he would have come from the direction of Lower Gorton. Having picked up his passenger – Kingsley had heard a car door slam *before* the exhaust had started making its racket – the driver had then turned in the lane. Across it, back again, at which point he'd buckled his exhaust pipe against the bank, before setting off again in the direction of Lower Gorton; and Henneker's farm.

'Couple of bootprints,' said Makins, up on the top of the verge now and down on his heels again. There were three clear depressions in the snow, and several scuff-marks, as if someone had stood there waiting. It looked as if whoever had left them had crossed the lane from the other side, just here, and stood about for a while to be picked up.

And at five o'clock in the morning, when few well-intentioned folk were about; but a pair of villains just might have been.

Chapter 13

Roper and Makins crossed Colin Snow's front garden. Prints and scuffs in the snow between the front door and the yellow Toyota indicated a lot of activity between now and the last time Roper had called here. More relevantly, the Toyota was standing on all four tyres and the snow had been scraped from it. Several sets of tyre depressions between the garden and the lane beyond also showed that the Toyota had been out at least twice since its front wheels had been put back.

Makins dropped down on his hands and knees behind it to look at the Toyota's exhaust, while Roper went on to the front doorstep and rang the doorbell. On the left, behind the Toyota, the sitting-room curtains were still closed.

Roper rang again. A couple of yards away, Makins had risen and was brushing the snow off the knees of his trousers.

'New, is it?' asked Roper softly.

'From the silencer box, and back,' said Makins, joining him under the porch. 'It can't be more than a few days old. If that.'

It sounded as if it boded ill for Colin Snow. He had a gammy right leg. He had a brand new exhaust on his Toyota. Although evidence of circumstances wasn't always evidence of proof; and this was one of the few occasions when Roper hoped that it was not. Colin Snow had just started to carve out a whole new life for himself; he had a lot to lose.

He stepped down from the porch as Makins thumbed the doorbell yet again. The upstairs front curtains were also closed. It was almost as if the house had been shut up. It was all very quiet.

'Think he's done a bunk?' asked Makins, from the porch.

'Could be,' said Roper. 'Except he'd have taken the car.'

But he'd scarcely said it when Makins suddenly cocked an ear towards the door. 'He's about,' said Makins.

And it was indeed Snow himself who opened the door. He was wearing a newly ironed shirt, the left-hand side of which wasn't quite tucked inside the front of his grey and neatly pressed trousers. He looked distinctly nervous.

'Sorry,' he said. 'You caught me on the lavvy.' He looked anxiously from one to the other of them.

'Can we come in for a few minutes, Mr Snow?' said Roper. 'If you're not too busy.'

'Yeah,' said Snow, although he didn't sound all that eager, hobbling back a pace to make way for them. 'Sure.'

He closed the door behind them. There was a small well-used red fibreboard suitcase standing against the hall wall where the tyres had been the other day. From the bulge of its lid it looked to be tightly packed.

'Going away, sir?' asked Roper companionably.

'It's for the missus,' said Snow. 'Along at the hospital. Clothes. She reckons on coming out tomorrow.'

'Complications?' asked Roper sympathetically.

'It came early,' said Snow. 'Yesterday afternoon. About four o'clock. A little lad. All on the quick, it was.'

'Can we look in the case, sir?' asked Makins.

'What for?'

'If we can just open the lid, Mr Snow,' said Roper. 'We'll leave it tidy.'

'What am I supposed to have done?'

'Hopefully, nothing, sir,' said Roper. Makins, down on his heels, had tipped the red case on to its bottom and sprung the catches and lifted the lid. Women's clothes; a grey woollen dress, some underclothes, a pair of shoes, tights in a plastic bag, an outer coat, some baby's woollen clothes, a tartan cot-blanket neatly folded at the bottom to wrap the new baby in to bring it home. It all looked very innocent and proper. Makins closed the case and stood it back against the wall.

'What's this all about?' gulped Snow, by now a deeply troubled man, and seemingly in as great a state of mortal terror as Roper had seen in a very long time.

'Perhaps we could talk more comfortably sitting, Mr Snow,' said Roper. 'Get the weight off your legs, eh?'

Snow seemed to have more trouble swallowing. He limped ahead of them into the darkened dining-cum-sitting room. He drew open the curtains. 'Haven't been in here since last night,' he mumbled unnecessarily. 'Haven't had a lot of time.'

Most of the presents had gone from the Christmas tree.

'Children gone away somewhere?' asked Roper.

'My sister's,' said Snow. 'Took 'em over when I got back from the hospital.'

'What time would that have been?'

''Bout half-six. Yesterday evening.' Snow limped back from the window to an armchair. 'All got done in a bit of a panic.' He lowered himself carefully, his right leg stuck out in front of him like a bowsprit. There was a sticking plaster on the ball of his right thumb. It looked new.

'Always had a dodgy leg?' asked Roper. 'Or is that something recent?'

'Day before Christmas Eve,' said Snow. 'I done my knee in getting out of the tractor. Twisted it . . . It's better now.' He looked down at the knee in question for a long time. 'Doctor said it'd take about a week.' But then he could contain himself no longer. 'Look,' he blurted miserably, 'I told the missus I'd be over the hospital again 'bout three. Today, like. With the clothes, for her and the kid. Then I promised to go over and see the other kids.' His unhappy eyes

155

lifted and met Roper's. 'At my sister's, like. Down at Swanage.'

Roper settled himself more comfortably, his loosely clasped hands hanging between his knees.

'You say you got back here yesterday at half-past six.'

'About,' agreed Snow.

'After you'd taken the kids to Swanage.'

'Aye,' said Snow. He eyed Makins nervously as Makins flipped to an empty page of his pocket book and wrote the date, and the time after a glance at his wristwatch. 'Look,' he broke in, 'if this is about . . .'

'About what, Mr Snow?' asked Roper.

Snow didn't answer, and Roper didn't press him. Snow had already begun to look pressed enough.

'You've got a push-bike,' said Roper.

'Aye,' said Snow. 'Buggered it. The front wheel.'

'When?' asked Roper.

'Yesterday morning,' said Snow. 'I went in to work for an hour. Early.'

'Mr Jackson's place?'

'Aye,' said Snow. 'Skidded on the way back and hit the kerb. The front wheel got buckled.'

'How about this morning? Did you go in by car?'

Snow shook his head. 'Fred said I needn't go in today. With the kid, an' all.' The quizzing about his bicycle had disarmed him, briefly, back to perplexity, but his anxiety quickly returned. 'You still haven't said what you're here for; not properly.'

'When did you last use your car, Mr Snow?' asked Makins.

'Yesterday night.'

'What time?'

'Told you,' said Snow. 'I drove the kids down to Swanage.'

'And you got back here at six-thirty,' said Roper.

'About,' said Snow. 'Told you, didn't I?' With the questions flying from two directions he was not sure which one of them to look at next.

'How about afterwards?' said Roper. 'Did you go out?'

There was a pause; it wasn't a long one, but it was long enough for Snow to back himself into the one corner from which Roper had no intention of letting him slip away.

'No. Didn't go nowhere.'

'You didn't go along to see Mr Henneker?'

Snow's Adam's apple rose and fell convulsively. Roper heard him swallow. 'Why should I have?'

He was, Roper decided, going to be a very poor liar. 'But you've seen Mr Henneker lately,' he insisted.

Snow shook his head. 'Not lately. Christmas Eve. Mornin'. The sheep business. I saw him then.'

'But not last night?' asked Makins.

'Or early this morning?' asked Roper.

'No.'

'Because he was out when you called?' Roper suggested.

'I didn't bloody call. I didn't go out nowhere. I was here. Watchin' the telly.'

'You know about the fire last night?' asked Makins.

'What fire?'

Neither answered him.

'You didn't hear the fire brigade? Or the explosion?'

Snow's head jerked up in alarm. 'Explosion?' he gasped. 'What bloody explosion?'

'The gas,' said Roper. 'I'm surprised you didn't hear it.'

Snow tried blustering. 'Told you,' he insisted. 'I *didn't* go 'long there.'

'Where?' said Makins.

'Henneker's place.'

'Who said the fire was there?' asked Roper.

'You said.'

Roper shook his head. 'Nobody said, Mr Snow. You must have imagined it.'

'But it was Henneker's you were going on about.'

'But we didn't say the fire was there. You said that.'

There was a hiatus. A rush of adrenaline had sent Snow lurching clumsily to his feet, one hand gripping

157

the edge of the shelf above the fire and knocking over a couple of Christmas cards. But he obviously realised that there was no one to fight and nowhere to run. All the blood had drained from his face. He would talk eventually; one way or the other.

'If you didn't intend to kill him, Colin,' advised Roper, 'the charge might only be arson.'

Snow's eyebrows shot up and his eyes looked as if they were going to pop out altogether. 'Christ!' he gasped. 'He's not bloody *dead*, is he?'

Neither Roper nor Makins offered him comfort.

'Somebody pay you to do it, Colin?' asked Roper. 'That it?'

Snow's head shook vehemently.

'All your own idea, was it?' asked Roper, helpfully but relentlessly.

Snow's head shook yet again, a barely perceptible shudder. It wasn't often Roper felt sympathy for miscreants, but Snow wasn't even a clever villain. If he was guilty he would probably go down for a couple of years – and that was only with an understanding judge on one of his more benevolent days, and a fast-talking lawyer.

'Wear a pair of wellies, this weather, do you, Colin?'

Snow let go of the mantelshelf and dropped back to his chair. He looked close to the end of his tether. His hanging head nodded.

'Where are they, Colin?' asked Roper.

'Out back. Kitchen door.'

Roper gave Makins a nod. While Makins was gone, Roper reached in his briefcase and brought out the two plaster-casts in their plastic bags.

Snow watched him apprehensively. 'What are those?'

'Casts,' said Roper, holding them out to show him, one in each hand. 'Somebody left some bootprints behind on their way to Henneker's house last night – or this morning. Yours, d'you think, Colin? Could be? Eh?'

Snow turned his head away. 'Told you, I didn't go 'long there.'

Roper laid the two casts beside him on the sofa. 'We noticed you'd got a new exhaust on your motor, on the way in. Get that fitted this morning, somewhere, did you?'

'Last week.'

'Where?'

'Did it myself. Just the back end. It was done when you came last time.'

Makins came back with two pairs of wellington boots, a new black shiny pair, and a pair of green industrials with reinforced toe-caps.

'Both yours, Colin?'

'Black ones are the missus',' said Snow, scarcely even bothering to look up.

Roper took the green ones and clamped the legs between his knees to look at the soles. Snow had little feet. Size 6. Roper compared the casts with the undersides of the boots. A jury would want the comparison made by an expert witness; but he would not have really needed to be all that much of an expert. Snow tended to walk on the inside of his left foot. And at some time lately he had trodden on a small nail that was embedded on its side in the middle of the left heel. The right-hand cast was too smudged to make a positive identification, but it looked near enough, and one human foot rarely went far without the other.

Roper stood the boots on the carpet beside him and repacked the casts, then glanced up at Makins.

'Go and make Mr Snow a nice cup of tea, George, eh?'

'Let's try again, Colin, shall we?'

Snow's cup rattled back on his saucer. He was frightened, and he knew something but he was hanging on to it like grim death. A half-hour had passed and he was on his second cup of tea and third cigarette.

'I'm telling you,' he said. 'I keep telling you, it was nothing to do with me. I didn't even know it had happened. Honest.'

'But you were there, Colin,' Roper insisted patiently. 'And we can prove it.'

'Everybody round here's got boots like that.' Snow picked up his cup again. Roper heard it chatter against his teeth.

'All right, Colin, I'll tell you what it all looks like, shall I?' Roper made himself more comfortable. He had moved into the armchair where Mrs Snow had sat the other day. His overcoat was draped over the back of it. 'About half-past four this morning, you got in your motor and drove most of the way to the village. Your mate was waiting for you, near the Kingsleys' place. You stopped. He climbed in. You turned round – that's when you bent your exhaust pipe – then you drove back to Henneker's farm. You parked at the gate to the cinder track and went the rest of the way on foot. Perhaps your mate went with you; we're not certain about him yet. With me so far?'

'Told you,' said Snow. 'I don't know nothing about it. *Nothing*. I had that exhaust pipe last week. It was on the car when you came *last* time.'

Roper affected to ignore him. 'You knew Henneker was out. One or both of you shifted his sofa close to the gas fire, which was either lit before or afterwards, then went out to the kitchen and opened the gas tap on the oven. How about the window?'

'Window?' said Snow, bewildered again. 'What bloody window?'

'The window in the sitting-room at Henneker's place,' said Roper. 'One of you opened it. Before you both scarpered.'

Roper waited for Snow to protest. He didn't.

'Then you drove him back to the village, dropped him off, and came back here. It must have worried you, though.'

'What must?' said Snow.

'Your exhaust,' said Roper. 'Woke half the village. Sounded like a machine-gun, that's what some say.'

160

Snow's cup and saucer went shakily down to the edge of the tiled surround under the gas fire.

'It all fits, you see, Colin,' said Roper.

'Just tell us who your accomplice was, Colin,' urged Makins.

Snow stayed silent and immobile, his back hunched, his hands clasped, in the long ensuing silence.

'Colin . . . ?' said Roper.

Nothing. The only sound came from a ticking, wind-up clock among the Christmas cards over the fireplace.

Roper rose from the armchair and beckoned Makins after him. In the passage, Roper drew the door closed quietly behind him.

'I'm getting bad vibes, George,' he said.

So was Makins.

'We've got his bootprints,' said Roper. 'He went there. So why's he saying he didn't?'

Makins shrugged. He didn't know, either. Roper eased the door open half an inch. Snow was still sitting exactly as they had left him, staring dully at the floor between his knees. Silently, Roper drew the door shut again. 'I reckon he knows something about it.'

'Got to, hasn't he?' said Makins.

But what? It didn't need a genius to start a fire, and Snow was certainly a long way from being one of those. But whoever had started that one last night had to be brighter than most to have thought about opening that window, and adding the grace note by turning on the gas at the oven. It indicated planning, or at least a modicum of nous.

On the face of it everything pointed to Snow. The bootprints certainly, the new exhaust on the Toyota possibly, and he certainly wasn't keen on Austen Henneker. But what pointed most inexorably was his denial that he had been anywhere near Henneker's house during the last few days, when copper-bottomed evidence showed that he had.

* * *

Roper sat down again and made himself comfortable. Snow hadn't moved, except to lift his eyes as the two of them had come back into the room. Roper turned the screw a little.

'What time's your missus expecting you?'

'Three,' said Snow.

'Doesn't seem likely now, does it?' said Roper.

Snow stole a glance at his wristwatch. It looked new.

'What time is it now?'

'One,' said Snow absently. 'Just after.'

'Present from your wife?'

Snow nodded. 'Aye,' he said.

'You must have had an expensive Christmas. With your car and all.'

'Aye,' agreed Snow. 'It was a bit.'

'Must have broken the bank.'

'Got a bonus,' said Snow. 'Old Fred always puts a bit of money about at Christmas. We'd have a job managing, else. With the kids and everything.'

'Did you proud, did he?'

'Two-fifty,' said Snow. 'He's good like that.'

So that was where all the money had come from. And if it wasn't, it was easily proved.

'Supposing I tell you we don't reckon you started that fire?' suggested Roper.

'I didn't,' said Snow. 'I don't know anything about it.'

'That's the bit we don't believe.'

'It's the truth.'

'But you went along there, didn't you, Colin?'

Snow shook his head.

Roper left him to sweat. He wouldn't be able to hold out much longer; he was too desperate to get across to the hospital to see his wife.

What he wasn't was Jack-the-lad. He hadn't known about the open window and he hadn't known about the gas tap. And if he had driven the Toyota into the village this morning to collect an accomplice he was unlikely to have left him in the car while he himself walked up the

162

cinder track alone; unless the other man's bootprints had been fortuitously obliterated, every one of them, by the tyres of the fire brigade, which didn't seem likely.

Makins made the ambience more oppressive by ambling to the window and looking out, as if he and Roper had all the time in the world. Snow's edginess grew, and eventually he had to take a look behind him to see where the silent Makins was.

'What's the time now, Colin?' asked Roper.

Snow tipped his wrist. 'Ten-past,' he said. 'Nearly.'

'Which hospital?' asked Roper.

'Dorchester,' said Snow.

'Fair old drive, that,' said Roper. 'This weather.'

The clock ticked. The sound of an aircraft came faintly down the flue of the gas fire. Snow began to fidget.

Makins came back to the sofa and flipped slowly, page by page, through his pocket book.

'I heard 'em,' said Snow abruptly, his hands clasped wretchedly tighter, their bony knuckles white.

Roper leaned forward. Makins poised his ballpoint over his open pocket book.

'I was in the feed shed, see. Upstairs. Fred'd asked me to wind down a couple of sacks before I went. Well, I was up there, see, having a quiet smoke, and I heard this whisperin'. Downstairs. It didn't sound right, see. Suspicious it was, like; like somebody was up to something. One of 'em said he'd pick the other one up near the Kingsleys' place at half-past four; and the other one said something about not keeping him hanging about because it was going to be bloody cold at half-past four in the morning. I'd thought they were talking about the afternoon half-past four, see. How we going to get in, one said. I got keys, the other one said. Then he said, you'd better bring gloves, leather ones, and a pair of shoes you can throw away afterwards. This time, we've really got to fix the sod. Well, it worried me, see. But when I got home, the missus had started, broken water and everything, up in the bathroom, so everything was a bit of a panic. The

163

ambulance came about one. I followed it with the kids, and we hung about there, like, because the sister said it looked as if it was going to be a quick 'un. It came about four. I went in to see the missus – knackered, she was, so I didn't stay long. Me and the kids saw the new little 'un, then I drove 'em down to Swanage, like we'd all arranged. Then I got back here.'

Snow was in full spate now, wringing and dry-washing his hands.

'That's when it started to get bad. Because I was all on me own, see, and I ought to be tellin' somebody, only if I did, and was wrong, Fred as like'd sack me. And it's a good job I've got over there. I had a couple of beers – I don't drink a lot, normal. And I watched the telly a bit, but none of it was going in. I was starting to get the shakes, an' all. Worrying, like, see. So I had a whisky; and that seemed to work so I had another one. I reckon I nodded off. Woke about ten o'clock. The telly was still on. I still had to go over and see Austen. Tell 'im, like – what I'd heard. But me and him don't get on, 'specially since the sheep business the other day, me telling Peasgood and everything.'

Snow was talking faster now and Roper was too shrewd to stop him.

Snow had put on his old overcoat and turned off the telly; but still had to fortify himself with another hefty Scotch before he could muster the courage to go and meet Henneker face to face.

'I didn't realise I was boozed till I got outside and the air hit me. And I couldn't afford to lose me driving licence, so I walked. He had no lights on. I went all round, knockin'. Front door. Back door. Windows. And when I had a look in the garage the Land-Rover wasn't in there – he'd left the doors open, see. So I knew he was out somewhere.'

'You didn't go and look for him?' asked Roper.

'Should've,' said Snow. 'I *knew* I should've. But I didn't know where to start. Could've been anywhere, couldn't he? And I was feeling rotten. All that booze. Must have been. So I come home. There's a phone-box down the lane by the bus stop. I went along there. 'Bout midnight, that was, and gave Austen a ring. About one o'clock I rang again, but he still wasn't there. I was going to keep on ringin' – all night if I had to. But I never did ring him after that second time. I woke up in this chair at half-past six this morning. In dread, I was. Still in me overcoat. I went over there. But it had happened, hadn't it? I never knew they were going to set fire to the place. Honest. I saw all the floodlights and the fire engines. So I turned, sharp, afore anybody saw me, and come back here. I haven't been out since. Was going to pretend I didn't know nothing. Stay stoom, like. None of my business, was it?' His outpourings finished at last and Colin Snow looked close to tears. 'I really have got to get to that hospital,' he said miserably. 'I really bloody have.'

'You'll be there,' said Roper. 'More tea, George. We'll have one, too.'

Makins collected Snow's cup from the hearth and returned to the kitchen.

Roper gave Snow a minute or so to draw breath.

'How did you know it was Henneker's place they were going to, Colin?'

'It was the talkin' about fixing him,' said Snow. 'And the talk about having keys.' He had taken a khaki handkerchief from his trousers pocket and was wiping the palms of his hands with it. 'I couldn't think of anybody else it'd be, 'cept Austen. Been at daggers drawn for a couple of years they have.'

'I want names, Colin,' said Roper. 'The two you heard talking. Who were they?'

'I don't want trouble,' pleaded Snow. 'If they knew it was me who'd told I'll be out on me bloody neck first thing tomorrow. Me job. The bloody lot. Honest.'

'Just you, me and Sergeant Makins, Colin. And if it never comes to court, nobody's going to be any the wiser. And if it does come to court we'll probably have enough evidence by then to keep your name out of it.'

Snow agonised over that for what seemed like an eternity. Then finally he wrenched it out.

'It was that Greg Painter,' he said. 'The landlord's lad along at the Arms.'

'And . . . ?'

'Henneker's boy,' said Snow. 'That bloody Trevor.'

Chapter 14

They held a brief conference in Roper's Sierra outside
Snow's cottage. That Snow was an innocent party was
almost beyond dispute. He had taken them to his garden
shed and shown them the silencer box and exhaust pipe
that he had taken off and replaced with new ones. Both
were perforated with rust and much repaired with asbestos
tape, but both were dead straight and showed no signs of
physical damage other than fair wear and tear.

What Snow had overheard passing between Greg
Painter and Trevor Henneker was only hearsay, about
whom they had been talking had only been guesswork,
plus a little imagination. That his guesswork and imagination were right on the button would take proof to turn
it into the kind of evidence to convince a jury. It would
take only Painter's and Henneker's strenuous denials to
have Snow branded a liar.

' . . . Unless one of Jackson's vehicles's got a dam-
aged exhaust pipe,' said Roper, around the cheroot he
was lighting. 'Let's go and look, shall we?'

Roper rose from the back of Jackson's mud-splattered
white Ford van which was parked in the Dutch barn where
he kept his stock of winter hay. The van's exhaust outlet
had floated freely when he had given it an experimental
rock; and shiny scars in the rusty metal looked as if they
had been made by the jaws of a pair of pliers, where someone had done their very recent best to turn the end of the
pipe from a crumpled oval back to a cylinder in an attempt

to disguise the damage. More pertinently, the rusty and paper-thin silencer box had been buckled by some kind of fore to aft impact, and had parted company at its front end with the pipe that came from the engine manifold. It was little wonder that Miss Kingsley had thought that the van had sounded like a motor-cycle in the early hours of this morning; because this van was what she had heard. Roper was certain of it, even if he had yet to prove it.

'Do you know how this happened, Mr Jackson?' asked Roper, touching the toe of his shoe to the tail-pipe and setting it wobbling again.

'Dunno,' said Jackson. His puzzlement looked genuine. 'Trevor was going to use it this morning when he went across to his father's place. But he came back in and said he couldn't get it started because the battery was flat: and could he borrow the Range Rover.'

'Perhaps we could try starting it now, sir.'

Jackson fished the keys from his pocket and climbed into the van. A touch of choke and twist of the ignition key and the engine leapt to life; with the ear-shattering racket of a pneumatic drill. Jackson quickly turned it off and climbed out again, looking even more puzzled.

'Who drove it last, sir?'

'I did, I suppose,' said Jackson. 'The night I went across to see Austen Henneker. I don't think it's been anywhere since.'

'Someone's driven it, sir.' Roper pointed out. 'Or the floor wouldn't be wet under the tyres. Right?'

Jackson could contain himself no longer. 'Look,' he said. 'Why d'you want to look at the van? Been involved in an accident or something, has it? I got some sort of right to know, haven't I?'

'We think it might be the vehicle a couple of witnesses heard on the road between here and the village round about the time the fire was started at Mr Henneker's place, Mr Jackson.'

Jackson had a long think about that. 'What d'you mean, *started*?' he countered. 'That's what you said,

168

wasn't it? The fire was *started*? Bloody hell, you're not saying someone did that on purpose, are you?'

'It could very well be, sir,' said Roper.

'Austen,' said Jackson. 'Did it for the insurance money, didn't he?'

'The house wasn't insured, sir.'

Jackson showed a momentary disappointment; to be followed by a slowly rising anger and another solution, and his quick shrewd upward glance made it plain that it was one he had considered before, and possibly at some length. 'That bloody boy,' he raged. 'Got to be, hasn't it? Becky don't drive and he's the only other one who's got a key to the van. It's him. It's been him all along. I've been trying to tell myself it wasn't, because of his mother. He's been trying to get me to buy Austen's place . . . and *she* has too—' Jackson had worked himself into a state where he was almost fighting for breath. 'She has . . . '

'Where is Trevor now, Mr Jackson?' asked Roper, not recognising that anything other than anger was amiss until Jackson's face screwed up with pain and began to go the colour of wood ash and he staggered sideways to steady himself on the bonnet of the van. 'You all right, Mr Jackson?'

'Angina,' wheezed Jackson. 'The lad's in the house.' But he could say no more because he was gasping for air and feeling frantically around the pockets of his jacket. He fumbled out a brown plastic phial of pills. Roper snatched it from him and prised off the cap. 'How many?' Jackson held up a finger. Roper shook a grey tablet on to his palm. Jackson plucked it off and popped it under his tongue, then, with Makins' help, subsided on to the passenger seat of the van with his legs hanging over the side.

Roper watched anxiously until the colour began to return to Jackson's face and his breathing started to ease.

'Get you a doctor, Mr Jackson?'

Jackson shook his head. 'Had it a couple of years,' he wheezed, the heel of one hand kneading up and down his breastbone. 'That's why I needed a young 'un to work the farm. And I picked a wrong 'un, didn't I?'

He wasn't faking. Fred Jackson was a genuinely sick man with a heart problem. Which made it highly unlikely that he would creep around the countryside at night re-arranging the local sheep population in pursuit of a personal vendetta. Nor was he likely to have been a party to the arson at Henneker's farm last night. And from the couple of hints he had dropped so far it also appeared that he had a passing suspicion or two regarding young Trevor Henneker.

'Go on,' he urged, looking up at Roper and Makins who were still hovering anxiously. 'You go and do what you've got to do. He's in the kitchen. The back door's open.'

Trevor Henneker almost choked on his cup of tea, and alarm fleeted across his face like sheet lightning.

'No need to get up, Mr Henneker,' said Roper, wiping the soles of his shoes on the kitchen doormat. It was thawing fast outside now. 'Unless you were going somewhere.'

'No,' said Henneker, quickly recovering his composure – almost – and carefully lowering his cup to the centre of his saucer. 'It was just that I was expecting you to come back in through the front door.'

'You knew we were here, then, sir?' said Roper, drawing out a chair for himself from under the kitchen table.

'I heard you talking to Fred in the hall. Where is he, by the way?'

Roper had to hand it to him. Trevor Henneker was as bold as brass and twice as shiny. 'We left him in the barn, Mr Henneker. He's just getting over an attack of angina.'

'Lord! He's all right, is he?'

'Yes, he seems to be,' said Roper. 'Stress does it very often, sir.'

'Stress?'

'Yes, sir. He got a bit upset. About the exhaust on his van.'

'What about the exhaust on his van?' Henneker did his level best to look puzzled.

'I was hoping you'd tell us, Mr Henneker,' said Roper grimly. 'Caution him, will you, Sergeant?'

Henneker laughed. 'It's my father you ought to be talking to.'

'We already have, Trevor,' said Makins, writing the time and date in his pocket book and underlining both, heavily.

'And young Painter,' added Roper, looking Henneker straight in the eye, although he omitted to mention that he had last talked to Greg Painter in his father's bar on Christmas Eve when he was not even remotely a suspect for anything.

Henneker's eyes narrowed and the smile froze from his face.

'The bastard,' he mouthed angrily. 'He bloody talked.'

'Everybody does, son,' said Roper sympathetically. 'In the end. All that honour among villains; it's a load of old garbage.' He glanced across at Makins. 'Give Mr Henneker a reading from your pocket book, Sergeant. Chapter and verse. Starting with the meeting in the feed shed.'

Makins licked his thumb and turned back a few pages of his notebook. 'Quote: "I'll pick you up near the Kingsleys' place at half-past four," ' he read. 'To which your colleague replied: "And don't keep me hanging about. How are we going to get in?" To which you replied something like: "I've still got keys. And you'd better wear an old pair of shoes; a pair you can throw away afterwards. This time we've really got to fix the sod." '

'That'll do,' said Roper. Not that there was a great deal more to what Snow had been able to tell them, but Henneker wasn't to know that. And that the brief extract had struck home was evident from the nervous tic that had started under Henneker's misaligned right eye. 'Ready to talk, are we, son?' asked Roper.

'You and Greg Painter both?' asked Roper. Henneker's emotions were going up and down like a yo-yo.

Trevor Henneker nodded tiredly. 'I rang him soon after eight yesterday morning and told him to come up to the farm. The back way. Along the service road. I told him I'd be in the feed shed.'

'Why did you finally decide you'd got to do it yesterday?' asked Makins. 'Some kind of rush, was there?'

'We were getting tight for time. There was some Welshman after the place. He was starting to push for an exchange of contracts by the end of January.'

'And you knew about that?' said Roper. 'How come?'

'Greg Painter works for my father's solicitor,' said Henneker. 'He's been keeping an eye for me as to how the business was going. He's been getting to see all the letters from the Welshman's solicitors as well.'

'Trying to stop this sale, were you?'

'I wanted the farm. I had a right. And Fred—'

'Mr Jackson?'

'—was coming round to thinking about buying it. He's always had his eye on that place. I just needed time.'

'*You* just needed time?' said Roper. 'Why was that, Mr Henneker? Because Mr Jackson's a pretty sick man? Because your father's place might soon get to be your place? That it?'

'Something like that.'

'And if your father's place was worth a bit less, Mr Jackson would be more persuadable. Something like that, too, was it?'

Henneker nodded, beginning to smoulder once more, a sure sign he was losing his self-control again.

'And you were going to make sure it was worth less. Right?'

'Yes,' snapped Henneker, crashing the edge of his fist down on the table in his temper. 'Christ! If you already know, why the hell d'you keep asking?'

'Because I want to hear it straight from the horse's mouth, laddie,' said Roper. 'What about all the sheep swapping? That down to you too, was it? Why?'

'To put the Welshman off,' said Henneker.

'How?'

Henneker's mouth twisted cynically. 'Nobody wants to move in next to a difficult neighbour, do they?'

'Like Mr Jackson?'

'Yes,' said Henneker.

'How about that bag of fertiliser in the stream at Mr Jackson's place?'

'I got Greg Painter to plant it for me.'

'And this Greg Painter . . . he does just what you tell him, does he?'

'He was in deep – to a bookie. I helped bail him out.'

'On condition?'

'More or less.'

'So you've been playing both ends against the middle?'

Henneker shrugged.

'Did Mr Jackson know all this was going on?'

'No,' said Henneker.

'How about your mother? Did she know?'

Henneker was adamant. His mother knew nothing. Roper didn't pursue it. However he couched that particular question he would only be wasting his breath. Henneker was never going to implicate his own mother, villain though he was.

'So without a house to live in, this Welsh farmer wouldn't want to buy,' said Roper. 'And the property would be worth less so that Mr Jackson might be more amenable to buying it. That was the idea, was it?'

Henneker nodded sullenly.

'Did you intend to kill your father last night, Mr Henneker?'

Henneker denied that hotly. 'God, no! Of course not!'

173

'You knew he was out, then?'

'Not until we got there. That's when we decided to make a proper job of it.'

'A proper job?' asked Roper.

It had only been going to be a small fire, just enough to make the house uninhabitable for a few months. 'We were going to start it, drive back, and I was going to make out I'd seen it from Fred's place and telephone my father to warn him. But when we got there, the Land-Rover was gone from the garage, so I knew he was out.'

They had left Jackson's van, now a noisy embarrassment since Henneker had rammed its exhaust into the verge after picking up Painter, out of sight in a side road near Henneker's gate. They had walked the rest of the way, carefully planting their feet in old tyre tracks, packed hard and frozen solid again during the hours of darkness, and since Snow had staggered up there, as far as Henneker's porch.

It had originally been their intention that Painter would act as an outside watchman, but with Austen Henneker safely out of the way the two of them had felt confident enough to go into the house together, letting themselves in with the key Henneker still had. It was at this juncture that Henneker first made mention of the bottle of petrol they had taken with them.

'That was the Johnnie Walker bottle, was it?' asked Roper, guessing, as he recalled the heat-crazed square bottle he had seen the Forensic technician hook up on the end of a ballpoint this morning in Austen Henneker's sitting-room.

'My God,' sneered Henneker. 'He really shot his mouth off, didn't he?'

Roper presumed he meant Painter; he didn't disillusion him.

The petrol had been strategically splashed on the curtains and sundry items of furniture, and the settee dragged closer to the fire. The icing on the cake – the idea of opening the sitting-room window and turning on the gas in the kitchen – had been Painter's.

'Why did you open the window?'

'Air,' said Henneker. 'Greg said air would make the fire burn faster.'

'Go on,' said Roper.

A lit match was tossed on to the settee. And when that had started to blaze – quicker than either of them ever thought it would – they had shut the sitting-room door on it to stop the fumes choking them. Henneker then dashed to the kitchen, opened the gas tap on the oven, and shut the kitchen door on his way out. Painter flung open the sitting-room door again on their final dash to the front door and fresh air. They didn't reach it—

'Where's the bottle?'

'You've got it!'

'No, you have!'

By now, dense black smoke was rolling from the sitting-room.

'It's in there!'

Painter had plunged back into the smoke. But only for a matter of seconds before he was charging out of it again and blundering into Henneker, blinded and coughing in the thick black fog.

'Leave it,' urged Henneker. 'All hell'll be let loose in a minute.'

Expecting the house to explode about their ears at any second, Henneker had dragged the gasping Painter after him to where they had left the van. Which was where the two of them engaged in another heated argument. Henneker had wanted Greg Painter, because of the broken exhaust on the van, to go back to the village on foot, but Painter had wanted none of that. He wanted out. Fast. He was still trying to haul air into his lungs and it was ten minutes' walk back to the village. Supposing the fire brigade came from that way? And someone spotted him? He had insisted on being driven back, at least as far as the Kingsleys' place.

So that's what had happened; but the brief exchange had cost more precious time, and they had already lost some in their run back to the van. And then the van refused to start, and already there was a bright glow in the direction of Henneker's farmhouse. There was a hasty discussion about ditching the van, but that was dangerous, too, especially if it was left where it presently was, close to the blazing farm. But still the starter motor wouldn't turn nor would the lights work, so the two of them had had to get out again and scrabble around frantically under the bonnet. The fault was elementary, a loose earth-lead from the battery to the chassis, but it needed a spanner and that had had to be got from the back of the van, and they had even argued about who was going to use it – and then the spanner had slipped and Painter's glove and hand were split open in what was now their mutually rising panic.

The van started then, but some twenty minutes had passed now since the settee had been ignited, and the sky was alight.

Nor were their troubles over yet. First came the explosion; they had felt the air heave, even in the van and a quarter of a mile away. And by the time they reached the Kingsleys' the van was making a racket that nobody was likely to sleep through and the lights were on in the Kingsleys' hall which might mean that someone was up and about in there and already yelling for the fire brigade.

Painter had baled out, still coughing and spluttering and clutching his bleeding hand, and had raced back to the Gorton Arms. Trevor Henneker, with a little more care on this second occasion, had turned the van in the lane and hared back to Jackson's farm where he had parked in the Dutch barn, then slipped indoors with, hopefully, neither his mother nor Jackson hearing him.

He was safely ensconced in his bed when he had heard the first wail of the sirens. Neither his mother nor Jackson seemed to have had their slumber disturbed; so he stayed where he was.

'How about your father's dog? Locked in the office.'

Henneker shrugged again. 'We left it there. It was kicking up hell. Couldn't let it out, could we? Somebody might have heard.'

'That'll be another charge, then, Mr Henneker,' said Roper, scarcely bothering to hide his contempt. He drew his own pocket book closer. 'Let's get down to the nitty-gritty now, shall we?'

'That was the nitty-gritty,' said Henneker. 'All of it.'

'I'm not talking about the fire, Mr Henneker,' said Roper. 'I'm talking about the shooting of Mr Komarowski.'

Henneker stiffened and blanched. '*Me*? You think I did that?'

'I don't think anything, son,' said Roper. 'I'm asking.'

'I told you,' said Henneker. 'I was up in Dorchester, at a disco.'

'With Greg Painter?'

'We were together all the evening. You can ask him.'

'You've already told us that Painter was your accomplice in the fire,' said Roper. 'So he's not going to be a great deal of help, is he?'

'How about girls?' asked Makins helpfully.

'We gave two a lift,' said Henneker. 'Afterwards.'

'Where did you drop them off?'

'Just outside Dorchester.'

'A big vague, that, Mr Henneker.'

'Look,' retorted Henneker. 'We didn't exchange names and addresses. They were just two girls we gave a lift to on the way out of the disco. We put them off at a bus stop on the road to West Stafford.'

'So they could live anywhere? And you don't even know their names?'

'Told you. We didn't ask.'

'What time did you drop them off?'

'We left the disco about a quarter past eleven . . . about twenty-five past, I suppose it was.'

'But you didn't get home until nearly a couple of hours afterwards. Why was that?'

Henneker didn't answer.

'Go along to see Mr Komarowski, did you?'

'Never went near the place.'

'So what *did* you do?'

'Shifting bloody sheep, weren't we?'

'And then you went home to bed?'

'Yes,' said Henneker.

'You've got a cricket-holdall,' said Roper.

The sudden change of direction had Henneker briefly confused.

'Well, have you or haven't you, laddie?'

'Had,' said Henneker. 'I threw it away.'

'Where?'

'The dustbin,' said Henneker. 'Where else?'

'When?'

'Six . . . seven months. Longer. I don't remember.'

'Try.'

The moment was spoiled by Jackson coming in through the back door. Roper glanced at his watch. Over half an hour had passed since he had left Jackson recovering in the barn. He looked like a man who had done a lot of thinking in the meantime.

'Feeling better, Mr Jackson?' asked Roper.

'Fine,' said Jackson, but his eyes weren't for Roper, only for Trevor Henneker's back hunched over the table. 'Been you all along, hasn't it?' he said contemptuously. 'You bloody little oick.'

'They're trying to say I killed old Komarowski,' pleaded Henneker, but the plea was ignored.

'I want you out,' said Jackson. 'Both of you. Don't want no more of either of you. Got that?' And so saying, he plucked off his cloth cap and stuffed it into his jacket pocket as he went on through to his hallway.

Jackson was in the mood for talking. Makins had taken Trevor Henneker out to the car, where they were waiting

178

for a transit van to take Henneker across to County HQ for his formal interrogation.

According to Jackson, Mrs Henneker had gone across to West Knighton to see how her mother was. The old lady had spent yesterday here at the farm, and when Trevor Henneker had driven her home yesterday evening she had complained of not feeling well. Mrs Henneker had left in a hire-car soon after breakfast this morning.

'She's not rung,' asked Roper, 'to tell you how the old lady is?'

'No,' said Jackson. 'Not yet. Reckon she's keeping low, eh?' He sat in the armchair opposite Roper. He was still wearing his jacket, his tweed cap still rolled up in the pocket, an unlit cigarette in one hand, his lighter in the other. He spoke his random thoughts as they came, the way a man does when he at last begins to see the light.

'I've had a sneaky feeling about him for a while,' he said. 'That lad of Becky's. And her,' he added. 'Should have seen it before; but I was smitten with her, wasn't I? A man don't see sense when a woman chucks herself at him the way she did.'

'This is Mrs Henneker, is it?' Roper prompted.

'Aye,' said Jackson. 'Kept on saying as how she was going to divorce old Austen; over a year it's been now. And she still hasn't got round to it. Funny, that. Eh?'

Roper tended to agree. It was indeed funny.

'They've been nagging on at me to buy Austen's place,' Jackson confided. 'And if it had been a few quid less I might have.'

'And now it is,' said Roper.

'Aye,' said Jackson. 'That's what I was out there thinking about. I was going to put Trevor in to run it; and perhaps take on another couple of hands to work the two places. Doctor's told me to take it a bit easier. Because of the old ticker.'

There was also the question of Jackson's will. 'Keeps on to me about changing it; in favour of her and the boy.'

Yes, she would have, thought Roper. And perhaps she and 'the boy' still figured prominently in Henneker's will; and that was why she was being so dilatory about instituting divorce proceedings against him.

'Got a solicitor, have you, Mr Jackson?'

'Aye,' said Jackson. 'Barkworth, Cutler and Roberts. Over Wareham. Same as Austen. He uses them, too.'

Roper felt his ears prick. It had been Mr Barkworth who had signed that letter to Komarowski. And if Trevor Henneker was right, it was for Barkworth *et alia* that Greg Painter laboured. He had had his hands on a lot of strings had young Mr Painter.

'Getting my affairs straight, she called it.' Jackson's mouth twitched wryly. 'No fool like an old fool, is there, eh?'

Roper changed tack slightly. 'You ever shifted any of Mr Henneker's stock? To get your own back on him?'

'Course I haven't,' retorted Jackson. He had lifted the unlit cigarette to his mouth, but lowered it again. 'Never. And perhaps he wasn't nicking mine, either. I'm beginning to wonder about that now, an' all. We were never friends exactly, me and old Austen, but we always used to rub along together . . . until I took that boy of his on. And his mother. My second mistake, she was.'

Roper waited while Jackson stuck the cigarette in his mouth and finally lit it.

'You used to play cricket, Mr Jackson.'

'Aye,' said Jackson. 'Long time ago, I did. Played at the Oval once. Austen did, too. And Harry Painter. All three of us.' Despite his present troubles, Jackson spoke with evident pride. 'Got to the quarter finals, we did. 1951. The only village to have three lads in the team, Gorton was.'

Painter had been the team's fast bowler, Jackson the highest-scoring bat, and Henneker a wickedly efficient keeper. It had been as much an outing as a cricket competition.

The team had spent the week touring the sights between matches. Up to Regent's Park to see the zoo. Half a day at Madame Tussaud's, Westminster Abbey, the long trek up to the top of the Monument to the Great Fire, an afternoon boat trip from Tower Bridge to Putney.

'Where did you all stay?' asked Roper. 'Hotel somewhere?'

'Some place near Charing Cross,' said Jackson. He tried to remember the name but too many years had passed. But what he did remember was travelling down from Charing Cross to the Oval on an electric tram on the playing days. Memorable because he, and the rest of the team, had never been on a tram before – or since.

'Do you remember the route number of the tram, by any chance?'

Jackson didn't remember that either. It was all too long ago.

'How did you carry your gear about?'

'Had a bag,' said Jackson. 'All three of us had one.'

Roper brought out his wallet. He took out the Polaroid of the cricket-bag that Makins had found at Allgrove's. He half rose and held it out to Jackson over the hearthrug.

'Like that, was it, Mr Jackson?'

'Aye, it was,' said Jackson, tipping it towards the window and the last of the daylight. 'Dead like.' He leaned forward and passed it back.

'How about the bag young Trevor had?'

'The very identical,' said Jackson. 'His father's, I think it was.'

'Seen it lately?'

Jackson shook his head. 'I think it went,' he said, dashing the remnants of Roper's hopes at a stroke. 'When he cleared his room out, a few months back. Saw him carting it down the stairs, full of old books. Haven't seen it since.'

'How about the one you had?'

'Gave it away,' said Jackson. 'It was on its last legs.

181

Didn't have use for it any more. Gave it to the local plumber. To carry his tools about in.'

'Is he still about, this plumber?'

'Aye,' said Jackson. 'He's still about. Lives along at Pitcher's Lane. Just the other side of Lower Gorton.'

Chapter 15

Pale and haggard, Harry Painter rose from the chair in the HQ annexe where he had spent the last three hours and, by the state of the ashtray, probably gone through the best part of a packet of cigarettes.

'Keeping them both here, are you?' he asked.

'Yes, sir,' said Roper. 'Pending further enquiries. They've both been charged with starting the fire at Mr Henneker's.'

'There's no sort of doubt?'

'No, sir. Sorry.' Both Henneker and Painter had made their confessions into the tape-recorders upstairs. More evidence had arrived a half-hour ago from Regional Forensic; the Johnnie Walker bottle found in Henneker's sitting-room still had the sooty residues of petrol lodged in its corners.

'These other enquiries . . . ' Painter hesitated. ' . . . That'd be about the Komarowski business, would it?'

Roper didn't answer – couldn't answer. So far, both lads had denied being anywhere near the caravan that night.

'No point in my hanging about, then?'

'No, sir,' said Roper. 'I'm sorry.' His sympathy was genuine. It was always an unhappy circumstance when the sins of a son were visited on the father.

Painter turned dejectedly to pick up his driving-coat from the back of the annexe armchair. Roper waited for him to slip his arms into it.

'There is one thing you might be able to help us with, Mr Painter.'

'What's that?'

Roper took out his wallet and from it the Polaroid photograph of the grey holdall. Painter took it with one hand and finished buttoning his coat with the other.

'Looks like the one I've got,' said Painter, handing it back again.

'Got, sir? Or had?'

'Got,' said Painter.

'Exactly like this one?'

'Spot on,' said Painter.

'Did it go to the Oval with you, sir? In 1951?'

'Yes,' said Painter. Like everyone else of whom the question had been asked, Painter could not quite see the point. 'What about it?'

'Did you ever go on a London tram with it?'

'A few times.'

'Before you went up to the Oval, I presume you and Mr Jackson and Mr Henneker all went out together to buy identical bags? Yes?'

'Didn't buy 'em,' said Painter. 'None of us did. My old dad gave me mine. Fred and Austen's fathers handed theirs down too.'

So the bags were even older than the fifty years Craig, at Forensic, had guessed.

'They were pre-war. You couldn't buy good bags like that afterwards. My old grandfather bought 'em. One each for all the team. He had a few pounds left over after he had the new changing-hut built. In nineteen thirty-eight, that was. Used to be a big thing, cricket, in Gorton, before the war.'

'And they were all identical, were they, Mr Painter, these bags your grandfather bought?'

'So far as I know.'

'And *your* bag, Mr Painter – you could show it to Sergeant Peasgood if he dropped in on you?' Roper glanced at his watch. 'About ten o'clock, say? Tonight?'

'Sure,' said Painter. 'If it helps.'

184

'And if you can spare a minute, sir,' said Roper. 'I'd like to know a bit more about those bags . . . '

Sergeant Peasgood was fortuitously at home, taking his evening-meal break, when Roper telephoned him a few minutes after Painter had gone.

'I want you to do a couple of checks for me, Sergeant. I'd like you to call in on Fred Jackson and Austen Henneker, and ask them both where their old cricket-holdalls originally came from. Second: there's a plumber. An Alan Hardisty. He lives in Pitcher's Lane, somewhere over Lower Gorton way. He should have a similar bag; and if he has, ask him where he got it from. Hopefully he'll say Fred Jackson. And ask to see it. Third: Harry Painter, the landlord along at the Gorton Arms. He's got a bag like it too. Give him a visit. Ten o'clock. He says he'll show it to you.'

And there was one more thing. When he and Makins had brought out Painter's son from the side entrance of the Arms earlier this evening, while they had been seeing him into the car, a little white van parked in front of the green opposite had been driven off in the direction of Lower Gorton.

'Any idea who could own that van, Sergeant?'

'Registration number?'

'Didn't get it,' said Roper. 'Too busy and it was too dark.'

'Fred Jackson's got a white van.'

'Not his. This was old. Could be an old Morris. Or an A-thirty-five. A collector's piece. Late fifties or early sixties. Could be. Makins reckons the driver's got it race-tuned.'

'Oh, *that* van, said Peasgood. 'That's a labour of love, that one, sir. Stan Rydz's van. It's got to be. Rumour has it he practically goes to bed with it. Want me to have a word with him, too?'

'No,' said Roper. 'I'll do that. Tomorrow.'

'Where'll you be when I ring back, sir?'

'Here,' said Roper. 'County.'

If a case could be said to break, the investigation into the death of Zygmunt Komarowski broke at half-past ten that same night when Sergeant Peasgood rang back. He was speaking from Alan Hardisty's cottage.

Painter had shown Peasgood his precious relic of a cricket-bag. It was an identical clone of the one Makins had found at Allgrove's. An earlier call on Austen Henneker, and another on Fred Jackson, had elicited the information that, like Harry Painter, the bags that they had once owned had previously been their fathers', all of whom had been members of the village cricket team for most of the decade before the war. And the bag presently in the possession of Alan Hardisty had been given to him by Fred Jackson.

But there was more than that – much more.

'Thing is, sir, I'm still with Mr Hardisty. And he might have come up with something useful, sir. About the shooting.'

'I'm all ears, Sergeant.' Sitting on the corner of his desk, Roper drew a notepad closer and uncapped his ballpoint between his teeth.

Peasgood seemed to have opened a whole new can of worms.

It was probably Alan Hardisty, the plumber, who had crossed the lane when he had seen Mrs Henneker coming towards him, the night Komarowski was shot. And at the time he had been carrying a cricket-holdall. And it was grey and old and tatty, and had been given to him by Fred Jackson. He usually drove around in a van but that cold night it had refused to start so he'd had to go out on foot. The job was urgent; a burst pipe in the attic of the vicarage. He wasn't sure what the time had been when he'd passed Mrs Henneker – he had not in fact recognised her in the dark, and had crossed the lane not to avoid her but because the vicarage was on that side – but the vicar's wife had rung him just before eleven o'clock, in some panic, and he had set off immediately, having lost some ten minutes trying to get his van started. It was a good twenty minutes' brisk walk so it had probably been about 11.30 when he crossed the lane towards the vicarage, which tallied, more or less, with the time when Mrs Henneker had told Roper she had got off the bus in the village.

But it was something that Alan Hardisty had seen some ten minutes *before* he had passed Mrs Henneker in the lane that night that had roused Peasgood's interest. Hardisty lived on the other side of Lower Gorton, just beyond the catchment area of the officers who had conducted the door-to-door enquiries, and to walk from his own house to Upper Gorton he had to pass the end of the lane that led to Charlie Allgrove's cottage.

Coming towards him, from the direction of Upper Gorton, weaving about the road, according to Hardisty, had been a solitary, feebly glowing lamp. As Hardisty reached the T-junction, whence the lane to Allgrove's branched off, the approaching shape resolved itself into a hunchbacked man on a bicycle. At the junction – Hardisty had heard the scrape of badly adjusted brakes – from Upper Gorton to the junction the road was slightly downhill, so the cyclist was travelling at some speed – the rider careered to the right, as Hardisty viewed him, and disappeared in the direction of Allgrove's cottage.

By this time Hardisty had drawn level with the junction and was about to cross the end of the lane that led to Allgrove's, and had thus been in a position to catch a brief glimpse of the cyclist's back.

'Thing is, sir,' said Peasgood, 'Hardisty reckons the bloke was bowling along without a back light; like old Komarowski was when he left Miss Kingley's. Could be nothing, of course; I choke off half a dozen idiots a week for not having lights. But it was *that* night, sir. And I was wondering if Hardisty might have seen Komarowski beetling about one last time. Just before he copped it.'

'So it would have been about twenty-past eleven when Hardisty saw this bike?'

'Near enough,' said Peasgood.

'And Hardisty said "careered", did he?'

'Fast, and all over the place,' said Peasgood. 'The bike skidded at the corner, and he thought the bloke was going to come off.'

The last person, positively, to have seen Komarowski alive, to date, had been Carslake the vet. That had been at 9.30 on the night in question. Was it just remotely possible that Alan Hardisty had seen the Pole two hours after that? And, if he had, where had Komarowski been cycling to at that hour of night? And why?

'He didn't get a *shufti* at the rider? Short? Tall? What he might have been wearing?'

'He hardly got a look at him,' said Peasgood. 'It was only me jogging his memory that got him to remember the bloke at all. All he does remember for sure is that the rider was a bit wobbly and he didn't have a back light on the bike.'

'And he was hunchbacked?'

'Hardisty said it might have been something like a rucksack, with a Christmas tree sticking out of it. He didn't see the shape exactly, except the top was sticking up above the bloke's head.'

'Man's bike, or a woman's?' Komarowski's bicycle had been a woman's.

'He isn't certain. Could have been either.'

'But he *was* headed for Allgrove's place?'

'That direction,' said Peasgood.

It might be significant, or it might not. The cyclist could have been anybody, and the fact that he had turned up the lane where Allgrove's cottage was sited was a long way from proof that he was on his way to visit Allgrove. There were a dozen cottages along that lane, and at the other end of it was the main road that led westward to Dorchester. It had been 11.20, and not too long after all the pubs had shut. He might have been just a drunk going home, a little the worse for wear, with a Christmas tree he had bought earlier in the day. Or he

188

might equally have had a grey cricket-bag slung across his back, with a twelve-bore shotgun in it.

Cheroot-smoke trailed behind him as he crossed the floodlit car park to his Sierra. It was midnight, and twenty minutes since he had ascertained that neither Gregory Painter nor Trevor Henneker owned a bicycle, nor had during the last few years. And despite his continuing suspicions, and the case against them, he had signed a bail-note for them both; conditional upon their reporting to Sergeant Peasgood at nine o'clock each morning until their case came before the magistrates. Painter's father was on his way back to collect them, both of them because Fred Jackson had refused outright to offer any further assistance to Trevor Henneker, even a bed for the night. More interestingly, Mrs Henneker had still not come back from her mother's at West Knighton, nor even contacted Jackson on the telephone.

In thirty-odd years Roper had made plenty of mistakes, and consigned many an unsolved case to files where they had been gathering dust ever since, but rarely had he allowed himself to be diverted like he had on this one. Feuding farmers and arson, and a death threat that was history now, had all conspired to lead him off the straight and narrow, and he should have known better. Whatever was spoken and written about murder, it was rarely complicated. In most cases, the victim knew his killer, often uncommonly well. The act was rarely planned, often not planned at all. The possible motives for murder could always be whittled down to four very basic human emotions: passion, panic, prejudice or greed, and the motive was the why. In the case of Komarowski the where was known, the how an immediate and undeniable conclusion, the when was spread over not too many hours of a cold winter night. All that remained were the who and the why and he was no nearer to either of those than he had been the other morning when he had stood in the snow with Wilson.

189

A lot had happened in the intervening days, and he had talked to a lot of people, although he was beginning to doubt now if he had come anywhere near talking to the right one.

It all hinged on an elderly shotgun, a scuffed and tattered cricket-bag with a London tram ticket, of almost equal antiquity, tucked away in the lining; and perhaps, just remotely, a rattling old bicycle that hadn't had a working back light.

And just supposing that bicycle Hardisty had glimpsed *had* been Komarowski's . . .

'Blast!' Metal tinkled somewhere by his feet in the black shadow of the Sierra. He crouched and felt about in the slush until he felt the familiar shape of his leather-tabbed key ring. He stayed crouched . . .

It wasn't just to do with a bag and a gun and a bicycle. It was to do with keys, as well. Four keys.

'Hell's bloody teeth,' he whispered aloud, as it suddenly occurred to him that he might no longer be supposing.

He rose creakily and started back to his office.

Four keys, and Komarowski's bicycle.

That's what it was *really* all about.

'Who are you, then?' asked Roper.

'Cody, sir. I'm the security guard.'

It had been unreasonable to expect anyone else to be answering the Forensic laboratory's telephone at ten after midnight. But it was disappointing, all the same.

'But you've got all the keys to the place?'

'Yes, sir.'

'I need a favour, Mr Cody. There's a yellow caravan across in your vehicle-testing bay. And hopefully not too far away, an old black bicycle. A woman's bicycle. And if somebody hasn't messed about with it, there ought to be a chain and a padlock that belonged to the bicycle—'

'It's all still chained together, sir. I've seen it.'

'Bully,' said Roper. 'I want to know what type of padlock it is. Got that?'

'Yes, sir.'

'Good,' said Roper. 'Ring me back as soon as you find out. Now, pencil and paper. Message for Mr Craig, or whoever's in charge there tomorrow. There were four keys in the cash-box found in the caravan. I want them here tomorrow morning. At the first crack. Write it large, Mr Cody, and put it on the reception desk. Ring me back about the padlock as soon as you like.'

Mr Cody was clearly a man with his wits about him.

'Cody, Mr Roper. You wanted to know about the padlock on the bicycle.'

'I did, Mr Cody. Does it operate with a key?'

'No, sir. It's one of those gadgets with four little wheels. You have to line the numbers up to open it. A sort of code, sir.'

'Thank you, Mr Cody,' said Roper. 'A Happy New Year to you.'

Roper and Price stood in the clearing where the caravan had been. The thaw that had begun yesterday had quickened; the trees were hung with dripping icicles and on the steeper ground the melting slush was turning into miniature rivers. Christmas had come and gone and it was ten o'clock in the morning of a new day.

'What was in it for Painter?' asked Price.

'Money,' said Roper. 'He put a lot of money he hadn't got on a couple of slow horses.'

'But what's it all to do with Komarowski?' asked Price. 'If you reckon Henneker and young Painter didn't kill him.'

'Nothing,' Roper admitted. 'Except that it got me talking to Harry Painter about grey cricket-bags. And he told me where they'd all come from; and I sent Peasgood along to check up on a similar bag that Jackson had given to the local plumber to carry his tools in. And it turned out that *he* was the bloke who crossed the lane the other night – the one Mrs Henneker saw. And when Peasgood got him to remember a bit better, this plumber thinks he

191

saw a bicycle go by, and it didn't have a back light.'

'Plenty don't,' said Price.

'The point is,' said Roper, 'the bike *he* saw was travelling in the direction of Allgrove's place. And the time was right.'

'So?'

'So everything,' said Roper. He brought from his overcoat pocket the four keys that had arrived at County for him at nine o'clock this morning. Holding them by the label, he dropped them into Price's hand. 'Still believe in fairies, Dave?'

Price weighed them in his gloved palm.

'Two look like ignition keys,' he said. 'The other two . . . they're too long. Could be keys to a couple of fancy padlocks.' The realisation dawned on him as suddenly as it had dawned on Roper last night in the car park. 'Charlie bloody Allgrove? And those two sheds he's got?'

'And his two vans,' said Roper. 'And if they are, that's how Jack-the-lad managed to get into Allgrove's garage to hide that shotgun.'

'So he *must* have known Allgrove was out.'

'Or the other way about,' said Roper. 'Perhaps he thought Allgrove was still in the chokey. And we weren't likely to go looking there. And when Allgrove did come out, and find the gun, he was hardly likely to hand it over to us, was he?'

Allgrove stood watching, unshaven, half-asleep, and shivering inside the old army overcoat he was wearing over a pair of lurid lilac pyjamas.

A padlock snapped open. Roper and Price moved on to the other shed. Allgrove shuffled after them in a pair of industrial boots with their untied laces trailing.

'Have a good Christmas, Charlie?' asked Roper, as he stuffed the second key into the second padlock.

'Good enough,' grumbled Allgrove. 'Till you two turned up.'

There was a soft click, a spring of metal.

192

'Look,' protested Allgrove. 'Ain't you blokes supposed to have a warrant or something? And where d'you get those bloody keys?'

'I'm doing you a favour, Charlie,' said Roper, squeezing the padlock shut again. He held out the keys for Allgrove's closer scrutiny. 'Ever seen these before?'

Allgrove went to take them; Roper drew them away. 'Just look, Charlie. It's important.'

Allgrove peered muzzily at the two dangling keys. 'They're mine,' he said. 'Got to be, haven't they?'

'And *you*'ve got a set?'

'Yeah,' said Allgrove. 'Course I have . . . Bloody hell,' he blurted as realisation dawned on him, too. 'They must be the ones I lost.' He reached for them again, but again Roper snatched them back out of his reach.

'Lost them where, Charlie?'

'Out on the heath.'

'When?'

'The day I got caught burying those dogs. I thought I must have dropped 'em in the grass somewhere. I had to hot-wire the van to get home. I could have sworn I'd left 'em in the van. In the ignition.'

'Perhaps you did,' said Roper.

Allgrove was still not at his brightest, but he was bright enough. 'That *bloody* Pole,' he said. 'He must have nicked 'em out of the van. Only way it could have been, wasn't it? To stop me shovin' off.'

'Which van?'

'The old ambulance.'

'Which Pole?'

'Komarowski, the one who bloody peached on me.'

'Why him?' asked Price.

'It was the day he took that picture of me up on the heath, wasn't it? I saw him belting off on his bike as I was going back to the van. And when I got there I couldn't find the keys. Thought I'd lost 'em, didn't I? Only he nicked 'em, didn't he, 'cause I must have left 'em in the van, mustn't I?'

193

Roper gave all that its due and proper consideration.

'Got that pantechnicon working yet?'

'The engine, I have,' said Allgrove.

'Mind if I try it?'

Allgrove stood aside. Roper unlocked the left-hand garage door again and went inside, and climbed up into the musty-smelling cab of the pantechnicon. The ignition key fitted, and when he turned it all the way the starter motor whined and the vehicle shook as the engine suddenly coughed to life. All of which left him in no doubt that the keys were indeed Charlie Allgrove's, and had been stolen from him by Zygmunt Komarowski and had been used, very lately, by Komarowski's killer in order to plant an elderly shotgun, in a holdall, in Allgrove's converted ambulance.

He glanced into the rear-view mirror. And unbuckled his seat-belt again. The little white van had reappeared while they had been in Allgrove's.

'Where're you going?' asked Price.

'Somebody to sort out,' said Roper, climbing out and slamming the door behind him, and squelching back through the slush some twenty or thirty yards to the white van.

He rapped on the roof of the cab. Rydz put down the paper he was reading and leaned across to wind down the nearside window.

'I am parked illegal or something, sir?'

'I'm sure you wouldn't do anything illegal, Mr Rydz,' said Roper. 'Keeping an eye on us, are you, sir? Be seeing a lot of you during the day, shall we?'

'I stick around a bit,' said Rydz. 'Things are movin', yes? Yesterday you pick up them two boys, and this morning you go up where the caravan was. Then you come chasin' up here to Allgrove and get him out o' bed. I reckon you on to something, sir.'

'Stay close, Mr Rydz. You might even find out. But not so close I can read your registration plates. Right?'

'Is promise,' said Rydz. He reached down to the seat beside him for his newspaper, folded it vertically twice, then leaned across to pass it out of the window. 'Is in paper today,' he said. 'About Ziggy. Is not much for a tombstone, eh? A couple o' lines in a bloddy newspaper.'

The couple of lines were nearer a dozen, but Rydz was right. It wasn't much to show for seventy years of a man's life. Roper handed back the paper.

'Yesterday's news, Mr Rydz.'

'I also know things it don't say there,' said Rydz.

'Like what?'

'Like a minicab with Mrs Henneker in it turns up at Jackson's place 'bout eight o'clock this morning. Driver dump a lot of suitcases in the back and Fred Jackson don't help none. She goin', I reckon. Or Jackson chuck her out. Went off towards West Knighton, she did. Where her mother is.'

It sounded likely.

'You ought to be a copper, Mr Rydz.'

'Is small place,' said Rydz, shrugging modestly. 'Also, 'bout half-past nine, I see Henneker's Land-Rover in Jackson's yard. And Jackson was helpin' Henneker carry stuff into the house. Cases and blankets and things. And if you take a ride up there now, you might get to see Henneker and Jackson repairin' that fence Henneker broke a bit back. Jackson's holding the wood and Henneker's knockin' the nails in. That's got to mean something, I reckon.'

'Sounds like good news, Mr Rydz,' said Roper. 'Anything else?'

'No, sir,' said Rydz. 'But perhaps later. I think o' something else, I tell you.'

'Yes, sir,' said Roper. 'You do that.'

Rydz began to wind up his window. Roper gripped the edge of the glass and pressed down on it.

'Sir?' said Rydz. 'You got some more to say?'

'Yes, sir,' said Roper, taking his hand away as the window started to go down again. 'You did a bunk on

195

us the other day. Scared of something, were you?'

'I was angry then,' said Rydz. 'Upset, see.'

'So?' said Roper.

Rydz looked shamefaced. 'I'd got a gun,' he said. 'Not loaded, though. I was just goin' to wave it about. Scare the bastard a bit.'

'Referring to whom, sir?'

'That Austen Henneker,' said Rydz. 'When you brought him out, I was going to stop you and point the gun in the window. Just to see the look on his face; like the look Ziggy must have had.'

'I'd have nicked you,' said Roper.

'So what?' said Rydz. 'It'd have been worth it.'

'Thought Mr Henneker was the villain, did you, sir?'

'For a bit,' said Rydz. 'Then yesterday, I see you pick up that Trevor Henneker. Only this morning, he's along at the pub. So I reckon it ain't him either. Then I see you come up here. To see Charlie Allgrove. Only you don't run *him* in, either. I was wondering where you might be going next.'

'Like I said, Mr Rydz: tag along. So long as you don't have that gun aboard again.'

Rydz shook his head. 'Not today,' he said. 'I got over it. You look if you want.'

'I'll take your word for it, Mr Rydz.'

'Thought you were going to tell him to push off,' said Price as Roper climbed back in beside him.

'I want him about,' said Roper, feeling around his pockets for his cheroots. 'Close . . . You want to hear a theory?'

'That's crazy,' said Price. They were still outside Allgrove's. The cheroot was half smoked.

'Is it?' said Roper. He belted himself in and turned the ignition key. In the mirror he saw a puff of exhaust come almost simultaneously from Rydz's van. 'Think about it. He was a friend of Komarowski.' He turned in the narrow lane; so did Rydz who then waited for Roper to overtake him before trailing on a respectable distance behind. 'He goes up to the caravan, probably on foot and carrying the gun in that holdall. He doesn't need to knock on the door because he knows about the key Komarowski keeps behind the wheel. And if Komarowski's hammering away at his typewriter, perhaps he doesn't hear a thing. The first thing he notices is the draught as matey opens the door, by which time it's too late. Matey takes one quick shot, probably from the doorway as Komarowski gets to his feet, and follows it up with the second one when Komarowski's flat on his back. Then he opens the cash-box, where he knows Allgrove's keys are, and takes them out – they're the most vital bit of his scheme those keys. Then he unlocks the bicycle padlock, of which he knows the combination. Then he wheels the bicycle down to the lane and goes hell for leather to Allgrove's to stash away the bag and the gun – because he's sure Allgrove's still in chokey and we're not likely to go looking there. Then he cycles back, padlocks the bike where he found it, and puts the keys back in the cash-box and walks back home; and prays to God nobody's seen him – or if they did, they wouldn't have recognised him.'

He dropped down a gear as he cautiously overtook a milk float. A quick glance in the mirror showed Rydz still behind.

'There's a snag,' said Price. 'The cash-box keys were inside Komarowski when Wilson opened him up. Mixed up with shotgun pellets. You saying the villain stuffed them in there after he came back with the bicycle?'

'There's another key, Dave,' said Roper. They had reached the junction where Hardisty the plumber had glimpsed the hunchbacked cyclist the other night. 'You always get two keys with a cash-box.' He turned right, towards Upper Gorton. He slowed down to make sure Rydz was still there. 'And matey knew where the spare one was. Bet your life.'

'How about a motive?'

'Don't know,' said Roper. 'But he must have had

one.' He checked the odometer on the speedo as they passed the old iron gate up to where the caravan had been. He was beginning to feel sick to his very gut at what the next few minutes were going to bring, if he was right; and he was fairly certain he was.

'But he *couldn't* have done it,' argued Price. 'Scudding around the country in the dead of night on a bike. He's an old man.'

'So was Komarowski. And *he* used to cycle everywhere. And what about old Rydz back there. He won't see his seventieth birthday again either, and he could probably bang our two heads together and we couldn't do a thing to stop him.'

'But Kingsley can't even bloody *walk*.'

'Can't he?' retorted Roper. 'We've never asked, have we?'

They were coming up towards the Kingsleys' cottage; where Makins' car was parked behind Peasgood's white Metro, and Makins was standing in the middle of the road, flagging his arms. It all looked very ominous. Roper drew into the kerb, where he took another odometer reading. A shade under a quarter of a mile. Some six hundred paces for a fit man . . . Rydz was pulling into the kerb behind him . . .

'What's up, George?' he asked, letting down his window.

'Been trying to get patched in to you on the radio,' said Makins. 'Kingsley's dead. Looks like an overdose job.'

Chapter 16

The chilly little downstairs bedroom was a shambles of junk, dusty old books, piled newspapers, magazines, and smelt as if the windows had not been open in months. Kingsley, toothless, wigless and still in his dressing-gown, striped flannel pyjamas and new tartan carpet slippers, lay on top of the rumpled bed covers in the sour stench of his own vomit, his eyes closed to slits and his mouth open. Peasgood, capless, pale and not yet master of the situation, was writing the time and date in his pocket book.

'Certain, are we?' asked Roper.

'Yes, sir,' said Peasgood sombrely, still writing.

Roper went across to the bed and lightly touched his fingertips to Kingsley's wrinkled neck, under his left ear. There was no pulse, The flesh was still warm, but not as warm as it would have been in life; but then the room was like a refrigerator. Whatever had gone on behind that gaunt twisted face during the last few days would now stay a secret for ever.

'Ambulance?'

'On its way,' said Peasgood.

'How about his sister?'

'Out, sir,' said Peasgood. 'Gone up to the sales in Dorchester; to buy some wool. I met her at the bus stop by the Arms. About quarter to nine.'

Roper bared his wristwatch. It was twenty to eleven now.

'How did you get in?'

'Door was open sir. Wedged-to with the doormat.'

'And you'd just dropped in, in passing?'

'No, sir,' said Peasgood. 'He rang me, or rather the missus. About nine o'clock. Asked if I could call by some time after ten-thirty. Said he'd got some information.'

'About what?'

'He didn't say,' said Peasgood.

It sounded very much as if Kingsley had wanted Peasgood to find him before his sister came back from Dorchester. And that was the least he had owed her.

Roper took in the near-empty whisky bottle on the dusty cabinet beside the bed, the torn fragments of its aluminium seal in the ashtray piled high with cigarette ends, the empty tumbler beside, and, more pertinently, close by, one lying on its side, two brown plastic pill containers with their caps off. Both were empty. Both had contained sleeping tablets, both had been dispensed by the chemist up in the village. One had been prescribed for Kingsley himself, the other for his sister. The latter had originally contained, according to the label, forty tablets, and bore the date of Christmas Eve. Kingsley's bottle had been dated the week before. That had contained sixty. Which was a lot of pills to down in one go, together with most of a pint of whisky.

'Any kind of note?'

'I haven't had a chance to look around yet. But I collected this from the postman earlier.'

'Thanks,' said Roper. It was a solitary letter, addressed to Komarowski. He stuffed it into his overcoat pocket, his mind, for the time being, on more immediate things. Without his wig and his teeth the old man looked all of his seventy years. His electric wheelchair stood near the door. A flimsy old wardrobe with its door hanging open was packed tight with more useless junk. A few war-time photographs hanging over the fading floral wallpaper. Everything brown with tobacco-tar, including the curtains. Dust everywhere. Compared with the rest of the house this room was a slum hovel. The scar tissue on the right side of Kingsley's face went right up into where his hair would have been, if he had had any. He was still wearing the one black glove, the little finger extended stiffly, like a prim old dowager's over a teacup handle.

'Get Wilson over, George,' said Roper to Makins who had followed him in. 'As quick as he likes. Be useful if we could get him out of here before his sister comes back.'

Makins returned to his car. Price took his place at Roper's shoulder. Roper untied the cord of the stained and frayed dressing gown wrapped around Kingsley, then unfastened the top button of the striped pyjama jacket. He had fully expected to see scar-tissue on the right-hand side of Kingsley's bony chest. There was none.

'Stinks in here,' said Price.

'Open the window a bit,' said Roper, gently probing now at the pale thin legs under the pyjamas. Thin; but not wasted, the way they ought to have been.

'Miss Kingsley have her dog with her?' he asked Peasgood, over his shoulder.

'No, sir,' said Peasgood.

'Have a look for it, will you?' He hoped it hadn't slipped out through the open front door. All Miss Kingsley had left now was that dog. The black wig was under Kingsley's left tartan-slippered foot . . .

'Dave . . . ?'

'What?'

'Come and look at these slippers.'

Kneeling on a precarious pile of old newspapers, Price finally managed to unjam the little casement window beside the wardrobe. Fresh cold air blew in as he joined Roper at the foot of the bed.

'What about 'em?'

'The uppers are damp,' said Roper. He leaned down and squeezed the toe of one. It was more than damp. It was soaking wet.

'Sir . . . ' Peasgood was quickly back. 'There's a whole

201

load of footprints out in the garden. Look like slipper prints. Man-sized.'

They were heel-less, so they probably *were* slipper prints. And as Peasgood had said, they were man-sized. They led from the kitchen door to an old brick potting shed at the far end of the tiny garden. A set of dog's paw prints ran, in the outward direction only, parallel with them.

They followed the tracks along the path. And if Roper was reading the signs aright, Kingsley had been able to walk with neither a stick nor a trace of a limp. Peasgood peered in at the cobwebbed window let into the brick-work.

'He's sitting in there, sir. Good as gold.'

Roper cautiously thumbed down the latch and opened the door an inch. The Labrador lurched to its feet expectantly and gave a tentative wag of its tail.

'Sit, boy,' said Roper. The Labrador sat, its tail swishing backwards and forwards over the stone floor like a duster. The metal disc on its collar gave its name as Max.

'You're the only witness we've got, Max, old son,' said Roper sadly, as the Labrador pushed its cold head up into the palm of his hand. 'And you can't tell us a bloody thing, can you, old lad?'

Wilson the pathologist was here now, and the Coroner's Officer; the ambulance had been sent away and the local undertaker's van would be here in a few minutes to replace it. According to Peasgood, the next bus from Dorchester would arrive in a little over half an hour; Peasgood and a WPC from County had driven along to the Gorton Arms to meet it. Hopefully, the bus would be running late.

'How long's he been dead?'

'About an hour,' said Wilson, sitting on the edge of the bed while he waited for the thermometer plunged into Kingsley's liver to register. 'Less, if anything.'

'Suicide?'

'It certainly looks like it. Cardiac failure, probably. All that vomiting.'

'Poor old sod,' said Roper.

'Quite,' agreed Wilson, sympathetically. He peered up at Roper over the top of his spectacles. 'How about you, Douglas? Are *you* certain?'

'More than I'd rather be,' said Roper. 'About sixty per cent. The odd forty per cent was what I was coming along to ask him about.'

'He must have been a very desperate man,' said Wilson.

'I think he was,' said Roper. 'And I think he could walk, too.'

'Really?'

'Yes,' said Roper. 'Really. Any way of telling? Here and now, I mean.'

'Yes,' said Wilson. 'Let's have a look, shall we?' He reached towards his case and took out a pair of surgical scissors. Moving down the bed, he cut up both the outside seams of Kingsley's pyjama legs. He parted the material and felt about the muscles of Kingsley's white and almost hairless legs, the right one first. 'A few square inches of replacement tissue,' he said. 'And a depressed scar on the outer thigh; might be an old bullet wound.' The tips of his fingers probed and kneaded. 'A bit varicosed here and there, but considering his age I'd say that was a fairly serviceable leg.'

'And the other one?'

'Feels sound,' said Wilson. 'No obvious injuries. Well-defined muscles. Really not bad at all. If I've got a leg like that when I'm seventy I don't think I'll complain too much.'

'Could he ride a bike, d'you think? Lately?'

'Assuming he'd ever learned I don't see any reason why not.'

'Can we look at his hand? The right one.'

Wilson sliced down the back of the black glove, then the back of each finger, except the stiff, extended one;

which was stuffed with cotton wool because the little finger was missing. The other three curled fingers straightened easily. There was a small patch of scar tissue on the right forearm, but in Wilson's opinion it had not been serious enough at the time to warrant a skin graft.

'But was it a working hand and arm?' asked Roper. 'Apart from the missing finger.'

'Yes,' said Wilson. 'I'd say so.'

'Looks like he was a con-artist too, then,' said Roper. Remembering it, belatedly, he took Komarowski's latest mail delivery from his pocket. It looked official. The address was typed, and the embossed black seal on the flap had what looked like a lot of Polish written around it and an address in Portland Place, London, underneath it. Roper slit the envelope open. The letter inside it might have been in Chinese for all that he could make of it.

'Rydz still outside, is he, Dave?' he asked Price, who, with Makins, was still rummaging around for a suicide note.

'Sitting in his van, the last I saw of him.'

'Good,' said Roper. 'Give him this and tell him I'd like a translation.'

Price went out to the hall. The touch at Roper's elbow was Makins. Nipped between two fingers, he passed Roper a folded and flattened sheet of white paper.

'Just found this, under the cushion of his wheelchair.'

Roper took the sheet of paper. It was white bond paper, good quality. And he did not need to unfold it to see that there was a semi-circular fragment torn from its bottom edge; as if it had been hurriedly ripped from a typewriter.

'You're certain about this, Mr Rydz?' asked Roper, holding the letter that Rydz had translated for him.

'Yes, sir,' said Rydz gloomily. Standing in the cramped little hallway he looked more massive than ever.

'And you didn't know about it?'

'No, sir,' said Rydz. 'He don't never tell me nothin' about that.'

'And it definitely refers to *two* people?'

'Yes, sir,' said Rydz. 'Definite. And the other one's Enid, I'll bet.'

Blessedly, Miss Kingsley had caught a later bus from Dorchester.

It was one o'clock in the afternoon. The body was gone, the photographs taken and the door closed on the room across the hall.

'We've logged it as a probable drug overdose, Miss Kingsley. There'll have to be an inquest, of course.'

'Yes,' she said. 'I understand. Thank you, my dear.' This last was to the WPC who, with Peasgood, had collected her at the bus stop and broken the news to her, and who had just brought in a trayful of assorted mugs, one with a slice of lemon floating in it. From the little casement window that Price had opened in Kingsley's bedroom, Roper had seen the white-faced Miss Kingsley arrive. She had stepped out of Peasgood's Metro and gone straightaway to Rydz, who had been standing by his van. They had talked closely, almost intimately, for several minutes and at the end of their conversation Rydz, clearly deeply moved, had taken up one of her gloved hands and pressed its knuckles to his mouth. It had looked like a moment of unbridled passion. Rydz was still out there, sitting in his van, with the Labrador.

Miss Kingsley sipped at her tea. Thus far, she had taken her latest tragedy with ice-cold stoicism, so much so that Roper was left with the distinct impression that however much she had wept for her lifetime lover she would weep for her brother not at all.

Roper prepared himself for the delicate skirmish which now had to follow. For fifty years the upright and dogged Miss Kingsley had been the victim of a supremely executed and cruel confidence trick. A few days ago she had plucked at his sleeve and pleaded earnestly with him to catch Zygmunt Komarowski's murderer; and he had assured her that he would; and he had, even though he had come an hour too late. It was a promise, now, that he would have preferred not to honour.

But then, as the right words finally came together and he was about to utter them, Miss Kingsley pre-empted him.

'Everyone has been very kind,' she said, sitting her mug on the palm of her hand. 'But if we could have a few moments together Mr Roper . . . Would you mind?'

'I'll give you a call, Dave,' Roper said to Price. Price rose. Makins and the WPC filed out. The door closed behind them.

Miss Kingsley lowered her mug to the hearth and sat upright again. She folded her hands on her lap, very calm, very cool, very composed.

'Forgive me, Mr Roper,' she said, 'but I'm a long way from being a helpless old woman. So whatever you have to say, I can bear it. I merely preferred the two of us to be alone when you told me. Did he – *could* he – have possibly done that terrible thing to Zygmunt? Because that's why you're *really* here, isn't it? I see you have his gloves – and a sock – and in the same sort of bag you took my scarf away in. I'm sure that must mean something.'

The bagged red woollen gloves lay on the arm of Roper's armchair. Makins had found them in a chest of drawers in Kingsley's bedroom; together with three elderly shotgun cartridges, with cardboard cases, tucked in an old sock among Kingsley's shirts.

'I'm afraid it might, Miss Kingsley,' Roper said. So there was, after all, no need to skirmish. 'We're not completely certain, of course . . . I need to know a few more things about your brother.'

'There was not much to him, Mr Roper,' she said. 'Believe me.' She spoke bitterly. 'But ask whatever you want.'

'The other evening, Miss Kingsley, I was up at the Gorton Arms. I noticed a photograph. The pre-war cricket eleven. Your brother was in it.'

'He was.'

'The team, according to Mr Painter, all had bags – cricket-bags. Mr Painter's grandfather bought them. Do you know if your brother had one?'

'Yes, he did.'

'Colour?'

'Grey, I think.'

Roper showed her the much-thumbed Polaroid photograph of the bag Makins had found at Allgrove's.

'Yes,' she said. 'It was exactly like that.'

'When did you last see it, Miss Kingsley?'

'Some time ago. Not lately. I didn't go into his room. I haven't for a long time. He forbade it.'

'Did your brother, Miss Kingsley . . . ever own a shot-gun?'

'Yes,' she said. 'A long time ago. Our father's.'

'How long?'

'Oh, years,' she said. 'Years since I saw it. Ten . . . twenty. I can't be sure. I thought he'd got rid of it.'

He asked her to describe it, as best she remembered.

'Two barrels,' she said. 'And the shoulder-thing – the stock – was split. My brother glued it back together and bound it with wire. He was still at school then.'

She did not, nor ever had, known what the gauge of the shotgun was, but descriptions rarely came better than that. Kingsley never had got rid of his father's old gun, until he had killed Komarowski with it.

'If you saw the gun again, you could identify it?'

'Yes. I'm sure I could.'

'If we can go back to that bag, Miss Kingsley; did your brother ever go to London with it?'

'No,' she said. She thought for a moment. 'But I did. A few years after the war. We were desperately short of money. We had a barometer. It was antique. Georgian. Ziggy told me he thought he could sell it for

207

us. I think he got three hundred pounds for it. That was a lot of money then.'

'So you took the barometer up to London in the cricket-bag?'

'Yes,' she said. 'It was the only thing we could fit it into.'

'And you travelled how? D'you remember?'

'Vaguely,' she said. 'A train to Waterloo, then, I think, a bus. Then I went from Charing Cross to Brixton on a tram.' She was certain about the tram ride. 'Zygmunt was lodging in Brixton then. He was just about to take his finals for his degree.'

'And you brought back the empty bag?'

'Oh, yes,' she said. Then, 'Look, if you really want to see the bag I could try to find it for you. I'm *sure* it's still about.'

He forebore to tell her that she had just been looking at a photograph of it.

'Mr Komarowski had a cash-box, Miss Kingsley.'

Yes. She knew it. She had the second key to it because she and her brother and Zygmunt had all agreed to act as each other's executors when the time came. The key was kept in the sideboard. The top drawer. Behind where Roper was sitting.

'And Mr Kingsley knew you kept it there?'

'Yes,' she said. 'Of course.'

'Mr Komarowski also had a bicycle . . . '

'Yes,' she said. 'It used to be mine. A long time ago.'

'There was a padlock on it . . . '

'We bought it for him. The Christmas before this one. A little make-weight present.'

'Could your brother have known the code that opened it?'

'Oh, yes,' she said. 'It was made in Taiwan. The instructions were in broken English and Zygmunt couldn't make head nor tail of them. It was my brother who worked out how to set the numbers up.'

'And the numbers . . . ?'

208

'Nineteen-twenty. Zygmunt's birth year. Easy for him to remember, you see.'

And Johnnie, thought Roper, although he didn't say so.

'We found some keys in Mr Komarowski's cash-box. The property of a gentleman who lives over Lower Gorton way. A Mr Allgrove. D'you know how Mr Komarowski came to have them?'

'Yes, I do,' she said. 'Zygmunt stole them. To stop Mr Allgrove driving his van away while he went for the RSPCA people and the police. Zygmunt saw Mr Allgrove burying some dead dogs. On the heath.'

Roper listened patiently while she told him the rest of the story, and a rider to it that he had not known. It was Komarowski who had flooded Allgrove's dog-pit with water, to stop Allgrove's friends using it while he was in prison. He had filled it using Allgrove's own hose and the standpipe outside the garage, the day after Mrs Allgrove had moved out. So Komarowski *had* been aware what the other two keys were for – and so, no doubt, had John Kingsley.

'Did you know Mr Allgrove was out of prison, Miss Kingsley?'

'Yes,' she said. 'I saw him. In the lane. The morning I sat in your car. I didn't know until then.'

'Did your brother know?'

'Yes. I told him.'

'When?'

'After you had gone. After lunch. I told him then.'

'And what was his reaction?'

'He was surprised.' She considered her answer again. 'No. More. Horrified . . . I remember now . . . he went straight to his room. He didn't even come out for tea. I thought that was very odd. But then he had *been* odd.'

'Since when?'

'Since the day before,' she said. Miss Kingsley had first noticed her brother's 'oddness' when she had come back from the chiropodist's clinic on the morning before

Zygmunt had been killed. Johnnie had been extraordinarily quarrelsome all that day, even snapping at Zygmunt when they had played chess together that afternoon.

'Anything particular happen that day, Miss Kingsley? While you were out, perhaps?'

She shook her head. She could remember nothing untoward that would have accounted for her brother's mood all that day.

'Could your brother ride a bicycle, Miss Kingsley? In the old days?'

'Oh, yes,' she said sadly. 'When he was a boy he was always having new bicycles. He was very spoiled. He had everything he ever wanted.'

'And could he walk . . . at all?'

'No . . . never . . . not since he came out of hospital . . . during the war.'

'Not even a few yards – a dozen paces, say – about the house?'

She shook her head.

'With a stick? Crutches?'

'He was helpless,' she insisted. '*Utterly*. He couldn't even cut up his food for himself. And he never used crutches . . . wouldn't . . . *couldn't*. The hand, you see. It wouldn't grip.'

'Did you ever see your brother's right hand, Miss Kingsley?'

'No,' she said. 'Never. He wouldn't show me. He wouldn't take that black glove off, even to sleep. That's why I used to knit him woollen gloves, so he could wear the right one over the leather one. The hand was useless, *quite* useless . . . ' Her voice tailed away. 'You must have seen . . . ' Roper watched the disbelief slowly flooding her . . . all those wasted years, pandering to his every need. He remembered what she had said to him once – 'Johnnie needed me more'.

'But I thought . . . when you said . . . I thought Johnnie had gone up to the caravan in his chair . . . but of course he couldn't have . . . he could only ever get up

210

there with Zygmunt helping him. Oh, dear God. I always thought it was the footrests on his chair . . . '

'What was, Miss Kingsley?'

'The way his slippers were always wearing out. I always seemed to be buying new slippers for him . . . '

At last Miss Kingsley was devastated; but at the great lie, not her brother's suicide. That death she could live with. 'Are you saying he *walked* up there, Mr Roper?'

'I think he did, Miss Kingsley,' said Roper. And choosing his words with great care he told Enid Kingsley what might have happened that night; about Kingsley's walk up to the caravan, the borrowing of the padlocked bicycle for the journey to Allgrove's to hide the gun in the garage, and finally his walk home after he had returned Allgrove's keys to the cash-box and padlocked the bicycle back on the caravan's towing bar.

'He was exhausted the next morning,' she said, remembering. 'I told Sergeant Peasgood . . . '

It was little wonder.

'We found two bottles of sleeping-pills in your brother's bedroom, Miss Kingsley. One was prescribed for you—'

'But I always kept mine upstairs,' she broke in. 'He couldn't *get* upstairs . . . ' But again her voice and her protest tailed away. It seemed that John Kingsley had been more than able to get upstairs.

She took a sleeping-pill every night. She couldn't sleep, otherwise. Her mind wouldn't stop working sometimes. The pills more or less laid her out for four or five hours. Both she and her brother turned in well before ten o'clock each night.

'So your brother could have gone out that night without your hearing him?'

'Well, yes . . . I suppose.' If she had any doubts now, it was only because she needed some hope to cling to. 'But you can't be certain, Mr Roper, can you?'

'We found your dog put away in the shed down the garden this morning, Miss Kingsley – and your brother's footprints out there. He waited until you'd gone out, phoned Sergeant Peasgood to come along about half-past ten, put the dog away, opened the front door for Peasgood . . . then went back to his bedroom. We know he could walk, Miss Kingsley. And I'm just as sure we've got your father's shotgun – and your brother's old cricket-bag; the one my sergeant found at Mr Allgrove's.'

He recounted what Harry Painter had told him last night: that there had originally been a dozen grey bags purchased for the Gorton cricket team in 1938. It had been intended that they would serve several generations of cricketers, but the war had intervened in the following year and many leaseholders of the bags had gone off in their different directions, taking the bags with them to serve as suitcases. The bags were never assembled as a set again, and of that 1938 cricket eleven only Painter's, Jackson's and Henneker's fathers – and John Kingsley – had chosen to stay in Upper Gorton after the war. 'So if there was another bag, it had to be your brother's.'

'And there was,' she said wistfully. 'Wasn't there?'

'I'm afraid so, Miss Kingsley,' said Roper.

'But still he had no *reason* to kill Zygmunt.'

'I think he did, Miss Kingsley,' said Roper. 'Or he thought he did.' He lifted Kingsley's gloves and the sock and took up the two letters lying beneath it on the arm of his chair. He handed her the one that Komarowski had been typing when he had been interrupted.

She unfolded the single sheet of paper on her lap. And read it twice with growing dismay.

Chapter 17

'It's addressed to a nursing home, Miss Kingsley,' said Roper. 'And it reads as if you were going to put your brother in there.'

'For two weeks,' she argued anguishedly. 'Only for two weeks.'

'But the letter doesn't say so,' Roper countered.

'Because it isn't *finished*,' she argued. 'It was only to be for two weeks. Two weeks in fifty years. Dear God, that wasn't much to ask, was it?'

'But you hadn't told your brother?'

She shook her head wearily. 'Things weren't settled. We'd only made tentative plans. We weren't going until late May, next year.'

'To Poland? You and Mr Komarowski?'

'Zygmunt wanted to go back. To Lodz. Just once more; before he was too old to go. We were going together. We were going to have a little holiday. Just the two of us. Just the once. We never did have. In all the years we never did have. And we *were* going to tell him. It was just a question of choosing the right time.'

'And your brother knew nothing about this trip?'

'Zygmunt had hinted that he was going. He thought it might soften the blow when Johnnie knew I was going too.'

'But Mr Komarowski had already made enquiries about applying for visas for you both. Yes?'

'Yes,' she said. She frowned. 'He had. But how could you know that?'

Roper handed her the letter that had arrived for Komarowski this morning and that Rydz had translated for him.

'It's no use,' she said, after only a glance at it. 'It means nothing to me.'

'It's from the Polish Embassy in London, Miss Kingsley. It tells Mr Komarowski that he and his travelling companion have to make an application for tourist visas at least two weeks before you intend to travel.'

She folded the letter carefully and slipped it back in its envelope.

'When your brother went up to the caravan that night, could he possibly have had any idea all this was going on?'

She remained insistent. Her brother had known nothing, only that Zygmunt had been going to visit Poland some time next year – and then only possibly.

Roper took her back step by step to the day before Komarowski had been shot, when her brother – she had not used her brother's given name once, Roper had noticed, during their entire conversation. Never Johnnie. Never Jack. Only 'my brother' – had suddenly become more spiky and argumentative than usual.

'And after the chiropodist?'

'I went into the newsagent's and bought some more Christmas cards. Mr Rydz was in there. He waited for me to finish my shopping then brought me back here in his little van. Zygmunt came in the afternoon. That's really all there was to it. Except that I took Max for a walk in the early evening.' She lifted a finger as another thought occurred to her. 'Oh, yes. I remember something else. My passport came. It came while I was along at the chiropodist's. In the post.'

'Could your brother have seen it?'

'No.' She shook her head, still insistent. 'It was lying on the doormat when I came back from the chiropodist's; and my brother was still in bed. So he couldn't have seen it, could he?'

'You ever had a passport before?'

'No,' she said. 'Never. I've never been anywhere. Not since the war.'

'May I see it, Miss Kingsley?'

She went upstairs to her bedroom to fetch it, a passport in a strong manila envelope that was slit along its top edge. The passport was new, the photograph inside a recent one. But what drew Roper's attention was the crinkled and grubby state of the envelope's flap. Something very significant indeed had happened while Miss Kingsley had been at the chiropodist's that morning.

'It's been steamed open, Miss Kingsley,' said Roper. 'Did you—'

But Enid Kingsley was already shaking her head again. So often, in the past, she had noticed the crinkled state of the flap of an envelope personally addressed to her. It had simply never occurred to her . . . She regarded Roper wretchedly.

'My brother must have opened them,' she said. 'Mustn't he?'

'You had no idea your brother was going to do what he did this morning?'

'No,' she said. 'None. I left him in bed. I knocked on his door to tell him I was going out; I hadn't seen him since last night.'

'And yesterday?'

'He was very quiet. And didn't want lunch. And he didn't eat all his supper. And he was drinking a lot. You must have noticed yourself when you came. And he was very grumpy with Mr Rydz—'

'Mr Rydz?'

'Yes,' she said. 'He called yesterday evening, with some bacon for us and a bottle of whisky for my brother. He often does. My brother hardly spoke a word to him. So rude.'

So that was it. Over the last few days nobody had

215

had his nose closer to the ground that Stanislaus Rydz.
'Mr Rydz stay for a chat, did he?'

'A few minutes,' she said. 'He always does.'

'What did he talk about? D'you remember?'

'Oh, everything. His grandchildren, the fire at Mr
Henneker's and how you'd been along and taken Mr
Allgrove away and let him go again . . . all the gossip.
Oh, dear . . . ' She broke off again. Like Roper, Miss
Kingsley, for all her years, was quickly able to put
two and two together. But still her sympathy was not
for her brother. 'Oh, poor Mr Rydz. If he were ever
to realise . . . He was so full of it . . . How you were
working so hard to catch . . . oh, you must *never* tell
him. Please, you won't, will you?'

'I can't promise, Miss Kingsley. The inquest . . . '

'Oh, yes,' she said sadly. 'The inquest. I'd forgotten
about that.'

She played absently with her handkerchief, screwing
it and unscrewing it on her lap, while all the pent-up
emotions of fifty lost years were at last let out into the
open.

'He was unconscious for three days. They thought
he might have suffered brain damage; but that was fifty
years ago, so they were never really certain. The doctors,
in the beginning, said that given time his hand and legs
would start working again. But they never did . . . We
all believed him, you see.'

For years afterwards, John Kingsley had lived the life
of a recluse, taking the air only in the garden where no
one but his sister could see him, eating the food that was
cooked and cut up for him, drinking, smoking, staring at
walls, saying little, becoming more unkempt, never taking
a bath but only washing himself in the kitchen because he
couldn't get upstairs to the bathroom, his toilet arrangements built into his chair . . . there had been that, too.

'Your brother never saw a doctor afterwards; somebody
who might have realised he was faking?'

'No,' she said. 'Except for little things. He was always saying he despised doctors.'

For nearly thirty years Miss Kingsley had managed her brother on her own—

'And then Zygmunt moved here to help me – the best friend my brother ever had.' It had been Zygmunt who had paid for the electric wheelchair, Zygmunt who had finally bullied him to go beyond the confines of the cottage in daylight, Zygmunt who inveigled him out for a drink in a public house where people were, and took him birdwatching, and came here every day to play chess and cards with him, and always brought a can of Guinness along for him. 'So many little things. All Zygmunt, you see. My brother gave nothing. Absolutely nothing. He only took. From both of us.'

The handkerchief was straightened out. 'A person is not always what she or he looks like, Mr Roper – but I expect you know that.' Her gaze lifted and went to the silver-framed photograph among the Christmas cards on the piano. 'He was such a beautiful boy on the outside,' she reminisced bitterly. 'But inside he was spiteful, always, even before he was wounded, even when he was only a little boy; and he loved playing the hero, swaggering about in his uniform, and all the killing, and the girls, and the medals, and his pictures in the newspapers and all the magazines. He was a hero, you see, to the people who didn't know him. And then it all stopped. He was nearly twenty-one. And he had a DFC and bar to it by then and he was soon to be gazetted to wing-commander. God forgive me, Mr Roper, I was never able to love my brother, but eventually I grew to hate him. And the only fine thing I ever had in my life was murdered by him. He was a cruel man, Mr Roper. He always was. Always.'

Roper waited patiently for more. But Miss Kingsley had purged herself at last.

'What will you do?' he asked, as the handkerchief was smoothed and folded meticulously on her tweeded lap. Miss Kingsley would never do anything less than meticulously. 'Stay here?'

'I am going to be outrageous, Mr Roper,' she confessed. 'When you've gone, I'm going to pack all my suitcases and Mr Rydz is going to put them in his van for me. I am going to keep house for him and help him with his pigs. I quite like pigs. And perhaps, later on, I might ask him to go to Lodz with me. Just the once. Am I being very preposterous, d'you think?'

Roper shook his head. Enid Kingsley would never be preposterous. 'No,' he said. 'I've always preferred happy endings myself, Miss Kingsley. Good luck to you.'

The ACC (Crime) came away from his hospitality-cabinet with a bottle of Scotch and two cut-crystal glasses.

'Never thought of you as sentimental, Douglas,' he said, as he stood the tumblers on the desk.

'He cheated her out of fifty years,' said Roper. 'I reckon she deserves a bit of luck.'

'Incredible piece of planning, though,' said the ACC, with frank admiration. 'Sister's passport arrives in the morning; our friend the squadron-leader puts two and two together and by the evening the chap's worked out a way to commit an almost perfect murder. Got to admire an old man who can think on his feet like that. Eh?' Roper waited for the pinched narrow face to smile coyly; but the ACC seemed quite unaware, this time, that he had come close to making a joke, albeit a grim one.

The neck of the bottle clinked against a glass. On the blotter nearby lay a green cardboard file. A typed label on its flap bore the terse instruction: NO FURTHER ACTION PENDING INQUEST; although Roper doubted that there would be any more action, inquest or not. The cartridges hidden in Kingsley's old sock were identical with the two found in Kingsley's old gun. The red gloves matched the fragment of red wool the SOCO had found snagged on the door-hinge of the caravan; and a grease stain on one glove matched the grease on the hinges, which was not of itself evidence of any-thing except that John Kingsley had visited the caravan during the preceding days and had been wearing the gloves at the time. Except that in the last half-hour, one of the technicians at the laboratory had found a wisp of an identical wool trapped in the hinge of one of the brake-levers of Komarowski's old bicycle, which Forensic had at last got around to examining. And that *was* evidence. The motive, brewed up amidst the mental turmoil of an unhappy old man who could not bear to face the ultimate tragedy, loneliness, even for a few days, was almost forgivable. Only a verbal confession was lacking, but that was impossible now. And perhaps the loose ends were better left untied . . .

The ACC swung himself in behind his mahogany raft of a desk, and raised his tumbler. 'Your continued good health, Douglas.'

'And yours, sir,' said Roper. The ACC always kept a good whisky. And, for once, the Speeding Spectre, as he was colloquially known among the lower orders, looked relaxed and leisurely as he lay back in his chrome and leather swivel chair and sampled his whisky.

'Tricky business,' he observed, after an appreciative lip-smack. 'Arresting a disabled war-hero. We could have got a damn dodgy press. Public sympathy. All that. And he'd have got away with it, too, bet your life. Wretched business all round.'

Roper agreed. Wretched summed it up exactly. This morning, driving towards the Kingsleys' cottage, he had felt sick to his very bones at the thought of facing John Kingsley with his suspicions, because they *had* only been suspicions then. All the real evidence had come along afterwards.

With his foot on an open drawer behind his desk, the ACC swung his chair gently from side to side and looked faintly amused about something.

'Time for another one, Douglas?' he said. 'Eh?'

Which Roper construed, or, rather, misconstrued, as

an invitation to another measure of the ACC's excellent malt.

'Still got a lot of things to do, sir,' he said, sipping. 'But thanks all the same.'

'I meant you've still got a few days left,' said the ACC. 'Time to wrap up another *villain* or two. Eh? Before you go swanning off to the Acropolis.' The pinched narrow face smiled coyly, and the ACC's eyes twinkled mischievously – or perhaps Roper had misconstrued yet again, and it was only the twinkling facets of the ACC's glass reflected in them. 'That was only a joke, Douglas,' the ACC laboured achingly to explain, in the face of Roper's inscrutable immobility. 'Really . . . But one never knows what even the immediate future might bring. Does one? Eh?'

'No, sir,' agreed Roper dourly, draining his glass. 'But one can always hope, sir. Can't one?'